A Sociological Perspective of Sport

Wilbert Marcellus Leonard II
Illinois State University

 **Burgess Publishing Company**
Minneapolis, Minnesota

Editorial: Wayne Schotanus, Marta Reynolds, Elisabeth Sövik
Art: Joan Gordon, Lynn Guilfoyle Dwyer
Production: Morris Lundin, Pat Barnes

Cover design: Lynn Guilfoyle Dwyer

Burgess Publishing Company
7108 Ohms Lane
Minneapolis, Minnesota 55435

0 9 8 7 6 5 4 3

To my wife, Dorothy Anne Donley,
and children, Marcelle and Marc,
with love and appreciation.

Preface

To argue that analysts and observers of the social scene have avoided focusing on sport as a societal phenomenon is partially true. Much of this literature, however, has been journalistic and anecdotal, and only a few efforts have been made to collect empirical data and test hypotheses. Furthermore, a consistent perspective or framework from which to study sport has been obviously lacking.

My purpose in writing this text was to contribute to the field by adopting a *sociological perspective* and demonstrating its utility in understanding sport as a societal institution. Until recently, sport as a social institution has been generally ignored by academicians.

Of the numerous ideas reflected in this book, three may be said to provide a central focus: (1) sport is a social institution and should be investigated and analyzed just as any other institution (marriage, family, economy, religion, etc.); (2) *sport is a microcosm* of the larger society—it can neither be isolated nor insulated from the broader social currents; and (3) there exist numerous *institutional interconnections* among the basic institutions of a society, and changes in one sphere of society reverberate into others.

To understand sport *sociologically,* I have chosen several pivotal sociological concepts—*social organization, culture, socialization, deviance, small groups, social stratification, prejudice, discrimination, minority groups, demography, collective behavior, mass media,* and *institutional interrelationships*—as focal points for discussion. Their usefulness and application to sport as a social phenomenon are amply demonstrated.

Chapter headings are organized around key sociological topics. In general, the sequence of chapters proceeds from a broad "macro" view to a more narrow "micro" view. Chapter 1 lays the foundation for a sociological perspective of sport by defining and illustrating critical sociological and sport concepts. Chapter 2 briefly surveys the history of sport in America, its diversity and social impact. After these two foundation chapters the sociological threads are made apparent in the following chapters: "Sport and Social Organization," "Sport and Culture," "Sport and Socialization," "Sport and Deviance," "Sport and Social Stratification," "Race and Sport," "Women in Sport," "Small Groups in Sport," "Sport, Economics, and Politics," "Sport and the Mass Media," and "Sport, Collective Behavior, and Social Change."

To make the book as interesting as possible, I have included a variety of materials. For example, each chapter begins with an introductory section which serves to locate the contents in an appropriate sociological context. Here, major issues, concerns, and queries are raised that are dealt with in the chapter proper. Similarly, each chapter concludes with a succinct summary of what has been discussed and attempts to answer some questions posed in the introductory section. Furthermore, each chapter ends with a section titled "Important Concepts Discussed in this Chapter." These concepts are distillations of the major conceptual tools invoked to describe and explain the essential concerns of the chapter. Moreover, the objective questions in the *Instructor's Manual* are "keyed" to these important terms. Hence, both student and instructor have common knowledge of what is considered germane. Also, endnotes which serve to refine a point, elaborate a meaningful matter, and/or provide a valuable supplement to the text proper appear at the end of each chapter.

Since sport lends itself to many inherently interesting illustrations, each chapter includes a variety of vignettes. The purpose of these "literary sketches" is to stimulate and motivate the student's interest in sport and society. Sometimes, as in chapter 5, the vignettes provide a personal component which allows the students to assess their "sports personality" by completing and scoring the questionnaire. This research instrument measures two traits associated with sport: (1) competitiveness, and (2) attraction to physical danger. In teaching sport sociology I have discovered this technique beneficial for generating excitement about socialization and sport. In other instances, the vignettes are more scholarly in nature. In chapter 3 a vignette hypothesizes the influence of sport social organization on the athlete's perceptions and experiences of failure, i.e., not making the team, being cut, or demoted. It is hoped that the vignettes serve as stimulating pedagogical devices for creating and maintaining student interest in the course material.

This text has been specifically designed for courses in the sociology of sport regardless of whether the courses are taught under the auspices of the sociology or physical education department. I have attempted to clearly define and illustrate all relevant concepts and terms. In addition to adoption for sport sociology courses, this text could also be used in courses such as sport and society, sport and culture, foundations of physical education, the study of social institutions, and American society.

Several individuals have aided me immensely in writing this text. I would particularly like to thank Wayne Schotanus, editor for this project, and Marta Reynolds, editorial assistant, for their patience, assistance, and encouragement in developing the book. Carolyn Cody, professor of physical education at the University of Northern Colorado, has graciously spent a great deal of time helping to mold the text into one that could be appreciated and understood by non-sociologists. Clinton Wesolik was primarily responsible for researching and writing the chapter on women in sport and kept me abreast of significant sport occurrences during the writing of the manuscript. Mary Schuneman typed the text and provided me with invaluable editorial suggestions.

Finally, my wife Dorothy and children, Marcelle and Marc, were most cooperative during the "highs" and "lows" in the production of this book. Their contributions are immeasurable. The final beauty of writing this text resides in the fact that one of my lifelong loves and interests—sports—could be fashioned into a professional piece of work.

Wilbert Marcellus Leonard II

Contents

1
Introduction to
the Sociology of Sport

INTRODUCTION

Sport permeates any number of levels of contemporary society and it touches upon and deeply influences such disparate elements as status, race relations, business life, automotive design, clothing styles, the concept of the hero, language, and ethical values. For better or for worse, it gives form and substance to much in American life . . .[1]

The social significance of sport[2] in American society is unparalleled. But America is not unique in the excitement, enthusiasm, dedication, and fanaticism engendered by participation and spectator sports. In many other parts of the globe there is a similar sport fervor, and to demonstrate the pervasiveness and penetration of sport in society is not difficult.

Many of us know from the time, money, energy, and emotion we spend on sport that our games are more than frivolous, spare-time activities. According to Beisser:

We prefer not to know too much about what we treasure. . . . This is the prevailing attitude of Americans toward their love affair with sports. But in sports, unless more than the surface is explored, men can become slaves, entrapped instead of (exercising) free will.[3]

Although our zeal is frequently clouded by doubts and contradictions, our love affair with sport is serious.

For example, billions of dollars are spent yearly to take part in sporting activities or to watch them, and probably an equal amount is bet, legally or illegally, on sporting events. This is an astronomical sum to devote to something related to "play." It is not common to hear people being apologetic for the huge resources expended on sport when compared to such areas as work, education, or health care.

"World-class" professional athletes have earnings that exceed those of the highest paid public officials, teachers, doctors, lawyers, dentists, and scientists. Sport news often receives at least as much coverage as news about business, culture, and public affairs. Sports are also given priority in the public budgets of many communities.

Sports are defended as the builders of physical and emotional health as well as esprit de corps and character. They are further justified for instilling national strength, social teamwork, patriotism—even nationalism and religious piety. Critics, on the other hand, debunk sport for being a kind of opiate—a sedative, if you will—for keeping people distracted from the more serious issues in life.

Typical sport buffs, however, display little interest and enthusiasm for serious debate over the merits and demerits of sport.[4] Though they hear of arguments over sport monopolies, betting and recruiting scandals, and athletic salary disputes, they are not likely to allow these to penetrate too deeply—nor to stir discontent. This kind of knowledge in and of itself does not make us sport literate. One of the goals of this text is to facilitate your literacy of sport in contemporary society.

Sociologists are quick to point out that reality is not always what it appears to be on the surface, or what people say it is, or what it is officially proclaimed to be. Social reality is like an onion. . . it has more than a single layer and must be peeled back if its true nature is to be exposed. In this text we will provide you with a broad perspective of sport in society, pointing out the sometimes difficult-to-see realities and uncovering a few of the myths and falsehoods that surround American sport life.

In this first chapter we will lay the foundation for a sociological perspective of sport by discussing the pervasiveness of sport in society; the relationships between sport and economics, politics, popular culture, and the mass media; sport as a concept (and how it differs from play and game); sport in the social/behavioral sciences; sport in sociology; and, finally, a brief chronology of sport studies in sociology.

Sport permeates virtually every social institution in the United States. The prevalence of sport can be witnessed in news coverage, financial expenditures, number of participants and spectators, movies, books, leisure hours consumed, and the time samplings of conversations.

Sports are among the most popular activities in American life today. Both personal experiences and impersonal statistics add substance to this statement. For many of us our indoctrination in sport began early in life—in the elementary grades or perhaps even before. For males, and increasingly for females, participation in organized sporting activities began in "little leagues," "pony leagues," "American Legion" baseball or the like. Few of us immersed in this sport environment escaped the hobby of collecting and trading bubble gum cards with sport personalities pictured on them. While disengagement from active participation takes its toll as one grows older, many adults still find sport significant even though the participant role frequently becomes subordinate to spectating.

SPECTATORSHIP AND PARTICIPATION

Statistically, attendance and participation figures are impressive. Table 1.1 contains the number of *spectators* at major sports events for 1965, 1974, and 1977 as well as the percentage change during each time period and attendance ranks for sports in 1977. Perhaps surprising, thoroughbred racing and auto racing occupy the first and second positions in terms of spectatorship. Figure 1.1 depicts the top ten adult *participation* sports and the millions of Americans engaged in such activities. More than 25 million people participate in swimming, tennis, fishing, bowling, and baseball or softball. It is estimated that nearly one-half of the U.S. population participate in some form of physical activity daily. Vignette 4.2 (p. 72) contains an account of this physical fitness mania.

Table 1.1
Number of Spectators at Major Sports Events
for 1965, 1974 and 1977

Sports Event	1965	1974	1977	Attendance Rank (1977)
Pro Boxing	1,743,000	2,675,000	3,000,000	12
Pro Basketball	2,356,000	8,229,000	8,247,609	11
Pro Football	6,956,000	10,236,000	11,070,543	10
Minor-league Baseball	10,194,000	11,032,000	13,000,000	9
Pro Hockey	2,823,000	12,006,000	23,000,000	7
Greyhound Racing	10,865,000	16,274,000	19,000,000	8
College Basketball	16,384,000	24,630,000	35,752,391	4
Harness Racing	26,899,000	29,976,000	31,225,600	6
Major-league Baseball	23,437,000	30,630,000	38,000,000	3
College Football	24,683,000	31,235,000	32,929,457	5
Auto Racing	39,000,000	47,500,000	49,000,000	2
Thoroughbred Racing	40,737,000	48,824,000	50,774,400	1
Total	206,077,000	273,247,000 Up 33% from 1965	315,000,000 Up 15% from 1974	

Source: *Rand McNally Marketing Atlas*, 1974 edition; Loy, McPherson, and Kenyon, 1978; and various media reports. Reprinted with permission of the Joint Council on Economic Education, from *The Economics of Professional Team Sports, Economic Topic* Series, ©JCEE 1976. All Rights Reserved.

SOME BRIEF OBSERVATIONS ON THE PERVASIVENESS OF SPORT

The Economic Impact of Sport

Sport is big business; it is a multi-billion dollar industry. Television contracts alone, which provide the lifeblood for many professional and amateur sports, cost millions of dollars per year. Advertising costs for major sporting events (Super Bowl) exceed a quarter of a million dollars per minute. University teams participating in some post-season bowl games (Rose, Orange, Cotton, and Sugar) are rewarded with million dollar kickbacks. It has also been estimated that Americans gamble somewhere between $15 and $50 billion annually on various sporting events (see Vignette 6.4). In short, the economic impact of sport is awesome and will be more fully discussed in chapter 11.

Sport and Politics

Many political figures have aligned themselves with sport and with good reason. Because the average person can easily identify with the tugs of war that take place on a local or national level, politicians have found it useful to make frequent comparisons between political life and sporting

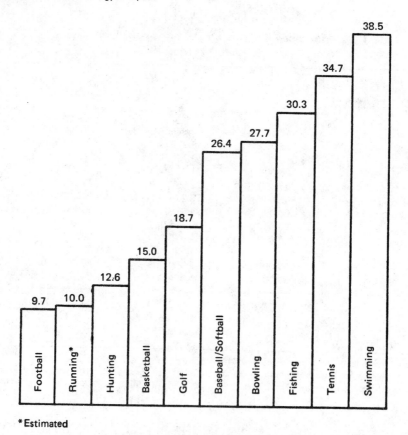

*Estimated

Figure 1.1
The Top Ten Adult Participation Sports (in millions)
(From Sindlinger's Economic Service, January 1978)

life—as well as to initiate changes in sport institutions. For example, midway through the 1905 football season, President Roosevelt became the catalyst for important changes in intercollegiate football. It is reported that after Roosevelt viewed a picture of a badly mauled football player, he threatened to abolish the game if remedial steps were not taken to modify its most objectionable aspects. His influence also had a great impact on the formation of the Intercollegiate Athletic Association, the forerunner of the National Collegiate Athletic Association (NCAA).

Former President Richard M. Nixon was so fond of his "No. 1" sport fan label that he did not hesitate to call coaches after dramatic football contests. In fact, Pennsylvania State University took him to task in the early 1970s when he declared that the University of Texas football team was number one when both teams had identical records and bowl games to play.

Former President Gerald R. Ford, himself, a former football "jock" at the University of Michigan, wrote an article (see p. 70) which appeared in *Sports Illustrated* attesting to the importance of sport competition. John F. Kennedy (1960) also used the *Sports Illustrated* forum to warn Americans that they were becoming "soft." Like Ford, he stressed physical fitness and claimed it provided the foundation for the "vitality of the nation."

Other political figures like former President Lyndon B. Johnson and Douglas MacArthur were consulted for their assistance in settling disputes between the Amateur Athletic Union (AAU) and the NCAA. Even the Supreme Court has had to act on decisions wrought by sport in American society (see p. 243). Furthermore, Congress has been the ultimate authority for determining the makeup of our Olympic teams and the courts determine who is exempt from federal antitrust legislation. Congress has also been instrumental in the formulation of blackout policies, the composition of Title IX (see pp. 202-203), and the State Department is involved with determining travel visas for U.S. teams.

Sport has also played a role, sometimes an undesirable one, in international sporting events. Vignette 1.1 describes the use of sport as a political tool in the 1936, 1972, and 1976 Olympic Games. Critics have argued that the intrusion of politics into sport has "bastardized" the sport ethic.[5] Politics has infused sport at the state and local levels as well. In short, sport and politics have been and continue to be intricately intertwined.

Popular Culture and Sport

Many expressions coined in sport have penetrated into non-sport contexts. Such sport idioms and figures of speech as *laying the ground rules, foul play, jumping the gun, bush league, cheap shot, dirty pool, toss up, touch base, out of bounds, spoilsport, go to bat, pinch hit, struck out, out in left field, ball park figure, not in the same ballpark, hit below the belt,* and facsimiles have become a daily part of our semantic lifestyles.

Literature and art have increasingly displayed sport themes. The intricacies of sport have been reported in "memoires" by such former athletes as Jim Bouton (*Ball Four*), Jerry Kramer (*Instant Replay*), Dave Meggyesy (*Out of Their League*), Gary Shaw (*Meat on the Hoof*), Peter Gent (*North Dallas Forty*), and Dan Jenkins (*Semi-Tough*). Other muckraking and exposé books have been written such as George Plimpton's *Out of My League, Paper Lion, The Bogey Man,* David Wolf's *Foul!,* Curt Flood's *The Way It Is,* Johnny Sample's *Confessions of a Dirty Ballplayer,* Robert Vare's *Buckeye, A Study of Coach Woody Hayes and the Ohio State Football Machine,* and Martin Ralbovsky's *Destiny's Darlings: A World Championship Little League Team Twenty Years Later.* While sport films as a general rule have never been "winners,"[6] a few recent films—"Rocky," "Roller Ball," "Semi-Tough," "Heaven Can Wait," and "The Champ"—have been quite lucrative. Sports have also provided the setting and themes for such famous writers as James Michener, Zane Grey, Ernest Hemingway, Norman Mailer, John Updike, and Ernest Thayer.

Motion pictures in recent years have captured sport themes and reflect the cultural values and heroes of the times. According to Loy, McPherson, and Kenyon:

> Generally, the movies have depicted or used sport as an autobiography of a particular hero or antihero (*Brian's Song, The Other Side of the Mountain, Fear Strikes Out, The Babe Ruth Story*); as an analysis of a subculture with its structure, rules, roles, and function (*Muscle Beach Party, The Endless Summer, Paper Lion, Downhill Racer, The Hustler, Rocky, North Dallas Forty, Semi-Tough, Pumping Iron*); as a comment on the ethics of sport that attempts to raise social consciousness (*The Loneliness of the Long Distance Runner, Roller Ball, Bad News Bears, Slap Shot*); or as a background or subtheme in advancing the main theme or plot of a movie (*Love Story, The Longest Yard, One Flew Over the Cuckoo's Nest, MASH, Black Sunday, Kansas City Bombers*).[7]

VIGNETTE 1.1
SPORT AS A POLITICAL TOOL

THE 1936 OLYMPIC GAMES

When the National Socialists (Nazis), led by Adolf Hitler, came to hegemony in 1933, the 1936 Games (sometimes called the "Nazi Olympics") had already been scheduled for Berlin (Richard Mandell, *The Nazi Olympics* (New York, NY: Macmillan, 1970). Hitler was reluctant to stage the games there but, on the urgings of his propaganda minister, was enticed to use them for propaganda purposes. In his preparation for war he took this opportunity to show the world the nature of Aryan (a non-Jewish Caucasian) supremacy both in and outside the Olympic stadium. The city of Berlin was given a "face lift" . . . cleaned up, repainted, and primed for the series of sporting events. The stadium itself was built to seat 105,000 and the Olympic village was an architectural ideal. Reports circulated regarding the impressive nature of Berlin and the Olympic site. The final gold, silver, and bronze medal tally was partial testimony to the superiority of the German athletes and their sport structure. But the real hero was a four-gold medal winner American black by the name of Jesse Owens. The Ohio State student won the 100 and 200 meter races, long jump, and kicked off the victorious 400 meter U.S. relay team. Not being fond of blacks (or Jews) Hitler vacated his special box seat when Owens took the winner's stand.

THE 1972 OLYMPIC GAMES

The modern Olympics reached their nadir during the 1972 Munich Games. It is a well-known political fact that the Middle East countries are constantly at each other's throats. On the 10th day of the 1972 Olympics eight Arab terrorists killed eleven Israeli athletes. Moreover, the German police eventually assassinated five of the eight Arabs. Meanwhile, athletes from Egypt, Kuwait, and Syria dropped out and went home immediately in fear of retaliation.

THE 1976 OLYMPIC GAMES

Like many other Olympics the 1976 Montreal Games were marred by political squabbles. Taiwan was ousted because the International Olympic Committee (IOC) only recognized mainland China. Additionally, 24-30 black African nations refused to participate because New Zealand did. Earlier New Zealand had sent a team to play rugby in South Africa where *apartheid,* the rigid racial segregation system operating there, reigns supreme. The black African nations did not condone this sporting occasion and registered their protest by withdrawing from the contests.

PING-PONG DIPLOMACY

A final example of the use of sport as a political tool concerns the restoration of diplomatic relations between the United States and China. In 1971, ping pong matches fostered relations between the two countries. This "ping pong diplomacy" stemmed from a team of table tennis players from the United States traveling to and competing against the Chinese. For a period of nearly 20 years (early 1950s to early 1970s) China had remained isolated from international sporting events, choosing to concentrate on domestic feats. International competition through table tennis was a catalyst to the revitalization of political negotiations between the two countries. A similar goal was achieved by basketball matches between Cuba and the United States in the mid-1970s.

Sport and the Mass Media

Sport coverage in the mass media (TV, radio, newspapers, magazines) has become a mainstay of daily life. On TV alone it is estimated that sporting events occupy about 15 percent (1,250 hours in 1978 on national networks for an average of 24 hours per week) of all telecasts. Similarly, the impact of the media has been felt in such changes as night (rather than day) baseball, Monday and Thursday night football rather than Saturday and Sunday afternoons, and the location of franchises. Even the timing, place, and manner of play is being determined by the media. The symbiotic relationship between sport and the media is more fully covered in chapter 12.

All this goes to underscore the observation that sport is a prominent feature of society, particularly American society, and that to ignore it is to ignore one of the most significant and pervasive aspects of social life. It has been said that if America has a religion, it is sport.[8]

SPORT AS A CONCEPT

Concepts[9] are the essential ingredients of scientific and everyday communication. [A concept might be thought of as a word or symbol representing an object (e.g., man) or a property of an object (e.g., intelligence).] They are abstract generalizations. All disciplines employ special vocabularies—jargon—that function to identify matters, issues, and ideas of central concern.

What Is Sport?

The meaning of sport, like love, marital success, time, life, satisfaction, or religiosity, is self-evident until we attempt to define it. Each of these terms is an idea—technically a *concept*—that undoubtedly means something to you. Although you have a casual understanding of these terms, this casual understanding is too general and imprecise for effective communication. Academicians are not afforded the luxury of using vague and ill-defined terms. Hence, there is a need for *conceptualization*, the mental operations through which a scientist refines, specifies, and homes in on what the concepts mean.

Generally speaking, sport as a concept is imprecisely defined. For example, the concepts *sport* and *game* are often used interchangeably. Few would argue that checkers is a sport; similarly, few would wager that boxing is a game. The line of demarcation between these two activities is fairly clear-cut. But what about orienteering, sky diving, chess, and poker? While the *physical* skill factor is paramount in distinguishing sports from games, there are semantic exceptions as in the case of ballet and modern dance which, while requiring high levels of physical skill, are catalogued as performing arts.[10] Consider professional wrestling. A large component of it is entertainment, but it also involves physical prowess. Finally, reports in the mass media discuss various "sporting" activities, such as bridge and rifle shooting which, in the strict sense of the term, are questionable. In short, sport as a concept is not easily distinguished from terms closely related in the mind of the layperson even though there is a fair degree of professional consensus on what is and isn't sport. The meaning of a concept like sport is socially constructed and results from humans' ability to create, use, and manipulate significant symbols.

Sport is a social symbol,[11] and one way of understanding the concept is to ask people what it means to them. Following this line of thought, Stone asked a sample of 562 Minneapolis residents to list the activities they thought of when they heard the word *sport*.[12] He discovered in excess of 2,600 activities associated with the term and an average (arithmetic mean) of 4.6 responses per respondent. Of those questioned, sport as a *spectator* activity was primarily associated with football (73%), baseball (67%), and basketball (43%). While most responses were conventional, such atypical activities as sex, movies, woodworking, and relaxing were also mentioned.

Leonard and Schmitt replicated and extended Stone's seminal inquiry.[13] The three most frequent sport mentions in their study were football, basketball, and baseball. These activities were mentioned by 86, 85, and 76 percent of the subjects, respectively (see Table 1.2). It is interesting that the three highest ranking sports—football, basketball, and baseball—were also the three highest ranking activities in Stone's study. Baseball, however, ranked second in Stone's research. It is of further interest that 11 of the 13 activities reported by Stone were found among Leonard and Schmitt's top twenty. These common sport activities were football, basketball, baseball, swimming, tennis, ice hockey, golf, snow skiing, wrestling, bowling, and boxing. Stone's report also included fishing and hunting, popular sports in Minnesota. The activities mentioned in Leonard and Schmitt's study, but not reported by Stone, were track and field activities, volleyball, soccer, gymnastics, badminton,

Table 1.2
Analysis of the Most Frequently Mentioned Specific Sport
Activities Cited in Response to Stone's Question

Specific Sport Activity	Percent of 128 Respondents Making One Mention	Percent of 73 Females Making One Mention	Percent of 55 Males Making One Mention*
Football	86	92	78
Basketball	85	94*	73
Baseball	76	80	71
Swimming	72	88*	51
Tennis	66	70	60
Track and Field	59	63	53
Ice Hockey	57	56	58
Volleyball	52	67*	33
Soccer	46	47	46
Gymnastics	38	48*	24
Golf	37	37	36
Snow Skiing	37	40	33
Badminton	27	36*	14
Softball	26	36*	13
Ice Skating	23	33*	9
Rugby	23	27	16
Wrestling	23	18	31
Bowling	18	20	14
Boxing	16	10	26*
Handball	12	14	11

*Chi-square significant at the .05 level. Asterisk is by category with highest percent. Wilbert M. Leonard, II and Raymond L. Schmitt, "Sport/Identity as Side-Bet," Paper presented at annual meeting of American Sociological Association (Boston, MA, August, 1979).

softball, ice skating, rugby, and handball. It is interesting to compare the similarities and differences between Stone's and Leonard and Schmitt's studies since their samples were distinct (gainfully employed adults in the former and college students in the latter). Table 1.2 contains the percentage of total respondents as well as the percentage of males and females who made specific sport mentions. Note the differential response of males and females to certain sport activities. Vignette 1.2 shows a comparison of a *national* survey (Harris) with the *regional* ones.

Ideal Types

In defining *sport, game,* and *play* we will enlist a methodological technique developed by the pioneering sociologist Max Weber. A very important concept with far-reaching implications in social science is the term *ideal type.* Weber (1864-1920), a major contributor to classic sociological theory and methodology, argued that attempts to understand the social world are aided by and necessitate the construction of conceptual models or mental constructs to analyze social phenomena. *Ideal* carries no connotation of importance or value (e.g., "better" or "worse"); instead, it refers to a concept constructed from the observation of the characteristics of the phenomenon under investigation. Nor does the term imply a direct correspondence with the "real world." For example, the triology of *play, game,* and *sport* may be thought of as ideal types which are useful in describing fundamental principles even though none of them adequately describes a specific type of physical activity. Ideal types are like statistical or mathematical models (the normal curve) in that they present a perfect "picture" of what should result if certain assumptions are true.

Acknowledging the conceptual morass surrounding sport and sport-related notions, it is imperative that at least general distinctions be made among three related concepts: (1) *play,* (2) *game,* and (3) *sport.* Since these terms have a cumulative property to them, we will begin with the basic notion of *play.*

Play

Roger Caillois advanced five distinguishing characteristics of play.[14] First, play is "free." This means that individuals choose to engage in particular activities as well as voluntarily starting and stopping their engagement in them. "Separateness," the second characteristic, refers to limitations in space and time. Play, unlike sport, is not restricted to the spatial milieu (bullrings, gymnasiums, golf courses, arenas, stadia, field houses or swimming pools); nor to specific times (quarters, halves, rounds, or periods). Third, play is "uncertain," in that the course, end result, or outcome cannot be determined beforehand. Such indeterminancy lends excitement and tension to the activity. Fourth, it is "unproductive" or "non-utilitarian" in both process and product. By unproductive is meant that the outcome does not result in the creation of new material goods. It is non-utilitarian in that the purpose of the activity is the game or contest itself. Finally, play contains a make-believe component. The player "takes on a role" voluntarily but does not identify with the role outside of the space/time confines of the activity. In brief, play is "a voluntary and distinct activity carried out within arbitrary boundaries in space and time, separate from daily roles, concerns, and influences and having no seriousness, purpose, meaning, or goals for the actor beyond those emerging within the boundaries and context of the play act itself."[15] "Play is voluntary activity characterized by minimal roles, spontaneity, and fantasy and is viewed by players and nonplayers as nonwork."[16] Pure play is difficult to identify although children's mimicry and pretense capture this notion.

VIGNETTE 1.2

Harris Survey

Football is rated No. 1 again

It is no surprise that interest in different sports shifts from season to season, but the latest findings indicates a greater seasonal swing than has been the case in previous years.

By Louis Harris

Football has regained its status as the country's No. 1 sport. In the latest Harris Sport Survey, 70 per cent of the nation's sports fans said they followed football, contrasted with 54 per cent who followed baseball. Back in July, baseball passed football in popularity for the first time since 1968 by a narrow 61-to-60 per cent.

It is no surprise that interest in different sports shifts from season to season, but these latest findings indicate a greater seasonal swing than has been the case in previous years. This may be an indication that the country's two top sports will have to fight during their respective seasons to hold on to the loyalty of their old fans and develop the interest of new ones.

A striking gain in this latest survey has been registered by soccer, which is now followed by 14 per cent of sports fans, a gain of 7 points since last July. This result points to the likelihood of further dramatic gains for soccer when its new season begins next spring. It is highly unusual for a sport to gain in popularity during its off-season.

Besides being the sport that is followed by the most fans, football heads the list when people are asked to name their favorite sport.

In this latest Harris Survey of 1,259 adults nationwide, taken at the height of college bowl games and just prior to the Super Bowl, football has widened its lead as the country's favorite sport to a substantial 26 to 16 per cent over baseball. Back in July, the margin was a narrow 22 to 21 per cent.

While the number of people who follow basketball rose from 39 to 42 per cent between July and January, those who name it as their favorite sport dropped slightly from 9 to 8 per cent. This may be a reflection of the growing violence in basketball and the aversion of many fans to such behavior.

Horse racing also showed a decline in popularity, with those who followed the sport dropping from 22 to 18 per cent over the six-month period and the number who named it as their favorite sport slipping from 4 to 2 per cent. Horse racing undoubtedly benefited last summer from the spectacular exploits of jockey Steve Cauthen and 3-year-old triple crown winner Seattle Slew.

Despite the ongoing controversy over Muhammad Ali and the staging of bouts on television, boxing continues to be very popular. The number who follow it has risen from 25 to 28 per cent since July and the number who name it as their favorite sport has gone up from 3 to 4 percent.

Bowling shows no recovery from its slow decline. From a high of 29 per cent who followed the sport in 1972, it now enjoys only a 22 per cent following. The number who named bowling as their favorite sport has dropped from 6 to 4 per cent since last July.

Tennis interest has not lagged, as some predicted it would. The number of fans who followed that sport has risen slightly from 30 to 31 per cent since July and the number who name it their favorite sport remains a constant 6 per cent.

Although the Olympics are still two years away, track and field events continue to show a good growth in following, from 18 to 21 per cent since July, with the number saying it is their favorite sport going up from 2 to 3 per cent.

Golf also rose slightly in popularity, from 19 to 20 per cent this year, while 3 per cent continue to name it as their favorite sport.

Reflecting another major seasonal trend, the percentage of fans following hockey has gone up from 12 to 17 per cent since last July, although the number of fans who name it as their favorite has remained a constant 2 per cent.

Between Dec. 27 and Jan. 10, the Harris Sports Survey asked the national cross section:

"Which of these sports do you follow?"

	Jan. 1978	July 1977	Nov. 1976	April 1975
	%	%	%	%
Football	70	60	67	59
Baseball	54	61	64	55
Basketball	42	39	43	48
Tennis	31	30	26	26
Boxing	28	25	28	22
Bowling	22	21	24	28
Auto racing	21	20	23	24
Track and field	21	18	17	21
Golf	20	19	20	22
Skiing	19	13	14	18
Horse racing	18	22	18	16
Hockey	17	12	19	17
Soccer	14	7	8	8
Boating	12	11	10	13

"If you had to choose, which one sport would you say is your favorite?"

	Jan. 1978	July 1977	Nov. 1976	April 1975
	%	%	%	%
Football	26	22	23	24
Baseball	16	21	20	16
Basketball	8	9	8	12
Tennis	6	6	4	4
Auto racing	5	5	5	5
Bowling	4	6	5	6
Boxing	4	3	3	2
Skiing	3	3	2	3
Track and field	3	2	1	2
Golf	3	3	2	4
Boating	2	3	1	3
Hockey	2	2	3	2
Horse racing	2	4	3	3
Soccer	2	1	1	1
None and not sure	14	10	19	13

Source: Lou Harris, The Harris Survey, Jan. 1978. Reprinted by permission.

Game

Games can be contrasted with *play*. Games are "nonseparate" in that the goals for participating originate outside the game itself. One may participate for the end-products of prestige, recognition, and status. Moreover, games are structured by rules, formal or informal, which players must abide by. Finally, games involve a seriousness—winning—and are collective in character. Games are not "free" in that rules define when the event is terminated and their perceived seriousness frequently begets preparation for the contest. A game may be defined as "an activity manifest in physical and/or mental effort, governed by formal or informal rules, and having as participants opposing actors who are part of or who represent collectivities that want to achieve a specific goal that has value beyond the context of the game situation, that is, prestige, recognition, influence . . ."[17] "Games are rulebound and competitive; they are won or lost by skill or luck or both."[18]

Caillois devised a fourfold classification of games which included the following elements:[19]

1. *Competition* ("agon"). Caillois' first category typifies games in which individuals or groups attempt to establish mental or physical superiority over rivals within the rule structure of the game. Games such as football, baseball, hockey, chess, and billiards exemplify this genre.

2. *Chance* ("alea"). This category refers to events like coin-flipping, dice, or roulette in which luck or fate become more important than ability or skill.

3. *Mimicry* or *pretense*. This classification refers to activities in which children and adults participate as part of their socialization experiences. For example, children love to role play as a mommy, daddy, cowboy, astronaut, or athlete. Adults, too, are fond of masquerading, especially on special occasions such as Halloween or Mardi Gras celebrations.

4. *Vertigo* ("ilinx"). Typical of vertigo are those experiences in which one transcends or loses self-consciousness (dancing, skiing, acrobatics, mountain climbing, meditation, and auto racing).

These game categories are not mutually exclusive but mixed. Caillois makes explicit the continuum of game forms from the childlike (which he calls "paideia") in which activity is spontaneous, reckless, and turbulent to the highly regulated or disciplined (which he calls "ludus") as in professional football.

Sport

Etymologically, *sport* is derived from the Latin root "desporto," meaning "to carry away." By logical extension, it implies diverting oneself from daily instrumental (economic and utilitarian) routines. In this sense it suggests recreation afforded through leisure pursuits. Sport, for many participants, implies a striking contrast to this root meaning. According to Coakley, three factors must be considered in defining sport: (1) *the types of activities involved,* (2) *the structure of the context in which the activities take place,* and (3) *the participants' orientations.*[20]

1. TYPES OF ACTIVITIES INVOLVED. According to Edwards, as one moves from play to sport the following occur:

1. *Activity* becomes less subject to individual prerogative, with spontaneity severely diminished.
2. Formal rules and structural role and position relationships and responsibilities within the activity assume predominance.

3. Separation from the rigors and pressures of daily life becomes less prevalent.
4. An individual's liability and responsibility for the quality and character of his behavior during the course of the activity is heightened.
5. The relevance of the outcome of the activity and the individual's role in it extends to groups and collectivities that do not participate directly in the act.
6. Goals become diverse, complex, and more related to values emanating from outside of the context of the activity.
7. The activity consumes a greater portion of the individual's time and attention due to the need for preparation and the degree of seriousness involved in the act.
8. The emphasis upon physical and mental extension beyond the limits of refreshment or interest in the act assumes increasing dominance.[21]

Sport may be thought of as a special type of game requiring physical competition (against other players, the "clock," or impersonal foes, such as Mt. Everest or the English Channel).

2.   THE STRUCTURE OF THE CONTEXT IN WHICH THE ACTIVITIES TAKE PLACE. Sport is generally thought of as a special type of game or contest. The essence of sport lies in its patterned and regularized form. It is through the social process of *institutionalization*—the formalizing and standardizing of activities—that sport is regulated. *Rules* constitute the major element in the institutionalization of sport. It is incumbent upon each participant to perform within a broader structure formalized by the "rules of the game." In other words, all participants are constrained by external rules that they impose upon themselves or have imposed by way of officials.

3.   THE PARTICIPANTS' ORIENTATIONS. The orientations of sport participants usually reflect a combination of *intrinsic* and *extrinsic* considerations. An activity which is engaged in for no apparent external rewards is said to be *intrinsically motivated*. On the other hand, when external rewards are the catalyst for an activity, it is said to be *extrinsically motivated*. The differential motivating forces can be captured in the orientation of *amateur* and *professional* athletes. The term *amateur* stems from the Latin word for "love" and refers to a sport participant who plays for intrinsic rewards. The term *professional* designates a participant who plays for external rewards, usually money. In reality, many amateurs and professionals are motivated by a combination of these factors although one may be more important than the other. The reason for this is simple: if the motivation were based solely on intrinsic rewards, the activity would become, by definition, some variant of play; if motivation were based exclusively on extrinsic rewards the activity would become, by definition, some form of work.[22] In reality, however, a dynamic balance between these two sets of motivating forces can be clearly seen.

Intrinsically motivated sport activities blend in with behaviors called *autotelic,* a word derived from two Greek words: *auto* ("self") and *telos* ("end" or "goal"), implying a behavior that is "self-motivated." Csikszentmihalyi interviewed people who devoted a great deal of time and energy to activities that were minimally extrinsically rewarded and maximally intrinsically rewarded.[23] Such individuals continued to involve themselves in autotelic activities out of a passionate concern for the activity and a sense of constant challenge; absence of boredom and anxiety, accompanied by relatively immediate feedback regarding their performances, was also noted. In short, people are capable of seeking peak performances in both sport and non-sport activities without external incentives.[24]

With some distinctions among play, game, and sport behind us, several caveats are in order. First, the defining characteristics of each are ideal-typical. Problems of categorizing a particular activity still remain although, hopefully, there are fewer problematic situations now than prior to the discussion. Remember, too, there are different conceptions of sport. Luschen, for example, defines sport as institutionalized competitive physical activity located on a continuum between work and play.[25] The continuum below locates sport in the middle between work and play.

work	sport	play

Several distinguishing features of sport emerge from Luschen's definition: (1) The activity is physical and thereby excludes activities of a sedentary nature (chess, cards, checkers, etc.). (2) The emphasis upon competition—striving against another—is an essential characteristic. (3) The agonistic or struggle aspect is also a feature of sport.

Others, notably Slusher, have maintained the sport is indefinable:

> The parallel between religion and sport might not be so far-fetched as one might think. As a result of mystical commitments sport and religion open the way towards the acceptance and actualization of being. A partial answer is now uncovered to our obvious difficulty in defining sport. Basically, sport, like religion, defies definition. In a manner it goes beyond definitive terminology. Neither has substance which can be identified. In a sense both sport and religion are beyond essence.[26]

Edwards formally defined sport as:

> Activities having formally recorded histories and traditions, stressing physical exertion through competition within limits set in explicit and formal rules governing role and position relationships, and carried out by actors who represent or who are part of formally organized associations having the goal of achieving valued tangibles or intangibles through defeating opposing groups.[27]

SPORT IN THE SOCIAL/BEHAVIORAL SCIENCES

Many disciplines—sociology, psychology, economics, anthropology, and physical education among others—have contributed to the fund of knowledge about sport in society. Not surprisingly, many of them have arrived at similar conclusions about the nature of sport. Let us consider, however, the purely sociological perspective on sport, the prevailing orientation of this book.

Sociology, one of several social sciences, is the study of human social life. Social life is very broad; so is the discipline of sociology. In fact, few fields have such broad scope and social relevance. "Sociology's subject matter ranges from the intimate family to the hostile mob, from crime to religion, from the divisions of race and social class to the shared beliefs of a common culture, from the sociology of work to the sociology of sport."[28] Social life can be studied from a variety of perspectives—not just the sociological. Furthermore, perspectives should not be construed as "good" or "bad," "better" or "worse," and "right" or "wrong," but as merely different. All perspectives or orientations—psychological, sociological, philosophical, or economic—contribute to the fund of knowledge about human social behavior. In studying sport as a social phenomenon, we will have occasions to approach it from a point of view other than the dominant sociological one.

Defining Sociology

Of the many definitions of sociology, one that is meaningful in the present context defines sociology as the scientific study of *social structures* and *social processes.* An elaboration of the *under scored* components is in order. *Social structures* refer to organizations of people, not in terms of their unique individualities, but in terms of the network of social relationships in which they are embedded. Social structures range in size from a dyadic relation (player and coach), to a small group (basketball or football team), to the entire institutional fabric of sports' organization (sport as a social institution). The different types of social structures in sport will be more fully discussed in chapter 3.

To capture the dynamic component of sport in society the notion of *social process* is salient. *Social processes* are the repetitive and somewhat standardized interactional patterns characterizing individual and group transactions. Some of the social processes relevant to the understanding of sport include: *institutionalization, industrialization, commercialization, bureaucratization, socialization, urbanization, mass communication, conflict,* and *change.* Throughout the book we will demonstrate the utility of these and other social processes for understanding the development, maintenance, and change in the institution of sport. In brief, *sport sociology* can be considered the scientific study of social structures and social processes in the world of sport.

Sociologists are professionals who study social life in a disciplined manner. Sociologists engage in three primary activities: (1) teaching, (2) research, and (3) policy administration. Frequently, they are found in institutions of higher learning although nonacademic employment has become an increasingly viable option for those formally trained in sociology. Because sociology embraces such a large social territory, sociologists tend to specialize in a few areas like family, sex roles, statistics and methodology, law, occupations, social gerontology, and the sociology of sport. Regardless of area of specialization the sociologist

> . . . is someone concerned with understanding society in a disciplined way. The nature of this discipline is scientific. This means that what the sociologist finds and says about the social phenomena he studies occurs within a certain rather strictly defined frame of reference. One of the main characteristics of this scientific frame of reference is that operations are bound by certain rules of evidence. As a scientist, the sociologist tries to be objective, to control his personal preferences and prejudices, to perceive clearly rather than to judge normatively. . . . Nor does the sociologist claim that his frame of reference is the only one within which society can be looked at. For that matter, very few scientists in any field would claim today that one should look at the world only scientifically.[29]

Wedding Sociology and Sport

The *sociology of sport* represents an application of sociological concepts, particularly those of social structure and social process, to the institutional nature of sport. Saying it differently, the sociological perspective is used to analyze sport as an element of the social order of society.

What is the *sport sociologist?* Melnick wrote:

> . . . someone who subscribes most passionately to a "value-free" orientation; . . . draws a distinction between himself as a working social scientist and as a private citizen; . . . leans

toward the functional systemic investigative paradigm; . . . views his professional task as helping to build a cumulative body of knowledge; and, lastly, . . . is someone who is very much concerned with gaining professional respectability within the academic community.[30]

Using Edwards' earlier definition of sport (p. 14), the sociological significance of sport includes the following elements: (1) "it is characterized by relatively persistent patterns of social organization, (2) it occurs within a formal organization of teams, leagues, divisions, coaches, commissioners, sponsors, formalized recruitment and personnel replacement, rulebooks, and regulatory agencies, (3) it is serious competition," i.e., outcomes are not predetermined, and (4) it emphasizes physical skill. The gamut of rules, roles, relationships, beliefs, attitudes, and behaviors constitute the sport institution.[31]

Structural Functionalism

The *sociology* of sport focuses upon the individual and social functions of sport. In other words, it attempts to answer the query, "How does sport maintain the larger social system (or society) and what is its contribution?" To appreciate this perspective, it is necessary to present a precis of the traditionally dominant theoretical orientation in sociology, *structural functionalism*.[32] According to this vintage of sociological analysis, society consists of interrelated and interdependent institutions (family, sport, education, religion, politics, economy), each of which makes some contribution to the overall social stability. Functionalism tends to focus more on equilibrium than social change, and, consequently, analyzes societal components in terms of their role in maintaining and sustaining social homeostasis (equilibrium).

According to Dahrendorf, functionalist theories assume:

1. Every society is a relatively persisting configuration of elements.
2. Every society is a well-integrated configuration of elements.
3. Every element in a society contributes to its functioning.
4. Every society rests on the consensus of its members.[33]

Within the functionalist perspective are several fundamental concepts that have significance in their own right as well as in considering sport as a social institution.[34] Eufunctions and dysfunctions are conceptual opposites. An *eufunction* refers to the positive consequences which make for adjustment and adaptation to the larger social system, while a *dysfunction* denotes consequences that tend to upset the stability of the society. Many *eufunctions* are incorporated into the "dominant American sports creed" (pp 67-73), whereby sport participation apparently performs a host of *individual* functions (builds character, cultivates discipline, prepares one for the competitive nature of life, promotes physical and mental fitness); and *social* functions (reinforces social cohesion through nationalism in addition to the reinforcement of traditional religious beliefs). Few would dispute that these claimed achievements are generally desirable.

Dysfunctions refer to practices that tend to disrupt the social homeostasis. Let us consider several examples. Excessive violence, cheating, gambling, brutality, aggression, and ruthless competition have undesirable ramifications. The infamous "Soccer War" (discussed more fully in chapter 13) between the Central American countries of Honduras and El Salvador was precipitated by the excessive on-the-field violence which "spilled over" to sever diplomatic and commercial relations between the two nations. Recent documentation of fan-player violence as an increasingly major problem in high school, collegiate, and professional settings is interestingly provided in several *Sports Illustrated* articles.[35] The Vince Lombardian ethic of winning at any cost has filtered down into the colleges and high schools and is, in part, responsible for questionable recruiting tactics. One last illustration of a dysfunctional feature of sport is its *commercialization*. Not only have the media influenced the place, playing, and timing of sport contests (see chapter 12), but the sport "spirit" has been subordinated to a position of secondary importance.

Functional theorists also distinguish between *manifest* and *latent* functions. The former are apparent, agreed-upon, anticipated, and generally recognized whereas the latter are frequently covert, unintended, unanticipated, and unrecognized. One of the *manifest* functions of sport is the belief that it affords those from humble social origins, but with highly developed physical skills, a channel of upward social mobility—a means to better oneself as depicted in the Horatio Alger "rags-to-riches" stories. A *latent* function of sport is that it perpetuates myths regarding the ease of social mobility achieved via sports when the statistical odds of success are very low. The following excerpts capture this point:

> In a typical year there will be 200,000 schoolboy seniors eager to win basketball scholarships at some college, but since there are only 1,243 colleges playing the game, the scholarships available cannot exceed 12,000. Four years later the colleges will be graduating about 5,700 seniors, most of them hoping for a professional contract. But there are only 25 professional teams, and they draft somewhere around 200 players each year, but they actually offer contracts to only a portion. About 55 college seniors will land salaried berths with the pros, but of them only about six will earn starting positions.[36]

Similarly,

> In the fall of 1968, there were well over 900,000 high school football players, but less than 30,000 college football players. Since only half of the college players were receiving athletic scholarships, less than two percent of high school football players are eventually supported in college. Of the group of college players only a handfull will ultimately sign professional contracts.[37]

Finally,

> About 400,000 young men played on high school baseball teams in 1970, another 25,000 were on college teams, and about 3,000 were in the minor leagues. However, only about 100 rookies made the 24 squads in the major leagues that year.[38]

These statistics give one an appreciation for the probability of making it in the collegiate/professional athletic arena. Further, they sober those who view sports as an easy escalator for social and economic gain.

Social system is the fifth concept in functional analysis. It is often used synonymously with social organization and/or social structure and highlights the systemic relation among individuals, groups, and institutions. In other words, the elements of society are interrelated so that an alteration in one component may have repercussions in other spheres. Examples of the social system's interconnectedness are legion. The politico-economic arena has affected sport through antitrust laws (see p. 243), blackouts (not telecasting a sport contest within a certain radius if the event is not sold out), reserve clauses (see pp. 243-245) and other judicial mandates.

Conflict Theory

Since the mid-1960s functional theory has been less influential and popular. Its critics assert that the emphasis upon equilibrium is essentially conservative and modern industrial societies are in a state of perpetual and rapid sociocultural change. *Conflict theorists,* the counterparts of functionalist theorists, address themselves to the causes and consequences of conflict and speculate about its resolution and regulation. Conflict theory is predicated on the virtues rather than the dysfunctions of societal disequilibrium and maintains that what may be dysfunctional for one group may be functional for another.[39]

Conflict theories focus upon the social forces producing instability, disruption, disorganization, and conflict. According to Dahrendorf, conflict theory is premised on the following:

1. Every society is subjected at every moment to change; social change is omnipresent.
2. Every society experiences at every moment social conflict; social conflict is omnipresent.
3. Every element in a society contributes to its change.
4. Every society rests on constraint of some of its members by others.[40]

Although conflict theory has a long history, its chief proponents have been Karl Marx (1818-1883) and Ralf Dahrendorf (1929-). Marx viewed social conflict in terms of the struggles between social classes over property and production. Dahrendorf sees the unequal distribution of power and authority as the bedrock of social conflict. Those with power and authority have vested interests in maintaining it while those without them attempt to alter the status quo. Hence, conflict is built into the very fabric of society.

Hoch, a scathing critic of the contemporary sport establishment, has advanced the following formula to underscore the exploitation of sport by the power elite.[41] It reads:

Both the functional and conflict perspectives facilitate our understanding of sport and society. Whereas functionalism sees equilibrium as the nature of social reality, conflict theory sees disequilibrium. Again, perspectives are not so much right or wrong as providing different viewpoints for studying and analyzing societies and their components.

A Brief Chronology of Sport in Sociology

The *sociology of sport*[42] is one of the most recent sub-areas to emerge within the mother discipline. Such newness inevitably bestows "growing pains" on the upstart field. For one, its scope and content are ill-defined and consensus is lacking as to the direction many believe it should take.

Historically, the play-game-sport triad has occupied a position in the scholarly writings of traditional sociologists. Such sociological pioneers as Max Weber, Georg Simmel (1858-1918), William

Graham Sumner (1840-1910), George Herbert Mead (1863-1931), and Thorstein Veblen (1857-1929) highlighted the triology's role in society and social relations. The first textbooks devoted to the study of sport as a social phenomenon were written by Germans. H. Steinitzer's *Sport und Kultur* (1910)[43] explained the connections between sport and culture, and H. Risse's *Soziologie des Sports* (1921)[44] examined sport as a social event capable of being investigated with the tools of sociological theory and methodology. These initial treatises failed to stimulate much interest in the formal study of sport since the next major publication did not appear until 1953 (Frederick Cozens and Florence Stumpf's *Sports in American Life*).[45] Further, much of this writing remained fragmented and unsystematic until very recently.

The serious study of sport sociology has been virtually nonexistent until the past couple of decades. Prior to the mid-sixties, there were not many articles devoted to the sociological analysis of sport. A concerted scholarly effort toward dealing with sport as a social phenomenon was stimulated by Kenyon and Loy's article, "Toward A Sociology of Sport."[46] Riley surveyed the academic specialities of sociologists who were members of the American Sociological Association (ASA) in 1950 and 1959.[47] There were so few designating this speciality area that a separate category was not warranted; instead, those practicing in this sub-field were placed under a miscellaneous rubric. Even as late as 1970 only 0.7 percent of sociologists classified their area as "Leisure Sports, Recreation, or Arts" (a category which obviously includes more than sport sociology) and ranked, in terms of membership, 30 out of 33.

Indications of a sub-area "coming of age" can be found in programs leading to advanced degrees in the field, publication of scholarly journals to disseminate theoretical and empirical knowledge, and professional workshops and seminars. In 1977, twenty universities offered advanced degrees (M.A. and Ph.D.) in "leisure, sports, and recreation" and approximately 150 members (1%) of the American Sociological Association (total membership of approximately 15,000) indicated this tripartite division as an area of academic interest. These curricula tend to be interdisciplinary in nature. The seminal journal in the field was the *International Review of Sport Sociology* (1966) followed by the *Sport Sociology Bulletin* (1976 and now called *Review of Sport and Leisure*), *Journal of Sport and Social Issues* (1976) and *Journal of Sport Behavior* (1978). The first sociology-of-sport session at the ASA meetings occurred in 1971 and several regional and international associations (Midwest Sociological Society and International Sociological Association) have also devoted sessions to this topic in recent years.

Several factors have contributed to the retarded development of sport sociology. Philosopher Paul Weiss traced the benign neglect of sport research to Aristotle some 2000 years ago who apparently shunned sports as too "common" and "low-class" to be worth serious thought. According to Weiss:

> Aristotle wrote brilliantly and extensively on logic, physics, biology, psychology, economics, politics, ethics, art, metaphysics, and rhetoric, but he says hardly a word about either history or religion, and nothing at all about sport. Since he was taken to be "the master of those who know" his positions became paradigmatic for most of the thinkers who followed, even when they explicitly repudiated his particular claims. . . . The fact that these subjects are studied today by economists, psychologists, and sociologists has not yet sufficed to free them from many a philosopher's suspicion that they are low-grade subjects, not worthy of being pursued by men of large vision.[48]

Another reason for this neglect may be due to the prejudgment that sport implies physical rather than social behavior. Hence, social scientists shied away from those areas believed to be devoid of social interactional components. Third, sociology has been notorious for its amoeba-like tendency to subdivide into numerous content areas under such headings as family, legal, occupational, industrial, minority, educational, or social-psychological sociology. Hence, there is a reluctance to continue this proliferation. Fourth, sports-related interests do not occupy the same level of prestige as sociological theory, methodology, and other substantive areas. Some believe it has been considered a part of children's, not adults', activity. In this regard, Dunning has speculated that the hesitancy of social scientists to study sport topics may reflect a Protestant Ethic orientation that considers studies of play, game, and sport as frivolous and unworthy of serious investigation.[49] Fifth, role models in sport sociology have been few in number. Since exemplars have been lacking, there is little opportunity to follow in the footsteps of more established scholars. When this is compounded by the generally inferior research and theorizing in the specialty, it is not difficult to surmise why the field has few practitioners.[50] Finally, until recently, sport, games, and recreation have been privileges of the elite. Now, however, they have become a mass phenomenon as we will see in chapter 2.

SUMMARY

In this chapter we have laid the foundation for a *sociological* perspective of sport. In doing so we have indicated the pervasiveness of sport by briefly mentioning the number of participants and spectators in various sporting events as well as the interconnections between sport and economics, politics, popular culture, and the mass media.

To initiate the discussion, we defined *sport* as a concept and distinguished it from two closely related activities, *play* and *game*. In defining sport, we considered three characteristics: (1) the types of activities involved, (2) the structure of the context in which the activities take place, and (3) the participants' orientations.

A discussion of sociology and sociologists followed. *Sociology* was defined as the scientific study of human social life and *sociologists* as individuals who study social life in a disciplined manner. Sociologists, like other scholars, specialize in various sub-areas; the sociology of sport is one of the most recent sub-areas to emerge within the mother discipline.

Two theoretical approaches in the discipline of sociology—*structural functionalism* and *conflict theory*—were considered and differentiated. Each of these is applicable to the analysis of sport as a social phenomenon.

Finally, we presented a brief chronology of sport in sociology and advanced reasons why its development has been so slow.

IMPORTANT CONCEPTS DISCUSSED IN THIS CHAPTER

Sport	Professional
Play	Sociology
Game	Social Structures
Ideal Type	Social Processes
Amateur	Sociology of Sport

Intrinsic Rewards
Extrinsic Rewards
Autotelic
Structural Functionalism
Eufunction
Dysfunction
Manifest Function

Latent Function
Social System
Conflict Theory
Institutionalization
Concept
Conceptualization

ENDNOTES

[1] Robert Boyle, *Sport—Mirror of American Life* (Boston: Little, Brown, 1963), pp. 3-4.

[2] Throughout this text we will frequently use the term *sport* rather than *sports*. The generic noun *sport* refers to sports in a collective sense rather than to specific activities such as football, baseball, basketball, or tennis. Some of the thoughts that follow appeared in *Sports in American Life* (Columbus, Ohio: Xerox Publications, 1974). Special permission granted, Xerox Education Publications © 1974, Xerox Corp.

[3] Arnold Beisser, *The Madness in Sports* (New York: Appleton-Century-Crofts, 1967), p. 227.

[4] Ray Kennedy and Nancy Williamson, "Money in Sports," *Sports Illustrated* (July 31, 1978), pp. 34-50.

[5] John C. Pooley and Arthur V. Webster, "Sport and Politics: Power Play," *Sport Sociology*, ed. A. Yiannakis, T. D. McIntyre, M. J. Melnick, and D. P. Hart (Dubuque, Iowa: Kendall Hunt Publishing Co., 1976). J. McMurty, "A Case for Killing the Olympics," ibid., pp. 51-55.

[6] William Johnson, "TV Made It All A New Game," *Sports Illustrated* (December 29, 1969), pp. 86-90, 92, 97-98, 101-102.

[7] John W. Loy, Barry D. McPherson, and Gerald Kenyon, *Sport and Social Systems: A Guide to the Analysis, Problems, and Literature* (Reading, Mass.: Addison-Wesley, 1978), p. 320.

[8] Harry Edwards, *Sociology of Sport* (Homewood, Ill.: Dorsey, 1973), p. 90.

[9] The term "concept" refers to a phenomenon that has a direct empirical referent (dog, football, baseball). Some concepts are more abstract in that they represent other concepts. Such sociological notions as *culture, value, norm*, and *social organization* have no immediate empirical referents and are called *constructs*. The social science literature, however, is not always consistent in such usage.

[10] Ronald W. Smith and Frederick W. Preston, *Sociology: An Introduction* (New York: St. Martin's Press, 1977), p. 427.

[11] The idea of "social symbol" emerges from interactionism theory in sociology and social psychology. This tradition was promoted by George Herbert Mead, Charles Horton Cooley, and William Isaac Thomas. According to interactionists, objects and events have no intrinsic meanings; instead, they are defined and refined by individuals in society. For a fuller treatment of symbolic interactionism see Jerome G. Manis and Bernard H. Meltzer, *Symbolic Interaction* (Boston, Mass.: Allyn and Bacon, 1978).

[12] Gregory P. Stone, "Some Meanings of American Sport: An Extended View," *Aspects of Contemporary Sport Sociology: Proceedings of C.I.C. Symposium on the Sociology of Sport*, ed. G. S. Kenyon (Chicago: The Athletic Institute, 1979), pp. 5-27.

[13] Wilbert M. Leonard, II and Raymond L. Schmitt, "Sport-Identity as Side-Bet" (Paper presented at the annual meeting of the American Sociological Association, Boston, Mass., August 1979).

[14] Roger Caillois, *Man, Play and Games* (New York, NY: The Free Press, 1961). Loy, McPherson, Kenyon, *Sport and Social Systems: A Guide to the Analysis, Problems, and Literature.*

[15] Edwards, *Sociology of Sport*, p. 49.

[16] John T. Talamini and Charles H. Page, eds., *Sport and Society: An Anthology* (Boston: Little, Brown, 1973), p. 43.

[17] Edwards, *Sociology of Sport*, p. 55.

[18] Talamini and Page, *Sport and Society: An Anthology*, p. 43.

[19] Roger Caillois, "The Structure and Classification of Games," *Diogenes* 12 (Winter, 1955), pp. 62-75.

[20] Jay J. Coakley, *Sport in Society: Issues and Controversies* (St. Louis: The C. V. Mosby Co., 1978), p. 7.

[21] Edwards, *Sociology of Sport*, p. 59.

[22] Coakley, *Sport in Society: Issues and Controversies*, p. 12.

[23] Milhaly Csikszentmihalyi, *Boredom and Anxiety: The Experience of Play in Work and Games* (San Francisco, Calif.: Jossey-Bass, 1975).

[24] Eldon E. Snyder and Elmer Spreitzer, *Social Aspects of Sport* (Englewood Cliffs: Prentice-Hall, 1978), p. 18.

[25] Gunther Luschen, "On Sociology of Sport: General Orientation and Its Trend in the Literature," *The Scientific View of Sport*, ed. O. Grupe, D. Kurz, and J. Teipel (Heidelberg: Springer-Verlag, 1972), p. 119.

[26] Howard S. Slusher, *Men, Sport, and Existence: A Critical Analysis* (Philadelphia: Lea and Febiger, 1967), p. 141.

[27] Edwards, *Sociology of Sport*, pp. 57-58.

[28] "Careers in Sociology" (Washington, D.C.: American Sociological Association, 1977), p. 3.

[29] Peter L. Berger, *Invitation to Sociology* (Garden City, NY: Doubleday, 1963), pp. 16-17.

[30] Merrill J. Melnick, "A Critical Look at Sociology of Sport," *Quest* XXIV (Summer, 1975), p. 47.

[31] Howard L. Nixon, II, *Sport and Social Organization* (Indianapolis: Bobbs-Merrill, 1976), p. 8.

[32] Talcott Parsons, *The Social System* (New York: The Free Press, 1951) and Talcott Parsons, *The Structure of Social Action* (New York: McGraw Hill, 1949).

[33] Ralf Dahrendorf, "Toward a Theory of Social Conflict," *Social Change*, ed. E. Etzioni-Halevy and A. Etzioni (New York: Basic Books, 1973), p. 103.

[34] Robert K. Merton, *Social Theory and Social Structure* (Glencoe, Ill.: The Free Press, 1957).

[35] Recent documentation of fan-player violence as an increasingly major problem in high school, collegiate, and professional settings is interestingly provided in several *Sports Illustrated* articles. See three-part series on Brutality in Football, Vol. 49 (August 14, 1978), pp. 68-82; (August 21, 1978), pp. 32-56; (August 28, 1978), pp. 30-41.

[36] James A. Michener, *Sports in America* (New York: Random House, 1976), p. 152.

[37] Howard L. Nixon, II, *Sport and Social Organization* (Indianapolis: Bobbs-Merrill, 1976), p. 43.

[38] U. S. Department of Labor Newsletter, June 21, 1973.

[39] Lewis Coser, *Continuities in the Study of Social Conflict* (New York: The Free Press, 1967); Dahrendorf, *Class and Class Conflict in Industrial Society*, (Stanford, Cal.: Stanford University Press, 1959).

[40] Dahrendorf, "Toward a Theory of Social Conflict," p. 103.

[41] Paul Hoch, *Rip Off: The Big Game* (Garden City, N.Y.: Anchor Books, 1972), p. 202.

[42] This brief chronology of sport sociology neglects the contributions of physical educators and Canadians. For their contributions see John W. Loy, "An Exploratory Analysis of the Scholarly Productivity of North American Based Sport Sociologists" (Paper presented at the IX World Congress of Sociology (ISA), Uppsala, Sweden, August 14-19, 1978).

[43] H. Steinitzer, *Sport und Kultur* (Munich, Germany, 1910); Edwards, *Sociology of Sport*.

[44] H. Risse, *Soziologie des Sports* (Berlin, Germany, 1921).

[45] Frederick W. Cozens and Florence Scovil Stumpf, *Sports in American Life* (Chicago: University of Chicago Press, 1953).

[46] Gerald S. Kenyon and John W. Loy, "Toward a Sociology of Sport," *Journal of Health, Physical Education and Recreation* 36 (1965), pp. 24-25, 68-69.

[47] Matilda Riley, "Membership in the ASA, 1950-1959," *American Sociological Review* 25, (1960), pp. 914-926; George H. Sage, *Sport and American Society* (Reading, Mass.: Addison-Wesley, 1974).

[48] Paul Weiss, *Sport: A Philosophical Inquiry* (Carbondale: Southern Illinois University Press, 1969), p. 5.

[49] Eric Dunning, "Notes on Some Conceptual and Theoretical Problems in the Sociology of Sport," *International Review of Sport Sociology* 2 (1967), pp. 143-153; Sage, *Sport and American Society*, pp. 10-11.

[50] In reviewing the state of the art of sport sociology Snyder and Spreitzer ("The Sociology of Sport: An Overview," *The Sociological Quarterly* 15 (Autumn, 1974), pp. 467-487) acknowledge the increasing sophistication of research in sport sociology. They see it as shaking off its "lumpen image." Snyder and Spreitzer, *Social Aspects of Sport*.

A Brief Historical Overview of the Rise of American Sport

INTRODUCTION

A review of the social processes and social history affecting the "rise of sport" in America could easily fill several volumes. Here, a synopsis of some of the more significant factors in this development will be outlined. The roots of American sport extend back to the colonial period. For instructional purposes, this chronology will be divided into five time frames: (1) 1600-1700, (2) 1700-1800, (3) 1800-1850, (4) 1850-1918, and (5) 1919 to the present.[1]

1600-1700

The settling of Jamestown, Virginia (May 13, 1607), the first permanent settlement in America, and Plymouth, Massachusetts (December 21, 1620), the colony of our Pilgrim forebears, provide a point of departure. Although life was less barren and monotonous than traditional accounts would have us believe, these early settlements, particularly New England, placed strong restrictions on play, game, and sport.[2] Two interconnected factors were primarily responsible for such prohibitions: (1) the harsh demands for survival (threat of starvation wrought by the unpredictable and unfamiliar wilderness and forays by the Indians) necessitated continual work and left little time, energy, or opportunity for recreation; and (2) strong religious regulations "in detestation of idleness" and "mispense of time."[3]

Puritan theology was particularly influential in New England. *Puritanism*, a social movement within England's established Anglican church, originated in the late sixteenth century and embraced a variety of groups such as the Congregationalists and Presbyterians. Puritans were dissenters from the Church of England (Anglican) and, dismayed by the crumbling of the church orthodoxy, desired to "purify" and reform some of its doctrines and practices. Dissatisfied with the church and state in England, the Puritans began emigrating to the New World where they hoped to form utopian-like communities. The Pilgrims were the first to arrive (1620), but the mass migration of this group did not begin until 1629. By 1640, some 20,000 people had settled in New England (see endnote 28).

The Puritans' official displeasure with "sports" was many-sided. They opposed all ceremonies and rituals that, in their view, obscured the direct spiritual relationship between humankind and God. But there was also a social class bias in their condemnation of worldly pleasure. Having emerged from the lower classes—poor, hard working, and struggling to enhance their social position—there was a note of resentment in their response to the amusements enjoyed by the wealthy, more leisured groups. Hence, these two influences—spiritual reform and economic envy—cannot be completely disentangled in understanding the Puritan influence on early American "sports."[4]

In 1618, two years before the Pilgrims set sail in the *Mayflower* for the New World, King James I, head of the Anglican Church, countered the Puritan ideology with a declaration in *The Book of Sports* that read

> ... that after the end of Divine Service, our good people be not disturbed, letted, or discouraged from any lawful recreation; Such as dancing, either men or women, Archeries for men, leaping, vaulting, or other harmless Recreation, nor from having of May-games, Whitson Ales, and Morris-dances, and the setting up of Maypoles and other sports therewith used. ... But withall We doe accompt still as prohibited all unlawful games to be used upon Sundayes onely, as Beare and Bull-baiting, interludes, and at times in the meaner sort of people by Law prohibited, Bowling.[5]

When the Puritans came to hegemony in Great Britain in 1643, the House of Commons ordered *The Book of Sports* burned publicly in major cities by the hangmen.

In New England the wayfaring Puritans were, officially, equally intolerant of all forms of amusement. Having sought religious asylum, they were determined to leave no trace of "worldliness." For the most part such a theology was functional. But, when conditions no longer demanded such a way of life, fissures began to appear, even though Puritanism's sway continued. The tavern became the site of social gathering and drunkenness became a social issue. Even at the peak of Puritan orthodoxy, people engaged in sport and recreation despite such condemnation. For example, hunting and fishing, because of their close connection with work and survival, were popular. On the other hand, the upper classes were already engaging in horse racing. In fact, the turf (horse racing) has the longest continuous history of any sport in America. Since as early as 1660 (the first horse race was held that year on Long Island, N.Y.), wealthy men from the Massachusetts Bay Colony were entering their horses in equestrian events.

Attitudes toward sport were not homogenous but varied according to geographical region.[6] New England settlers were the most adamant in their condemnation. The Middle Atlantic states, displaying little religious uniformity since Catholics, Lutherans, and Quakers were prevalent, did not display the same degree of intolerance. The Southern states with their single-crop economy revealed a more permissive attitude. Since many plantation owners were members of the liberal Anglican Church or other tolerant groups, games of all types were generally not scorned. The impact of religious restrictions was considerably less effective on the frontier. Gambling on horse races, cock fights, and bear-baiting were widespread. Fistfighting, wrestling, and rifle shooting were popular as well as rough and brutal. The most popular sport, however, was horse racing.

Despite the varied religious condemnation of play, game, and sport, the sport spirit was not completely squelched. The tavern became a social center in which drinking (sometimes competitively), cards, billiards, bowling, rifle and pistol shooting provided lively competition and entertainment. In colonial Williamsburg, Virginia, the three most popular sports were horse racing, cock fighting, and dancing.[7]

1700-1800

In the larger settlements of the early 1700s there was a suspicion that sports like running and swimming were harmful to health. At the same time, however, sports were amusing after-work activities in which rural peoples convened for such purposes as barn-raising, logging bees, or quilting parties.

Benjamin Franklin (1706-1790), an early advocate of sport, wrote essays on the benefits of sport. As early as 1743 he wrote:

> The first drudgery of settling new colonies, which confines the attention of people to mere necessities, is now pretty well over; and there are many in every province in circumstances that set them at ease, and afford leisure to cultivate the higher Arts . . .[8]

But Franklin was not a proponent of sheer frivolousness since he insisted that "leisure be a time for doing something useful." He also drew an analogy between life and games when he wrote: "Life is a kind of game, in which we have points to gain and competitors or adversaries to contend with. . . ." He advised that "You must not, when you have gained a victory, use any triumphing or insulting expressions, nor show too much pleasure . . ."[9]

A wide range of sporting festivities surfaced during this epoch. They included walking races, hopping and leaping contests, throwing axes, turkey shoots, gander pulling, and quoits (a rudimentary form of horseshoes). In most cases winners received prizes and/or cash, and drinking and gambling often accompanied such bouts.

In 1732 the first sport social club, the Schuylkill Fishing Company, was organized in Philadelphia and was followed by the formation of a fox hunting club in Gloucester City, New Jersey in 1776, a golf club in Charleston, South Carolina, and a cricket club in New York City in the late 1700s. Most of these organizations, however, remained out of the reach of the common person. The "commoner" was pretty much confined to spectating at boxing matches, bull and bear baiting, and cock fighting. While these latter events were part of the tradition of rural Americans, they quickly became commercialized at hotels, inns, and taverns.

Collegiate sports during the period were only in their infancy and characterized by brutality. Students at such Ivy League schools as Yale, Columbia, and Harvard engaged in wrestling and prototype football games but these contests were generally so destructive that college officials discouraged them. In 1787 the Princeton faculty banned such contests because they were deemed ungentlemanly, excessively rough, and of dubious value.

During this century America was primarily agrarian (about 90 percent were engaged in agricultural pursuits) and the population was geographically dispersed. Furthermore, transportation facilities were crude and many people spent their entire lives within a twenty-five-mile radius of their birthplace.[10]

1800-1850

While the attitude toward sport and recreation during this antebellum period (pre-Civil War) reflected ambivalence, mass media reports and distinguished personalities began to acknowledge the benefits of sport engagement. Tom Molyneux, a black, made the news in 1810 when he traveled to London to defend his informal heavyweight boxing championship against Tom Cribb, the English champion. The reporting of this event stirred the sporting spirit. By 1830 boxing clubs in such major cities as New York, Philadelphia, and Washington, D.C. offered instruction in "the art of self-defense" or "the manly science of pugilism."

Newspapers and periodicals applauded this trend and kindled interest in other forms of participation. Footracing tracks, the English game of fives (a forerunner of handball), and racquets (fives played with paddles) gained wide currency. Ninepins and skittles (variations of bowling) were popular at taverns and inns, and improvements in ice skates made skating and figure skating of interest. Classes in swimming (1827) and archery (1828) were being taught in Boston and Philadelphia, respectively.

For the most part, the elitist orientation of sport participation maintained its foothold. Prosperous men, not women or men of humble financial means, occupied the front stage of sport participation. For example, a group of Philadelphia gentlemen organized a town ball (baseball) club, a refined version of one-old-cat, in 1831 and, fourteen years later the Knickerbocker Club played a more sophisticated version of the game that was destined to become America's "national pastime."[11]

This *elitist* orientation is depicted in Seymour's account of the Knickerbocker Club: "It was primarily a social club with a distinctly exclusive flavor—somewhat similar to what country clubs represented in the 1920s and 1930s, before they became popular with the middle class in general. . . . To the Knickerbockers a ball game was a vehicle for genteel amateur recreation and polite social intercourse rather than a hard fought contest for victory."[12] Wealthy individuals sponsored a number of sporting events (rowing, sailing, and footracing) which were attended by large numbers of spectators from all social classes. A rowboat race in 1824 drew 50,000 spectators while a footrace attracted 29,000. The fervor over horse racing and betting is illustrated in Stephen Foster's (1826-1864) song "Camptown Races." This appears to have been the first popular song composed around a sporting theme and ends with "I'll bet my money on da bob-tail nag, Somebody bet on da bay."

1850-1918

The development of modern sport accelerated between the Civil War (1861-1865) era and the First World War (1914-1918). During the former time, industrialization, coupled with the loosening of religious restrictions, revolutionized the life style of the populace. Sport began to be seen in a positive light and Paxson noted that sport had become a "safety valve" (a theme which continues to this day) for people deprived of the freedom of frontier life and the opportunities it offered.[13] Unlike America's agrarian era in which recreation was centered in the family, the movement to urban living shifted the recreational function to secondary institutions.[14]

Since camp life was filled with games, notably baseball, the return of Civil War veterans hastened the sport expansion. By 1868 baseball had become so popular that admission fees were charged. Moreover, in 1869 all members of the Cincinnati Red Stockings, the first professional baseball team, were playing for season salaries between $500 and $1,400. Popularity combined with the profit motive stimulated the formation of the first baseball league, the National League, in 1876. Sport became more businesslike with the shift in control from the players to managers and club owners. By 1880 team owners had instituted reserve clauses restricting players' movement from club to club. Despite attempts of players and other owners to start new leagues, only the formation of the American League (1900) proved viable. In 1903 the warring factions (over players and cities) between the two pro baseball organizations agreed to authorize and play a World Series.[15]

The post-Civil War period witnessed concern over amateur and professional issues. Wealthy and genteel men of the New York City Athletic Club helped organize the National Association of Amateur Athletes of America in 1868 and in 1888 reorganized it as the Amateur Athletic Union (AAU).

Intercollegiate athletics began to blossom during this period. The first collegiate competition took place between rowing crews of Harvard and Yale in 1852.[16] Rowing rivalries (often with track meets as "side events") became commonplace.

Intercollegiate sport gained a foothold in higher education during the 1870s and 1880s. Even the popular sport of football, promoted by Walter Camp, maintained an aristocratic flavor since college students were generally from the upper classes. By the turn of the century football had become a mass national sport with an appeal that cut across social class lines.[17] Football's development, however, was more problematic since it was characterized by ruthless violence and fierce partisan loyalties. News about the abuses of the game (brutality, injuries, deaths) and use of players who were not even enrolled at the college ("trampathletes"), reached as far as the White House. President Theodore Roosevelt, an avid sportsman, called a conference for representatives from thirty colleges to "save" the game. Among the significant outcomes of this meeting was the authorization of the forward pass as a means of reducing the amount of bodily contact. This meeting also culminated in the formation of the National Collegiate Athletic Association (NCAA) in 1906 to regulate football and other collegiate sports. With these events, the purely recreational aspect of sport became secondary to formalized competition.[18]

Prep schools became organized on the collegiate model. The New York Public School Athletic League began in 1903 with organized competition for high school students in track, football, baseball, basketball, soccer, cross-country, swimming, ice skating, roller skating, and rifle shooting.

The modern Olympics was reinstituted (after 1500 years of dormancy) in 1896 by the Frenchman Pierre de Còubertin (1863-1937). His actions were premised on the belief that England's (and to a lesser extent Germany's) emergence as a world power was promoted by integrating sports and education.[19]

During this time sport took on a more formalized appearance with national championships in such activities as chess (1857), billiards (1859), rifle shooting (1871), archery (1870), croquet (1879), bicycling (1880), canoeing (1880), horsemanship (1883), fencing (1891), golf (1894), bowling (1895), handball (1897), logrolling or birling (1898), skiing (1904), and lawn bowling (1915).

Females became active participants, too; first in croquet, then lawn tennis (first introduced from Bermuda in 1875), roller skating, bicycling, and golf. The bicycle, known as the "high wheeler" because its front wheel was as much as five feet in diameter, was exhibited at the Centennial Exposition in Philadelphia in 1876. It ultimately "liberated" females because it provided them with mobility and produced changes in their clothing (from skirts and dresses to shorts). Regarding Olympic competition, women made their debut in 1900 in Paris and were confined to tennis and golf; but in 1928 they were also allowed to participate in track and field events.

Newspapers, beginning with the *New York Journal* in 1895, began to provide coverage of such games as polo, lacrosse, squash, volleyball, field hockey, basketball, and water polo; and in the same year, the first auto race was promoted by the *Chicago Times-Herald* as a publicity stunt.

The first "superstars" were also created by newspaper and magazine sports journalists. The in- and outside-the-ring conquests of John L. Sullivan, heavyweight boxer, made the front-page and he was even boosted as a candidate for Congress. Walter Camp's selection of All-Americans, commencing in 1889, placed outstanding college athletes in the limelight. Similarly, U.S. newspapers heralded the nation's victory in the 1896 Athens Olympics when students from Harvard and Yale captured 9 of 12 gold medals. Famous sport personalities like Jack Johnson (first black heavyweight boxing champion in 1908), Eleanora Sears (first famous female athlete, accomplished in swimming, tennis, golf, boating, and auto racing) and Jim Thorpe (hailed as the greatest athlete in the world after winning both the pentathlon and decathlon gold medals in the 1912 Stockholm Olympics) received favorable recognition from the press.

1919-Present

The years 1919 to 1930 have been applauded as "Sports' Golden Age."[20] Three social factors seem to have been responsible for the surgency of pro and amateur sport: (1) affluence, (2) the increased popularity and significance of the automobile in the lives of people, and (3) the newspaper industry. America's sportsmania was also invigorated by more leisure time, amateur and professional sport organizations, technology (see pp. 29-32), dramatic publicity and promotion, and the possibilities of fame, fortune and big money.[21] It was during this time that the athlete as a national hero—a *celebrity*—emerged.

The gallary of sport personalities included such household names as "Babe" Ruth (baseball), Jack Dempsey, Gene Tunney, Joe Louis (boxing), Will Tilden (tennis), Johnny Weismuller (swimming), "Red" Grange, George Halas, Knute Rockne (football), Cliff Hagen, Bobby Jones (golf), and Tommy Hitchcock (polo), among others.

Female athletes also became popular. In 1925, Hellen Wills Moody captured the fancy of the tennis world, while Mildred "Babe" Didrikson became one of the most versatile athletes of all times; she was accomplished in running, hurdling, javelin throwing, high jumping, swimming, diving, golf, baseball, basketball, billiards, and rifle shooting. In the same year Gertrude Ederle won instant fame as the first female to swim the English Channel. Sonja Henie became one of the richest sport heroes of all time (she has made in excess of $40 million) after winning her third consecutive Olympic gold medal in figure skating. She later entered show business and produced her own Hollywood Ice Revue.

Black professional athletes broke the "color bar" in the late 1940s when Branch Rickey signed Jackie Robinson to a professional baseball contract. In amateur sports Jesse Owens won four gold medals in the 1936 "Nazi Olympics." Although blacks had been stellar boxers prior to this time, it has only been in the past decade or so that their proportionate makeup in certain team sports has exceeded their percentage makeup of the total population. Since much of the discussion in later chapters deals with sport after Robinson's monumental entry, this brief synopsis of America's sporting heritage will end here.

From the 1920s to today, sport has become an increasingly pervasive feature of society. It permeates virtually all educational levels and has filtered into social agencies, private clubs, and business. The last generation has seen two significant developments in sport that we considered briefly in chapter 1 and that we will document more fully in later chapters: (1) the growth of amateur and professional spectator sports, and (2) the accelerated interest in mass participation.[22] The time line printed on the inside of the book cover contains a chronicle of significant sport "events" from 776 B. C. to the present.

INDUSTRIALIZATION, URBANIZATION, AND MASS COMMUNICATION

Three social forces—*industrialization, urbanization,* and *mass communication*—have been instrumental in the development of American sport. These *social processes* are sufficiently important that a separate discussion of them is warranted.

Technology and Sport

The application of scientific knowledge to the production of goods and services and the tools employed in their production is known as *technology.* In short, technology includes both the "know-how" and "wherewithal" of a society. Technological developments in agricultural and industrial production (industrialization), transportation, and communication have been among the most conspicuous catalysts in the rise of sport in America.

Betts provides an excellent summary statement of the impact of *technology* on the development of sport:

> Technological developments in the latter half of the nineteenth century transformed the social habits of the Western World, and sport was but one of many institutions which felt their full impact. Fashions, foods, journalism, home appliances, commercialized entertainment, architecture, and city planning were only a few of the facets of life which underwent rapid change as transportation and communication were revolutionized and as new materials were made available. . . .
>
> The first symptoms of the impact of invention on nineteenth century sport are to be found in the steamboat of the ante-bellum era. An intensification of interest in horse racing during the 1820s and 1830s was only a prelude to the sporting excitement over yachting, prize fighting, rowing, running, cricket, and baseball of the 1840s and 1850s. By this time the railroad was opening up new opportunities for hunters, anglers, and athletic teams, and it was the railroad of all the inventions of the century which gave the greatest impetus to the intercommunity rivalries in sport. The telegraph and the penny press opened the gates to a rising tide of sporting journalism; the sewing machine and the factory system revolutionized the manufacturing of sporting goods; the electric light and rapid transit further demonstrated the impact of electrification; inventions like the Kodak camera, the motion picture, and the pneumatic tire stimulated various fields of sport; and the bicycle and automobile gave additional evidence to the effect of the transportation revolution on the sporting impulse of the latter half of the century. Toward the end of the century the rapidity with which one invention followed another demonstrated the increasingly close relationship of technology and social change. No one can deny the significance of sportsmen, athletes, journalists, and pioneers in many organizations, and no one can disregard the multiple forces transforming the social scene. The technological revolution is not the sole determining factor in the rise of sport, but to ignore its influence would result only in a more or less superficial understanding of the history of one of the prominent social institutions of modern America.[23]

Industrialization

Industrialization, the bedrock of these social factors, is a stage of social and technological development characterized by mass production of goods in large factories employing power-driven machinery and a specialized division of labor. Such societal changes began in Western nations, particularly England, between 1760 and 1860.[24] The production of such sports as volleyball, basketball, baseball, football, hockey, tennis, and golf was greatly facilitated by certain technical developments—transportation and communication facilities and electronics. These developments were by-products of industrialization.

One of the socially significant offshoots of the *Industrial Revolution* was the factory system. The textile industry was the first to feel its impact, largely due to the invention of the sewing machine by Elias Howe (1819-1867). The sewing machine wrought dramatic changes in the production of clothes, shoes, and assorted leather goods. Consider the impact of these technological byproducts on sport. The modern baseball era began around 1920. The "jack-rabbit" ball was made from stronger and stouter Australian yarn. Since the ball could be wound and sewed tighter, it traveled farther when hit and bounced higher and quicker. Babe Ruth's home run production doubled from 29 to 58 with this change. Furthermore, during the "deadball era" (1900-1919), fans saw about one homer every four games. During the modern baseball era (1920-1945), daytime play only, spectators saw almost two per game. In short, the number of home runs multiplied eight times.[25]

Transportation

Technological developments also had a monumental impact in the area of transportation.[26] During the colonial period transportation of any kind was difficult and cumbersome. Movement from one vicinity to another was restricted to foot, horse, and water. During the early 1800s the swiftest form of travel was the steamboat. Of course, even its development depended upon the invention of the steam engine, and when Robert Fulton (1776-1815) built the first steamboat, the *Clermont*, it took in excess of 24 hours to complete a 150 mile journey up the Hudson River. Steamboats carried horses to various cities located along the major waterways, but it was a relatively slow mode of transportation and was inept for transporting participants and spectators (to horse races and prize fights) to locations not stationed along the major waterways.

The smelting of iron set the stage for the production of steel to be used for the rapidly growing railroad system. The upshot of these developments was to facilitate movement of persons and goods from one location to another. Even railroads made their contribution to the development of organized sport (see the quotation from Betts on p. 29).

Prior to the Civil War the railroad nurtured Americans' interest in horse racing by transporting both horses and crowds from track to track. Similarly, participants and spectators for boxing and footraces could be carried to the site of the event by the railroads. In many areas prize fighting was prohibited, necessitating the scheduling of the event in some remote area. The railroad once again provided the means of transportation.

Both collegiate and professional sport were the beneficiaries of the railroad system. For example, the first intercollegiate athletic event—a crew race between Harvard and Yale in 1852—greatly enhanced the sporting spirit through a promotional stunt. Participants received an expense-paid, two week vacation for the visibility they afforded the railroad superintendent regarding the area serviced by his company. Similarly, the first intercollegiate football game between Rutgers and Princeton in 1869 was attended by students taken to the playing area where the event was to be staged. Professional baseball also took advantage of the expansion of the railroad system. Teams tended to locate along the network of railroad lines so that access to the cities would not be difficult.

During the 19th century the technology of the steamboat and railway were among the most significant forces in the rise of sport. But it was the internal combustion engine that revolutionized transportation during the 20th century. The automobile (Henry Ford, 1863-1947) and the airplane (Wilbur, 1867-1912, and Orville, 1871-1948, Wright) were the direct descendents of the internal combustion engine. While auto racing eventually developed into a sport of its own (first Indianapolis 500 occurred in 1911), the automobile is notable for the manner in which it facilitated movement from town to town and city to city at the owner's discretion. People could now travel to ski resorts, beaches, golf courses, and tennis courts when they had the desire, time or money. While airplane races have never been particularly popular sporting events, air travel now enables teams from any location to travel to some distant land to stage a sporting contest. Hence, interregional sport competition today is a commonplace occurrence.

Communication

Paralleling the improvements in transportation were those in communication. The invention of the *telegraph*—the electrical device for transmitting messages or signals over a distance through wires—by Samuel F. B. Morse (1791-1872) around 1844 was instrumental in transmitting sport information since newspaper publishers had telegraphic installations in their offices. During the 1850s it was not uncommon for the outcomes of various sporting events—prize fights, horse races, and yachting events—to be reported by this medium. About the same time, the *printing press* was being improved and literacy rates were rising.[27] Both the telegraph and printing press catapulted sports journalism into the limelight.

International sports received a boost with the laying of the *transatlantic cable* by Cyrus Field (1810-1892) in 1858 and 1866. In the last quarter of the nineteenth century, the most significant invention was the *telephone* by Alexander Graham Bell (1847-1922). Now the human voice could be transmitted over wide geographical areas. The newspaper industry in general and sporting departments in particular reaped extensive (and obvious) benefits from the addition of the phone.[28] Such technical inventions also fed the burning fires of sport journalism.

Mass communication, another social process, is the simultaneous transmission of a message via the mass media to a spatially dispersed and anonymous audience. The printed *newspaper*—press— became an important agent of sport development around 1830. Later *radio* (1920) and particularly *television* (1940s) became almost synonymous with sport. Today, television is so significant in the fiscal considerations of sport that some critics feel it has become the lifeblood of sports, an issue we will consider more fully in chapter 12.

Other Technological Inventions

Other technological advances that influenced the course of sport include the *still camera* (which provided pictures for newspapers and periodicals), *photography, motion pictures,* and the *incandescent light bulb.* Before the lightbulb, sporting events were by necessity restricted to the daylight hours. Shortly after the invention of the light bulb various sporting events—prize fights, walking contests, horse shows, wrestling matches, and basketball games—were being played during the nighttime hours. The famous Madison Square Garden in New York City was staging night sport events during the mid-1880s.[29]

Outdoor sports, notably baseball, did not utilize artifical light until the 1930s. While night baseball was being played in various minor league locales (Des Moines and Wichita), it wasn't until 1935 that the first major league night baseball game was played between Cincinnati and Pittsburgh in Cincinnati. Nevertheless, it wasn't until the 1940s that night baseball gained a firm foothold in the major leagues, although to this day, Wrigley Field in Chicago (the home of the Chicago Cubs) does not have facilities for night events. On August 9, 1946, for the first time in major league history, every game scheduled that day was played at night. A consequence of night baseball was a general lowering of batting averages. Another possible reason for this reduction, however, was the expansion of franchises, which tended to dilute the quality of teams.[30]

Urbanization

Urbanization is a concept referring to two different but interrelated social processes: (1) the movement of people from rural to urban areas and the resulting disproportionate concentration of the population in the urban rather than rural areas, and (2) the impact of urban styles and cultural patterns on life in the rural areas.[31] At the moment we are concerned with the first process. The "movement" of people from rural to urban areas was facilitated by transformations in communication, transportation, and other technological advances.[32]

The first concentrations of the population sprang up around seaports and were associated with transportation and merchandising. Most of the early cities developed around transportation nexuses, e.g., Boston, New York and New Orleans (harbors), Buffalo (canal), and Omaha (railroad). Since industry tended to concentrate around trans-shipment areas (Chicago, New York), the factory system became responsible for bringing together large numbers of people who ultimately created our urban centers.[33]

At the time of the American Revolution (1775-1783) only about five percent of the U.S. population of 3½ million lived in urban areas. By 1860 the increasing concentration of the population in urban centers and the drudgery of routinized mechanical work created a demand for recreational outlets. According to Betts, "*urbanization* brought forth the need for commercialized spectator sports, while *industrialization* gradually provided the standard of living and leisure time so vital to the support of all forms of recreation."[34] In 1890 about 35 percent of the population of 62 million was urbanized. During the early twentieth century the population was 50 percent urbanized and by 1975 about 75 percent of the 225 million population lived in urban settings.

Such early cities as New York, Louisville, New Orleans, Boston, Chicago, and St. Louis became centers of organized sport. Betts summarizes the impact of the city on sport as follows: "Urban areas encouraged sport through better transportation facilities, a growing leisure class, and the greater ease with which leagues and teams could be organized."[35]

In summary, urbanization, a correlate of industrialization, refers to *how* people live as well as to *where* they live. Professional teams tended to develop and locate in large metropolitan areas because the potential market—ticket purchasers, advertisers, and food franchises looked very favorable. Even today the size of the market area (see p. 251) is one of the most important considerations in the location of professional sport franchises.

DEMOGRAPHIC CONSIDERATIONS IN THE RISE OF SPORT

Since urbanization is a demographic process, let us illustrate the application of some demographic concepts to sport. *Demography* is an eclectic field concerned with the *distribution* (the arrangement of the population in space—geographically and residentially—at a given time), *composition* (distribution of population by various bio-social characteristics (age, sex, ethnicity), *size* (number of units—persons—in various categories), and *growth* and/or *decline* in the total population or subpopulations. Demographic analysis[36] assists us in answering such queries as: In what areas does the excitement over a particular sport reach its pinnacle? Why do some sports appear more popular in some regions and other sports more popular in other regions? From what states are student athletes recruited for specific sports? Why have women's sports been most popular in rural America? Why have some sports diffused rapidly while others have not? Where—central city or suburbs—should sport complexes be built? Such questions as these help us understand the significance of sport and facilitate an awareness of the changing role of sport during its historical development.

Once the origin point of a sport has been reasonably established, it is of interest to trace its diffusion into other areas. Basketball, because it was somewhat unique, spread throughout the United States, being promoted by the YMCAs and quickly adopted by colleges and universities. Other sports, notably rugby, were confined to three counties in England and had a much more difficult time spreading (due to a strong amateur rugby league).

After a sport has spread, it undergoes a process of *spatial organization*. Facilities, modes of transportation, geographical distribution of capital, as well as level of interest in the sport, affect this process. For example, during the formative years of the National Football League, most of its members were located in the midwest—Illinois, Ohio, and Indiana. Later on, however, sport franchises were "housed" in other major American cities.

Once a sport had been established, a tendency toward regionalization appeared. For example, basketball is extremely popular in Indiana, Illinois, Kentucky (acronym: "IllInky") and Eastern cities; football is a major sport in Pennsylvania, Ohio, Texas, Oklahoma and other parts of the Southwest; baseball is associated with the Southwest, particularly Arizona, California, and the southern states.

Spatial Organization

The geographical organization of professional American sport is currently in a state of dynamic flux as new leagues and franchises vie with the old for the paying customer (World Hockey Association vs. National Hockey League; National Basketball Association vs. American Basketball Association—but now merged). Baseball provides a clear-cut case of stability in the location of franchises. For more than 50 years the location of teams was stable; then, in 1953, the Boston Braves moved to Milwaukee followed by the transcontinental migration of the Brooklyn Dodgers to Los Angeles and the New York Giants to San Francisco. The most recent additions to pro baseball are the Toronto Blue Jays and the Seattle Mariners. Today there are 26 baseball franchises spread out through the United States and two located in Canada (Toronto and Montreal). Similarly, pro football (28), basketball (22), and hockey (18) have significantly increased the number of franchises.

Historically, the spatial distribution of American sport evolved around lines of transportation. During the embryonic days of baseball's expansion, the existence of transportation facilities and capital were key factors in the location of franchises. More recently, economic matters have become increasingly salient for their establishment and maintenance. Baseball, unlike basketball and football, was from the beginning a professional rather than a collegiate sport. Pro basketball and pro football did not blossom until they were firmly entrenched and accepted at the collegiate level. To this day, in some nooks of the country, college/university basketball and football are as prestigious as their pro counterparts.

To comprehend the spatial organization of America's sport triology—baseball, basketball, and football—it is necessary to consider the relationship between college and professional sports. First, decisions to embark upon these programs were made by college and professional organizations at different times. Whereas the development of collegiate sports took place between 1890 and 1930, pro sports development in basketball and football occurred later. The location of big-time colleges commenced around 1862 when President Lincoln signed the historic Morrill Act, bequeathing public land to each state for creating colleges of agriculture and mechanical arts. Almost seventy colleges, many of them now major state universities, resulted from this legislation. Many states now have at least one school with a "big time" athletic program. Many colleges have elected to join some type of athletic conference, and this membership heightens competition among the constituency. What is of interest, however, is that some of the "hot beds" of collegiate football activity are somewhat removed from professional circles—examples are Columbus, Ohio (Ohio State University), University Park (Penn State), South Bend (Notre Dame), Norman (Oklahoma), Tuscaloosa (Alabama), and Fayetteville (Arkansas).

Sport Regions

Interest, participation, and emphasis in various sports is *not* uniformly distributed across the American terrain. To identify different sports areas, it is practical to determine the *origins* of athletes in various sports. Rooney has documented the origins of players in various sports.[37] In assessing regional concentration of players, two approaches can be taken: (1) simply count the *absolute number* of players from a given region in a particular sport, and (2) control for population of area by constructing an index based upon *per capita* figures. Per capita figures would appear better since they adjust for unequal population sizes. For example, in 1960 there were approximately 14,500 football players with a total population of 180 million.[38] By dividing the former figure by the latter, a crude index for the nation of 1/12,500 is produced. Hence, areas with smaller ratios are producing less than the national average, areas with larger ratios more.

Football

On a *total output basis,* it was discovered that urban areas, particularly Los Angeles, Chicago Pittsburgh, and Cleveland, are producing the bulk of football players, although smaller towns, particularly in the Southeast and throughout the Southern Plains, are noteworthy, too. On a *per capita* basis, however, most of the cities producing large absolute numbers are found to be at the national average or even below. Using this latter index, the high production regions include Western Pennsylvania, Eastern Ohio, Southern Mississippi, Texas, the East Bay near San Francisco, and the Wasatch Valley of Utah—each having two-to-four times the national average. Regions producing relatively few players include Southern Missouri, Northern Arkansas, Kentucky, Southern Illinois, Southern Indiana, the Great Plains, and Rocky Mountains. By state, the flourishing football areas include Texas, Louisiana, Mississippi, Idaho, Montana, North Dakota, and Ohio. See Vignette 2.1 for a view of where high school players come from and where they go.

Basketball

The origins of basketball players are dissimilar to those of football. On a *per captia* basis, the states of Illinois, Indiana, and Kentucky are the primary producers. This region also extends into southern Ohio, West Virginia, and Pittsburgh. Other significant basketball regions include the eastern metropolises of Washington, D.C., New York, and Philadelphia, the cities of Detroit and Chicago as well as areas of Utah and western Oregon. The South and North Central belts (stretching from Minnesota to New England) were well below the national average. By state the most prosperous basketball regions include Illinois, Indiana, Kentucky, Ohio, Pennsylvania, Utah, Idaho, and the Dakotas.

Baseball

Focusing upon the origins of major league baseball players, we find a strong association between population of region (area or state) and the production of players. California leads the pack, followed by Massachusetts, New York, New Jersey, Pennsylvania, and Ohio. Missouri, Oklahoma, Texas, North Carolina, Alabama, Florida, and Louisiana follow. On a *per capita* basis, California leads the group with Nevada and Idaho contributing above the national average. Also above the average are Oklahoma, Missouri, Arkansas, Alabama, North Carolina, and Louisiana. Poor producing states include New York, New England, Michigan, Wisconsin, Minnesota, and the Northern Plains. Surprisingly, the "sun belt" states—Arizona and New Mexico—are not major producers of baseball talent.

Soccer

Soccer, historically, has been region-specific. It thrives in the Northeast and in the St. Louis area. The greatest amount of participation is in New England, New York, Pennsylvania, Maryland, and Missouri. It has spread throughout the United States but has had difficulty in establishing and maintaining a foothold in the South.

Sport Car Racing

This sport originated in the Carolinas and to this day witnesses the most sophisticated facilities and development along the southern Atlantic seaboard and southwestern regions.

Equestrian Events

The American horse show was imported from England and thrives in New England, Virginia, and Kentucky—in those areas dominated by the English colonials. Quarter horse racing is popular in the West (attributed to the influence of cowboys) and in the states of Illinois, Indiana and Iowa.

VIGNETTE 2.1
FOOTBALL: WHERE THEY COME FROM (HIGH SCHOOLS),
WHERE THEY GO (COLLEGES)

WHERE THEY COME FROM

Over the years, certain high schools have turned out far more than their share of star football collegians. Here are ten of the most consistent suppliers of football talent:

Moeller High School, Cincinnati, Ohio
Odessa High School, Odessa, Texas
Bremond High School, Bremond, Texas
Valdosta High School, Valdosta, Georgia
Mountain Brook High School, Mountain Brook, Alabama
Brockton High School, Brockton, Massachusetts
Loyola High School, Los Angeles, California
Brother Martin High School, New Orleans, Louisiana
Cardinal Mooney High School, Youngstown, Ohio
Lakewood High School, Lakewood, Colorado

WHERE THEY GO

Similarly, certain colleges have garnered more than their share. Here, in the order of their effectiveness in bringing football talent to their campuses in 1977 are the top ten colleges:

University of California, Los Angeles
University of Oklahoma
University of Houston
University of Florida
Ohio State University
University of Pittsburgh
University of Washington
University of Colorado
Auburn University
University of Michigan

Source: Terranova, Joe, "Is This the Next Joe Namath," Flightime (September, 1977), p. 48.

Accounting for the diversity and emphasis of different sports regions seems to call for a multi-theoretical explanation. The emphasis upon football in Ohio and Pennsylvania appears to be correlated with a host of economic, ethnic, traditional, demographic, and political variables. Football in the Texas and Oklahoma areas appears to thrive on a different set of socioeconomic variables; the climate, too, is more amenable to the playing of the game. Organizational features (sophisticated run-offs and tournaments), among other features, would seem to help explain basketball fever in "IllInKy." Some regions are single-sport oriented while others are more generally sport conscious. The income and priority accorded by education to sport is still another factor. For example, some states provide extensive opportunities for participation while others provide only a few. In the end, there appears to be no single factor that sufficiently explains the various types of sport programs blossoming across the country.[39]

SUMMARY

The emergence of modern sport is the product of many events, social forces, and people. The roots of American sport extend back to the colonization of North America. During the 1600-1700 period, *Puritan theology* was a dominant force. The harsh demands for survival accompanied by strong religious regulations "in detestation of idleness" and "mispense of time" restricted the early settlers' quest for recreation and amusement. Nonetheless, the sporting spirit was not completely squelched during this century and varied according to geographical region.

During the 1700-1800 period, a wide range of sporting festivities surfaced. Various sport social clubs were founded and the few collegiate sports that existed were characterized by brutality (particularly rudimentary forms of football) and discouraged by faculty and administration alike.

Between 1800 and 1850 newspapers and periodicals began to applaud the sport trend and kindled interest in other forms of participation. Just the same, the elitist orientation in participation sports continued to prevail.

Between the Civil War and the First World War (1861-1914), developments in modern sport accelerated. Intercollegiate sporting events surfaced during this epoch and national championships in many areas were instituted.

From 1919 to 1930 this country witnessed the first "Sports' Golden Age." Affluence, the increased popularity and significance of the automobile, and the newspaper industry helped to kindle the surgency of collegiate and professional sport. From the 1920s to today sport has become an increasingly pervasive feature of society. A time line appearing on the inside of the cover depicts some significant sport "events" from 776 B.C. to the present in the rise of American sport.

Three social forces—*industrialization, urbanization,* and *mass communication*—have been instrumental in the development of American sport. These social processes are sufficiently important that a separate discussion of each was undertaken. Special attention was focused on demographic analysis of sport patterns for the light it sheds upon the rise of sport. The discussion in this chapter facilitates understanding the historical factors contributing to the rise of present day sport.

IMPORTANT CONCEPTS DISCUSSED IN THIS CHAPTER

Puritanism

Industrialization

Urbanization

Mass Communication

Technology

Transportation

Demography

ENDNOTES

[1] This chronology and some of the following observations are gleaned from *Sports in American Life* (Columbus, Ohio: Xerox Publications, 1974); and George H. Sage, *Sport and American Society* (Reading, Mass.: Addison-Wesley, 1974), pp. 61-103. Special permission granted, Xerox Education Publications, © 1974.

[2] John Betts, *America's Sporting Heritage: 1850-1950* (Reading, Mass.: Addison-Wesley, 1974), p. 4.

[3] Foster Rhea Dulles, *A History of Recreation: America Learns to Play* (New York: Appleton-Century-Crofts, 1965).

[4] Ibid.

[5] King James I, *The Book of Sports* (London, England, 1618).

[6] Dulles, *A History of Recreation: America Learns to Play;* Sage, *Sport and American Society.*

[7] William C. Ewing, *Sports of Colonial Williamsburg* (Richmond, Va.: The Dietz Press, 1937), p. 1.

[8] *Sports in American Life*, p. 27.

[9] Ibid., pp. 27-28.

[10] C. W. Hackensmith, *History of Physical Education* (New York: Harper and Row, 1966).

[11] The origin of baseball is still controversial. Some, like A. G. Spalding, a fine pitcher of his day and the founder of a sporting goods company by that name, contended that baseball was uniquely American. On the other hand, Henry Chadwick, the inventor of the box score and an acknowledged authority on baseball, maintained that baseball evolved from "rounders," a girl's game played in the British Isles before Spalding was born. Although Abner Doubleday is often credited with inventing the game, he never claimed that achievement.

[12] Harold Seymour, *Baseball* (New York: Oxford University Press, 1959).

[13] Frederic L. Paxson, "The Rise of Sport," *The Mississippi Valley Historical Review* 4 (1917), pp. 144-168.

[14] Typically, family pastimes grew into organizations and competitions, and then often became profit-makers for manufacturers and/or promoters of public contests. A. G. Spalding, a professional baseball stalwart, co-founded the National Baseball League, promoted a sporting goods business, and sponsored many athletic contests and sports awards. Edwards, *Sociology of Sport*, p. 25.

[15] Paul Hoch, *Rip Off: The Big Game* (Garden City, N.Y.: Anchor Books, 1972).

[16] The first collegiate baseball game was played in 1859 between Amherst and Williams; the first collegiate football game was played in 1869 between Rutgers and Princeton; the first modern intercollegiate basketball game was played in 1897 between Yale and Penn.

[17] Betts, *America's Sporting Heritage: 1850-1950*.

[18] Dr. James Naismith, inventor of basketball in 1891, echoed this sentiment when he declared that adults as well as children preferred contests over sheer physical exercise. Gymnastics had been promoted by the YMCAs by 1860 and the turner (*turnverein*) societies of German immigrants but never became particularly popular.

[19] James A. Michener, *Sports in America* (New York: Random House, 1976).

[20] John Durant, *Pictorial History of American Sports* (New York: A. S. Barnes and Co., 1952).

[21] In 1924 Fordham University took in over one-half million dollars in football gate receipts. In 1926 Stanford University received nearly $200,000 from its intercollegiate sport program; in 1927 Ohio State University grossed nearly $276,000 (Harry Edwards, *Sociology of American Sport*, (Homewood, Ill.: The Dorsey Press, 1973), p. 33.

[22] D. Stanley Eitzen and George H. Sage, *Sociology of American Sport* (Dubuque, Iowa: Wm. C. Brown, 1978), pp. 29-30.

[23] John Betts, "The Technological Revolution and the Rise of Sport," *Mississippi Valley Historical Review* 40 (September, 1953), p. 256.

[24] *Encyclopedia of Sociology* (Guilford, Conn.: Dushkin Publishing Group, 1974), p. 137.

[25] Min S. Yee and Donald K. Wright, *The Sports Book* (New York: Holt, Rinehart and Winston, 1975), pp. 14-15.

[26] Some of these observations are gleaned from Eitzen and Sage, *Sociology of American Sport* (with permission).

[27] Frederick W. Cozens and Florence Scovil Stumpf, *Sports in American Life* (Chicago: University of Chicago 1953). Eitzen and Sage, *Sociology of American Sport*.

[28] *Encyclopedia of American History* (Guilford, Conn.: Dushkin Publishing Group, 1973).

[29] Eitzen and Sage, *Sociology of American Sport*, pp. 39-41.

[30] Yee and Wright, *The Sports Book*, p. 15. Eitzen and Sage, *Sociology of American Sport*.

[31] *Encyclopedia of Sociology*, p. 301.

[32] Betts, *America's Sporting Heritage: 1850-1950*, pp. 173-203; 308-325.

[33] *Encyclopedia of American History*.

[34] Betts, *America's Sporting Heritage: 1850-1950*.

[35] Ibid., p. 30.

[36] The approach of demography and geography are similar. Most material on pp. 33-36 has been excerpted from John Rooney, *A Geography of American Sport* (Reading, Mass.: Addison-Wesley, 1974), with permission.

[37] Ibid. The empirical generalizations for basketball and football were based upon two data sets. The first (covering 1961-1967) consisted of 14,500 football players (136 university division teams) and 4,200 basketball players (161 university basketball teams); the second (covering 1971-1972) contained over 24,000 players.

[38] Joe Terranova, "Is This the Next Joe Namath," *Flightime* (September, 1977), pp. 47-49, wrote: ". . . there are some 29,676 high schools in this country, almost half of which fielded football teams (in 1976 alone, more than 1,058,533 players competed on eleven-man teams at 14,740 high schools) . . ."

[39] John Rooney, *A Geography of American Sport*. See also Rooney's book *The Recruiting Game* (Lincoln, Nebraska: University of Nebraska Press, 1980).

3
Sport and Social Organization

INTRODUCTION

As a scientific endeavor sociology commences with two basic facts: (1) human beings are *social* animals, and (2) human behavior exhibits *repetitive* and *recurrent* patterns. The concept of *social organization* is vital in explaining and understanding these statements. Social organization refers to the ways in which human conduct is regulated and organized as a result of the *social conditions* in which individuals are embedded rather than their physiological or psychological characteristics. It underscores the stable patterns of rules, roles, and relationships in a society or in one of its parts.[1]

According to Blau and Scott, the influence of social conditions can be further subdivided into two categories: (1) the structure of social relations in a group or collectivity, i.e., the network of social relations in which people are involved and sometimes called the *social structure,* and (2) the shared outlooks, beliefs, or perspectives that societal members share and that, in turn, provide "blueprints" for their behavior, i.e., the culture (discussed in chapter 4).

An Example of a Sport Social Organization

Figure 3.1 represents the social organization of a baseball team. Anyone knowledgeable about baseball knows that the diagram represents the basic defensive alignment. Each position carries with it certain behavioral expectations. For example, the first baseman is expected to cover first base when a ground ball is hit to the other infield positions when no one is on base. Within limits, one can predict the probable behavior of any particular player in various situations. All kinds of human groups—not just sport teams—function within a framework of general rules that every member is expected to follow. Further, there are specific expectations for individuals who occupy different positions in the social group. Social organization may be thought of as the process through which social life becomes recurrent, patterned, and orderly.[2]

Consider the 1979 Oakland Athletics. As any pro baseball fan knows, the personnel of this team was radically different from that of the team that previously won three successive World Series (1972, 1973, and 1974). Their manager was no longer Dick Williams and many key players—"Catfish" Hunter, Joe Rudi, Sal Bando, Rollie Fingers, Reggie Jackson—had been traded to other clubs; yet, in spite of this player turnover, the basic social organization of the ball club remained the same.

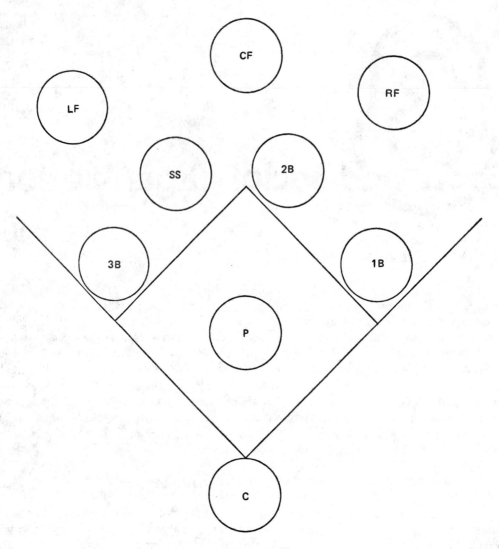

Figure 3.1
Baseball's Social Structure

From year to year there is generally a slightly different crop of players due to trades, sellings, injuries, retirements, and the promotions of minor-league aspirants. As in the past the "front office" and management made new policies (or stressed the old) and instituted changes. But no one would deny that there was a recognizable entity called the Oakland As. The social relationships among management and players, players and coaches, and any combination of categories remained essentially the same. In other words, even though the *individuals* comprising the team changed, the general *social organizational* nature of the baseball club remained similar and therefore analyzable.

The relative enduring quality of the As was its *social structure*. The team was stable because it was organized; all categories of persons—players, coaches, manager—knew, in general, what was expected of them—their duties, obligations and rights.

Levels of Social Organization: Interpersonal, Group, and Societal

Sociologists have found it helpful to distinguish three levels of social organization: (1) *interpersonal*, (2) *group*, and (3) *societal*.[3] These echelons move from the concrete to the abstract. The *interpersonal* level is the most elementary social bond and refers to social relationships existing between two persons when they stand in some kind of relationship with each other. In sport it could be player/coach, fan/player, manager/front-office president. The *group* level refers to interactions between groups as in the National Football League Players Association's dealings with the front offices (labor vs. management). The most abstract level is the *societal* or *social order* which refers to the structure of social relations in the society as a whole.

At the broadest level—the *societal*—sport is a social institution comprised of the totality of associations, organizations, and groups which organize, facilitate, and regulate human activity in sport contexts. Included in this cadre are manufacturers of sporting goods, sport clubs, athletic teams, regulatory and governing bodies of amateur and professional sports, the mass media of the press, radio, and television.[4] Following Caplow's lead, four levels—(1) primary, (2) technical, (3) managerial, and (4) corporate—of social organization within the sport social order can be distinguished.[5]

Primary, Technical, Managerial, and Corporate Levels of Social Organization (Loy, 1968, and Caplow, 1964)

(1) The *primary* or interpersonal level permits firsthand face-to-face association and contact among participants. An informally organized baseball "sandlot" team would be illustrative of the primary level of social organization since leadership has not been formally delegated to specific persons.

(2) The *technical* level is characterized by delegating authority to specific persons who perform in an administrative leadership capacity. Unlike the primary level, the organization is generally sufficiently large to preclude simultaneous face-to-face association among all the members but, at the same time, small enough to allow participants to know of each other. High school and college athletic teams would qualify as technical organizations with coaches and athletic directors functioning in the administrative capacity.

(3) *Managerial* level social organizations are too large for the participants to know every other member but small enough so that all members know one or more of the administrative leaders of the organization. Professional sport tends to exemplify the managerial level social organization.

(4) The *corporate* level of social organization is typified by the general characteristics of bureaucratic structures. Bureaucracies are distinguished by: (1) a clearly defined division of labor specifying the decision-making power of position incumbents and producing an unambiguous chain-of-command among the hierarchy of position occupants; (b) rationality of the operations and impersonal relations of the officials so the goals of the organization can be implemented; (c) an impersonal application of the rules regardless of person or circumstance; and (d) routinization of tasks so that specific individuals are replaceable.[6] Amateur sport organizations (Amateur Athletic Union, National Collegiate Athletic Association, National Association of Intercollegiate Athletics, Association for Intercollegiate Athletics, Association for Intercollegiate Athletics for Women, International Olympic Committee, United States Olympic Committee) and professional sport organizations (such as the Professional

Golf Association, Ladies' Professional Golf Association, National Football League, and National Football League Players' Association) at the national and international levels illustrate the corporate level of social organization.

In summary, the social organization of sport includes congeries of primary, technical, corporate, and managerial associations which arrange, facilitate, and regulate human activity in sport settings. The analytical significance of this delineation permits a macro-level perspective of sport and the social order. Hence, the social organization of sport can be compared and contrasted in both an historical and cross-cultural manner.[7] Vignette 3.1 attests to the social significance of sport social organizations with respect to "failures."

SPORT ORGANIZATIONS AS ASSOCIATIONS

The word *association* is a synonym for *formal organization.* We use the former term instead of the latter to minimize confusion with the sociological concept of "social organization." This latter term is much broader than what we wish to convey in the present discussion. An *association* is a special-purpose group which is deliberately constructed to seek specific objectives, goals, and values such as profit, public service, and entertainment. Considering the number and size of organizations in modern industrialized societies and their pervasive effects on the character of people's lives, social scientists sometimes use the phrase "organizational society" in referring to the modern world.

Let us demonstrate how sport can be understood from this perspective. A brief chronology of sport ownership, baseball in particular, will prove enlightening. Originally, professional teams were "owned" by the players.[8] The players themselves determined when, where, and how they would play as well as how the profits would be distributed. Apparently, the players liked this arrangement and it existed until the latter half of the 19th century. Prior to the formation of the National League in 1876, pro baseball players moved from team to team depending on where they could command the largest salaries. The success and growth of the sport presented problems which sowed the seeds of organizational change.

As payrolls became larger and larger, as the need for more than part-time administration of the program grew, and as the cost of equipment and facilities spiraled, the players grudgingly permitted owners and "front offices" to take care of the off-the-field business affairs. The players did not like the loss of control over the clubs' operations and profit distribution, nor did they appreciate the "strings" attached to such negotiations. It was at this time (about 1880) that owners insisted that players sign contracts containing reserve clauses (see pp. 243-45), giving the owners virtual control over the players' destinies.

When the American League was formed in 1900, there was a short period of time during which players could choose between the two leagues. This meant the owners in the respective leagues had to compete for them. The owners quickly realized this state of affairs was not in their best mutual fiscal interests so they agreed not to hire each others' players. This usurpation of self-determination put the players back into their "powerless" bargaining position. It is this set of historical occurrences that provides the backdrop against which the contemporary structure of sport can be understood and will be expanded upon in chapter 11.

Sport franchises today are *associations*—special purpose groups—aimed at seeking profits and providing entertainment. They are *formal organizations,* colloquially referred to as *bureaucracies.* Like other bureaucratic structures, they possess identifiable elements such as specialization, a system

VIGNETTE 3.1
SOCIAL ORGANIZATION AND FAILURE

The impact of failure in professional sport can be understood, in part, in terms of a sport's social organization (Donald W. Ball, "Failure in Sport," *American Sociological Review* 41 (August, 1976), pp. 726-739). Consider the organization of professional baseball and football. Baseball is built upon a two-caste hierarchy of leagues: (1) the "majors" and (2) the "minors." The majors are comprised of 26 teams, each team belonging to either the American or National League. Under this top crust are various minor leagues occupying different positions on the baseball ladder. The classification of minor league teams (AAA, AA, A, and rookie) has significant consequences, e.g., player salaries, facilities, prestige, and player ability. Many minor league teams are owned outright by their major league counterparts and serve as "farm" teams from which players can be recruited. Because of these structural arrangements mobility in baseball can be *between* leagues or *vertical*. In this sense baseball failures stick with you and you with them as one moves up and down the baseball hierarchy.*

The organization of professional football differs from that of baseball. It comprises one unstratified league of 28 teams (since the AFL and NFL have merged and the WFL did not prove viable) and minor league facsimiles—"semi-pro" clubs—are not affiliated with a "parent" club. Players are generally recruited from colleges and universities. Mobility in pro football is *intra*league and *horizontal* or out. Hence, failures in football are more likely to produce an exodus from the game rather than movement from one organization to another. Furthermore, since pro football players are more likely to have gone to college and graduated, the costs of failures may be less traumatic for them than for their baseball counterparts.**

In brief, the contrasting social organizations of professional football and baseball shed light on the differential experience of failure by pro baseball and football athletes.

*The social organization of professional hockey resembles that of baseball and, theoretically, failures may operate similarly.

**The structure of field hockey in Brazil is analogous to that of football in the states and failure may have similar ramifications.

---

of rules and regulations, hierarchy of authority, and impersonality. The *formal organization* or official organizational chart of a typical baseball team is depicted in Figure 3.2. Scrutinizing Figure 3.2 highlights the bureaucratic characteristics of baseball's formal organization. Most obvious is the hierarchial "power" arrangement with the owner at the top and the players at the bottom. Those at the top are generally in a position to pass judgment on the fate of those below. Cutting across the vertical dimension is a horizontal one which includes the positions of ticket manager, traveling secretary, scouting supervisor, public relations director, director of player personnel, etc.

Each slot in the organization is specialized in that a set of rules and regulations—a job description—specifies what each incumbent is and is not expected to do. The players, for example, cannot "fire" the manager but the owner can. The manager, on the other hand, decides who should play at the various positions and when. A system of rules such as dress codes or curfews specifies the attitudinal and behavioral requirements and taboos. Finally, the structure is impersonal in that, theoretically, decisions—hiring, firing, demoting, or trading—are made for the larger good of the organization.

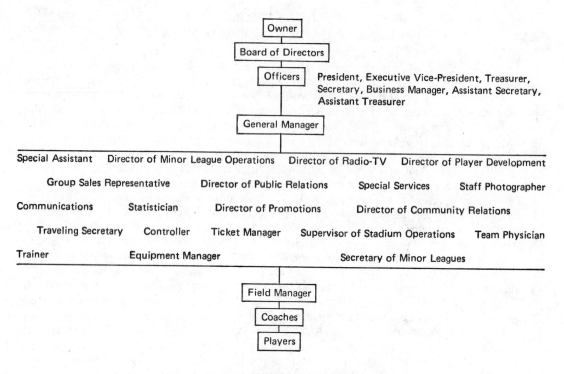

Figure 3.2
Formal Organization Chart For a Typical Major League Team
(Constructed from various professional baseball teams' press, radio, and TV guides)

The nature of the bureaucracy that we have been discussing must be understood in "ideal-typical" terms (see p. 9). Theoretically, these characteristics and operations apply but, in practice, do not always so neatly match up with locker-room realities. Bureaucracy has another "face," what sociologists call the *informal structure* or *informal organization*. This arises, sometimes spontaneously, to fulfill needs the formal organization cannot meet and can be understood as behavior patterns that develop when persistent problems are confronted. Some issues which inevitably seem to produce the informal organization are lag (the gap between rules and actual operations), generality and abstractness of rules (which in individual cases may be bent or modified), and the impersonality which goes against the "social grain."

SPORT AS A SOCIAL INSTITUTION

Just as the survival of human organisms requires the operation of certain vital functions, societies, too, have tasks or activities that must be performed if they are to exist and flourish.[9] This biological point of view is referred to as the *organic model* of society, and in it society is viewed as an organism with certain "needs."[10] When individual and societal "needs" are adequately met, the "organism" maintains a state of equilibrium or homeostasis (see structural-functionalism in chapter 1). Similarly, when such needs are malfunctioning or inadequately served, disequilibrium results.

The life-sustaining chores of a society are carried out by the *institutions,* cultural patterns organized around the central needs of individuals in society. The five fundamental social institutions are: (1) marriage and family, (2) polity, (3) education, (4) religion, and (5) economy. Institutions are classified in terms of their functions. The function of the economy lies in the production, distribution, and consumption of goods and services; the functions of the marriage and family system are those of reproduction, socialization, and position maintenance; education is responsible for the formal transmission of the cultural heritage; the polity is a means of establishing laws and protecting citizens from one another and foreign countries; and religion provides the vehicle through which humans relate to the supernatural.

But what is the function of sport? Like the other social institutions, sport does not have a single function, nor are its functions independent from other institutions. However, two of the chief functions of sport are: (1) a *value receptacle,* and (2) a *safety valve.*[11] The *value receptacle* function is a description of the way in which general cultural values are mirrored through a particular institution, in this case, sport. Carefully investigated, sport can be seen to reflect the general values society holds important. In this regard, sport provides a *microcosm* of society at large.

The *safety valve* function of sport implies that sports provide an arena in which hostility, violence, and aggression may legitimately be expressed. Sport thus becomes a medium for the expression, catharsis, and displacement of pent-up aggressions that would otherwise disrupt the homeostatic and dynamic balance of society. In making this latter statement, the dominant theoretical paradigm in sport sociology is, again, made explicit. As we saw in chapter 1, the structural/functional model has, historically, been given conceptual priority over conflict theory.

Institutions develop in one of two ways. They are either *crescive,* that is, naturally and spontaneously emerge in the routine course of social interaction or *enacted,* that is, deliberately and concertedly formed. Sport has witnessed the operation of both these developmental processes. The earliest intercollegiate sports had a crescive flavor to them. The fragmented collegiate sports that existed between 1850 and 1875 were student-created endeavors. College administration and faculty did not oversee them nor were they particularly interested in students' leisure time activities. Later, when colleges and business people began to acknowledge the commercial potential of sport, administrators took specific steps to control intercollegiate athletics. Sports that have been deliberately enacted include snowmobiling, superstar competition, rollerderby, demolition derby, and box lacrosse. The reason for such enactment generally stemmed from the anticipated profit-making nature of the sport.

Institutionalization of Sport

Sport, today, is institutionalized. *Institutionalization,* a social process, refers to procedures becoming organized, systematized, and stabilized. *Organization* denotes a delineation of positions, roles and role relationships; *systematization* indicates the specification of tasks and duties to be performed by the role incumbents; and *stabilization* refers to the tendency of the process to exist beyond the life of any given participant. *Sport as a social institution may be thought of as a system of social relationships or a network of positions and roles* (athlete, coach, manager, athletic director, cheerleader, and owner), *embodying the ultimate values people hold in common* (R.C. Angell, *The Integration of American Society,* New York: McGraw-Hill, 1941). Figure 3.3 is a partial list of the positions embodied in the institution of sport.

Athlete	Cheerleader
Superstar	Band Member
Starter	Alumni
Substitute	Owner
Captain	Sport Equipment Wholesaler
Coach	Sport Equipment Retailer
Manager	Concessionaire
Physician	Fan
Trainer	Spectator
Athletic Director	Timekeeper
Referee	Scorekeeper
Umpire	Statistician
Line Judge	Public Address Announcer
Field Judge	TV, Press, and Radio Reporter

Figure 3.3
A Partial List of Social Positions in the Institution of Sport

Position, Role, Norm, Role Set, and Role Strain

To understand the individual's place in a social institution, two sociological concepts are of fundamental importance: (1) *position,* sometimes called *social status,* and (2) *social role.* A *position* is the niche one occupies in the larger society. Most often these niches are occupational (professor, doctor, lawyer, professional athlete) or kinship-based (mother, father, brother, sister, aunt, uncle). A *social role,* on the other hand, is the behavior expected/required/anticipated from the occupant of a social position. Roles are governed by *social norms,* the expectations the larger society—or sub-groups within a society—have for the position incumbent's rights and duties. To give substance to these sociological concepts, consider the position of professional baseball players. They occupy an occupational niche in society called "professional athlete." All those who occupy such positions are expected to conduct themselves in certain ways, on as well as off the field. For example, the Cincinnati Reds, like other pro clubs, have a dress code. Among other things, it places restrictions on length, amount, and neatness of head and facial hair. The duties or obligations of the Reds' players require adherence to this code. The rights or privileges of players include a salary that is generally an incentive for abiding by these regulatory dictates. On the general level, individuals, theoretically, become unimportant in the analysis since the norms—expectations for players on fans', management's and front office's part—apply to all individuals. Hence, these two ingredients—*position* and *role*—of social organization become significant in a sociological analysis.

Implicit in the position-role scheme is the principle that roles are *reciprocal* or *relational* in nature. Rights and obligations for a social category are always in reference to other categories. The role of player is not isolated from the role of manager, coach, owner, or even fan. The reciprocality of roles is further testimony to the fundamental importance of social relationships in human conduct.

To the keen reader, it has probably occurred that the flow of social interaction does not always proceed in the smooth and orderly fashion suggested above. Sometimes players refuse to follow the rules. Richie Allen, Joe Namath, Derek Sanderson, Duane Thomas, Curt Flood, Chip Oliver, Vince Matthews, Muhammed Ali, Wayne Collett, and Al Hrabosky have been notorious for deviating from their official duties. Such individuals are referred to as *deviants* (*deviance* is more fully discussed in chapter 6), a generic name given to persons who depart, usually significantly, from the expectations for their behavior. What happens in such cases? First, roles are not straight jackets; rather, they define a *range* of more-or-less acceptable behaviors. Hence, there is some leeway permitted. Second, star performers frequently accrue "idiosyncrasy credits";[12] if their performances are superior to the rest, then they are allowed a greater range of departure from the norms. Of course, too much deviation and by too many individuals (for example, the Athletic Revolution of the 1960s) threatens the stability of a social group or organization.

Each individual in society plays numerous roles and, similarly, is an occupant of numerous positions. The pro athlete may also hold the positions of father/mother, husband/wife, son/daughter, uncle/aunt, or brother-in-law/sister-in-law. With each one of these positions there are social norms influencing the nature of the interaction with other specific positions. Such multiple position-occupancy and role-performance is called a *role set*. Often in the course of acting out the various roles we play we confront an impasse . . . sometimes the expectations of different roles or even the same role are inconsistent. Take managers as an example. On the one hand, they are expected to make decisions, cultivate a respect for rules, and discipline their players. On the other hand, they are expected to be sensitive to the needs and idiosyncrasies of their players. Not infrequently the two expectations conflict with one another. In the course of role behavior, the individual may be subject to conflicting pressures and strains arising out of incompatible behaviors required or expected of the incumbent. This phenomenon is known as *role strain*.

Ascribed and Achieved Positions

Positions in society may be either *ascribed* or *achieved*. *Ascribed positions* are those secured involuntarily. For example, sex, age, race, and ethnicity are social categories to which all of us belong through no choice of our own. We do not choose to be male, white, 34, or WASP. *Achieved positions* are those over which we have some control. They are secured voluntarily; we choose to be a doctor rather than a lawyer, a ditch digger rather than a sociologist. Attaining professional athletic status is generally considered to be an achieved position although both ascribed and achieved features play a facilitating or inhibiting influence. For example, certain physical/physiological/genetic factors (of an "ascribed" nature) are extremely important in achieving certain positions. Short stubby individuals are not likely to appear on pro basketball rosters; weak and frail individuals are not likely to do well in football, hockey, or boxing.

Of the several social positions listed in Figure 3.3, we will isolate one—that of the participant or *athlete*—for subsequent discussion. In other sections of this book we will consider some of the other sport positions outlined in this figure.

THE ATHLETE: PROFESSIONAL, COLLEGIATE, HIGH SCHOOL, AND JUNIOR HIGH

One dictionary (Random House *College Dictionary*, 1973) defines an *athlete* as a person trained to compete in contests involving physical agility, stamina, or strength. Athletes are not a homogenous mass; instead there are different types (male vs. female, white vs. non-white, amateur vs. professional, high school vs. collegiate vs. professional). These considerations are significant when talking about the ambiguous phrase "the athlete role." It should be obvious that the rights and responsibilities of athletes are affected by the level at which they perform. Sand-lot players in contrast to professional athletes have different skills, expectations, and motivations for playing (see the discussion of the distinguishing characteristics of sport, game, and play in chapter 1 on pp. 9-14).

The modern day athlete is on one hand a cherished idol, subject to adulation but, interestingly, neither well nor fully understood. Take a moment and jot down the characteristics and traits you attribute to athletes. Does a certain stereotyped image prevail?

Literary Perspectives of the Athlete

According to Wiley Lee Umphlett,[13] American fiction conveys a three-part image of the athlete. The fictional stereotype describes athletes as: (1) anti-urban in mind set and mentality and striving for a life closer to nature (Bill Walton, professional basketball player, might be thought of as epitomizing this image); (2) anti-feminine and incapable of coping with women. Johnny Bench of the Cincinnati Reds, described in the following news brief, conforms to this characterization:

BENCH HAS 'NO RESPECT FOR WOMEN'

CINCINNATI—On his wedding night, Johnny Bench played ping-pong with his best man, says his now divorce-bent bride, Vicki Chesser, who claims the Cincinnati Reds' slugger has "no respect for any woman and probably for any man."

In an exclusive interview with the Cincinnati *Enquirer* Tuesday to give her side of the breakup of "poor Johnny Bench's marriage," Miss Chesser said, "Johnny broke my heart, my spirit and my health."

She is asking $100,000 a year in temporary alimony while her divorce goes through.

Miss Chesser said when she received an offer to pose in the nude for *Hustler* Magazine for $25,000 Bench told her, "Why not, it's good money."

She said the incident proved to her that Bench wanted a "whore in the bedroom," not a wife, and that he had "no respect for any woman and probably for any man."

(Vidette, Illinois State University Daily Newspaper (March 3, 1977), p. 8.)

(3) A victim of prolonged adolescence clinging to poignant memories of bygone days of glory and incapable of grappling with adult problems, issues, and concerns. Several former players have experienced emotional, social, and economic crises after their disengagement from sport (see pp. 50-53).

Several excerpts from literary works capture the popular social stereotype of Umphlett's triology. Michener wrote:

The fact that success in athletics does not always mean success in business or life provides Philip Roth in *Goodbye, Columbus* and Irwin Shaw in "The Eighty-Yard Run" with a convenient means for satirical expression. We discover that Roth's Ron Patimkin and Shaw's Christian Darling as ex-college athletes are unable to involve themselves with the realities of life. Instead, they continue to live in the idealized world of "the game"; consequently their lives exemplify still another theme in modern literature—the search for maturity.

Like a child, he cannot see himself in relationship to his environment, and in this so-called innocent state is compelled to relate everything to his own ego-centered world. The result is lack of self-awareness and a failure in communication, not only in marriage but in social dealings as well. The only real world for him is, and always will be, we recognize, the world of the game. As early as F. Scott Fitzgerald's portrait of Tom Buchanan in *The Great Gatsby* (1925), we are given an important clue to the reason for such an outlook. Tom as an All-American football player at Yale is described as "one of those men who reach such an acute limited excellence at twenty-one that everything afterward savors of anticlimax." For the star athlete, nothing in life can ever again approach the significance of the lost world of the Big Game.[14]

The thesis advanced by the fictional version of the athlete is that sports provide a vehicle through which one can ascend to greatness, followed by a sickening descent into social, economic, and psychological oblivion. Kennedy and Williamson lucidly illustrate this process:

In 1972 the Philadelphia Blazers of the WHA signed Sanderson (Derek) to a five-year, $2.65 million contract. At $500,000 a year he was the highest paid athlete in the world, but eight games into the season the Blazers bought back his contract for $1 million—or $333,333 a goal. Sanderson then bounced to six teams in six years. Last December he was hospitalized, ostensibly for burns suffered in a kitchen accident, but really to dry out from overuse of Valium, sleeping pills, and alcohol. During his 10-year career, Sanderson grossed approximately $2 million. Now most of it is gone: $1 million to taxes, $100,000 to uncollectible loans to acquaintances, $100,000 to his agent, $32,000 for a Rolls-Royce, $35,000 for a single trip to Hawaii, $120,000 for his house in Fort Erie, Ontario, $45,000 for apartment renovation and thousands more on booze, broads, and costly hotel suites. "In one year I spent $117,000 just living," says the out-of-work center, who figures he has simply "blown" $600,000. To be sure, Sanderson is self-destructive, but in the megabucks world of sports he has lots of company.

"I don't know how long I'll be around this league, but while I've got cash, I've got to splash," says Houston Rocket guard Rudy White, who in three years splashed from a Chrysler, to a Cadillac, to a Mercedes. After Marvin (Bad News) Barnes signed his $2.1 million contract with St. Louis of the ABA in 1974, he spent $125,000 in six weeks. A silver Rolls-Royce, a diamond ring for each hand, a ruby necklace spelling NEWS and 13 telephones were musts for Barnes, then 21 years old.[15]

In short, the social and economic gains achieved through sport are quickly wiped out after (generally) short careers terminate. The problem lay people confront when thinking of the athlete is that the successful ones (pro football players Jimmy Brown and Joe Namath, baseball players Willie Mays and Mickey Mantle, golfer Arnold Palmer, hockey player Bobby Orr, boxers Joe Louis and Muhammad Ali, and tennis players Jimmy Connors, Chris Evert and Billie Jean King) stand out. Only when the careers of "typical" participants within a sport are carefully examined is the full truth disclosed. Let us proceed to examine, then, the *scientific* rather than *fictional* accounts of amateur and *professional* athletics.

THE PROFESSIONAL ATHLETE

Individual Sports

Participants in *individual* sports—boxing, horse racing, auto racing, bowling, golf, tennis—typically confront a distinct set of problems in transiting to the "big time." In *team* sports the expenses associated with training are typically underwritten by professional or collegiate organizations. In individual sports participants must secure financial backing on their own. Their problems go beyond the paying of expenses. They must have access to the means for becoming involved in matches, contests, events, tournaments, and meets. For example, boxers need sponsors and agents; automobile participants need to be recognized by other participants; bowlers, golfers, and tennis players must maintain membership in professional organizations and sometimes await special invitations.[16]

Boxing

The classic example of problems faced by individual athletes is boxing. Generally the boxer has arisen from humble socioeconomic origins and his financial status inevitably requires some sponsor, in addition to a trainer and manager, to meet the financial cost of training and travel. Such external financial backing has greatly reduced the prize money received by even recognized champions and contenders. Boxers have often negotiated contracts in which the bulk of the "purse money" went to their sponsors. Studies of boxers[17] have found that relatively few are able to maintain professional careers, save money, and become wealthy, and many are exploited by managers. Studies of boxers, initially called pugilists, have consistently shown that boxing draws its performers from the lower social classes. Weinberg and Arond's research documents this contention.[18] In both 1909 and 1916 Irish and German boxers were most prominent. In 1928 these ethnic minority groups were replaced by boxers of Jewish and Italian descent. From 1948 to the present black and Mexican boxers, particularly the former, have been in greatest abundance. These data demonstrate that boxing has appealed to ethnic minorities who are generally stationed at the lower rungs of the social stratification system (see chapter 7 for a definition and discussion). Hence, it is tempting to see this avenue of mobility as more worth to minority ethnic groups than, in fact, it has been. Weinberg and Arond's research offers convincing evidence that *vertical mobility,* movement up the social class ladder, via boxing is more apparent than real.[19] In one inquiry they analyzed what happened to ninety former boxing champions who earned more than $100,000 when that sum was large and taxes were low. Virtually none of them had a substantial job—they worked in bars and taverns, held unskilled laborer jobs, were ticket takers in movie houses, bookies, janitors, gas station attendants, and the like.

Additionally, the career patterns of boxers shed light upon this arena as a *social mobility mechanism* (a channel through which improvements—social and economic—can be made). Regardless of period—1938 or 1950—the overwhelming majority of fighters (more than 90 percent) were restricted to local and preliminary fights (which are generally poor paying and of less social significance) and only a small minority (less than 10 percent) received recognition brought by being national contenders.

Let us relate the fate of several heavyweight boxing champions.[20] Three of the ex-champs since Joe Louis are dead: Rocky Marciano was killed in a plane crash in 1969; Sonny Liston died of drug overdose in 1970; and Ezzard Charles succumbed to the same debilitating disease (sclerosis involving a degeneration of brain and spine) that killed baseball's Lou Gehrig.

Joe Louis, 63, captured the heavyweight crown from James J. Braddock in 1937. He successfully defended his title 25 times and scored 21 KOs. Although it is reported that he made $5 million during his reign, ill-advised business adventures, a costly divorce, and a tendency to live "high" left him in debt. For example, by 1956 he owed $1¼ million in taxes. In 1970 he was committed by his family to a psychiatric hospital, and more recently is learning to walk after suffering a stroke following a heart attack.

Jersey Joe Walcott, 64, beat Ezzard Charles for the title in 1951. Fourteen months later, after being KO'd by Marciano, he retired. Today he lives in New Jersey where he has gained high acclaim as a community organizer for handicapped and retarded children. Walcott says he never earned a purse larger than $300 during the first fifteen years of boxing and concedes that some of his later winnings "could have been better invested."

Ingemar Johansson, 45, was driven out of Sweden by high taxes after his fights with Floyd Patterson. After retiring in 1963, he dabbled in real estate and the restaurant business before moving to Florida. Since his retirement from boxing he says: "I haven't done anything, really. I am like a used-car dealer; I stick my nose in everything I can make a profit on."[21]

Other surviving champions like Floyd Patterson, 43, Joe Frazier, 34, and George Foreman, 30, appear to have fared better than either Louis or Johansson. Patterson has achieved what he's always been looking for—"piece of mind." Frazier invested his money wisely and experiences no financial problems; and Foreman, after losing to Jimmy Young, has become a religious convert and is now preparing himself for religious work. Muhammad Ali, one of the greatest, successfully retired in 1979.

Golf

When golf buffs think of golf personalities, the Arnold Palmer's, Jack Nicklaus's, Tom Watson's, Nancey Lopez's, and Jerry Pate's come to mind. During their prime such athletes have won thousands each week. What most golf fans fail to realize, however, is that hundreds of others—the "rabbits" (those who haven't made it)—live from "hand to mouth" in a constant struggle for a chance to make the big time. Let us briefly discuss these unglamorized players and their lives.[22]

Consider the Professional Golf Association. There are about 420 golfers on the tour. In 1977 the leading money winner, Tom Watson, made $310,653. But 190 players (45%) earned not a single cent and about the same number made some money, but not even enough to cover expenses.

Gaining a slot on the tour is not easy. Most players gain admittance to the tour through the Tour Qualifying School in Pinehurst, N.C. Although there are lectures on finance, tournament etiquette, and player rules, the school is not a school in the traditional sense of books, classroom lectures, and written exams. Instead, the school is one of on-the-job training: six rounds of golf subject to elimination after elimination. PGA official Jack Stirling describes the process by which golf players reach the qualifying school.

> Most players . . . learn the game as preteens, play all through high school and college, then practice in earnest. The ideal training process means hitting about 600 balls a day. That means . . . swinging a club every 45 to 60 seconds and doing it for four hours in the morning, breaking for lunch, then another four hours in the afternoon—day after day. All the while he is analyzing his grip, his swing, his stance.[23]

Once a golfer has gained a slot on the tour, most have to qualify for each tournament. The number of golfers competing in weekly tournaments varies according to the number of daylight hours. During daylight savings time about 156 can compete; during standard time about 144. The deck is stacked against the substar players since it is traditional for the top players to have the first opportunity to secure these spots and sometimes as few as five are available for qualifiers. It is the rabbits—the low or non-earning players—who are most prone to travel each week from one tournament to another around the country. Stirling says: "It is a demanding life . . . Monday is for qualifying, Tuesday is the practice round, Wednesday is the pro-am, Thursday through Sunday, the tournament—that is, if he makes it."[24]

Golf, like so many other sports, presents a constant challenge. Since the big winners are the ones most clearly impregnated in our minds, it is necessary to look behind this facade to catch a glimpse of what the sport is really like.

Team Sports

The legal status and career training of athletes who participate in *team* sports is unlike that of individual sport participants. Rather than duplicate our discussion of team sport participants (chapter 11), we will directly begin with some empirical data regarding the sports of baseball and football.

Baseball and Football

The idolization of pro athletes frequently reaches its apex with baseball and football players. Empirical data reveal a relatively short professional career for most of these athletes. Statistics show that the average playing career of both professional baseball and football players is less than five years.[25] This means two significant things: (1) they retire before 30, and (2) most do not play long enough to qualify for a pension. Using the mean salary in baseball (for 1978) as $76,349 (the mean salary using the starting lineups for the 1977 opening game was $93,000)[26] consider the modal player. If he plays five years he grosses $381,745 but, of course, there are agent and other fees that siphon off some of this amount (not to say anything about taxes). Then what? Typically, the athlete will be economically downward mobile. "Doc" Medich, a second-year resident in general surgery at Pittsburgh's Allegheny Hospital and a pitcher for the Texas Rangers, says that athletes in general and baseball players in particular are foolish not to prepare themselves for a second career while they are active. Medich has argued that (McNaught, 1979)

> Once they are through the drop in pay scale is precipitious. . . . Most of them have the attitude that the high living will go on as usual. What they don't realize is that with inflation increasing by leaps and bounds, their nest egg may be almost negligible by the time they need it.

In fact, John Paisios, a psychologist, has a consulting firm for helping athletes' transition from the sport world to the world at large. It is not uncommon for athletes to experience a temporary identity crisis when they disengage from this glamorized social role. Jerry Kramer, the ex-All Pro offensive lineman of the Green Bay Packers, wrote:

> Giving up football is giving up . . . the hero's role. I worry about that, I wonder how much I'll miss being recognized, being congratulated, being idolized. For years, as an

offensive lineman, I worked in relative obscurity, but with the block against Jethro Pugh and with the success of *Instant Replay,* I became as well known as a running back. I was recognized in restaurants, on the golf course, in the streets, and I loved the strange sweet taste of recognition.

I know that the fan's memory is not long, that my name will fade quickly, that in a few years I'll sink back into anonymity. I have to wonder how I'll react to that . . . . You get spoiled being a celebrity . . . I was pursued just enough to keep my ego well fed. I hope I don't need that ego gratification to survive, but I just don't know. I won't know for a few years.[27]

In 1977 the mean salary of a professional football player was $55,288. In five years (the average playing career) he earns $276,440. Again, at an early age, he moves from a familiar and socially supported role to another for which he may be very ill-prepared.

Another perspective for viewing the professional athlete's financial lot is to contrast his role with that of other professions. Consider college teachers. Let's say that over a life-time they average $25,000 per year. If they begin teaching at 30 and retire at 65 they earn about $875,000. Of course, superstars can accrue a considerably larger sum than this but superstars are relatively rare. On the other hand, mediocre free agents have been commanding and getting exorbitant financial deals (see pp. 247-48). The long-term financial conditions and job-related accompaniments are perhaps more desirable for the college professor than the pro athlete. And, of course, other professionals (lawyers, physicians, dentists) earn appreciably more than the college teacher. All this goes to suggest that a myopic vision frequently intrudes into the realities of professional athletes and athletics.

The reality of the duration of careers of baseball and football players is often only partially understood since it is the players who play for a decade or two—the Hank Aaron's, Willie Mays', Lou Brock's, and Ken Holtzman's—that gain a firm foothold in the public's mind. Similarly, regarding financial matters, it is the highly paid and publicized athletes who remind us of the inordinate rewards associated with professional sport. But money is not all; there are also psychological and social status factors that sometimes play determining roles in a player's choice to go or stay professional.

In Andreano's work, athletes were hypothesized to feel "a direct and psychic association with the legendary players of the past; he is a part of American history and therefore above the din of the average guy who works for a weekly or hourly wage."[28] This metaphysical assertion did not meet the scientific test. Charnofsky tested these assumptions by asking major league baseball players how they viewed their role.[29] Contrary to Andreano's thesis, they did not see themselves above the average worker nor did they identify with the bucolic tradition of the greats of yesteryear. In fact, while still acknowledging their extraordinary physical skills, they saw themselves as similar to the average worker in values, intelligence, and personality. Moreover, money ranked considerably above the fun, challenge, prestige, and love of the game. Players perceived their jobs as exciting but with undesirable job-related characteristics like traveling, separation from family, and job insecurity.

THE COLLEGE ATHLETE

In our review of the history of sport in the United States (chapter 2), we saw that college sports began in the latter half of the 19th century primarily as a diversion and escape from the tedium and boredom of classroom work. Initially, students were in control of these extracurricular activities. Today, however, students have much less input since coaches and administrators make most of the

major decisions. Intercollegiate sport programs have been criticized primarily for reflecting entertainment and public relations values rather than those associated with the educational mission of
institutions of higher learning. Today, intercollegiate athletic programs are an integral part of higher
education. But before embarking on what we know about college athletes, let us consider the pro and
con arguments for intercollegiate sports programs.

The pro agruments, according to Coakley,[30] include:

1. Schools have to compete for students and respectable athletic programs help generate
   applications for admission—hence, sport serves as an advertising vehicle.
2. Since funding is more variable, it is important to have the school recognized by legis-
   lators, business community, foundation administrators, and alumni—sport is a publicity device.
3. Sport is a source of spirit and tradition that makes the program of the entire school
   viable.

The con arguments, according to Coakley,[31] include:

1. Expense of maintaining the program.
2. Irrelevance of sports to the academic mission of the school.
3. Restricts opportunities of student body for involvement in sports and recreation.
4. Destructive public relations stemming from mediocre or losing records.
5. Commercialization destroys purpose of university.

Since our focus is upon the role of the athlete, let us turn to the research data bearing upon the
consequences of *intercollegiate* sport programs for the participant. The scientific literature on college
athletes is very diversified and must be carefully scrutinized for time period covered, institution
examined, and sampling procedures. Some of these studies shed light on sport as a social and economic escalator (see pp. 152-53). A piecemeal synopsis of some research on collegiate athletes will be
discussed.

Litchfield and Cope located 1,678 former University of Pittsburgh lettermen who played intercollegiate athletics between 1900 and 1960.[32] A questionnaire regarding their present lifestyles was
mailed to them and 83 percent (1393) of the former athletes responded. Their findings were indicative of success: 37 percent of the Pitt athletes had received advanced degrees. They cross-tabulated
the success of the athletes in several professions (medicine, law, engineering, education, management,
business, sales, dentistry) and the sport in which they participated. There were striking relationships
between golfers going into sales, swimmers into engineering, baseball players into education, and
football players into dentistry. Only 8 percent had gone into coaching. Although the data appear to
be promising of success, data on the original socioeconomic status of these athletes were not available and thus made it impossible to determine the extent of social mobility.

Randy Jesick also studied Pitt athletes.[33] He focused exclusively on the 71 players on Pitt's
1963 football squad (9-1). He asked: "What were the players doing a decade later?" Ninety-three
percent (n=66) had graduated and 33 had earned advanced graduate or professional degrees. Among
the players who had done postgraduate work, three were physicians, fifteen were dentists, five were
lawyers, seven were educators, and two were ministers. Additionally, twenty-eight ex-Panthers had
advanced positions in industry.

A similar study of 223 Stanford University male athletes who participated in baseball, basketball, football, track, and swimming revealed that 88 percent graduated versus 82.5 percent for the entire student body.[34]

McIntyre sought to determine the social backgrounds of varsity athletes at Penn State.[35] He confined his study to participants during the 1958-59 school year in football, basketball, gymnastics, and wrestling. He discovered that 69 percent of the fathers of football players had not completed high school in comparison to 35, 31, and 31 percent respectively of the fathers of baseball, wrestling, and gymnastics participants. The liability of this study is the reverse of the former one, namely, we do not know—socioeconomically speaking— where these athletes are today.

Loy[36] criticized past studies of the social mobility of athletes on the grounds that, for the most part, starting and ending points were not simultaneously considered (as Litchfield/Cope and McIntyre's studies underscore). Hence, he tried to remedy this oversight by focusing upon the social backgrounds and subsequent future occupational roles of a select group of UCLA athletes. The athletes were recipients of at least three varsity letters during four years of sport competition. Of approximately 1,386 "Life Pass Holders" sent a questionnaire, 83 percent returned it. Loy discovered that college athletes, regardless of sport, were generally upwardly mobile (as determined by a comparison of father's occupational prestige with that of his son's first job).

Webb studied 300 Michigan State athletes on tenders—scholarships—between 1958 and 1962 and discovered several significant outcomes:[37] (1) five years after their classes' graduation, 49 and 60 percent of team and individual athletes, respectively, had received their MSU diplomas. For comparative purposes, consider that the graduation rate for all Michigan State students was 70 percent and for the nation as a whole 75 percent. Apparently, then, athletes at MSU were less successful than nonathletes in relation to academic success. However, we must reserve our final judgment because several salient factors—academic backgrounds and IQ's—were not accounted for and these variables may have had an important mediating impact.

In our highly educated society, degrees are important mechanisms for achieving social mobility. Athletic scholarships provide the wherewithal—the means and financial incentives—for higher education matriculation. Without such inducements, individuals from certain social origins, particularly lower and working classes in our society, may find it virtually impossible to attend (and graduate from) colleges. Webb's data speak to this matter since 64 percent of lower class white athletes versus 52 percent of upper class athletes eventually received degrees. One may speculate that while the 64 percent figure is smaller than the overall 70 percent graduation rate, it may be higher than for nonathletes of similar social origins. The graduation rate for black athletes was 38 percent.[38]

Sage studied two groups of former high school students.[39] One group continued their athletic participation in college while the other did not. He found that the nonparticipants had higher grade point averages, were less likely to join a fraternity, and were more occupationally oriented (in comparison to socially oriented) than the participants. His data suggest that athletes tend to be less academically oriented than nonathletes.

Two pieces of information permit us to conclude that college participants earn more after they leave the university than non-participants. Husband studied the 1926 graduates of Dartmouth.[40] Twenty years after their graduation, letter winners were earning about $18,000 annually in contrast to nonathletes who were earning about $14,280. Scrupp compared letter winners with non-letter winners among a sample of Minnesota students.[41] The incomes of the letter winners averaged about $1,360 higher than the incomes of non-letter winners.

The empirical literature on college athletes is not, as we have seen, always consistent. We must remind ourselves of the pitfalls listed in the fourth paragraph of this section. Take, for example, the high graduation rates of athletes at Pitt and Stanford vs. the considerably lower rates at Michigan State. The former universities are private schools (Pitt is *now* a public institution) with fairly high academic standards while the latter is a state university with generally less stringent entrance requirements. Hence, the differences may be due, at least in part, to the academic nature of the institutions studied. Although college athletes may have difficulties in taking their studies seriously and doing well,[42] there is evidence that if they graduate from college they'll do well in their careers.

THE HIGH SCHOOL AND JUNIOR HIGH ATHLETE

The impetus and model for interscholastic sports were sport programs in the colleges and universities. Intercollegiate sport programs began to flourish in the early part of this century and provided models for their high school counterparts. Cozens and Stumpf (see chapter 6) report that school officials encouraged such extracurricular activities for two essential reasons: (1) the need to upgrade the physical fitness of American youth since an excessive number of post-high school students were discovered to be poorly conditioned when given physical exams during the First World War, and (2) educators believed that sports provided a medium through which positive traits such as citizenship or character could be cultivated[43] (refer to the dominant American sports creed, pp. 67-73). Today, interscholastic sports are an important component, some say the most important component, of contemporary high school education. Consider the following vignettes. One author recently spoke to a high school principal who told him that he would probably receive more negative feedback from the community if he abolished the sports program than if he abolished the English department. While this personal experience may be somewhat atypical, it may not be too much of an exaggeration. A more impersonal story may add some objectivity to this notion. In 1971 a budget shortage in Philadelphia led to the elimination of 600 teaching jobs and all extracurricular activities including sports. "Local officials and the general public seemed to accept the loss of teachers, but the pressure to reinstate athletics was so great that it became a campaign issue in city politics." Part of the problem was alleviated when Leonard Tose, owner of the Eagles, put up $79,000 to temporarily fund varsity football.[44]

What are the supposed consequences of interscholastic sport programs? On the one hand they have been considered meaningful adjuncts to traditional instruction; on the other hand, they have been criticized for being unnecessarily disruptive. Kniker and Schafer and Armer have summarized the traditional arguments for and against interscholastic sport programs.[45] The *pro* arguments include:

1. Sport and other activity participants increase their interest in school in general and academic pursuits in particular.
2. Prepares participants to participate as citizens in American society.
3. Stimulates interest in physical activities among all students.
4. Generates school spirit and unity necessary to maintain the school as a viable organization.
5. Evokes school support from teachers, parents, alumni, and community.

The *con* arguments:

1. Distracts attention from academic pursuits.
2. Focuses athletes on values that may no longer be appropriate in American society.
3. Relegates most students to a spectator rather than a participant role.
4. Creates an anti-intellectual spirit among students which has nothing to do with the educational goals of the school.
5. Deprives educational programs of resources, facilities, personnel, and community awareness and support.

While both sides of the argument lack empirical support, the pro position tends to hold sway over the con, certainly in terms of public sentiment.

Since high school athletic programs are promoted or criticized on the basis of the consequences for the participant, we will focus on some representative research regarding the consequences of *interscholastic* sport programs for the participant. The empirical investigations will be presented in chronological order.

James Coleman's work on adolescent society reached one bold sport conclusion: athletic participation (in high school) was more important than scholarship.[46] This finding was reached from scrutinizing ten Midwest high schools of varying sizes, locations, and socioeconomic compositions during the 1957-58 academic year. This research is sufficiently significant that an analysis of his methodology is warranted. Coleman wished to determine "why" and with "what effects" this outcome was produced.

Students at the high schools were asked to name the best student and the best athlete. He found that steller athletes were easier to identify than good students. The students were queried as to whether they would prefer to be remembered as a "brilliant student" or "star athlete." Most preferred "star athlete." Students were also asked to name members of the leading crowd and Coleman found that participants in scholastic sports, particularly basketball and football, were pegged as the leading clique. When the students were questioned as to what it took to be a member of the leading crowd, the rank order of characteristics was: personality, good reputation, athletic ability, good looks and success with girls, and brains and good grades. Finally, students were asked who they would like to be like. Not surprisingly, the athletes outdistanced the scholars.

Why are athletes accorded this enviable social status? Coleman attributed it to the *value system* of the school and community. Parents, teachers, peers, and community opinion leaders channeled males into spheres of sports activity through social rewards and reinforcements. The social significance of sports to the high schools led to cohesion, esprit de corps, and identification. In summary, Coleman discovered that sports and athletes were of utmost importance in high schools, perhaps at the expense of scholarly pursuits. He contended that adolescents formed a *subculture,* a group with distinctive and somewhat contradictory values to the larger society and the formal educational goals.

Rehberg and Schafer examined the relationship between participation in interscholastic sports and college expectations.[47] They sampled 785 male seniors from six urban Pennsylvania high schools in 1965. The *dependent variable* (the factor they were interested in studying) in their analysis was educational expectations operationalized (measured) by: "Do you or do you not expect to enroll in a four-year college?" Responses were trichotomized into yes, no, and no response. The *independent variable* (the factor presumably accounting for variation in the dependent variable) was dichotomized into athletic participation and no athletic participation. Overall, 62 percent of the athletes and 45 percent of the nonathletes said yes to the query, a difference of 17 percentage points. The researchers then elaborated[48] this relationship by asking, "Could this relationship be incidental or spurious?" Three *control variables*—variables believed to have a potential mediating effect on the original two—were studied: (1) social status, (2) academic performance, and (3) parental educational encouragement. They discovered that for both athletes and nonathletes of high social status, high grades, and high parental encouragement there was little difference in educational expectations. However, there was an *interaction effect* with those in the lower categories of the control variables. More particularly, for athletes low in status, performance, and encouragement, there were significantly higher collegiate expectations than for nonathletes with those same characteristics. Diagrammatically:

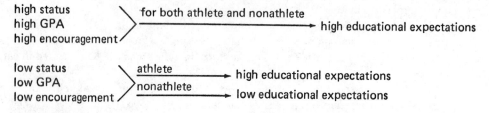

Rehberg and Schafer concluded:

> Our data have shown that a greater portion of athletes than nonathletes expect to enroll in a four-year college, even when the potentially confounding variables of status, academic performance, and parental encouragement are controlled. This relationship is especially marked among boys not otherwise disposed toward college, that is, those from working-class homes, those in the lower half of their graduating class, and those with low parental encouragement to go to college.[49]

Before becoming overly optimistic about Rehberg and Schafer's conclusions, several qualifications are in order. Of the 270 athletes in their sample, only 16 percent were found to be low in status, GPA, and encouragement (the remaining 84 percent had characteristics favorably predisposing them to attend college). Coakley presented the following sobering comment:

> If we can estimate that about 30 percent of the males in any given high school participate in the interscholastic sport program, it is reasonable to use the Rehberg and Schafer study to conclude that sport participation has a significant impact on the educational aspirations of about 5 percent of the males in the student body and 2.5 percent of the total students in the high school. In other words, if we were talking about a school of 2000 students, 1000 of whom were males, there would be about 300 (at the very most) participants in the interscholastic sport program. Of these 300, only 16 percent or . . . 48 . . . students would have mediocre academic records and would come from families offering little academic encouragement. Those 50 students, constituting only 5 percent of the males in the school and only 2.5 percent of the total students, are the ones most likely to experience increases in aspirations apparently resulting from sport participation.[50]

Schafer and Armer compared the grade point averages of senior athletes with a matched sample of nonathletes in two midwestern high schools.[51] They found that success was greatest for the athletes who participated in either football or basketball and for three or more years. What is of interest in their research outcomes was the fact that sport participation per se was not a guarantee of academic success. Instead, it appeared to be dependent, in part, upon the number of years played and the sport participated in.

Jerome and Phillips in a comparative study of Canadian and American high school athletes discovered that sport participants in Canada were generally not accorded the same degree of prestige as athletes in the United States.[52] Moreover, the academic achievement and goals of Canadian athletes were not especially favorable to success; in fact, the athletes had poorer academic records than nonathletes. Jerome and Phillips concluded: "In the absence of a differential reward structure favoring athletics, one cannot expect athletes, as a group, to excel in their school work to a greater degree than other students."

Phillips and Schafer advanced in the following differences between high school athletes and nonathletes:

1. Athletes receive slightly higher grades and are more likely to aspire to attain more education than nonathletes. This is particularly true for the athlete from blue collar families.
2. There is a modicum of evidence suggesting that athletes are less likely to become delinquent than nonathletes. Research has not established whether this results from the direct benefits of sport participation or from self-selection factors (individuals with delinquent tendencies may not go out for sports and, conversely, individuals with nondelinquent tendencies may go out for athletics).
3. Athletes from blue collar families are more prone to be upwardly mobile than nonathletes from the same type of families.[53]

Why these differences are found has not been clearly established but may result from one or a combination of factors. For example, athletes may receive special attention and assistance from teachers and administrators and this may provide added incentive for doing well scholastically. When this possibility is combined with the minimum GPA requirements, one can logically speculate why grades may be slightly higher for the athlete. Another reasonable explanation is that the habits cultivated in the sports realm (hard work, discipline, and perseverance) may spill over into academic circles. Finally, the self-selection factor must be considered. It may be that conforming, able, and ambitious persons engage in scholastic sports while those lacking these traits do not. While these explanations do not exhaust the possibilities for explaining differences between athletes and nonathletes, they must be entertained since the relationships alluded to above may be quite complex (Schafer and Armer).

A decade and a half after Coleman's investigation, Eitzen replicated it by studying fourteen schools of different sizes and located in communities of varying sizes.[54] In regard to the question, "How would you like to be remembered?" Coleman discovered 31, 44, and 25 percent wishing to be remembered as a brilliant student, athletic star, and the most popular. Eitzen found 25, 45, and 30 percent, respectively, indicating these categories of response. Hence, the importance of athletic stars appeared to persist over the sixteen year interlude. Similarly, Eitzen found that being an athlete played a major role in being perceived as popular among one's fellow students.

Spreitzer and Pugh discovered an interesting twist to the connection between athletic participation and educational aspirations.[55] They collected data from 704 seniors in thirteen Connecticut high schools. They found that the positive correlation between athletic participation and educational plans after graduation could not be accounted for by socioeconomic status, parental academic encouragement, grade point average, or intelligence. Hence, athletic participation appeared to have real positive effects. The significant mediating variables between athletic participation and educational expectation were the school "value climate" (in which athletic achievement was highly valued relative to academic achievement) and perceived peer status (in which the perception of high peer status facilitated and created a desire for continued recognition, perhaps through college attendance). In other words, a strong relationship between athletic participation and educational aspirations existed only in those schools emphasizing athletics as a source of rewards. In schools which did not hold athletics in such high esteem there was no such correspondence. For example, among those schools emphasizing scholarly excellence with little emphasis upon athletics, the relationship between athletic participation and educational aspirations was nonexistent.

More recent studies of the relationship between athletic participation and academic achievement do not support a causal connection between the two variables.[56] These findings are consistent with those of Stevenson who demonstrated that differences between athletes and nonathletes are due to their initial dissimilarity rather than to the positive influence of sport socialization.[57]

When these data are put together to form a composite picture of the consequences of athletic participation, they appear to lead to the conclusion that only when athletes are held in high esteem and shrouded with prestige are there positive academic aspiration and achievement effects. Moreover, the skimpy evidence available suggests that the United States, perhaps more than other countries, such as Canada or England, bestows greater prestige on athletes. Furthermore, this prestige is likely to vary from school to school and sport to sport.

For *junior high school athletes* Buhrmann's longitudinal study (1959 to 1965) in southern Oregon revealed that athletic participants received higher grades (GPA) and higher standardized achievement test scores than nonparticipants.[58] When this relationship was "elaborated" by controlling socioeconomic status (SES) and prior scholarship (grade point averages at the end of elementary grades), the correlation between grade point was weakened (although it remained statistically significant) and the association with standardized achievement test scores was "wiped out." This means that SES has an effect on grade point beyond that due to athletic participation and no direct causal link exists between athletic participation and scores on standardized test batteries. In other words, the original relationship may be spurious.

Importantly, Buhrmann discovered differential effects of these variables depending upon the social class of the athlete. For example, the relationship between athletic participation and educational attainment was reduced for middle-class individuals after controlling for previous scholarship but not for individuals from low social class moorings. He suggests that athletics may be very important, particularly for less privileged youth, in terms of social recognition, acceptance, and scholarship.

In summarizing the section on "The Athlete: Professional, Collegiate, High School, and Junior High," our attention is called to the importance of the level of performance under consideration. A gap in the present discussion is that females and nonwhites—two socially significant categories of athletes—have not been systematically accounted for. These "types" will be dealt with in chapters 8 (nonwhites) and 9 (females).

SUMMARY

This chapter was devoted to a discussion of sport and social organization. *Social organization* refers to the ways in which human conduct is regulated and organized as a result of the social conditions in which individuals are embedded rather than their physiological and psychological characteristics. To understand the individual's place in the social organization, two key sociological concepts—*position* (the niche one occupies in the larger society) and *role* (the expected/required/anticipated behavior of a position occupant)—were defined and illustrated.

Positions in society are either obtained voluntarily (called *achieved positions*) or "thrust" upon the individual (called *ascribed positions*). Because individuals occupy more than a single position and because they play more than a single role, the notion of *role set* signifies this multiple position occupancy and role performance. Finally, when individuals experience different and contradictory pressures to behave in certain ways, they may experience *role strain.*

The various levels of social organization—*interpersonal, group, societal, primary, managerial, technical,* and *corporate*—were discussed and defined within a sport context. Sport organizations as *associations*—special purpose groups deliberately constructed to seek specific objectives, goals, and values—were singled out for our attention.

In this chapter we conceptualized sport as a *social institution,* a system of social relationships or a network of positions and roles (athlete, coach, manager, athletic director, and cheerleader) embodying the ultimate values (the dominant American sports creed) people hold in common. The functions of the institution of sport include, among others, that of *value receptacle* and *safety valve.*

Finally, we isolated one of the many social positions in sport—the *athlete*—for attention. Athletes at the professional, collegiate, high school and junior high school levels were considered. Hence, much of the empirical literature revealed the interconnections between the institutions of sport and education.

IMPORTANT CONCEPTS DISCUSSED IN THIS CHAPTER

Social Organization
Position (Social Status)
Role
Social Norms
Deviants
Role Set
Role Strain
Ascribed Positions
Achieved Positions
Levels of Social Organization:
  Interpersonal
  Group
  Societal
  Primary
  Technical
  Managerial
  Corporate
Association
Formal Structure

Informal Structure
Social Institution
Organic Model
Value Receptacle
Safety Valve
Crescive
Enacted
Institutionalization
Professional Athletes
College Athletes
High School Athletes
Junior High School Athletes
Functional Imperatives:
  Tension Management
  Integration
  Adaptation
  Goal Attainment
  Pattern Maintenance
Mobility

ENDNOTES

[1] Peter M. Blau and W. Richard Scott, *Formal Organizations* (San Francisco: Chandler, 1962), p. 2.

[2] Melvin L. Defleur, William V. D'Antonio, and Lois B. Defleur, *Sociology: Human Society* (Glenview, Ill.: Scott, Foresman, 1976). Reece McGee et al., *Sociology* (Hinsdale, Ill.: Dryden Press, 1977).

[3] Leonard Broom and Philip Selznick, *Sociology* (New York: Harper and Row, 1968), pp. 15-16.

[4] John W. Loy, "The Nature of Sport: A Definitional Effort," *Sport, Culture, and Society,* John W. Loy and Gerald S. Kenyon (New York: Macmillan, 1968), pp. 56-71.

[5] Theodore Caplow, *Principles of Organization* (New York: Harcourt, Brace and World, 1964), pp. 26-27.

[6] *Encyclopedia of Sociology* (Guilford, CT: Dushkin Publishing Group, 1974), p. 30.

[7] Loy, "The Nature of Sport: A Definitional Effort."

[8] Paul Hoch, *Rip Off: The Big Game* (Garden City, N.Y.: Anchor Books, 1972).

[9] According to the structural-functionalists, society has five needs—called *functional imperatives*—which must be satisfied: (1) *pattern maintenance* refers to the societal need for value socialization by which social patterns are maintained and perpetuated; (2) *tension management* refers to the societal need for regulating tension, conflict, and hostility in a socially acceptable manner and thus helps maintain social equilibrium; (3) *integration* is the need for societal solidarity, stability, and cohesiveness; (4) *goal attainment* is the means by which societal values are translated into goals to guide day-to-day behavior; and (5) *adaptation* refers to the societal need to adjust to both the social and physical environment. The institutions of society, including sport, help meet and satisfy these societal needs (Coakley, *Sport in Society*, pp. 17-21).

[10] Mavis H. Biesanz and John Biesanz, *Introduction to Sociology* (Englewood Cliffs, N.J.: Prentice-Hall, 1973).

[11] Hoch, *Rip Off: The Big Game.*

[12] Edwin P. Hollander, "Conformity, Status, and Idiosyncrasy Credit," *Psychological Review* 65 (1958), pp. 117-127.

[13] Wiley Lee Umphlett, *The Sporting Myth and the American Experience: Studies in Contemporary Fiction* (Lewisburg, Pa.: Bucknell University Press, 1975); Michener, *Sports in America,* p. 225.

[14] James A Michener, *Sports in America* (New York: Random House, 1976), pp. 225-226.

[15] Ray Kennedy and Nancy Williamson, "Money in Sports," *Sports Illustrated* 49 (July 24, 1978), p. 48.

[16] Jay J. Coakley, *Sport in Society: Issues and Controversies* (St. Louis, Mo.: C. V. Mosby Co., 1978), p. 196.

[17] D. Kirson Weinberg and Henry Arond, "The Occupational Culture of the Boxer," *American Journal of Sociology* 57 (1952), pp. 460-469; J. Orr, *The Black Athlete: His Story in American History* (New York: Lion Press, 1969).

[18] Weinberg and Arond, "The Occupational Culture of the Boxer."

[19] Janet Lever, "Soccer as a Brazilian Way of Life," *Games, Sport, and Power,* Gregory P. Stone (New Brunswick, N.J.: Transaction, 1972), pp. 36-43. Lever's study of professional Brazilian soccer players also revealed that the social and economic gains brought by sport to these athletes were short-lived.

[20] "Where Are the Ex-Champs Now?," *Time* (February 27, 1978), p. 79.

[21] Ibid.

[22] Arlene Garbett, "Pro Golf's Rabbits—The Guys Who Haven't Made It," *Family Weekly* (February 19, 1978), p. 19.

[23] Ibid.

[24] Ibid.

[25] Wilbert M. Leonard, II, "Mortality Ratios of Professional Baseball Players and Managers (1876-1973): An Investigation in the Sociology of Sport," (Unpublished manuscript, 1978); Michener, *Sports in America.*

[26] The salary data are skewed as evidenced by a median and mode of $75,000 and $40,000 respectively.

[27] Jerry Kramer, *Farewell to Football* (New York: Thomas Y. Crowell, 1969), pp. 9-10.

[28] Ralph Andreano, *No Joy in Mudville* (Cambridge, Mass.: Schenkman, 1965), p. 144.

[29] Harold Charnofsky, "The Major League Professional Baseball Player: Self-Conceptions versus the Popular Image," *International Review of Sport Sociology* 3 (1968), pp. 39-53.

[30] C. R. Kniker and P. M. Keith, "The Perceived Values of Physical Activity Programs in Elementary and Secondary Schools of Iowa" (Paper presented at the Western Social Science Association Meetings, Denver, Col., 1975); Coakley, *Sport in Society,* p. 179.

[31] Walter E. Schafer and J. Michael Armer, "Athletes are not Inferior Students," *Transaction* 5 (1968), pp. 21-26 and 61-62; Coakley, *Sport in Society,* p. 179.

[32] Edward Litchfield and Myron Cope, "Saturday's Hero is Doing Fine," *Sports Illustrated* 17 (October, 1962), pp. 66-80.

[33] Randy Jesick, cited in Michener, *Sports in America*, p. 237.

[34] Michener, *Sports in America*, p. 237.

[35] T. D. McIntyre, "Socioeconomic Background of White Male Athletes and Four Select Sports at Pennsylvania State University" (M. Ed. thesis, Pennsylvania State University, 1959).

[36] John W. Loy, "The Study of Sport and Social Mobility," *Aspects of Contemporary Sport Sociology*, ed. Gerald S. Kenyon (Chicago, Ill.: The Athletic Institute, 1969), pp. 101-133.

[37] Harry Webb, "Success Patterns of College Athletes" (Paper presented at the National Convention of the American Association of Health, Physical Education, and Recreation, St. Louis, Mo., 1968).

[38] Howard L. Nixon, II, *Sport and Social Organization* (Indianapolis, Ind.: Bobbs-Merrill, 1976).

[39] John J. Sage, "Adolescent Values and the Non-Participating College Athlete" (Paper presented at the Southern Section of CAHPER Conference, San Fernando Valley State College, Los Angeles, Calif., 1967).

[40] R. W. Husband, "What do College Grades Predict," *Fortune* 56 (1957), pp. 157-158.

[41] M. H. Schrupp, "The Differential Effects of the Development of Athletic Ability of a High Order," *Research Quarterly* 24 (1952), pp. 218-222.

[42] Several books report that athletic preparation is sufficiently demanding on time and energy so that it severely limits study time. Under such circumstances, maintaining the minimum average required for athletic eligibility would seem to be the basic academic orientation. See John Underwood, "Three Part Series on the Desperate Coach," *Sports Illustrated* 36 (August 25 and September 1, 8, 1969); Dave Meggyesy, *Out of Their League* (Berkeley, Calif.: Ramparts Press, 1971); Jack Scott, *The Athletic Revolution* (New York: The Free Press, 1971); Gary Shaw, *Meat on the Hoof* (New York: St. Martin's Press, 1972).

[43] Frederick W. Cozens and Florence Scovil Stumpf, *Sport in American Life* (Chicago, Ill.: University of Chicago Press, 1953), chapter 6.

[44] Coakley, *Sport in Society: Issues and Controversies*, p. 124, 156.

[45] C. R. Kniker, "The Values of Athletics in Schools: A Continuing Debate," *Phi Delta Kappan* 56 (1974), pp. 116-120; Schafer and Armer, "Athletes are not Inferior Students," *Transaction* 6 (1968); Coakley, *Sport in Society*, p. 126.

[46] James S. Coleman, "Athletics in High School," *Annals of the American Academy of Political and Social Science* 338 (1961), pp. 33-43.

[47] Richard A. Rehberg and Walter E. Schafer, "Participation in Interscholastic Athletics and College Expectations," *American Journal of Sociology* 73 (1968), pp. 732-740.

[48] "Elaboration" is a statistical technique whereby an initial relationship between two variables is rigorously tested to see if it "holds up" when other variables, called test factors or control variables, are systematically introduced into the analysis.

[49] Rehberg and Schafer, "Participation in Interscholastic Athletics and College Expectations," p. 739.

[50] Coakley, *Sport in Society: Issues and Controversies*, p. 140.

[51] Schafer and Armer, "Athletes are not Inferior Students."

[52] Wendy C. Jerome and John C. Phillips, "The Relationship Between Academic Achievement and Interscholastic Participation: A Comparison of Canadian and American High Schools," *Journal of Canadian Association of Health, Physical Education, and Recreation* 37 (1971), pp. 18-21.

[53] John C. Phillips and Walter E. Schafer, "Consequences of Participation in Interscholastic Sports: A Review and Prospectus," *Pacific Sociological Review* 14 (1971), pp. 328-338.

[54] D. Stanley Eitzen, "Athletics in the Status System of Male Adolescents: A Replication of Coleman's 'The Adolescent Society'," *Adolescence* 10 (1975), pp. 267-276.

[55] Elmer Spreitzer and Meredith Pugh, "Interscholastic Athletics and Educational Expectations," *Sociology of Education* 46 (1973), pp. 171-182.

[56] Lloyd B. Lueptow and Brian D. Kayser, "Athletic Involvement, Academic Achievement, and Aspirations," *Sociological Focus* 7 (1973), pp. 24-36; William J. Hauser and Lloyd B. Lueptow, "Participation in Athletics and Academic Achievement: A Replication and Extension," *Sociological Quarterly* 19 (1978), pp. 304-309.

[57] Christopher L. Stevenson, "Socialization Effects of Participation in Sport: A Critical Review of the Research," *Research Quarterly* 46 (1975) pp. 287-301.

[58] Hans C. Buhrmann, "Scholarship and Athletics in Junior High School," *International Review of Sport Sociology* 7 (1972), pp. 119-128.

4
Sport and Culture

INTRODUCTION

The concept of *culture* is as fundamental in understanding human social behavior as the concept of gravity is in physics or disease is in medicine. In fact, it is so pervasive that it is easy to lose sight of its influence on our attitudes and behaviors. There is a proverbial story about a fish that suggests the last thing it would be aware of would be the water in which it swims. In less dramatic fashion, humans everywhere are immersed in a culture. Because it is second nature, it takes a special effort to become cognizant of the many ways in which it channels behavior. As Berger said: "The fascination of sociology lies in the fact that its perspective makes us see in a new light the very world in which we have lived all our lives."[1]

What Is Culture?

Culture is the changing patterns of learned behavior and the products of learned behavior (including attitudes, values, knowledge, beliefs, and material objects) which are socially shared and transmitted among members of a society.[2] Whereas laypersons tend to think of culture in terms of "refinement," social etiquette, niceness and manners, social scientists use the concept in a non-evaluative sense. Instead of only some people having culture ("high-brow"), all people have (or more appropriately *learn)* culture, although their "cultures" may differ in content.

Culture, then, is the way of life of a social group, the distinctive characteristics—values, norms, institutions—which set it off from others. Culture can also be dissected into *material* and *nonmaterial* modes. *Material culture* includes tangible objects like stadia, swimming pools, baseballs, bats, tennis rackets, nets, hockey sticks, uniforms, gloves, running shoes, turnstiles, skis, "exploding" scoreboards, and the like. Many of these material objects are the products of technological development. In sport, one of the most interesting components of material culture is the stadium. Michener maintains that architectural symbols have significance far beyond their functional purposes.[3] He says first we had the "Age of Pyramids," then the "Age of Temples," followed, in chronological order, by the "Age of Cathedrals, Bridges, Railroad Stations, Skyscrapers, Traffic Circles, Airports, and Shopping Centers." Today we are in the "Age of the Stadium." The keen observer of the sport scene is well aware of the construction of multi-million dollar sport palaces such as the Superdome (New Orleans), Astrodome

(Houston), Harry S. Truman Sports Complex (Kansas City), Hackensack Meadows (New Jersey) and the refurbishing of existing stadia such as Yankee Stadium (New York City) and Soldier Field (Chicago).

Nonmaterial or *ideational culture* consists of "intangibles" like values, attitudes, norms, and beliefs. In the next section we will examine the significance of social *values* in understanding sport.

CULTURE AND VALUES

Values are conceptions of what is desirable. They are the underlying assumptions by which individual and social goals are chosen. We evaluate our own behavior and that of others in terms of these criteria. People will ordinarily work hard, strive for, and expend energy to achieve those dimensions of social life deemed important.

One of the recurring themes emerging from the sociology of sport literature is that sport can be viewed as a *microcosm* of the larger society. As a social institution, it can neither isolate nor insulate itself from broader social events. The nature of sports, their organization and structure, tell us a great deal about the society in which they exist. Sport permeates and mirrors many levels of society (see opening quote to chapter 1). Voigt suggested that the evolution of American baseball from an amateur to a corporate structure reflected the socioeconomic changes occurring in the larger society.[4] Similarly, Riesman and Denney traced the evolution of rugby football into American football by noting the manner in which it had to be changed in order to be consistent with the dominant American ethos.[5] Nixon wrote:

> . . . one could interpret the introduction of running, the minimum yardage rule, mass play, and the forward pass as responses to the need of American spectators for constant excitement and visible action. The emergence of clear, standardized, formal rules could be seen as a result of the increasing diversity of the social backgrounds of participants in football. This expansion of participation, which was consistent with American democratic ideology, demanded formalization of the rules to prevent differences of opinion that informal collegiate, class, or local interpretations could produce. The rationalization of the game could be viewed as a partial outcome of the capitalistic emphasis on productive efficiency in American society . . . . the sports arena will accommodate itself and its culture to the rules and themes embodied in the broader culture of the society . . . . the culture of sport and the process of sports socialization bear some important similarities to the patterns of culture and socialization in the broader societal context.[6]

Hence, there is a reason to argue that sport provides a means of expressing the dominant values of society. Edwards succinctly summarized this theme when he wrote:

> sport . . . has primary functions in disseminating and reinforcing the values regulating behavior and goal attainment and determining acceptable solutions to problems in the secular sphere of life. . . . This channeling affects not only perspectives on sport, but, . . . affects and aids in regulating perceptions of life in general.[7]

The Values of Social Integration and Social Control

For societies to function effectively, it is necessary to integrate the masses and provide social control. Each of these values—*social integration* and *social control*—can be fostered by sport. Many national governments have recognized the importance of sport and have systematically utilized it as a means to achieve various ends. For one, sport is used to produce *social integration*. The social, political, and economic instability of emerging nations like Uganda and Ghana are stabilized, to some extent, by a superordinate interest in sport. In the geographically dispersed provinces comprising the Commonwealth of Canada, sport is also used for social assimilation. In brief, sport is and continues to be used to accomplish social integration in countries of diverse national, religious, ethnic, racial, and sociopolitical peoples. Herein lies some of its social significance (Pooley and Webster).

Sport has also been used to foster *social control*. Particularly in the socialistic and communistic countries, sport is used as a lever of social control whereby the interests, activities, and leisure pursuits of the citizenry are carefully channeled into state-inspired goals. The Soviet Union, China (PRC), East Germany, and the Union of South Africa are notable in using sport to achieve such ends.[8]

Two *attitudes* appear to pervade the employment of sport in international affairs: (1) the socialistic and communistic countries use sport as a vehicle of social control channeling activity to party-inspired goals (in fact, this theme has become an aspect of the "Cold War"); (2) the West has historically had a rather naive understanding of the sociopolitical implications of athletics. Organizationally, these recurrent themes can be supported by the following allegations. In the communistic countries sport is directed and administered at the national level through Ministries of Sport, social structures equivalent to our cabinet positions. Apparently, sport is too important to leave to casual, unsystematic control. In the United States, to use an example of a Western country, there exist no parallels at the national level. The President's Council on Physical Fitness and Sports is essentially advisory, and the NCAA and AAU are responsible for collegiate and amateur sport, respectively, and frequently end up at loggerheads.

VALUES IN AMERICAN SOCIETY

If sport is a microcosm of society, we would expect it to reflect and transmit some of the key elements in the larger culture. Since we have seen that one of the major elements of culture lies in its value system, let us consider the major *value orientations* of American society and see what correspondence exists between those values and the values perpetuated in the sport realm.

Robin Williams, a contemporary sociologist, listed the following values he believed characterized American society in general:[9]

1. Achievement and Success
2. Activity and Work
3. Moral Orientation
4. Humanitarian Mores
5. Efficiency and Practicality
6. Progress
7. Material Comfort
8. Equality

9. Freedom
10. External Conformity
11. Science and Secular Rationality
12. Nationalism and Patriotism
13. Democracy
14. Individual Personality
15. Racism and Related Group-superiority Themes

Several qualifications regarding these value orientations merit attention. First, some of these values are inconsistent (individual personality vs. external conformity; racism and related group-superiority themes vs. freedom, equality, and democracy). Second, the values receiving "lip service" are not always reflected in actual behavior. This is not unique. In all cultures there are cleavages between "ideal" and "real" culture. For example, while most Americans endorse the value of equality, in practice some act as if some individuals and groups are "more equal" than others. Finally, specific subgroups (see pp. 143-52) in a society may not pay homage to the culture's official values. In short, variations in values are commonplace and vary from one segment of society to another.

Does the Public View Sport in a Positive Light?

Is sport defined in positive terms? Do the values expressed in sport operate as eufunctions? Spreitzer and Snyder's research provides some answers.[10] They asked a sample of 500 people residing in a large midwestern metropolitan community what the consequences of sport were. Almost 90 percent of the sample believed sport was of value because it taught self-discipline, 80 percent felt sport cultivated fair play, and about 70 percent believed sport nurtured respect for authority and good citizenship. Their study revealed similar value conceptions regarding sport from both males and females. The sex differences that emerged "revolved around a tendency for females to emphasize the social control functions of sport (that is, to teach discipline and respect for authority), while the males were more likely to emphasize the value of sports as a means of relaxation and getting away from the tensions of the day."[11] With the increasing equality of sport opportunities, it will be interesting to see if male and female attitudes in the future are similar. Since there is evidence that sports are perceived in positive terms, let us examine the specific values attributed to sport.

VALUES IN SPORT

Harry Edwards has categorized the social values attributed to sport in the *dominant American sport creed.*[12] Statements of opinion, belief, and principle were culled from newspapers, magazines, and the *Athletic Journal* (the alleged first professional sports journal) for the light they shed upon the presumed benefits of sports. Through content analysis he categorized the themes into seven basic categories (listed below) reflecting the dominant value orientations in sport.

Character Building

Probably the dominant value attributed to participation in sport is character building. *Character* in this context refers to positive or desirable personality traits like integrity, responsibility, wholesomeness, maturity, red-bloodedness, objectivity, and cleanliness. During the latter 60s and early 70s facial and head hair became volatile issues in both collegiate and professional circles. The *symbolic* importance of such adornment can hardly be underestimated. Long hair, beards, moustaches, and headbands have been (although today they are commonplace) traditional trademarks of the *counterculture*—a culture that is often explicitly defiant of mainstream values. The juxtaposition of long hair (a symbol of defiance) with athletics (which apparently built character) was incongruent.

It seems rather ludicrous that so much was made of the "hair" issue. Upon deeper inspection, it appears that the brouhaha was essentially symbolic—long hair, beards, and mustaches had been symbolic of revolt during the late 1960s and early 1970s. There is sufficient evidence that "hair" and playing ability are not causally connected. For example, ex-Cincinnati manager Sparky Anderson won the 1972 National League pennant but the "clean-cut" Reds were defeated in the World Series by a group of long-haired, mustachioed Oakland Athletics.[13]

But does sport really build character? According to Tutko and Bruns "sports don't build character—they build characters."[14] They wrote:

> For the past eight years we have been studying the effects of competition on personality. Our research began with the counseling of problem athletes from every sport, at every level from the high school gym to the professional arena. On the evidence gathered in this study . . . we found no empirical support for the tradition that sport builds *character* (italics added). Indeed there is evidence that athletic competition limits growth in some areas. . . . the personality of the ideal athlete is not the result of any molding process, but . . . the ruthless selection process that occurs. . . . Sport is like most other activities—those who survive tend to have stronger personalities.[15]

Where did the notion that sports build character come from? Firstly, people who have been athletes and become successful outside of sports have often provided testimonials (see ex-President Ford's comment on p. 70). Secondly, some people who have made their livelihoods in sport have justified its role in society. To illustrate, Jess Hill, when athletic director at USC, said: "Athletes develop a dedication and a desire to excel in competition, a realization that success requires hard work and that life must be lived according to rules. . . ."[16] Thirdly, banquet speakers constantly bombard their captive audiences with the virtues of sport participation and use the metaphor that it is a preparation for life.

There is no mistaking that one of the significant justifications for engaging in athletics is that it builds character. Sometimes it does; other times it doesn't. Even as early as the 1920s there was a suspicion that the whole linkage between athletic participation and character building was a hoax, or at least over-generalized. During the "roaring twenties" sportswriter John Tunis wrote:

> The "Great Sports Myth . . . is a fiction . . . newsgatherers . . . tell us that . . . sport is . . . *character building* . . . [italics added]. Why not stop talking about the noble purposes which sports fulfill and take them for what they are?[17]

Discipline

Some social critics of today maintain that young people lack discipline. *Discipline* in this context means obedience to authority. They say that such an undesirable trait stems from overpermissiveness. According to the sport ethic, participation in athletics is conducive to self-discipline and

VIGNETTE 4.1
WHEN DISCIPLINE BECOMES YOUR EPITAPH

On November 21, 1977, Bob Vorhies, a Virginia Tech freshman halfback, collapsed and died approximately an hour after he was administered a punishment drill. This brutal drill went as follows: "Ten 50-yard sprints; ten 100-yard sprints, with both the sprint and the return to the starting line to be completed in thirty seconds; fifty pushups; fifty sit-ups; two 100-yard bear crawls, in which the player "runs" on his hands and feet without allowing his knees to touch the ground; four other 100-yard runs of various kinds, and an indeterminable number of laps around the field."

The punishment was for a minor drinking incident in Vorhies' dormitory room the previous Saturday following Tech's victory over Wake Forest, a game in which Vorhies gained twelve yards in his first, and only, collegiate carry.

There are quite a few unusual aspects surrounding Vorhies' death. First, the university administration seemed to sweep the case under a rug. Of the 1500 people attending the funeral, no one came on behalf of Virginia Tech. The coaches did send flowers, but not one member of the alumni club sent even a note.

Second, the assistant coach who issued the punishment did not administer it. Another assistant coach put Vorhies through the paces. He is now coaching at a Virginia high school and refuses to discuss the case.

The only other witness, a fieldhouse janitor, says Vorhies fell several times in exhaustion. A local sheriff saw Vorhies having difficulty breathing just after the drill, but said he recovered soon and returned to his dormitory.

Dr. David W. Oxley, the county coroner, announced Vorhies had died of cardiac arrhythmia, a disturbance of the heartbeat. Oxley said, "There was probably some relationship between the drill and Vorhies' death, but there was no way to prove it."

A grand jury "found no basis to conclude that anyone acted in bad faith, or with a disregard for the safety and health of Robert Vorhies, or deliberately caused him any harm."

However, the strangest twist to this morbid affair was the fact that Bob Vorhies was probably one of the most disciplined athletes you could ever meet. He wanted more than anything else to be a major running back and he worked hard to reach that goal. "Most players would have dreaded the drills, but Vorhies joked about the prospect." A friend recalls, "he'd do the punishment to the letter. There was nothing a coach could do to make him quit." Another teammate said, "Bob never took any drugs, so everybody knew it wasn't that. People were saying they must have run him pretty hard. Bob was in pretty good shape. He didn't die easily."

It is pointless to make Vorhies out to be more in death than he was in life. Many of his teammates were puzzled because Bob never paid much attention to a secret in running punishment drills called "sucking wind early." One player says "you act like you're tired in the beginning so they won't run you so hard." It is a shame that discipline became Bob Vorhies' epitaph!

William Taff, "A Teen's Brutal Run-to Death," *Chicago Tribune,* February 19, 1978.

---

social control. The asceticism of the Protestant Ethic is very much in evidence in the importance attached to self-dicipline. Woody Hayes, the curmudgeon former football coach of the Ohio State Buckeyes, in a pregame interview before the 1977 Orange Bowl, spoke of the need to cultivate discipline in student athletes. See Vignette 4.1 for a tragic account of over-discipline.

Ray Mears, a successful basketball coach at the University of Tennessee, spoke of his role as disciplinarian in the following way:

> I'm a disciplinarian. There isn't a boy on my team that has a beard or mustache. A lot of people say it's the style. Black athletes come and say it's part of their culture. I show them pictures of some nice looking, All-American black athletes who don't wear a mustache and beard and say, "What about their culture?" I want our boys to look like the All-American boy. To my way of thinking, and that's who's coaching the team at Tennessee, the All-American boy is clean cut, clean shaven and his hair is in order. This is how I expect them to look.
>
> Coaches must hang on to the discipline which is part of their profession. . . . When I say a meeting is at 2:30 I don't mean 2:32. . . . You have to make exceptions and shade a bit and I will, but I'm not going to let anybody else run the ball club. A boy's got to understand right from wrong.[18]

Obedience to authority is very much in evidence even in pro sports. For example, when baseball superstar Reggie Jackson refused to follow the manager's orders, he was suspended for five days. This suspension occurred during the summer of 1978. Similarly, the Cincinnati Reds management impose a restrictive code on facial and head hair. Players are forbidden to wear mustaches and beards or have hair longer than a predetermined length. Again, these practices existed in the late 1970s. Strict obedience to authority can have and has had dire consequences. Take the case of Bob Hayes, former superstar receiver of the Dallas Cowboys. In the spring of 1979 he was found guilty of selling narcotics to an undercover agent. After psychiatric examination the psychiatrist declared: "Bob Hayes is a victim of his own existence as a celebrity . . . he is emotionally incapacitated . . . he has a difficult time sustaining himself as a person of value . . . he has a need to be liked . . . he lived a life as a person under discipline, controlled and managed . . . he didn't learn any social skills" (Denne H. Freeman, AP sports writer).

Competition

Another view of the value of sport is almost Darwinian. Life is struggle; the fittest survive. Accordingly, sport participation prepares one for the competitive nature of life. Sport advocates suggest that it cultivates fortitude, perseverance, and courage . . . desirable traits by our society's definition. According to Douglas MacArthur (1880-1964) the competitive character of sport develops tomorrow's leaders. He said that sport "prepares young men for their roles as the future custodians of the Republic."[19] Gerald Ford, when Vice-President, echoed testimony to the social significance of competition. He said:

> Broadly speaking, outside of a national character and an educated society, there are few things more important to a country's growth and well-being than competitive athletics. If it is a cliche to say athletics build character as well as muscle, then I subscribe to the cliche. It has been said, too, that we are losing our competitive spirit in this country, the thing that made us great, the guts of the free-enterprise system. I don't agree with that; the competitive urge is deep-rooted in the American character. I do wonder sometimes if we are adjusting to the times, or if we have been spoiled by them.[20]

American games are highly competitive. Measures are usually taken to ensure that one team (or individual) emerges victorious. The American people are generally dissatisfied with "ties" and "draws." To circumvent this possibility, sporting contests climax in "sudden deaths," World Series, Super Bowls, and championship playoffs in almost every sport.

Physical Fitness

Physically healthy and fit bodies are often—but not always—the result of athletic participation. Americans subscribe to the importance of physical fitness (see Vignette 4.2). Even the late John F. Kennedy (1917-1963) admonished Americans for becoming soft (see pp. 4-5). Virtually any sporting activity requires limbering exercises and calisthenics which contribute to developing and maintaining muscle tone. Exercise that accompanies some sports not only firms up the muscles and makes the body look good, but it can also bring about positive changes in the cardiovascular system, reduce cholesterol and triglyceride levels in the blood, produce weight loss through caloric consumption, reduce blood pressure readings, and reapportion body fat.[21]

Mental Fitness

Mental alertness, often presumed to have direct educational benefits, is another frequently mentioned by-product of sport participation. Not only do many believe that sport prepares the body, but they also believe it prepares the mind for doing battle in the mental marketplace. A slogan capturing this notion was used at Illinois State University. Locker rooms, banners, towels, and even uniforms were labeled with the abbreviation "MTXE" (Mental Toughness and eXtra Effort). This abbreviation was the coach's formula for success, namely, victory.

Religiosity

Sport reinforces traditional religious beliefs. Eighty-one percent (21 of 26) of the professional football teams in 1973 had pre-game mini religious services. Similarly, team chaplains are not uncommon and an interesting incident is that of the Pittsburgh Steelers prior to the 1975 Super Bowl. The Steelers' management flew their good-luck priest over from Ireland since he had brought them victory in many crucial games over the years.[22]

Sport and religion have been intertwined for centuries. In the beginning sport held elements of a religious cult and served as a preparation for life. In writing on the origins of sport Brasch said: ". . . I was amazed, . . . to discover how greatly religion, and even humble clergymen, have influenced sports. It is a fact that many modern sports descend from ancient religious rites."[23] When the first recorded Olympic Games were convened in 776 B.C. delegations from all over the Greek world met in honor of twelve honored guests—12 gods spearheaded by Zeus. These gods were thought to inhabit Mr. Olympus, which overlooked the fertile plain where the stadium was constructed. For the gods' satisfactions and entertainment, participants held religious pageants and competed not only in sports but also in oratory, poetry, and music.

During the present century there are numerous indications of the close relationships between sport and religion. Churches and church-related organizations like the YMCA, YWCA, and CYO (Catholic Youth Organization) have sponsored a wide assortment of sport and recreation programs.

VIGNETTE 4.2

America's Physical Fitness Boom

By Mark Leepson
Editorial Research Reports

Washington—In Alfred Lord Tennyson's day, spring turned a young man's fancy to thoughts of love. This spring, a young man's fancy—and a young woman's, too—is very likely turning to thoughts of physical fitness.

Never before have so many Americans spent so much time, energy and money to get into shape and stay there. Tens of millions of men and women have made physical fitness a part of their lives, regularly setting aside time for tennis, swimming, bicycling, jogging and the like. Young affluent adults are in the vanguard of the movement, but nearly all segments of American society are participating in the physical fitness boom.

Exercise authorities are encouraging parents to take their children to gym classes even before they're old enough to enter school. At the other end of the age spectrum, senior citizens are active in sports and exercise activities that only a few years ago were thought to be the exclusive domain of the young. One of the most important trends in the fitness boom is the marked increase in women sports participants.

According to Richard O. Keelor, director of program development for the President's Council on Physical Fitness and Sports, "America is going through a physical fitness renaissance that can make a real dent in degenerative diseases, not to mention the quality of life."

Keelor is one of many who believe that exercise is a form of preventive medicine that leads to better physical and mental health.

Nearly half of all Americans—47 percent—participate in some form of daily physical exercise, according to a Gallup Poll taken last fall.

This is twice the percentage recorded in 1961. Sindlinger's Economic Service, a marketing and opinion research firm in Media, Pa., estimates that 38.5 million adult Americans participate in swimming, 34.7 million play tennis and 27.7 million in bowling—the three most popular sports in the United States.

Many are turning to exercise for reasons other than physical conditioning. Long distance running, for example, has been used as a form of psychological therapy. They say that running brings them tranquility, enabling them to forget everyday troubles. Running has been called a "mental exercise, a kind of ambulatory yoga."

Moreover, physical conditioning is highly personal and, unlike team sports, non-competitive. The only goal is self-improvement. Exercising thus fits in with a social philosophy that has become prevalent in the 1970s, described by social critic Tom Wolfe as the "Me Decade" and by others as the "New Narcissism."

Improved physical appearance through exercise frequently is part of this preoccupation with the self.

Then, too, physical fitness has become a chic pastime in places like New York City, Chicago, and Los Angeles. Seventy-five-dollar designer running suits have replaced rumpled cotton sweat suits for many. And movie stars' publicity photos are likely to show the actor or actress dressed in the latest jogging or tennis attire.

Many observers of the fitness movement are convinced that it is not a passing fad. "I've wondered whether the fitness movement was just another flash-in-the-pan American craze—whether today it's fitness, tomorrow it's some therapy, diet, political movement, or whatever," Richard Kipling, director of The Sports Project of Santa Barbara, Calif., told Editorial Research Reports.

"But I've watched this thing closely for three years now and it looks like it's become part of a new American lifestyle. It certainly fits Americans' vision of themselves as vigorous, healthy, active and on the go."

There is no question that the number of Americans exercising regularly is at an all-time high. It is doubtful that every American adult will soon be a regular jogger or tennis player. But with an increasing number trying to stay in shape through serious exercise programs, those who choose not to participate may soon become an out-of-shape minority.

Source: Bloomington Normal (IL) *Pantagraph,* May 14, 1978. Reprinted by permission.

The famous evangelist Billy Graham is fond of using sport metaphors in his preaching. He has said: "The Bible says leisure and lying around are morally dangerous .... Sports keep us busy."[24] Church-supported institutions of higher learning like Notre Dame, Brigham Young, Texas Christian, Southern Methodist, and Oral Roberts, more recently, have used sports to advertise their religious stance. Of the many religious organizations that exist for athletes, a few of the more popular are the Fellowship of Christian Athletes (FCA), Athletes in Action (the "AIA" is a division of the Campus Crusade for

Christ), and Pro Athletes Outreach (PAO). Deford proclaimed that the use of athletes as amateur evangelists is sufficiently widespread that a new denomination—"Sportianity"—has evolved.[25]

Nationalism

Athletes, particularly Olympic ones, are billed as ambassadors of good will. Sports reinforce patriotism, a form of *ethnocentrism.*[26] When George Foreman traipsed around the ring after winning the heavyweight boxing championship in the 1968 Mexico City Olympics, Americans were ecstatic. He toted a miniature American flag, a cultural symbol glorifying the Unites States. On the other hand, when track stars Tommie Smith and John Carlos gave the black power salute on the victory podium at the same Games, Americans looked on with consternation and horror and the duo was banned for life from future Olympic competition.

In 1938 Joe Louis, an American boxer, and Max Schmeling, a German fighter, fought for the heavyweight championship of the world. The "brown bomber," as Louis was known, was twenty-four years old, had been fighting professionally for four years and had lost only one previous bout . . . to Schmeling in 1936. In fact, in the previous match Louis had been so decidedly beaten that some boxing experts did not believe Louis would win the rematch. The nationalistic and racial overtones were highly significant. For one, Adolf Hitler (1889-1945) was at the height of his power in Germany and the United States was beginning to be seriously disturbed by his proclamations that Germans were a "master race" destined to rule the world. Schmeling was explicit in his disdain for blacks and referred to Louis as a "stupid black amateur." On a hot humid night on June 22, 1938 Louis explosively knocked out Schmeling in a little over two minutes of the first round amidst the screams of some 70,000 fans, while millions of others listened to the climax on their radios.[48]

In summary, a moment's reflection suffices to capture the essence of the individual and social good that has traditionally been associated with sport. Edwards even sees the sport creed in ideological terms, a set of beliefs aimed at convincing people of the virtues of sport.[27] But, like other social institutions, sport is not immune from the distortions of self-praise nor the exaggerations of the media. The problem is one of balance—balancing out the myths against the realities (see Vignette 4.3).

Winning?

It is ironic that *winning* is not explicitly mentioned in the dominant American sport creed. Is winning of no import? Obviously not. In fact, many sport critics wager that the Lombardian ethic—"Winning is not everything—It's the only thing"—is the motherlode of sport. At the professional level there is no denying the importance of winning, as the following quotes of pro coaches explicitly express:

> "Winning is living." (George Allen, Washington Redskins) "Everytime you win, you're reborn; when you lose, you die a little." (George Allen) "No one ever learns anything by losing." (Don Shula, Miami Dolphins).[28]

Even at the high school level the emphasis upon winning is explicit through such sport slogans as:

> "A quitter never wins, a winner never quits." "Never be willing to be second best." "The greatest aim in life is to succeed." "Win by as many points as possible."[29]

VIGNETTE 4.3

Contradictions in Sport

I recently met a visitor from Denmark who was full of wonderment because we Americans take our sports so seriously.

Initially, I was surprised at this observation, but of course I shouldn't have been. Is there any other country with so many athletic teams, so many sporting contests, and so many hours of television devoted to sports? Surely sports occupies a more important place in our society than any other in the world.

But we Americans don't always consciously accept this fact, and so perhaps it takes a visitor's casual remark to bring us back to reality. Only then does our vision of a mere game yield to the truth, that sports is serious business. This disparity between our ideals and our reality is one of the recurrent themes of United States history; thus it is probably inevitable that American sports should embody such a contradiction.

The more popular sports become, the more we are confused about their role in our society, the more we proclaim one thing and practice another.

We say it's not whether you win or lose, it's how you play the game. But in reality, only athletes who win games get scholarships to college and fat salaries to play professional ball. Only winning coaches get their contracts renewed, sometimes even on the high school level. Only winning teams draw big crowds, and if they lose the audience may boo or toss debris at players and referees.

The stereotype of the pushy parents who demand victory from their Little League son is all too real, and now we can expect the same pressure to be applied to their daughters. In Milwaukee, a parochial grade-school league voted against a proposed rule that would require coaches to evenly divide playing time between all the players on the team. Apparently, these coaches feel it's too important to win the game than to worry about how it's played.

We say that sports programs build "character." But do they? I still vividly remember my eighth grade coach. He was the darling of the priests and nuns at the parish school, an imposing, dedicated man.

His players were manhandled during practice and were told to quit being "nice guys" and become "dirty, mean" football players. But his teams always won. Is this what we mean by character? What about the high school coach who subjects every player who errs to verbal abuse? What about Al McGuire, who badgered referees tirelessly, or Woody Hayes, who attacked a TV cameraman? What about the routine recruiting violations by big-time colleges? What is the collective effect of this kind of sportsmanship on the character of our nation's youth?

We say that school sports programs promote physical fitness. But how many students actually benefit from these programs? Only a minority of students try out for the teams, and of these less than half play regularly. Yet even as early as fifth or sixth grade, some schools spend big money on glamorous uniforms and next to nothing on general physical education.

It's not surprising a President's physical fitness program was started, apparently to help the many young people who didn't make the team. As for those who did, their growing bodies could be injured for life by the premature stress of organized athletics.

To be sure, some youngsters may thrive on a steady diet of team sports, and may eventually develop into powerful physical machines like Dick Butkus, who terrorized pro football opponents for years. But even Butkus is nowadays just another former athlete, minus most of his kneecaps. So many former athletes have earned a lifetime disability along with their fame.

We say that sports fosters the competitive spirit. But how "spirited" must the competition become before we begin to question the truth of this ideal? A noncontact sport like basketball has become a brutal battle where the object is to be as physical as possible. The amount of violence allowed in hockey had led to judicial suits for damages, and now other sports are beginning to enter the legal arena.

In pro football, a former coach regularly instructed his players to physically punish the rival team's place-kicker, so the threat of a long-distance field goal would be "eliminated." Other teams use the same approach on the opposing quarterback to "eliminate" the threat of a pass. Fights between players, players and coaches, players and fans have become increasingly commonplace.

Perhaps this is to be expected in a nation that reveres players who "like to hit." Increasingly, it seems contradictory to expect opponents to give 100 per cent, yet draw a fine line between legal and illegal assult.

We say that athletics is a sport or game. But countless professional teams are turning a tidy dollar, and even college sport is ultimately justified because it earns money for the alma mater. Big-time sports is big business. Yet we condemn franchises for disloyally moving to another city when the business begins losing money. We become outraged at sports stars who, like good businessmen, ask for a raise.

Millionaire movie stars or corporation executives with similar salaries are somehow more acceptable to the public. Apparently, we want pure, selfless athletes to satisfy our need for heroes. A noble ideal, but one that has no relationship to reality, and probably hasn't since the day of the highly paid Babe Ruth.

"Where have you gone, Joe DiMaggio? A nation turns its lonely eyes to you?" asks Paul Simon rhetorically. In fact, Joe never really left us. Like any good businessman, he chases a buck wherever possible, once upon a time as a Yankee Clipper, now as the official Mr. Coffee.

We say an endless number of things about sports, most of which are not necessarily true. As a result, the American sports world is one of countless contradictions. Perhaps we are all of us aware of the negative side of the sports ledger, but choose to close our eyes and enjoy what we can, thereby assuring the continuity of these contradictions. For all my misgivings, despite my amusement at the spectacle of adults angry about a meaningless defeat, I eagerly participate.

I can't miss the big games on TV, I can't help starting with the sports section of the daily newspaper, I can't refuse a pickup basketball game, or a Ping-Pong match. While no one's yet asked, I probably couldn't refuse an invitation to arm wrestle. Sports is such an irresistible phenomenon, that today, when doubts and disagreements about it have reached a crescendo, it is more successful than ever before, seemingly thriving on its own contradictions.

What is the impact on society of this kind of success? Isn't there cause for alarm at the disparity between our ideals and our reality? I believe there is, and I would very much like to see what's good about sports preserved before it is too late.

I still have happy memories of many childhood hours spent playing pickup games, and find it hard to imagine a better way to have passed the time. But the organized institutions of sport have little to do with this kind of innocent fun. This is the reality we must eventually confront.

Various reforms of sport have been urged before but true reform seems unthinkable until we concede the fact that big-time sports rarely embody the ideals of sportsmanship, physical fitness, and good clean competition.

I speak as one who enjoys sports, both as spectator and participant. It is we sports lovers who must be honest about the deficiencies of our national pastime, in hopes of preserving its better side. We must attempt the painful process of reconciliation of our ideals and our reality before we can ever attempt meaningful reform. However difficult such a process, it seems an inevitable necessity if we are indeed as serious about sports as our Danish visitor has suggested.

*By Bruce Murphy, *Chicago Tribune,* June 10, 1978, Section 1, p. 1. Reprinted by permission.

CROSS-CULTURAL DIFFERENCES

We have seen that the values attributed to American sport overlap with the value orientations existing in American society. But if sport is genuinely a microcosm, it is necessary to demonstrate this claim in other cultural complexes. A data archive known as the *Human Relations Area Files* contains ethnographic information on various topics for more than two hundred societies. These "files" permit social scientists to engage in comparative research in a large number of areas. We will consider some comparative data for sport.

Sport and game, as we saw in chapter 1, are not synonymous concepts. Anthropological investigations have advanced a three-category classification of games:[30] (1) *games of strategy*, (2) *games of chance,* and (3) *games of physical skill*—based upon such cultural components as child-rearing practices, nature of the economy, and complexity of the social structure.

Games of *physical skill* tend to be associated with tropical regions where the economy is one of subsistence. Child-rearing practices are relatively easy-going and relaxed. Conflict and war also tend to be minimal. Sex roles tend to be highly differentiated. For example, games of spear throwing and archery are typically engaged in by males but not by females. Games of physical skill are associated with permissiveness and high conflict over nurturant and self-reliant behavior.

Games of *chance* are found in regions marked by seasonal changes in the temperature. Child-rearing practices are more authoritarian and strict. The games played in such regions tend to be more diversified and subject to the changing climatic conditions. Games of chance appear to be related to high frequency of responsible behavior and high frequency of achievement behavior.

Games of *strategy* predominate in regions characterized by advanced technology and social organization. They are correlated with low permissiveness in child training, severity in bowel training, and extensive rewards for obedience behavior.

In most developed societies all three types of games are found. Games of strategy have been linked with the learning of social roles (mastery of the social system), games of chance with responsibility and achievement (mastery of the supernatural) and games of physical skill with self-reliance (mastery of both self and environment).

Zurcher and Meadow correlated national sports and socialization techniques.[31] For example, the national sport in Mexico is bullfighting. According to the researchers, both the national sport and the Mexican family reflect such cultural themes as death, dominance, personal relationships, respect, fear, hatred for authority, and passive-aggressive character structures. In recent years bullfighting has undergone change as a result of the criticisms of inhumane treatment of animals as well as excessive violence and destruction. Zurcher and Meadow explain this transition by pointing to alterations in the macho ("virility") complex in the culture and the decline of authoritarianism in the Mexican family.[32] In short, changes in sport and the larger society tend to reinforce each other.

Another cross-cultural account illustrating the manner in which games and cultural values mutually reflect each other is the game of *taketak*. This game resembles bowling and is practiced by the Tangu of New Guinea. *Taketak* is described by Light and Keller as follows:

> The game is played with a top that has been fashioned from a dried fruit and with two groups of coconut stakes that are driven into the ground (more or less like bowling pins). The players divide into two teams. Members of the first team take turns throwing the top into the batch of stakes; every stake the top hits is removed. Then the second team steps to the line and tosses the top into their batch of stakes. The object of the game, surprisingly, is not to knock over as many stakes as possible. Rather, the game continues until both teams have removed the *same* number of stakes. Winning is completely irrelevant.[33]

The nature of *taketak* reflects the dominant values of the Tangu culture. They value equivalence. The idea of defeating opposing parties through competition bothers them since they believe winning and losing breed ill will and contempt. Not surprisingly, when Europeans introduced the competitive game of soccer into their culture, they modified the rules so that the object of the game was for the two "opposing" sides to score the identical number of goals!

A final illustration of the manner in which dominant cultural values influence the character of sport is illustrated by Ruth Benedict's ethnographic observations of a "model" Zuñi Indian runner. She wrote:

> The ideal man in Zuñi is a person of dignity and affability who has never tried to lead, and who has never called forth comment from his neighbors. Any conflict, even though all right is on his side, is held against him. Even in contests of skill like their foot races, if a man wins habitually he is debarred from running. They are interested in a game that a number can play with even chances, and an outstanding runner spoils the game: they will have none of him.[34]

Apparently, then, the Zuñi emphasize cooperative over competitive contests. Hence, those individuals who stand "above" the field are victims of societal rebuke and wrath.

In summary, sports tend to promote and be consistent with the values of the culture as a whole. If contradictions and paradoxes exist in sport values, it is probably because inconsistencies exist in the larger culture as well.

SPORT HEROES AS REFLECTIONS OF DOMINANT CULTURAL VALUES

It is common for societies to personify their cultural ideals into specific "people-types." The *cultural heroes* typically manifest the major value orientations and symbols that the society holds in highest esteem. Earlier we indicated that values provide directives and motivation for action. Hence, cultural heroes who personify these values will be objects of admiration and emulation. Smith suggested that heroes functioned to maintain the social structure through the perpetuation of societal values and norms and, in doing so, contributed to social solidarity.[35] He suggests the following:

Hero worship in sport is common. It manifests itself in autograph seeking, acquiring and memorizing sport statistics, reading feature stories, collecting bubble gum cards with sport personalities pictured, attending publicity events, and making pilgramages to sports' halls of fame (Canton, Ohio, and Cooperstown, N.Y.). Let us trace the changing nature of sport heroes in the United States during the present century for the light it sheds upon dominant cultural values.

Frank Merriwell was probably the best known sport figure around the turn of the century. He was a fictional baseball character who appeared in dime store novels between 1896 and 1914. Merriwell was truly the All-American boy. He was a good student, gentlemanly, educated, brave, handsome, wealthy, admired, clean-living, and an excellent athlete. Boyle said:

> Frank Merriwell in the words of his creator, Gilbert Patten, stood for truth, faith, justice, the triumph of right, mother, home, friendship, loyalty, patriotism, the love of alma mater, duty, sacrifice, retribution, and strength of soul as well as body.[36]

When Merriwell disappeared from the social scene, he was supplanted by new idols of worship. With the advances in technology during the 1920s and 1930s, the hero of strength was superseded by the hero of persistence, finesse, and guile. The heroes during this period—Jesse Owens, Red Grange, Babe Ruth, and Johnny Weismuller—reflected a change in cultural values.

During the early 1940s the heroes of the previous era were replaced by those with military connections. Ted Williams, a baseball player and ex-Marine fighter pilot, and Felix "Doc" Blanchard and Glenn Davis, stellar football players at West Point, were catapulted to the hero podium. Maurice Richard, even though he refused to join the army, still remained a Canadian hockey star idol.

The 1950s and 1960s saw football players emerge as objects of adultation. Smith said: "It was a sport for the times, the highly complex organization, specialization and division of labor in the game coincided with exactly the key characteristics of a highly industrialized society. The sport heroes were the equivalent of business executives."[37] Quarterbacks Johnny Unitas and Bart Starr epitomized this breed, and it was during this time that Vince Lombardi gained popular acclaim. The New York Yankees, Boston Celtics, Green Bay Packers, and Montreal Canadiens—teams depicting efficient and conservative business organizations—were glamorized.

With the social movements of the 1960s and early 1970s, the nature of the sport hero changed to accommodate the change in society's social atmosphere. Such sports personalities as Joe Namath, Derek Sanderson, Dick Allen, Dave Meggyesy, Jim Bouton, Muhammad Ali, and Duane Thomas depicted the anti-establishment type in tune with the times. Sport commentator and writer Robert Lipsyte[38] wrote:

> Sports is an unsparing mirror of our life and fantasies. Nowhere is this easier to see than in sports' choice of its super heroes.

The Gold-Plated Age of American sports, that mid-sixties to late seventies era of instant legends and sudden millionaires and overnight bankrupts, was dominated by the images of three celebrity athletes whose impact on the nation's psyche was as deep and significant as their effect on the games they played.

Joe Namath, Billie Jean King, and Muhammad Ali were supreme performers at their peaks, now past, but each had something more. Call it magnetism or sex appeal or charisma, it allowed people to use them as extensions of their hopes and daydreams, as living symbols of the ultimate.[39]

THE CULTURAL ROOTS OF SPORT

Let us examine the cultural roots of sport and games. Frederickson wrote: "There is no society known to man which does not have games of the sort in which individuals set up purely artificial obstacles and get satisfaction from overcoming them."[40] What accounts for this universality?

In all human societies, rituals, festivals, dances, music, pictorial art, sports and games, not only provide pleasure from participating and/or spectating but provide outlets for creativity and reinforce *social identity* and *solidarity*. These activities are intimately tied into social, religious, economic, and political phases of life. Among the oldest organized games, the ancient Olympics, these multi-faceted interconnections can be seen.

The Olympic Games began in ancient Greece. Historians date the Games from 1453 B.C. with the first formal event, a 200-foot footrace, staged in 776 B.C. In the Greek mind, sport reigned supreme. Early in Greek history the importance of a healthy body and mind was a dominant cultural value, and the glorification of sport can be seen in epics, poems, and art—as the writings of Homer (*Illiad* and *Odyssey*) testify.

The Greeks believed that athletic contests not only invigorated the body but cultivated the mind; they were not simply peaceful athletic preparations for winning wars (of which there were many) but they helped to renew the spirits of the deceased and win the approval of the gods. Many myths and legends have arisen regarding the inception of the Olympics but it is fair to say that the original (ancient) Olympics were multi-purpose and multi-faceted social events with cultural, theological, political, and practical purposes.[41]

Some have attributed the universality—what sociologists call *cultural universals*—of sports and games to a primordial instinct embedded in humans' phylogenetic or evolutionary history. For example, ethologists—scientists who study the social behavior of nonhumans and then attempt to draw parallels between human and nonhuman behavior—have pointed to purposeful play among animals. These observers frequently suppose that young animals tumble and wrestle about in anticipatory training for the time when they must battle in deadly earnest for food or for mates. These same ethological observations have noted "rules of the game" existing for adults and not just the young.[42]

Acknowledging a tendency to anthropomorphize, some observers of animal behavior have suggested that certain congregations of birds are much like tournaments, mock battles, and flying contests. Other animals (antelopes and bowerbirds) display "arena behavior" during the mating season. Bowerbirds of the South Pacific construct elaborate shelters out of vines, twigs, and flowers while antelopes vie for territories. In both cases the female members of the species gravitate to the most outstanding performers amongst these animals. Though these acts have adaptive and survival value (to the species), it is difficult to escape the play-like character and rule-observation accompanying them.

The problem with this evolutionary explanation for humans' play and games is that it fails to consider the extent to which biologically-based impulses are molded, modified, and conditioned by culture. That is, without an understanding of culture, how would one explain the elaborate sport social organization that exists in North America and many European and Asian countries? In brief, whether humans at any time in history play for fame, self-expression, prestige, power, glory, financial gain, or political advantage, it is culturally conditioned.

As a preparation for life the roots of sport can be traced to man's desire for victory over foes, seen and unseen, to influence the mysterious forces of nature, and to promote fertility among crops and livestock. The functional necessity of sport and sport-related skills can easily be viewed in terms of humans' earliest need for defense. Thus, some sports grew naturally out of martial training since strength, speed, and guile served to repulse or conquer one's foes. Man's wish to survive and prosper explains the origins of some early sports.

Many sports began as *fertility magic,* to ensure birth, growth, and the return of spring. In studies of primitive societies a connection between play and magic—the methods devised to influence the forces of nature and the gods—has been discovered.[43] For example, the variety of jumping games today (jumping rope to high jumping) has been traced back to ancient crop planting festivals in which it was believed that the grain would grow as high as the best jumper could leap.

While these may be the ancient origins of games and sports, today some sports are artificially created and often have no direct link with the original reasons. No matter what their origin however, sports must be understood as cultural phenomena.

The Dutch historian Johan Huizinga argued that play is the very foundation of human culture. He wrote: ". . . culture arises in the form of play, that it is played from the very beginning."[44] In elaborating this thesis, he started with the idea of *agon,* a Greek word meaning "contest" but also implying gathering and playing together. He revealed that social differentiation in societies—clans or totems, male or female units—was carried out for competitive play. The magical importance of such groups is reflected in the following excerpt:

> the earliest phase is one in which rural clans celebrate the seasonal feasts by contests, designed to promote fertility and the ripening of crops. It is a well-known fact that such an idea underlies every primitive ritual. Every ceremony well-performed, every game or contest won . . . fervently convinces archaic man that a boon and a blessing have thereby been procured for his community. The sacrifices have thereby been procured for his community. The sacrifices have been successfully executed, and now all is well, the higher powers are on our side, the cosmic order is safeguarded, social well-being is assured for us and ours . . . . It is a life-feeling, a feeling of satisfaction crystallized into faith.[45]

In Huizinga's mind, play is the bedrock upon which social institutions are built . . . religion, law, government, arts, and society in general. While the element of play may be masked or obscured, it nevertheless remains:

> As a rule, the play-element gradually recedes into the background . . . but at any moment, even in a highly developed civilization, the play instinct may reassert itself in full force, *drowning the individual and the mass in the intoxication of an immense game.*[46] (italics added)

While Huizinga's perspective is a bit grandiose, it is of interest to speculate about the truth of the *underscored* words. May they not be applicable to many individual and social features of sport today? In fact, some see sport as a kind of opiate for the masses.[47]

SUMMARY

In this chapter we have shown the relationships between sport and culture. In general, sport is a *microcosm* of the larger culture. *Culture* is the changing patterns of learned behavior and the products of learned behavior which are socially shared and transmitted among members of a society. In short, culture is the way of life of a social group, the distinctive patterns—values, norms, institutions—which set it off from others. Culture can be dissected into two components—*material* and *nonmaterial.*

Material culture includes "tangibles." In sport it would include such artifacts as stadia, swimming pools, tennis rackets, hockey sticks, turnstiles, and uniforms. *Nonmaterial culture* includes "intangibles" like values, attitudes, norms, and beliefs. The "dominant American sport creed" devised by Edwards was used to demonstrate the *social values*—conceptions of what are desirable—attributed to sport. The values espoused in the sport creed include: (1) *character building,* (2) *discipline,* (3) *competition,* (4) *physical fitness,* (5) *religiosity,* (6) *mental fitness,* and (7) *nationalism.* Each of these presumed values was illustrated and discussed. Although winning is not explicitly mentioned in the sport creed, there is sufficient evidence that it is extremely important in sport (and life in general).

In societies other than our own linkages exist between sport values and values held in high regard in the general culture. Several cross-cultural illustrations corroborate this assertion. These include observations of sport behavior in Mexico, New Guinea, and among the Zuñi Indians.

Sport heroes tend to reflect the dominant cultural values. We traced the popular sport heroes from the turn of the century to the present to demonstrate the manner in which the two—sport heroes and cultural values—tend to change together.

Finally, we considered the cultural roots of sport. We discussed the inception of the ancient Olympic Games and the Games' multi-purpose and multi-faceted nature.

IMPORTANT CONCEPTS DISCUSSED IN THIS CHAPTER

Culture

Material Culture

Nonmaterial Culture

Values

Dominant American Sport Creed

Character Building

Discipline

Competition

Physical Fitness

Mental Fitness

Nationalism

Ethnocentrism

Human Relations Area Files

Games of Physical Skill

Game of Chance

Game of Strategy

Taketak

Sport Heroes

Cultural Universals

Agon

ENDNOTES

[1] Peter L. Berger, *Invitation to Sociology* (Garden City, N.Y.: Doubleday, 1963), p. 21.

[2] John F. Cuber, *Sociology* (New York: Appleton-Century-Crofts, 1968), p. 76.

[3] James A. Michener, *Sports in America* (New York: Random House, 1976).

[4] David Q. Voigt, "Reflections on Diamonds: American Baseball and American Culture," *Journal of Sport History* 1 (May, 1974), pp. 3-25.

[5] David Riesman and Reuel Denney, "Football in America: A Study in Cultural Diffusion," *American Quarterly* 3 (1951), pp. 309-319.

[6] Howard L. Nixon, II, *Sport and Social Organization* (Indianapolis: Bobbs-Merrill, 1976), p. 14.

[7] Harry Edwards, *Sociology of Sport* (Homewood, Ill.: Dorsey Press, 1973), p. 90.

[8] John C. Pooley and Arthur V. Webster, "Sport and Politics: Power Play," *Sport Sociology*, ed. A. Yiannakis, T. D. McIntyre, M. J. Melnick, and D. P. Hart (Dubuque, Iowa: Kendall-Hunt, 1976), pp. 35-42.

[9] Robin M. Williams, Jr., *American Society: A Sociological Interpretation*, 3d edition (New York: Alfred Knopf, 1970), pp. 454-500.

[10] Elmer Spreitzer and Eldon E. Snyder, "The Psychosocial Functions of Sport as Perceived by the General Population," *International Review of Sport Sociology* 10 (1975), pp. 87-93.

[11] Eldon E. Snyder and Elmer Spreitzer, *Social Aspects of Sport* (Englewood Cliffs, N.J.: Prentice-Hall, 1978), p. 28.

[12] Edwards, *Sociology of Sport*, pp. 63-69, Appendix A.

[13] The Barnesboro Star, November 19, 1972.

[14] Thomas Tutko and William Bruns, "Sports Don't Build Character—They Build Characters," in *Sport in Contemporary Society*, ed. D.S. Eitzen (New York: St. Martins, 1979), pp. 232-237.

[15] Ibid., pp. 232-33.

[16] Ibid., p. 234.

[17] Ibid., p. 232.

[18] Ray Mears, "Staff Organization," *The Basketball Bulletin* (Fall, 1976), p. 38.

[19] Edwards, *Sociology of Sport*, p. 121.

[20] Gerald R. Ford (with John Underwood), "In Defense of the Competitive Urge," *Sports Illustrated* (July 8, 1974), p. 17.

[21] Kenneth H. Cooper, *Aerobics* (New York: M. Evans and Co., 1968).

[22] Michener, *Sports in America*, pp. 385-386.

[23] Rudolph Brasch, *How Did Sports Begin?* (New York: David McKay, 1970), p. x.

[24] "Are Sports Good for the Soul," *Newsweek* (January 11, 1976), p. 51.

[25] Frank Deford, "Religion in Sport," *Sports Illustrated* 44 (April 19, 1976), p. 92.

[26] Ethnocentrism is the practice of judging "foreign" cultural practices by the standards of one's own culture. Hence, others' behavior is frequently judged to be "unnatural," "wrong," or "bizarre," while one's own is judged "natural," "right," and "proper."

[27] Edwards, *Sociology of Sport*.

[28] D. Stanley Eitzen and George H. Sage, *Sociology of American Sport* (Dubuque, Iowa: William C. Brown Co., 1978), pp. 66-67.

[29] Eldon E. Snyder, "Athletic Dressing Room Slogans as Folklore: A Means of Socialization," *International Review of Sport Sociology* 7 (1972), pp. 89-102.

[30] John Roberts, J. Malcolm, and Robert R. Bush, "Games in Culture," *American Anthropologist* 61 (August, 1959), pp. 597-605; Brian Sutton-Smith, John Roberts, and Robert M. Kazelka, "Game Involvement in Adults," *The Journal of Social Psychology* 60 (June, 1963), pp. 15-30; Eldon E. Snyder and Elmer Spreitzer, *Social Aspects of Sport* (Englewood Cliffs, N.J.: Prentice-Hall, 1978).

[31] Louis Zurcher and Arnold Meadow, "On Bullfights and Baseball: An Example of Interaction of Social Institutions," *Sport: Readings From a Sociological Perspective*, ed. Eric Dunning (Toronto: University of Toronto Press, 1972): Nixon, *Sport and Social Organization*.

[32] Ibid.

[33] Donald Light, Jr. and Suzanne Keller, *Sociology* (New York: Alfred A. Knopf, 1975), p. 74.

[34] Ruth Benedict, *Patterns of Culture* (New York: Mentor Books, 1934), p. 95.

[35] Gary Smith, "The Sport Hero: An Endangered Species," *Quest* XIX (January, 1973), pp. 59-70.

[36] Robert Boyle, *Sport—Mirror of American Life* (Boston, Mass.: Little, Brown, 1963), p. 242.

[37] Smith, "The Sport Hero: An Endangered Species," p. 62.

[38] Robert Lipsyte, "Sports: Instant Legends and Super Heroes," Copyright © 1977 by the Regents of the University of California. The material was excerpted from an article written for the eighth Course by Newspaper, "Popular Culture: Mirror of American Life." Reprinted by permission.

[39] Ibid., p. 1.

[40] Florence Stumpf Frederickson, "Sports and the Cultures of Man," *Science and Medicine of Exercise and Sports* (New York: Harper and Bros., 1960), p. 634; *Sports in American Life* (Columbus, Ohio: Xerox Publications, 1974). Used with permission, Xerox Education Publications © 1974, Xerox Corp.

[41] Brasch, *How did Sports Begin?*.

[42] *Sports in American Life* (Columbus, Ohio: Xerox Publications, 1974).

[43] George Gmelch, "Baseball Magic," *Transaction* 8 (June, 1971), pp. 34-41, 54; Brach, *How did Sports Begin?* and *Sports in American Life.*

[44] Johan Huizinga, *Homo Ludens—A Study of the Play Element in Culture* (Boston, Mass.: Beacon Press, 1938); *Sports In American Life*, p. 19.

[45] *Sports in American Life*, p. 18.

[46] Ibid., p. 19.

[47] Edwards, *Sociology of Sport;* Arnold Beisser, *The Madness in Sports* (New York: Appleton-Century-Crofts, 1967).

[48] Jack Orr, "The Black Boxer: Exclusion and Ascendence," *Sport and Society,* ed. John T. Talamini and Charles H. Page (Boston, Mass.: Little, Brown and Co., 1973).

5
Sport and Socialization

INTRODUCTION

Socialization is the general process by which humans become participating members of society. It refers to the various mechanisms through which a biological organism is fashioned into a social being. It is a kind of "social metamorphosis," a metaphor emphasizing that what is human is due to the *learning* experiences persons have from other persons in the social environment. Socialization can be viewed from two different angles: (1) the transmission of cultural values, attitudes, and norms; and (2) the development of personality. It is a life-long process although much of the literature has typically focused upon the early years of life.[1] Further, it entails an interplay and interaction among biological, psychological, and social forces.

It is common to hear of someone being a "natural athlete." This declaration is misleading and belies the fact that individuals must learn a host of ideas, attitudes, and movements associated with a particular physical activity. As McNeil's model suggests (discussed below), virtually any role—physician, college professor, athlete, or dentist—necessitates acquiring the appropriate emotional, social, cognitive, perceptual, and behavioral skills.[2] In a controversial article regarding the need to *learn* how to play, Gilbert wrote:

> Play, I think, is very close to being an innate characteristic of man, and for that reason as long as man is man, it is never going to be forgotten or abolished, but there are times when we get very grim and serious, and the whole style of society tends to make it harder for people to play. When this happens—and we are in that kind of period—people languish, become spiritually spindly as they might physically if they did not have sufficient or proper food. I think play is an essential element for spiritual well-being.[3]

When individuals are referred to as "natural athletes," it typically means they possess the "tools"—coordination, agility, speed, power, and stamina—to perform sport feats with relative ease. On the other hand, studies have shown that physical characteristics are essential components but so, too, is the acquisition of relevant psychological characteristics (Snyder and Spreitzer, 1978, p. 55).

A helpful scheme for understanding the complexities of the *social learning process* called socialization has been proposed by Elton McNeil.[4] It contains three components: (1) the *individual dimensions* along which socialization occurs, (2) the *agents of socialization,* and (3) general and specific *acquisitions* or *learned consequences.* The model applies to socialization in general and will be adapted to the learning of sport roles, values, and attitudes.

In this chapter it is important to distinguish between two types of sport socialization: (1) *socialization into sports,* and (2) *socialization via sports.* Each of these will be discussed.

SOCIALIZATION INTO SPORT

Of the array of socializing stimuli (see Figure 5.1) the individual will selectively experience a few, and the significance and influence of these will vary from one person to another and from one time period to another. The select few who have the most telling impact upon the individual are termed *significant others* or *reference groups,* those individuals and groups whose attitudes, values, and/or behaviors are decisive in the formation of one's own attitudes, values, and behavior. Regardless of these specific significant others—parents, peers, siblings, relatives, coaches, teachers—the social learning mechanisms operate similarly. There are several theoretical perspectives for understanding the learning of social roles (*psychoanalytic, cognitive-developmental, social learning*), but *social learning theory* is probably most salient in understanding the acquisition of sport roles.

Social Learning Theory

How individuals acquire and perform social behaviors is the focus of social learning theory.[5] Three features of this approach—(1) *reinforcement,* (2) *coaching,*[6] and (3) *observational learning*— are useful for comprehending the learning of sport roles.

Reinforcement

"Reinforcement" highlights the role of *reward* and *punishment* in the acquisition and performance of social roles. The initial socializing agents for most infants are their parents. Later on in

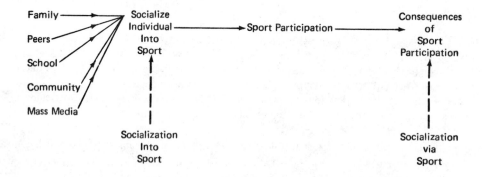

Figure 5.1
A Model for Conceptualizing Socialization into Sport and Socialization via Sport

the life cycle siblings, peers, teachers, and coaches become increasingly important. These agents of socialization dispense and/or withhold rewards and punishments. Furthermore, behavior positively reinforced (i.e., rewarded) tends to reoccur while behavior negatively reinforced (i.e., punished) tends to be inhibited.[7]

Parents pressure children, sometimes subtly, unknowingly, and selectively in the acquisition of "appropriate" sex role behavior. For example, young boys are given toy soldiers, trucks, doctors' kits, footballs, baseballs and bats while young girls are given dolls, toy kitchens, and nurses' uniforms. Hence, some of the basic differences in the acquisition and performance of sport roles can be traced to the differential and selective social experiences and social expectations of boys and girls. It is axiomatic that direct rewards and punishments will influence the kinds of behavior learned and performed. In addition to controlling reinforcement contingencies, parents can provide verbal and nonverbal "hints" about what they think is appropriate.

Coaching

"Coaching" is a deliberate teaching or exposure of the socializee by the socializer. Parents who are fond of a sport frequently coach their offspring in the behaviors required in performing specific athletic skills. This direct tutelage has at least three effects on the socializee: (1) new knowledge about the range of behaviors the "coach" thinks appropriate is acquired, (2) new skills and responses are learned, and (3) greater motivation often results from the rewards extended to the learner.[8]

One aspect of coaching that is important involves the issuing of challenges or dares. When children accept a challenge, they make a commitment to act in a particular manner in the present and it will likely carry over to their future behavior as well. When the challenge is successfully met, the child gains recognition and reward, and becomes more committed and motivated to perform the behavior.

Observational Learning

While "coaching" entails a direct approach to role learning, not all behavior is acquired in this fashion. "Observational learning" refers to the learning and performance of a task resulting from observing the behavior of another and then acting similarly. The basic notion is that exposure to some behavior produces a disposition by the observer to behave similarly.

Albert Bandura, a proponent of *observational learning* or *modeling,* proposes three different effects of exposure to models:[9] (1) novel response patterns may be acquired (learning how to hold a baseball bat, golf club, tennis racket); (2) existing responses may be strengthened or weakened by attending to the act resulting from that behavior (line drives are more likely to be hit when holding the bat a certain way, taking a particular stance, and swinging at certain pitches); and (3) distinguishing among stimuli (the concentration of black athletes in the outfield in baseball today is attributed by some to the relative abundance of role models at those positions when blacks first entered professional baseball).[10] Apparently blacks distinguished among those positions "open" (outfielder) and "closed" (catcher) to them. Similarly, females' historical lack of participation in sport can, in part, be attributed to the scarcity of role models (see chapter 9).

In summary, exposure to models can provide new behavioral skills, information about the probable outcome of engaging in a certain act, and knowledge about various situations.

Agents of Sport Socialization

Since socialization is the process by which skills, traits, dispositions, values, and attitudes for the performance of certain roles occurs, it is apparent that someone or some things must initiate the process. The entities responsible for such transmission include a myriad of individuals, groups, and institutions.[11] Here we will examine the influence of some *agents* of socialization.

The Family

Since socialization commences at birth, a highly significant part of the process occurs within the *family/kinship unit*. The importance of the family in the acquisition of any roles and skills, particularly those learned early in life, has received wide attention. This early learning may be the result of direct teaching as, for example, when a father, mother, or older sibling deliberately teaches a youngster a particular sport skill, or may be the consequence of role modeling as when a parent or older sibling participates in sport with a child's knowledge of it. The fact that many former athletes have offspring (McKay, Doby, Cassidy, Murtaugh, Berra, Howe, Rote) who are athletes themselves can, in part, be explained by the model provided by the parent.

The family's location in the social structure of society—its social class mooring, structure, and patterning of activities—has been shown to affect socialization in general and sport socialization in particular.[12] Since social class is determined by education, occupation, and income, it is not surprising that some sports (golf, tennis) have traditionally drawn their constituency from "higher" social classes while other sports—basketball, boxing, football, and baseball—have drawn their "clientele" from "lower" social classes. In summarizing the influence of the family on sport socialization, Loy, McPherson, and Kenyon wrote:

> . . . the family as an institution is intimately related to sport in a variety of ways. The family serves as a socializing agent for the learning of sport roles (especially mothers for their daughters); it provides a structure from which ascribed and achieved attributes impinge on an individual in a sport system, and it uses sport as an expressive microcosm of the larger society in its attempt to socialize children. Moveover, there is little evidence to support the myth that participation in sport contributes significantly to family integration or solidarity.[13]

The Peer Group

During adolescence one generally finds the family's influence subordinated to the *peer group*. During the teen years the reference group of many youths switches from mother and father to age cohorts (companions of the same age), although this change of influence is affected by such factors as social class background, relationships within the family, and the importance attached to the "youth" or "teen-age" subculture. The powerful socializing force of the peer group is highlighted in Axthelm's book, *The City Game*.[14] In this tome the author describes how playground basketball in Harlem—among working and lower class blacks—captures the interest and energy of young boys. This same phenomenon is duplicated in other metropolitan areas across the country as well. In summarizing the influence of the peer group on sport socialization, Loy, McPherson, and Kenyon wrote:

. . . there is little question but that peer pressure operates to influence sport-related facets of our life style. During childhood, peer groups are found in the immediate neighborhood and tend to be somewhat similar in values to the individual; during the adolescent years, peer groups (youth subcultures) are located within the high school and therefore may include individuals with different values and interests; and during adulthood, influential peer groups are normally comprised of peers at the place of employment, providing an even greater likelihood of there being diversity in interests and values concerning sport. However, despite this influence throughout the life cycle, it is still not possible to determine whether an individual selects a peer group to "fit" with their previously established life style or whether an individual can experience dramatic changes in life style because of the influence of the peer group.[15]

The School

Most schools have physical education classes and intramural and interschool athletic programs which provide sport socializing experiences for many young people. See chapter 3 for a more thorough discussion of the relationship between education and sport. With mass education and mandatory gym classes, many people learn the fundamentals of a variety of sporting activities. In summarizing the influence of the school in sport socialization, Loy, McPherson, and Kenyon wrote:

. . . the school, along with the family and peer group, is an influential institution in the process of sport-role socialization. However, like other social systems, the role of the educational system in the process varies by sport, by roles within sports, by sex, and stage in the life cycle. For example, professional female golfers are largely socialized into their sport role by agents (that is, parents and friends) outside of school settings.[16]

The Community

Many communities sponsor sport programs for males and females alike. Baseball has been one of the oldest and more highly developed programs, and many males are familiar, either directly or indirectly, with Little Leagues, Ban Johnson, Pony Leagues, Babe Ruth Leagues, and American Legion baseball. Add to this compendium Pop Warner football programs, Bittie basketball, youth hockey leagues and track, soccer, and swimming programs, and one can easily infer the importance of these in providing opportunities for the socialization of youth into sport. In summarizing the influence of community sport programs, Loy, McPherson, and Kenyon wrote:

. . . there are many apparent problems in voluntary sport associations that are ostensibly organized for children. Most of these are possible to solve because they result from the overemphasis on competition and the over-organization imposed by adults. If children are given the opportunity to participate spontaneously and at their own level of ability and interest, it is quite likely that more individuals would be socialized into a variety of sport roles that would continue to be enacted throughout the life cycle. At the present time, many children are forced out of sport at an early age and never return. These individuals likely remain sedentary throughout life and may never be interested in socializing their own children to participate in sport. Thus, noninvolvement becomes a self-perpetuating cycle in which future generations become less likely to be socialized into sport roles.[17]

The Mass Media

Television, radio, and the press—the mass media—play a dramatic role in sport socialization. Through them many youngsters become acquainted with sports and are exposed to sport heroes who function as role models.[18] Many young boys and increasingly, young girls, can name the top teams and players in various sports. Moreover, sport personalities are among the most endeared idols of contemporary youth (see pp. 74-78). In summarizing the influence of the mass media, Hoch wrote:

> This brings us to the other main socializer for consumption—the mass media. As Marshall McLuhan has obliquely pointed out in his book *Understanding Media,* almost all news, views, and entertainment heard over the media are essentially advertisements for the consumption-oriented way of life favored by media advertisers and owners. Sports news, for one, has never really been much more than a bit of razzamatazz for promotional purposes, and the bribery of the media-men by professional promoters has long been institutionalized.[19]

In chapter 12 we will examine more deeply the role of the mass media in sport. For now, it suffices to say that it is one of the major socializing agents in contemporary society. It socializes one to *participate in* as well as *consume* sport.

While the family, peer group, school, community, and mass media do not exhaust the sport socializing agents in our society, they are among the most profound influences on young people.[20] It is a rare person who is not affected in some way by sports during the early socialization years.

A review of sport socialization studies by Kenyon and McPherson led them to conclude that sport participation is an outgrowth of early involvement in sports activities, rewarding and successful sport experiences, positive encouragement from significant others, and accessibility to adequate facilities and instruction. The researchers advanced a model to summarize the overall process of socialization into sport.[21]

Factors Contributing to Participation in Sport

With the theoretical discussion of the significant agents of sport socialization behind us, let us consider some empirical evidence regarding some of these contentions. Kenyon and Grogg studied background factors that were important to University of Wisconsin athletes' participation in sport.[22] Two outcomes of their investigation merit attention: (1) of such socializing agents as mother, father, brother, sister, relatives, male friend, female friend, classroom teacher, school coach, school counselor, nonschool personnel, and "others", the parents emerged as the most significant socializing agents. Further, their influence was slightly greater at the high school and collegiate levels than it was during the pre-high school period; and (2) the influence of the agents of socialization varied according to the particular sport of involvement during the pre-high school years.

Spreitzer and Snyder, not surprisingly, found that adult sport participation for members of both sexes could be traced back to "rewarding" experiences during childhood.[23] The following factors correlated with adult sport participation: (1) parental interest in sport, (2) parental encouragement to participate in sport, (3) participation in formal sport programs as a youth, (4) self-perception of athletic ability, and (5) involvement in sport by one's spouse.

Other Factors in Sport Involvement

The following observations on other factors affecting sport involvement were derived principally from an article by Howard L. Nixon II, entitled "Sport, Socialization, and Youth: Some
Proposed Research Directions" (*Review of Sport and Leisure* 1, Fall 1976, pp. 45-61).

In American society there are diverse opportunities for children and youth to be exposed to
sport socializing experiences. There is no dearth of studies attesting to the central role occupied by
sport in the youth culture.[24] In order for people to become involved in sport roles, the desire for
participation must be translated into concrete behavior through attention and muscular effort.
According to some,[25] the motivation to participate in sport is affected by three variables: (1) socioeconomic background, (2) the prestige and power of various socializing agents, and (3) the perceived
structure of opportunities for participation.

As important as these factors may appear, they are not sufficient to explain socialization into
sport. To these must be added personality and physical characteristics, although this dyad does not
receive much emphasis in the present discussion. Kenyon and McPherson advanced several propositions aimed at specifying sociological variables leading to greater sport participation.[26] The inventory
includes: (1) coming from families of higher socioeconomic status with more male than female
children; (2) having fathers employed in entrepreneurial occupations who tend to be highly achieve-
ment-oriented; (3) having parents who are democratic, permissive, warm, and nurturant and place
more emphasis on independence during child-rearing, and who have provided direct encouragement
for athletic participation; and (4) have friends who participate in sports.

More generally, athletic participation will be more likely if: (1) the past experience and future
prospects of material, social, and psychological rewards outweigh the costs; (2) athletic achievement
itself has been rewarding; and (3) the quality of available equipment and facilities is perceived as
satisfactory.

The above conceptual framework for explaining sport socialization appears to be most applicable to *white males* in American society. There is a spate of evidence that *female* and *nonwhite* sport
socialization requires alterations in this scheme. For example, Snyder and Spreitzer found parental
(particularly father's) sport interests positively correlated with sport involvement for both male and
female offspring.[27] For other types of involvements—reading, talking, watching—the sport interest of
the opposite-sex parent appeared more significant. The inquiry suggested the need for separate analysis of male and female sport socializing experiences. According to McPherson, sport socialization for
minority groups, especially blacks, has a differential pattern and outcome.[28] Some of these differences include socializing agents, social structure, and group-influenced individual traits and expectations and will be discussed further in chapter 8.

Types of Involvement

Involvement in sport varies in several respects (degree, frequency, duration, intensity and
kind).[29] There are two generic involvement categories—(1) *primary,* and (2) *secondary*—that are further dichotomized into *direct* and *indirect* subdivisions. *Primary involvement* refers to direct participation (formally prescribed and audible or visible participation) in the staging of an athletic contest
or intermission activities. Primary involvement may be further subcategorized into *direct* and *indirect*
types. To add substance to these conceptual distinctions, consider a football game. The most obvious
role is that of the contestants themselves (quarterbacks, ends, tackles, etc.). These persons are the
direct primary involvers or actors in the event. Nevertheless, there exist other roles, some of which are

vital to the staging of the contest. For example, there are coaches, officials, trainers, physicians, score-keepers, timekeepers, public address announcers, TV and radio sportscasters, cheerleaders, band members, and the like. These latter roles reflect *indirect primary involvement* and, as a totality, consist of primary activities other than those of the athletic participants.

Secondary involvement comprises a residual category encompassing activities not qualifying as primary in nature. *Direct secondary involvement* includes the roles of financial controllers such as professional club owners, promoters, alumni, members of athletic committees, regulators and administrators (e.g., rules committees, sport governing bodies, athletic directors), entrepreneurs (e.g., sports equipment manufacturers, retailers, concessionaires), technical production staff members (e.g., ground crews, mass media production crews), reporters/analysts (e.g., sports writers, TV and radio personnel, sport sociologist) and public relations personnel. The consumers of the sporting events, fans, fall into the category of *indirect secondary involvement*.

In short, there are different types and kinds of sport involvement and the above scheme is an attempt to classify some of the more-or-less identifiable social positions in sport (see Figure 3.3). Moreover, a particular person may fall into several categories of involvement at different times.

Another way of analytically distinguishing categories of sport involvement was suggested by Kenyon.[30] Involvement in sport can be other than behavioral; it may also be cognitive and/or affective. The following trichotomy is useful: (1) *behavioral involvement* includes active (participation in sport) and passive (watch and talk sport, read the sports page, subscribe to sport journals) components; (2) *affective involvement*[31] refers to a person's feelings and attitudes about sport (whether they are deemed cathartic, a waste of time, satisfactory, or unsatisfactory); and (3) *cognitive involvement*[32] refers to a person's knowledge about sport—its rules, personalities and facsimiles. Although these dimensions are likely to be mutually reinforcing, they can be differentiated for analytical purposes.

The Fan

The potential *fan*[33] is generally socialized into this sport role at a very young age. It is not uncommon for parents, as fans, to purchase sport paraphernalia—stuffed footballs, miniature basketballs, toy baseballs and bats, sweatshirts, jackets and caps bearing the insignia of their favorite team—as gifts for their children. As the child matures, he or she is frequently provided with more appropriate "symbols" of various sports—plastic bats, small rubber footballs, basketballs, cheerleading outfits, roller skates, etc. Having been exposed to sport stimuli since birth the motives for fan involvement take on different forms. Two *personal functions* for fan involvement have been advanced:[34] (1) it engenders a feeling of belonging, and (2) it provides a socially acceptable outlet for vicarious hostile and aggressive feelings. Not all would agree to these functions, and a reading of Vignette 5.1 suggests some professional differences of opinion.

Beisser argued that sport enthusiasm stemmed from the nature of mass society and the subsequent form of social interaction wrought by it.[35] He contended that the increasing prevalence of secondary forms of social interaction (due in part to family ties being extenuated and an increase in geographical mobility), affective neutrality (emotional blandness), and social isolation of individuals forced them to search for more permanent roots from which a sense of belonging could be nurtured. Additionally, fan zeal emerges from a desire to share feelings with others in an urban setting.

Schafer advanced a tripartite explanation for fans' motivations. "One must ask, why do fans give their energy and interest to athletics to the extent they do?"[36] He proposed three reasons: (1) Normative influences are one. *Normative social influence* indicates what is important, what should be done, where interest should lie, etc. This reasoning is circular, yet valid. Since "success breeds success," one might argue that sports are popular; therefore, many people participate in and identify with them. As a result, many people emulate and idolize sport figures, and, consequently, sports are popular. Fans' interest in sport has become a preoccupation because of the snowballing effects of its initial popularity. (2) Sports provide a sense of belonging and an identification with a social group beyond the immediate family or kinship group. The "affiliative motive" for "fandom" may be of considerable significance. (3) Team identification may represent an extension of self. This explanation is a double-edged sword in that when the team wins one's self feelings are enhanced; when it loses one's self feelings are strained (see Pierce's statement in Vignette 5.1).

While these explanations for fan involvement appear to have face validity, several conspicuous questions remain unanswered. For example, why does sport and not other institutions fulfill these needs? Secondly, why are fans predominately males rather than females? Edwards' provocative thesis is of interest:

> As an institution having primary socialization and value maintenance functions, sport affords the fan an opportunity to *reaffirm the established values and beliefs defining acceptable means and solutions to central problems in the secular realm of everyday societal life.* But this fact does not stand alone; particular patterns of values are expressed through certain intrinsic features of sports activities; in combination, the two aspects explain not only fan enthusiasm but sport's predominately male following. Sports events are *unrehearsed,* they involve *exceptional performances* in a situation characterized by a degree of *uncertainty* and a lack of total control, and they epitomize *competition for scarce values*—prestige, status, self-adequacy, and other socially relevant rewards.[37]

In other words, Edwards argues that the modus operandi of the typical working man is unrehearsed, the worker cannot hope to control all the myriad forces affecting his life, and activity is characterized by striving for scarce resources. In short, sport reaffirms the viability of the values or rules of the game under which the fan must operate in the instrumental pursuits necessitated by the workaday world. Thus, sports have personal significance to the fan insofar as reinforcing the values, beliefs, and ideologies existing in other institutional spheres, particularly the economic.

SOCIALIZATION VIA SPORT

According to the values expressed in the dominant American sport creed, involvement in sport produces desirable consequences and outcomes (builds character, teaches discipline, prepares one for the competition of life, facilitates moral development and good citizenship, and cultivates desirable personality traits). Does scientific research bear out these admirable claims?

Webb's evidence suggested that the value of winning is enhanced and correlated with the institutionalization of athletic activity.[38] Using a quasi-longitudinal research design (studying a variable at different points in time to determine change, growth, and/or stability), he drew random samples of students (over 1200 in all) in Battle Creek, Michigan, from grades 3, 6, 7, 10, and 12 and had them

VIGNETTE 5.1
FOOTBALL'S EFFECT ON FANS: SOME EXPERTS' VIEWS

NO CONSENSUS
The Football Fan— What Drives Him?

BY SHEILA MORAN
Times Staff Writer

For 20 years, Ralph Richmond has gone dove hunting on Sept. 1, opening day of the season. This year, there was a conflict: the Rams vs. San Diego.

A season ticket-holder for 30 years, Richmond wrote the Rams demanding to know "what idiot in your organization" was responsible for the scheduling.

"Now you people have forced me to charter an airplane from the Imperial Valley to fly back to Los Angeles to see you play the Chargers," Richmond wrote.

Jack Teele, a club executive, wrote to explain that the scheduling allowed fans to have the long Labor Day weekend free.

Richmond finally changed his mind about chartering a plane because "it's just too much of a hassle." He skipped the dove hunting and instead drove the 80 miles from Redlands with his wife, Luella, to see the game.

"I hunt ducks all winter long," Richmond said, "and I can go dove hunting the whole month of September."

Richmond is a football fan, one of millions who attend pro and college games each autumn. Their attachment to the sport and its mystique—and the ways they manifest it—has prompted studies and analyses by psychologists and other students of the human condition. They don't always agree.

Some experts say watching a football game is a catharsis; that by witnessing the violence on the field a fan rids himself of his aggressions. Others say it's the other way around; that a guy is more likely to belt his wife after watching a football game. Still others say that football is one thing for one person and something else for another.

Dr. William Beausay, president of the Ohio-based Academy for the Psychology of Sports International, interviewed 800 football fans in a study four years ago that also included auto racing and wrestling addicts.

"We were curious about why people would want to go to an auto racing event and watch people get killed," he said. "From there, we went into football, and from football into wrestling."

A clinical psychologist and professor at Bowling Green State University, Beausay concluded that watching a football game was "far more therapeutic than six months of psychotherapy for a lot of neurotic people."

"You feel spent after watching a game, like after taking a shower," he said.

Beausay said the football fans were questioned at Ohio State and Michigan games and at a Detroit-Chicago pro contest. Some of the questions included "items we lifted from a psychological test to measure hostility and tolerance, impulsivity and self-discipline."

"The women tended to be tolerant; the men, hostile and aggressive. The same trend showed in auto racing, but in wrestling, which is the best example in sports of fans venting hostility, the men and women were identical psychologically."

In football, he said, about 70% of the women most enjoyed the esthetics—the colors of the uniform, the half time ceremonies, the fashions worn by other women.

"There was no significant difference between the women at the pro game and the college games," Beausay said.

"We discovered that about one-fifth of the men were what we call technicians. They loved the strategy, the tactics, the playing style. Of the other 80%, 55% were hostile and, of those, half would be further agitated through watching the game and the other half would feel satisfied. The remaining 25% were the guys with the flasks in their pockets who didn't care who won. They were just out with the gang.

The football fans also were asked if they "got into trouble" after the game. Of the more than 50 who did, 35 said they got a traffic ticket. Others said they got into a fight about the game with someone in their own group.

Fan hostility tends to be higher if the home team loses. And it increases with the temperature.

"If the Jets played the Rams and the Jets won, your highways outside the Coliseum wouldn't be safe for an hour," Beausay said.

Football ranks fourth on the Academy's Sports Violence Index, behind hockey, rugby, and auto racing," Beausay said.

"Baseball fans are much more docile. There are many more technicians. Whether a team gets beat or not isn't that much of an issue. And one of the things that kills basketball is that they have games every day. The teams are smaller and there are more of them than in football, so the loyalty is more diffused."

Dr. Jeffrey Goldstein, a Temple University psychology professor, surveyed 150 male spectators before and after the 1969 Army-Navy game in Philadelphia and concluded that watching football—or any contact sport—increases spectator hostility, regardless of which team wins.

As a control for the experiment, Goldstein asked the same questions of male spectators at the Army-Navy gymnastics meet, where there was no body contact. The statistics indicated that hostility did not significantly increase over the meet, he said.

Anthropologist Christie W. Kiefer of UC San Francisco leans toward the opposite viewpoint: that football has a cathartic effect.

"If a viewer feels really frustrated, maybe watching a game could provoke him to violence. But if a person is basically civilized that won't happen," he said.

Kiefer regards football as a "ritual of renewal" that can make a fan feel better. He compares it to ancient Greek dramas designed to "cleanse the soul."

"When I go to a game, I come out feeling good. I often get a lift. I think most people do because you get rid of frustrations. You feel closer to your fellow Americans; more tied in.

"Americans are not encouraged to show their emotions in public. If you yell and curse on the street you'd be hauled to the looney bin. You can do things in a football stadium you can't do on the street."

Kiefer said many societies have rituals in which people gather in large groups and experience an emotional high.

Japan, he said, has "an emotionally repressed society like ours, and the national male ritual there is to periodically go out and get drunk together. Once drunk, anything goes. They sing, cry and tell sad stories. A football game is like that."

Women are sometimes involved in the rituals, Kiefer said, and in Japan are allowed to show their emotions more than men.

Dr. Stuart Miller, a Maryland psychology professor and Baltimore Colts fan, said that the effect of football on spectator violence is an open question, but most evidence supports the theory that watching a violent sport stimulates rather than quiets aggressions.

In a 1973 study of 400 students at Towson State College, where he teaches, Miller said no differences were noted between male and female hostility.

"One thing that did come out was that female fans tended to be sensation seekers—the sort of individuals who sought out novelty, variety, unpredictability, risk," he said.

Dr. S. Harvard Kaufman, a Seattle psychiatrist and sports fan, believes violence is part of football's spectator appeal. An even bigger part, he said, is the escape from boredom and daily routine.

"People are looking for some excitement outside of themselves and want to grab onto something. People are looking for heroes. The Rams have Namath. Hell, with his wobbly knees, if he stands up and throws a touchdown pass, they'll carry him around on their shoulders for weeks."

"Football is bang-bang, clashing miniwars," Kaufman said. "The players don't get killed but they practically do. Indoor stadiums take away the excitement. There's no wind to deal with, and no rain, so the ball doesn't slip out of the players' hands. It's too predictable. It's like you know what they're going to do on third down."

"Football stimulates action, sex. Most players are sexually active after a game. All kinds of people are attracted to football. The nicest woman you ever met can look at the players sexually and have a helluva time. The beer drinker can yell and holler while the players get hurt instead of him."

In his book "The Madness in Sports" Dr. Theodore Beisser, a Los Angeles psychiatrist, said that watching any sport can fulfill psychic needs. The fan, he said, "can project onto the players the whole gamut of his emotions as they enact the competitive drama. In sports, unlike the theater, all things are possible in any role with which the spectator may identify, for there is no script. The outcome is always in doubt; as long as it continues, the game can still be won."

Beisser added: "Regression, the return to simpler and more elemental stages of adjustment, is acceptable within the matrix of sports watching. Grown men carry banners or wear hats denoting their favorites, in the same way youngsters emulate their idols . . . Regression, if controlled, tends to refurbish the individual for return to the monotony of his daily life."

According to Beisser, Los Angeles fans are different from those in other cities. Los Angeles is a melting pot of transplants, a "fluid, centerless mass." It's not surprising," he said, that "the citizens seek, sometimes desperately, groups they can identify with."

While ardent supporters, Rams fans are "less antagonistic toward visiting teams than fans in other cities," said the Rams' Teele who has attended games in every NFL city except Tampa. "That could be because so many of our fans used to live somewhere else."

He rates Philadelphia fans as the most hostile. He said Ram players are told to keep their helmets on while they're on the bench in Philadelphia because "the fans throw golf balls and you can get clobbered."

From their seat near the 50-yard line, Tom Pierce, a stockbroker from Tarzana, and his wife, Jan, watched intently as the Rams and the Philadelphia Eagles matched running games on the field below.

"If the Rams win, I feel great," Pierce said. "If they lose, it's a long drive home."

He likes the game, he said, because it's more exciting than other sports.

"If you watch the last five minutes of a basketball game, you've seen it all," Pierce said. "And baseball puts you to sleep, it's so slow."

For Marvin Simmons, a Los Angeles County probation officer, football is "like a chess game. There are a lot of intricate plays and it's fast moving. That's why I like it."

For other fans, such as a Beverly Hills management consultant in her 30s who asked that her name not be used, football is "an outlet. You can yell and scream."

The sport offers social benefits too.

"I became interested in football in college at UCLA," the businesswoman said. "The best-looking men were either playing the game or they liked it a lot."

VIGNETTE 5.2
PATERNO ONE-OF-KIND IN COACHING PROFESSION

To the modern college football coach, bowl-game invitations and national rankings are many times more important than molding boys into men.

But Penn State mentor Joe Paterno, 51, is an exception. He is one of a kind in one of the most demanding professions on the contemporary scene.

Paterno is one of the winningest coaches in the nation. His Nittany Lions have been ranked in collegiate football's Top Ten nine of the last 11 years.

Statistics and rankings, however, tell only part of the story of the skinny-legged Italian kid from Brooklyn who made good.

"I cannot commit myself to having to win every game," he said recently. "I can still enjoy a great game, whether we win it or lose it."

Paterno speaks of "keeping the fun in football." He speaks of the importance of the young man who lurks beneath the helmet.

He came to Penn State with Charles A. (Rip) Engle in 1950 from Brown University as an assistant coach. It seemed a move likely to be short-lived, for Paterno was a city boy who grew up playing stickball in the streets and he was coming to a school known as "the cow college" to Ivy Leaguers. But instead, in 1966, he assumed the helm of Penn State's football program and has remained there despite periodic offers to join the pros.

Paterno believes Penn State students—from the fresh faced country kids of rural Pennsylvania to the hard-bitten natives of the coal regions—are in a class by themselves.

He respects the players he coaches and demands the very best they can do.

"I believe in perspiration," he said, sitting in his plush office in front of book-lined shelves. "You get better by doing things 100 per cent, over and over—whether it's writing, farming or playing football. It's important to pay attention to little things.

"You can go out and play with a lot of emotion. It might work for 20 minutes, but you better know what you're doing."

Part of Paterno's uniqueness is that he never forgets that football ought to take a back seat to academics. Too much attention to football can be bad for a young man, he said.

"A lot of them get so wrapped up in football their whole personalities change. They get depressed, sometimes violent when things aren't right. They sulk. Sometimes I have to tell a kid it's not the end of the world. There are a lot of other things to life."

Paterno isn't just talk. Since he has been head coach, Penn State has graduated more than 94% of its football lettermen. Last year it was 100%. Among major football colleges, only Notre Dame can match that standard.

rank what was most important: (1) to play as well as you can (called "skill"); (2) to beat your opponent (called "victory"); and (3) to play the game fairly (called "fairness"). Webb discovered a positive correlation between grade level and importance attached to winning—as year in school increased, so, too, did the importance attached to beating one's opponent. In other words, as students progressed through the various grades, their attitudes toward playing a game became more professional (skill and the importance of victory became more important than fun or fair play) and achievement oriented.

Mantel and Vander Velden's research[39] corroborated Webb's findings. These investigators believed that sports function as cultural models and, consequently, hypothesized that the professionalization of attitude toward play (operationalized like Webb by having each subject rank the importance of "skill," "victory," and "fairness") was related to participation in organized athletics. Only pre-adolescent males, aged 10 and 11, were used in hope of avoiding the confounding influences that correlate with age (recall that Webb used several age/grade cohorts). The total sample of 133 was carefully divided into two groups. An experimental group (n=73) included individuals who had participated in baseball or football for a minimum of two years while members of either a local Boy's Club or Catholic Youth Organization (CYO). A control group (n=60) included individuals who never had participated in organized athletics.

Mantel and Vander Velden found empirical support for their hypothesis. Professionalization of attitude toward sport was positively related to participation in organized sport (see Table 5.1) and, conversely, nonparticipants ranked fairness as more important than did participants (see Table 5.2). Whereas participants ranked skill and victory as most important, nonparticipants stressed fairness.

Table 5.1
Skill or Victory Responses Among Participants and Nonparticipants

		Participants			Nonparticipants		
		n	%		*n*	%	χ^2 = 5.38
Rank Skill	1	39	53		20	33	P < .05
or Victory	0	34	47		40	67	C = .20
		73	100		60	100	

Source: R. C. Mantel and L. Vander Velden, "The Relationship Between the Professionalization of Attitude Toward Play of Preadolescent Boys and Participation in Organized Sport," Third Annual Symposium on the Sociology of Sport, Waterloo, Ontario, Canada, August, 1971.

Table 5.2
Fair Responses among Participants and Nonparticipants

Rank Fair	Participants			Nonparticipants		
	n	%		*n*	%	χ^2 = 7.19
1	34	47		40	67	P < .05
2	29	40		18	30	C = .23
3	10	14		2	3	
	73	101		60	100	

Source: R. C. Mantel and L. Vander Velden, "The Relationship Between the Professionalization of Attitude Toward Play of Preadolescent Boys and Participation in Organized Sport," Third Annual Symposium on the Sociology of Sport, Waterloo, Ontario, Canada, August, 1971.

Despite the positive correlation, the specific mechanisms accounting for this relationship were not isolated and, although sport is a socializing agent, it is but one of several factors shaping attitudes, behaviors, and values.

Richardson's study of 233 male physical education majors suggested that positive attitudes toward sportsmanship and fair play are *not* the result of involvement in organized collegiate sports.[40] Dichotomizing his sample into letter and non-letter winners, he discovered that letter winners had lower regard for sportsmanship than non-letter winners, scholarship recipients had less concern with sportsmanship than non-scholarship recipients, and football players vis-a-vis other sport participants had the lowest scores of all. It appears, then, that involvement in sport does not produce the desirable consequence of fair play and sportsmanship—attitudinally at least—alluded to in the "sport creed."

The major benefits of sport involvement are widely believed to be health, character development, and training for the competitive character of the adult world. More and more evidence indicates serious questioning of these alleged functions. In the context of sport socialization the query: "Do sports develop character and personality?" has significance. On some test batteries it has been found that athletes vs. their nonathlete counterparts do score higher on measures of self-discipline and other traits as well. For example, on the IPAT test (Institute for Personality and Ability Testing) athletes were compared with the average male college student and found to be above the norm on outgoingness, trust, and control, but less intelligent.[41] While differences existed between black and white athletes, such differences will not concern us here.

The unanswered riddle, however, is whether sports produce these effects or whether the athlete comes to the sports arena with these traits as a result of self-selection factors. In commenting upon the self-selection factor, Coakley wrote:

> Allow me to illustrate this point by using a reference to physical rather than character traits. If we had data to clearly indicate that participants in sport were stronger, faster, and more coordinated than nonparticipants, would it be reasonable to conclude that the strength, speed, and coordination of participants were acquired as a *result* of their involvement in sport? Obviously . . . not. It is rather clear that youngsters with certain physical attributes will be attracted to sport, and, once involved, it is likely that they will be continually encouraged by peers, parents, and coaches. It should also be obvious that youngsters who lack strength, speed, and coordination may never try out for an organized team. . . . Those possessing the desired attributes will probably stay involved and further develop those attributes through continued participation. This does not mean that sport participation has no effect on the development of physical attributes, but it does mean that the effects of sport participation are likely to be limited to a select group of individuals who are physically predisposed to that development.[42]

Sport psychologists Ogilvie and Tutko maintain that some sport traits are characteristic of "athletes who survive the high attrition rate associated with sports competition. . . . Competition doesn't seem to build character, and it is possible that competition doesn't even require much more than a minimally integrated personality."[43]

A substantial minority of athletes have achieved success or near success despite severe personality disorders. Ogilvie and Tutko wrote:

> We know from our work hundreds of outstanding competitors who possess strong character formation that complements higher motor skill. . . . But we found athletes who possessed

so few strong character traits that it was difficult on the basis of personality to account for their success. . . . There were gold medal Olympic winners in Mexico and Japan whom we would classify as overcompensatory greats. Only magnificent physical gifts enabled them to overcome constant tension, anxiety, and self-doubt. They are unhappy, and when talent ages and fades, they become derelicts. . . .[44]

Another consequence of sport retrieved from their annals is *success-phobia*—the anxiety and fear arising from anticipated success in sport. Track athletes who break records in practice but not in meets as well as athletes who "choke" at crucial times are cases in point. Examination of the personal and social histories of success phobics uncovers two major precipitants: (1) the athlete feels he will "kill" his competitor by beating him, and (2) the athlete feels he will not be able "to live up" to the expectations of parents, friends, and peers as a result of prior stellar performances.

The poignant case history of the following success phobic is gleaned from Ogilvie and Tutko's files.[45] The father of one "success phobic athlete" spent many hours coaching and teaching his son a particular sport skill. As part of the training the father would compete with his son and virtually always beat him because of his superior size, strength, and speed. However, the athlete was informed that he was improving rapidly and would soon be able to compete with dad. A few years later when the son could consistently defeat his father, the father became disturbed and, as a consequence, became overly critical of his son's play. Training now became punishment, and verbal rewards were few and exhortations many. The boy's pressure was eased only when dad beat him . . . only then did he receive recognition and love. Hence, the success phobic athlete pretended to go all out to beat his father but relinquished because of the need for social recognition, reward, love, and acceptance. The conflict over winning and being punished soon gave way to losing and being loved, and this same pattern followed the athlete in his college sport involvement.

The preponderance of evidence does *not* support the presumed positive consequences of sport personified in the dominant American sport creed. We still do not know if the Battle of Waterloo was won on the playing fields of Eton. Orlick nicely summarized this research when he said:

> For every positive psychological or social outcome in sports, there are possible negative outcomes. For example, sports can offer a child group membership or group exclusion, acceptance or rejection, positive feedback or negative feedback, a sense of accomplishment or a sense of failure, evidence of self-worth or lack of evidence of self-worth. Likewise, sports can develop cooperation and a concern for others, but they can also develop intense rivalry and a complete lack of concern for others.[46]

Are Sport Experiences Generalizable?

Professionals often ask the following query of any social experience: Does the experience—skills, values, attitudes, or motivation—generalize beyond the specific context in which the learning initially took place? In the sports realm the question becomes: "Does socialization via sports develop *generalized* and diffuse role skills or merely the ability to play *specific* roles?" Advocates of physical education and sport programs frequently claim that desirable traits ("democratic citizenship," "moral character," "adjusted personality," "respect for constituted authority," "cultivation of discipline," "the ability to win and lose graciously") result from athletic participation. As we have seen, the "dominant American sport creed" encompasses these and other virtues attributable to sport.

Theoretically, socialization involves past, present, and anticipated future interactions between an individual and his/her significant others (parents, siblings, girl/boyfriends, peer groups, coaches, teachers). These significant others—or reference groups—are the "audiences" for which we play. Social psychologists say that reference groups serve two functions:[47] (1) they provide us with a frame of reference for guiding our behavior; we see in them norms, values, and behavioral blueprints; and (2) they serve as a standard or "measuring stick" against which we can judge or evaluate ourselves. Technically, the former function is called *normative social influence*, and the latter *informational* or *comparative social influence*.

According to Snyder, much sociological literature suggests that attitudes and behaviors learned in specific contexts (in sport activities) may *not* carry over to more general settings (family and work).[48] The research suggests that such "spill over" occurs only when *situations* are similar.

Since humans do not automatically absorb social influences, five variables crucial to socialization experiences have been forwarded. These factors—what Snyder calls "dimensions of social interaction"—have been known to produce differential learning on the socializee's part. First, the degree (frequency, intensity, and duration) of involvement is crucial. As concrete illustrations, consider the differences between a team captain and subs in organized sport versus pupils in a required PE class, intramurals, or a sandlot game. Since the commitment of these different participants is probably variable, the development of specific and diffuse role traits will likely be a function of the degree of involvement.

A second important factor would be whether the participation is *voluntary* or *involuntary*. Although it seems reasonable to conclude that free choice is valuable to general role learning, a branch of social psychological theory called cognitive dissonance might argue that *forced compliance*, nevertheless, may have some beneficial end results.[49]

A third factor is the nature of the socialization relationship. More specifically, one might reasonably expect differences in outcomes when comparing *instrumental* vs. *expressive social* interaction. Some sport researchers have advanced the notion that blacks who have been reared in matriarchal families (see pp. 178-79) are superior athletes because the coach provides a surrogate father—an expressive social relationship. Instrumental relationships, on the other hand, provide a means to a desired end without the same emotional overtones between interacting parties.

The *prestige* and *power* of the socializer is the fourth factor. As we know from socialization in general, prestigious, powerful, and affective persons generally have more influence over the socializee than do their counterparts.

The fifth key variable addressed by Snyder is actually dual in nature. It refers to the *personal and social characteristics of the participant.* In sport not only is the participant's skill important but so too is one's perception of that skill. How persons define their skill may be as important as the actual level of the skill itself since self-perception motivates present and future behaviors. The social characteristics of participants—their social class, race, and ethnicity—mediate present participation and the adoption of future diffuse roles. The intended boycotts of the 1968 Olympic Games can be viewed as a struggle between conflicting loyalties. Black athletes had to decide whether to forego individual recognition to protest prejudice and discrimination against blacks in sport in American society.

In summary, whether traits, skills, and values learned in a specific context will carry over to other contexts depends upon several dimensions of social interaction. These crucial variables mediate between the specific and general contexts.

VALUE ORIENTATIONS, PERSONALITY PROFILES, AND
SOCIAL CHARACTERISTICS OF ATHLETES

Schendel studied the personality characteristics of over 300 athletes and nonathletes in high school (ninth and twelfth grades) and college.[50] He concluded that on the traits of dominance, responsibility, sociability, self-acceptance, well-being, and tolerance athletes in the ninth and twelfth grades displayed more positive personality characteristics than nonathletes (only self-control was "better" for nonathletes in these two grades). However, these findings were reversed for college students, and nonathletes scored more positively on all seven dimensions than athletes. Further, there were few differences among athletes of different ability levels. The few differences that emerged tended to favor the nonathletes over the athletes.

Rehberg and Cohen's study of 937 male seniors from eight New York high schools found: (1) a positive relationship between participation in extracurricular activities (sports and others) and acceptance of authority, (2) athletes in comparison to nonathletes were more likely to believe that the American way of life was superior to all others, (3) athletes were less likely to endorse the belief that American society was in need of fundamental change, and (4) athletes were more likely to perceive draft evasion as morally wrong than were nonathletes.[51]

Snyder and Spreitzer report on a secondary analysis of data collected by *Playboy* magazine.[52] The *Playboy* sample was a representative one (on such variables as sex, age, class level, family income, and GPA) in which randomly selected students (about 3,700) were surveyed from twenty randomly selected colleges and universities in the United States. Some of their noteworthy findings included: (1) athletes were *not* more likely to have lower GPA's than nonathletes, (2) athletes were *not* more likely to be enrolled in easy academic programs, (3) athletes were slightly more likely to be members of campus organizations that were vocationally oriented, (4) athletes did *not* rate themselves higher than nonathletes on religiosity, (5) athletes did *not* rate themselves more politically conservative than nonathletes, (6) athletes were more conventional in the sense that they were more likely to join sororities and fraternities, to agree that having a good time socially was important, and indicated that parties and sporting events were preferable leisure activities, (7) both male and female athletes were less likely than their nonathlete counterparts to be co-habitating, (8) male athletes had slightly higher rates of sexual intercourse (although female athletes had lower rates of sexual intercourse than their counterparts), (9) both male and female athletes were less accepting of homosexual practices than nonathletes, (10) male and female athletes were more likely to be nondrinkers than nonathletes, and (11) male athletes reported less drug usage, e.g., marijuana, amphetamines, barbiturates, and LSD (while female drug usage was not significantly different from female nonathletes). Snyder and Spreitzer summarized their findings as follows:

> In sum, the *Playboy* survey showed more similarity than dissimilarity between athletes and nonathletes at the college/university level. Perhaps the only clear difference shows up in rate of membership in fraternities and sororities and the associated propensity for athletes to place a higher value than nonathletes on socializing as a component of college life. Consequently, once again popular stereotypes are chastened by social scientific data. As is repeatedly noted . . . the world of sport is pervasive and is shared by no particular social or psychological group.[53]

Norton's research on college students found some of the same basic outcomes.[54] Athletes in contrast to nonathletes were more conservative, less interested and active in politics, more tolerant of civil liberties violations and repressive action taken to calm campus unrest. On the other hand, Petrie and Reid discovered an interesting cross-cultural difference when Canadian athletes were found to be more liberal than nonathletes.[55] Hence, once again, we must be sensitive to cultural differences regarding the by-products of sport participation.

Since the consensus of research supports the notion that American athletes tend toward conservatism, let us attempt to answer why this is so. First, at many schools athletes occupy the limelight. Since they are the beneficiaries of the status quo, their vested interests do not motivate them to be critical of the establishment. Second, because athletics are time consuming activities there is less time to become knowledgeable and active in social criticism. Third, since athletes must generally "toe the line" by deferring to authority, they are probably less questioning and critical of authority structures. Fourth, it is difficult to remain in sport when one adopts a radical stance. Athletes who are vocally critical of the existing state of affairs tend to be dismissed (or quit) at all levels of performance.[71]

Nonconforming athletes—sometimes called "troublemakers"—are handled in several ways. Amateur athletes may be benched, suspended, socially ostracized, removed from the team ("cut"), and/or forced off financial aid. Professional athletes are dealt with in a similar manner but may also receive fines, demotions to second teams or minor leagues, salary cuts, and unconditional releases, or be subject to blackballing. The experiences of Bernie Parrish, Walter Beach, Johnny Sample, Steve Wright, Duane Thomas—pro football players—and Jim Bouton, Jim Brosnan, Clete Boyer, and Joe Torre—pro baseball players—are testimony to the consequences of asserting oneself when it is clearly inconsistent with the organization's position on an issue. Although there is no research evidence regarding the political orientations of professional athletes, we would speculate that they, too, are probably conservative in outlook.

Role Strain Among College Athletes

Since college athletes are also students, the tension or *role strain* between the two social categories—*athlete* and *student*—is apparent. What needs to be known, however, are the value orientations of athletes per se since it is possible that years of sport socialization may make them more like their coaches than would be the case for nonathletes.

Some evidence suggesting *personality* differences between athletes and nonathletes exists. Using the IPAT test battery, Ogilvie found (using the "average male college student" as a reference) athletes scoring *above* the norm on "outgoingness," "trust," and "control" and *below* the norm on intelligence (although there were some differences between black and white athletes).[56] On two other personality test inventories (Edwards Personal Preference Scale and Jackson Personality Research Form) athletes in comparison to nonathletes scored above the norm on "exhibitionism," "impulsivity," and "understanding/intraception." While these latter traits are not directly comparable to the value orientation research, they do allow us to make inferences as to where the "outlooks" of coaches and athletes are likely to dovetail.

Sage found no differences in the personalities of athletes participating in different sports.[57] He compared athletes at the University of Northern Colorado between 1962-1971 (n=532) in eight sports (basketball, football, baseball, wrestling, gymnastics, swimming, track, and tennis). The non-significant personality traits included achievement, deference, order, exhibitionism, autonomy, affiliation, intraception (introspection), succorance (helping others), dominance, abasement (humiliation), nurturance, change, endurance, heterosexuality, and aggression.

VALUE ORIENTATIONS, PERSONALITY PROFILES, AND SOCIAL CHARACTERISTICS OF COACHES

It is reasonable to conclude that a major socializer for athletes is the coach. Coaches have recently come under heavy fire from sport critics, fans, athletes, and others. Frequently these criticisms have accused coaches of being rigid, authoritarian, Machiavellian, unsympathetic, and cruel.[58]

Many coaches, certainly not all, have gained tough reputations. Frank Kush, head football coach at Arizona State, is one. In late August he takes his "troops" to football camp, a private camp he owns on the edge of the desert, and puts his rookies and veterans through rigorous drills. Near to the camp is a 450 foot high rock pile euphemistically christened "Mt. Kush." Players, particularly those guilty of numerous or major infractions, are required to scale this miniature mountain. Mike Tomco, a former Arizona State football player, provided the following character reference for Kush:

> College football is an ugly business. . . . Kush does what he thinks is necessary to win. I can take what he hands out—and it's helped me—but a lot of kids can't handle it. They go through the gate. We all hate him now, but later, most guys see he's really made them play their best. You know, I've seen him do some awful things—stamp on hands, humiliate and emasculate guys till they quit football and left school, call 'em "wops" and "dagos," and drive kids till they passed out. Still, aside from my father, there's nobody I respect more. . . . He's a different guy after the season. Like Jekyll and Hyde. Last winter I was broke, but I wanted to take out my girlfriend. I called Kush to see if he knew somebody who'd loan me a car. He gave me his car and ten bucks for dinner.[59]

Gary Shaw, former University of Texas football player, wrote an account of football while Darrell Royal was mentor at that school. His book, *Meat on the Hoof* (1972), described how football players were recruited and then abused when they didn't make the first team and shamed into voluntarily surrendering their scholarships. Shaw wrote:

> Our coaches would tell us about the necessity for self-discipline, but what they really meant was obedience. . . . (The) threat of punishment reinforced our total dedication and tacitly demanded that we should never question our coaches' authority. Like good soldiers, our job was to follow orders, not think about them.[60]

There have appeared numerous documentaries describing coaches. John D. Massengale wrote:

> Coaches as a group are aggressive and highly organized, seldom paying attention to what others say. They display unusually high psychological endurance, persistence, and inflexibility. Coaches appear to dislike change and tend to be very conservative politically, socially, and attitudinally. They are often formally educated in the field of physical education. Physical education majors tend to have little in common with other students in the field of education. They have a more traditional philosophy of education and a

slightly lower social class background. They tend to be more dogmatic and appear to have different social values from other prospective teachers.[61]

Sport psychologists Ogilvie and Tutko wrote:

> We know that coaches are aggressive people, self-assertive; we know that they are highly organized and ordered; . . . they will listen to others—pay little attention to what others say, but they will listen; and they have fierce psychological endurance. . . . But they are also inflexible in their profession as coaches; they dislike change and experimentation; and they are extremely conservative—politically, socially, and attitudinally.[62]

The "split-personality syndrome" of coaches is revealed in the person of Woody Hayes, the colorful and controversial former coach of the Ohio State Buckeyes. Having coached at the university since 1951, he had the third longest tenure of any coach at a major institution (only Amos Alonza Stagg, 41 years at Chicago and Bob Zuppke, 29 years at Illinois survived longer). The by-products of his coaching are undeniably superb: Hayes has turned out more All-Americans (39) and has sent more players to the pro ranks than any other mentor. His former assistant coaches (Bo Schembechler, Bill Mallory, Gary Moeller and Bo Rein among others) have gone on to become big-time coaches in their own right. He has won three national championships and 13 Big Ten Titles (more than any other league coach in history); has twice been coach of the year and twice runner-up; has had more Rose Bowl invitations (nine) than any other coach and achieved a 205-60-10 record at the perennial football-power school.

Woody Hayes was a demanding task master, and his on-the-field antics are well known as well as questionable. Amidst a great deal of media and public relations brouhaha recently, Hayes was summarily dismissed shortly after the 1978 Gator Bowl game for striking a Clemson player on the head. But there was another side to Hayes, and Bronfield relates one noteworthy occasion:

> One morning during his busy recruiting season, Woody got a letter from a former player who had entered Harvard Medical School that year. The young man said he couldn't take the grind and pressure and was dropping out. He wanted Woody to know before he heard it from other sources.
> Hayes grabbed his hat, hurried out to the airport and caught a plane to Boston. Two hours later, he barged into the startled student's room. Woody rudely thrust the boy onto a chair and laid it on him, furiously. In essence, he wasn't going to allow the boy to disappoint his family—and no former player of his was going to be a quitter. He was going to stay there and finish medical school.
> Without even waiting for a response or a reaction, Woody stalked out and headed for home. He hadn't even removed his coat or hat. The boy stayed. Today, he is a prestigious midwestern neurosurgeon and has often told why he was able to finish at Harvard.[63]

The moral of the story is that coaches, like people in all walks of life, have different images. Their public image should not allow us to forget that there is often another side. See Vignette 5.2 for a profile of coach Joe Paterno.

Much of the tongue-wagging regarding coaches has had a nonempirical anecdotal basis, or has been the result of a single (or few) incident(s). Since coaches' value orientations are likely to permeate their social interaction with players, it is of interest to examine, empirically, their value orientations.

"Values," we've seen, are conceptions of "right" and "wrong," "good" and "bad," "desirable" and "undesirable." This concept is valuable in understanding social behavior since values are used in evaluating and regulating one's own and others' behavior in a wide variety of contexts, particularly in political, social, educational, economic, and personal/moral affairs. It is assumed that values provide a basis for guiding, directing, and orienting one's behavior and usually are thought of as being located along a conservative/liberal continuum. A *conservative* value orientation refers to values giving priority to "loyalty to tradition, respect and obedience to established authority, normative standards of conduct, and strong religious commitments." A *liberal* value orientation, on the other hand, refers to values which stress social change and equality in political, social, and economic matters. A *moderate* value orientation would fall midway between these poles. With these distinctions in mind, let us turn to a systematic study of the value orientations of college coaches, college students, and business-people (Sage, 1972).

Sage conducted a scientific study of the value orientations among this triad.[64] His sample consisted of 330 college coaches randomly selected from *Official Collegiate Guides* in football, basketball, and track, and their value orientations were compared to previously collected data on college students and business leaders. The coaches executed an instrument known as the Polyphasic Values Inventory (PVI) developed by Roscoe (1965). The questionnaire covered such areas as philosophical, political, economic, educational, social, personal/moral, and religious dimensions. Table 5.3 contains a summary of statistics along with specific value arenas tapped by the instrument. Comparing college coaches *with students,* note that on items 1, 7, 8, 9, 10, 11, 13, 14, 15, 16, 17, 18, 19, and 20 coaches were more conservative; on items 2, 4, and 5 coaches were more liberal. On the other hand, when coaches were compared to *business leaders* they were more conservative on items 7 and 17, while the coaches were more liberal on items 3, 4, 5, 6, 8, 9, 10, 12, 13, 14, 16, and 20. These data suggest that college students were "moderate," coaches were "moderately conservative," and business leaders were basically "conservative." What appears significant is that coaches' and students' values are likely to clash in their differing beliefs about "authority structures."

Another interpersonal response trait, Machiavellianism, has been explored and contrasted among college and high school coaches and college students. *Machiavellianism* is a personality characteristic characterized by exploitation, opportunism, expediency, and deception in interpersonal encounters. Sage's sample included 150 randomly selected college coaches from each sport, 100 randomly selected high school coaches from each sport in Colorado, and 764 college students from 14 different institutions. He discovered no "Mach" differences between college and high school coaches and male college students. Additionally, he found no differences in "Mach" scores among college football and basketball coaches and high school football and basketball coaches with regard to age or head coaching experience. Nor were there differences between college football and basketball coaches and high school football and basketball coaches with winning records (over 60 percent victories) and coaches with win/loss records below 60 percent.[65]

Snyder compared the political orientations of high school coaches, farm operators, and college students.[66] On items regarding civil liberties and social welfare the farmers were found to be most conservative, the students most liberal, and the coaches in-between. Relative to the comparison groups the researcher concluded that coaches were moderately conservative.

It has been traditionally assumed that the development of winning athletic teams is based upon strict adherence to discipline and conformity to the coach's instructions. Do authoritarians make successful coaches? The evidence is not at all consistent. Penman, Hastad, and Cords administered an authoritarianism scale to 30 head football coaches and 34 head basketball coaches in several large high

Table 5.3
Value Orientations of College Athletic Coaches Compared to Male College Students and Businessmen

Chi-square Goodness-of-Fit

Item #	Value Orientations	Male College Students				Businessmen			
		Football coaches	Track coaches	Basketball coaches	All coaching groups	Football coaches	Track coaches	Basketball coaches	All coaching groups
1	Nature of science	6.56	7.25	12.24	17.88*(S)	2.38	6.42	10.49	12.29
2	Right-to-vote	43.09*(C)	6.13	20.23*(C)	54.56*(C)	13.35*(C)	4.70	5.77	8.20
3	Treatment of communists	12.65	4.20	4.66	10.93	16.50*(C)	45.31*(C)	29.44*(C)	70.12*(C)
4	Military action	7.39	14.42*(C)	7.94	27.10*(C)	4.98	11.02	4.27	17.23*(C)
5	International relations	5.85	6.97	13.05	23.09*(C)	14.77*(C)	9.19	9.65	29.93*(C)
6	Private enterprise	3.41	8.89	7.47	7.39	10.70‡(C)	3.22	19.65‡(C)	25.02‡(C)
7	Labor unions	9.50	8.64	7.77	17.79*(S)	5.09	6.07	7.09	15.45‡(B)
8	Citizenship education	35.26*(S)	9.42	22.59*(S)	60.41*(S)	24.11†(C)	6.31	7.69	29.34†(C)
9	Nation's schools	24.02*(S)	4.76	3.42	23.01*(S)	32.32*(C)	26.76*(C)	35.71*(C)	78.83*(C)
10	Academic freedom	88.46*(S)	57.15*(S)	65.76*(S)	208.52*(S)	45.21*(C)	25.30*(C)	46.29*(C)	114.01*(C)
11	Equality of man	8.70	3.82	4.84	13.87*(S)	6.84	2.63	1.81	6.89
12	Race relations	1.33	4.88	5.32	7.25	20.76*(C)	23.93*(C)	23.93*(C)	65.32*(C)
13	Treatment of criminals	4.99	3.90	8.00	14.32*(S)	17.27†(C)	10.64	7.82	33.05†(C)
14	Final authority for ethical conduct	32.42*(S)	15.91*(S)	15.32*(S)	54.91*(S)	4.34	9.36	14.03*(C)	22.01*(C)
15	Cheating on tests	11.16	14.72*(S)	8.67	31.97*(S)	2.36	1.11	5.85	7.19
16	Sexual behavior	31.27*(S)	22.12*(S)	30.40*(S)	82.61*(S)	8.85	6.08	9.07	22.53*(C)
17	Use of alcohol	16.93*(S)	19.89*(S)	14.23*(S)	48.88*(S)	60.15*(B)	51.16*(B)	63.92*(B)	169.39*(B)
18	Nature of God	38.25*(S)	13.62*(S)	16.32*(S)	62.71*(S)	7.40	1.60	4.97	7.90
19	The Bible	17.21*(S)	2.68	18.64*(S)	31.41*(S)	5.45	1.86	3.17	5.07
20	Man's responsibility for his deeds	15.12*(S)	8.11	20.15*(S)	35.22*(S)	8.23	8.26	3.72	13.90*(C)

*$df = 4$; significant at .01 level
†$df = 3$; significant at .01 level
‡$df = 2$; significant at .01 level

(S) = Students more liberal
(B) = Businessmen more liberal
(C) = Coaches more liberal

Source: George H. Sage, *Sport in American Society* (Reading, MA: Addison-Wesley, 1974), p. 213. Reprinted by permission.

schools in Minnesota and Washington.[67] The coaches were divided into three categories based upon their winning percentages over the years. The result: the most successful coaches (i.e., the "winning-est") were discovered to have high authoritarian scores.

Why are coaches authoritarian? First, some believe it stems from the personality structures of coaches while others (particularly sport sociologists) believe it emanates from the institutional context (i.e., the role expectation of winning under conditions of minimal direct control) in which coaches perform. A more moderate position would attribute such authoritarianism to both selectivity (weeding out non-authoritarian types) and to the social conditioning occurring in sports contexts.

Second, when the social backgrounds of coaches are compared with that of other faculty, it has been discovered that they come from lower socioeconomic positions.[68] This revelation is significant in that social-psychological research has indicated that childrearing patterns differ by social class.[69] The lower the social class, the more likely is physical punishment to be used and the more likely are parents to be authoritarian and conventional. Moreover, working class parents tend to value "law and order," obedience to authority, and political conservatism. Hence, it may be through socialization experiences that coaches come to be conservative and authoritarian.

Third, since many coaches have been former athletes, and since athletes tend to be conservative, the pattern is self-perpetuating.

Fourth, since coaching may be viewed as an occupational subculture with distinct values, it may be that coaches seek out occupations in which the value system dovetails with their own.[70] The other possibility is that through years of apprenticeship—what sociologists call *anticipatory socialization*—coaches come to internalize and act out those characteristics they have been exposed to at earlier periods of time. Additionally, group pressures will direct and channel coaching styles into certain avenues through the application of social sanctions, i.e., rewards and punishments. In chapter 10 we will consider coaches "leadership" behavior.

In this chapter we have related results of various studies of the personality profiles, social characteristics, and value orientations of coaches and athletes. We thought it would be of interest to you, the reader, to determine your own sports personality. While we make no claim to the reliability and validity of the "sports quiz" in Vignette 5.3, we offer it to you for your own amusement and use.

SUMMARY

In this chapter we have discussed sport and socialization. *Socialization* refers to the various mechanisms through which a biological organism is fashioned into an adult social being. Sport roles require learning just like other occupational roles. It has been necessary to distinguish two types of socialization: (1) *socialization into sport,* and (2) *socialization via sport.*

To explain *socialization into sport* we considered *social learning theory.* How individuals acquire and perform social roles is the focus of this conceptual framework. Three features of this approach—*reinforcement, coaching,* and *observational learning*—were addressed and expounded upon in regard to sport socialization. We also considered various *agents of sport socialization* such as the family, peer group, school, community, and mass media. Studies focusing upon factors contributing to participation in sport and factors in sport involvement also occupied our attention.

Involvement in sport may be *behavioral, affective,* and/or *cognitive.* Since much sport involvement is of a secondary nature special attention was paid to the role of fan and the personal functions of fan involvement.

VIGNETTE 5.3
SPORTS QUIZ REVEALS ALL!
By Scot Morris

If you'll take the time to pick the 30 sports you'd most like to try, we'll tell you what your choices reveal about the kind of person you are.

If you wouldn't mind laying down your glove, ball, club, racquet or bat for a few minutes, we'd like you to take our sports questionnaire. Assuming that you have the time, money and ability to do well in any of the 75 sports listed below, please pick the 30 you would most enjoy participating in. Which would be the most fun? (In some cases you may need a little imagination, since you probably haven't tried some of the sports. Imagine yourself as a skipper or crewperson on a racing yacht, or fantasize that you're behind the wheel of a Grand Prix racer or that you're a karate black belt or hang-gliding enthusiast.)

We'd like you to score your preferences this way: mark "10" in the space next to your first three choices; mark "9" next to the next three; "8" by the next three—and so on 10 times, until you've marked "1" next to the last three of your chosen 30.

Don't worry about being super precise. It might make it easier, incidentally, if you go through and check your favorite 30 without thinking about ranking at all, and then go back to rank your choices.

Disregard the numbers and letters in front of the spaces. They'll be explained to you later.

1d ___	Archery	1d ___	Golf	1a ___	Poker
3c ___	Arm Wrestling	5e ___	Grand Prix Racing	4A ___	Polo
1a ___	Badminton	4d ___	Gymnastics	1a ___	Pool (billards)
3A ___	Baseball	2a ___	Handball	5e ___	Powerboat Racing
3A ___	Basketball	5b ___	Hang-Gliding	2E ___	Relay Racing
4e ___	Bicycle Racing	3e ___	Harness Racing	2D ___	Road Rally
2b ___	Bicycling	3d ___	High Jump	3C ___	Roller Derby
5D ___	Bobsled, 4-man	4b ___	Hiking	2E ___	Rowing (crew)
1d ___	Bowling	3e ___	Horse Racing	4C ___	Rugby
5c ___	Boxing	3e ___	Hurdles	2E ___	Sailing (crew racing)
1A ___	Bridge	4C ___	Ice Hockey	3b ___	Sailing
3B ___	Canoeing	3b ___	Ice Skating	2d ___	Shot Put
1a ___	Chess	1b ___	Jogging	5d ___	Ski Jumping
1d ___	Darts	4c ___	Judo	3b ___	Skiing
3c ___	Demolition Derby	5c ___	Karate	4b ___	Skin Diving
4d ___	Diving (10 meters)	4C ___	Lacrosse	5b ___	Sky Diving
2c ___	Fencing	2d ___	Long Jump	3d ___	Slalom
3D ___	Fig. Skating (cpls)	3e ___	Marathon	3C ___	Soccer
3d ___	Fig. Skating (indv)	5e ___	Motorcycle Racing	3E ___	Sled Dog Racing
1b ___	Fishing	5B ___	Mountain Climbing	3A ___	Softball
4C ___	Football (tackle)	1a ___	Ping-Pong	3e ___	Speed Skating

5e ___	Stock Car Racing	2A___	Tennis (doubles)	2A___	Volleyball
4b ___	Surfing	2a ___	Tennis (singles)	3C ___	Water Polo
2b ___	Swimming	3C ___	Touch Football	4b ___	Water Skiing
2e ___	Swimming (100 M free-style)	2A___	Tug-of-War	4c ___	Wrestling

Risk Factor____   Aa ____   Bb ____   Cc ____   Dd ____   Ee ____

* *

Now for the scoring. What we've tried to score with this quiz are two traits associated with sports: (1) *competitiveness* (which is related to aggressiveness), and (2) the *attraction to physical danger.*

You total up your scores this way: first, add up all the code numbers (not the rank numbers you wrote in) next to the 30 sports you chose. Divide the total by 30 and write the result in the blank next to "risk factor score." This is your "risk quotient."

Then, add up your scores for each of the five capital and small letters, using the rank numbers you wrote in. You will have totals for five different letters, all written in the space provided.

It's impossible to say with certainty what personality traits are common to those who prefer one class of sport over another. Still, there are enough transparent differences between the sports to allow one to make some general observations. You should judge for yourself whether the statements accurately fit your character or not.

The risk-factor score is fairly easy to analyze. The average score is three; so any score much above or below that means you have a more-than-average attraction to—or aversion to—physical danger.

Now for your one-to-10 rankings: if you were absolutely evenhanded in your preferences, you would end up with 33 points in each of the five categories (you had 165 points to distribute altogether). In looking over your scores, then, you should note any marked deviation from that average—either above or below it—and pay special attention to the discussion of the sports in that particular category.

First, the 25 capital-letter sports on the list are *team sports;* the 50 small-letters designate *individual sports.* If you checked more than 10 capital letters your preference for playing on a team, rather than by yourself, is above average, and less than five is below average. There's an element of sociability in team sports, you have to be able to cooperate and get along with others to pilot a yacht or a baseball team to victory. A high small-letter score may mean that you're shy in social situations, that you're asocial or independent, or that you're so competitive you'd rather not share the glory with anyone else if you win; of course if you lose, you have to be big enough to take the loss alone—you can't blame an inept teammate if you lose a footrace. It may be that for you victories are more exciting and defeats less crushing when both can be shared with others.

The sports have been divided into five classes according to the type of competition involved: that is, how important it is to beat the opponent, to win, or to avoid losing.

The five categories are: (1) *active contact* (Cc); (2) *active competition* (Aa); (3) *passive competition* (Ee); (4) *delayed competition* (Dd); and (5) *no competition* (Bb). The five classes are roughly in the order of decreasing competitiveness. If your score in any category is very much greater, proportionally, than your score in others, then you tend toward that competitive type, described on the following page.

Cc: contact sports. There are 15 physical contact sports on the list, including eight team sports (touch and tackle football, ice hockey, lacrosse, roller derby, rugby, soccer, and water polo) and seven individual sports (arm wrestling, boxing, demolition derby, fencing, karate, judo, wrestling). Physical contact is the most immediate, personal form of competition. It's head-to-head, "I'm stronger, you're weaker, and I'm not afraid to put my body on the line to prove it." If your score was more than 40, you like the feeling of physical striving against other bodies, and may like to see your opponents beaten by your own hands. You may feel there is virtue in physical strength, and you may enjoy venting your hostilities by direct physical force. (A low Cc score, on the other hand, doesn't mean you're not hostile—you may have learned more subtle ways to express it.)

Aa: active competition. There are 15 Aa sports listed, eight team efforts (baseball, basketball, bridge, polo, softball, tennis—doubles, tug-of-war and volleyball) and seven individual competitions (badminton, chess, handball, Ping Pong, poker, pool and tennis—singles.) The only difference between Cc and Aa sports is that the former involve physical contact, and so are more personally, immediately competitive. Both types involve direct, active competition: you win by making your opponent lose. To play these games you must try to prevent your opponent from doing well—trick him, outsmart him, get in his way, defend your goal, block his shots, return his serve, capture his pawn or otherwise cause him to make a poor showing, while at the same time prevailing over his efforts to do the same to you. More than 75 points here is above average and indicates your preference for direct, personal confrontation, short of physical contact.

Ee: passive competition. Three team sports of the passive-competitive sort are listed (relay racing, rowing and sailing—crew racing), and 11 individual sports (bicycle racing, Grand Prix racing, harness racing, hurdles, marathon, motorcycle racing, powerboat racing, sled dog racing, speed skating, stock car racing and swimming), making 14 in all. Participants in these sports aren't necessarily passive people, but their competition is based on winning through their own individual efforts and merits rather than by directly confronting an opponent. Those partial to this type of sport may be shying away from the personal confrontations of A and C sports: they would rather win by outshining their opponents than by "beating" them as such. When they do play an A or C sport, they'd rather play offense than defense. Opponents may see each other, but generally don't interfere; Mark Spitz and Eddie Arcaro may wish for their opponents to lose, but there is not much they can do to affect it directly. It's "You do your best, I'll do my best, and we'll see who crosses the finish line first."

If C sports are head-to-head and A sports are face-to-face, E sports are side-by-side. The competition is still simultaneous: the winner can look back and see those he has beaten, the loser knows he has lost as soon as he crosses the finish line. In the next sport category, passive competition is made even more passive, through delay.

Dd: delayed competition. Fifteen delayed competition sports are listed, including three team sports (four-man bobsled, figure skating—couples and road rally), and 12 individual (archery, bowling, darts, diving, skiing, figure skating—individual, golf, gymnastics, high jump, long jump, shot put and ski jumping). In these sports, the competition may be intense, but it is impersonal; it's not so much me against you, as both of us against some agreed-upon standard: a stopwatch, a measuring tape, par or a judge's decision. The competition is not simultaneous: "I'll take my best shot, then you can take yours, and then we'll measure to see who won." The joy of winning is still there, but it is a matter of individual pride in achievement rather than in beating someone else; and the pain of losing is tempered by the fact that one may never have to face the person who has beaten him.

Bb: no competition. Sixteen are listed, including two team sports (canoeing and mountain climbing), and 14 individual sports (bicycling, darts, fishing, hang-gliding, ice skating, jogging, mountain climbing, sailing, skiing, skindiving, skydiving, surfing, swimming and water skiing). These are the activities usually played "for the fun of it," with little or no competitiveness involved. There may be winners and losers (e.g., darts) and any of them can be performed competitively, but the emphasis, for most people, is on sociability, amusement, and self-improvement. If you have a high Bb score then competing with others doesn't interest you much; you'd rather be a friend than a hero, and you probably don't get much kick out of seeing others proven inferior to you. You reject the competition-ethic for some reason: perhaps it's insecurity and a fear of losing or seeing others beaten. At any rate, you'd rather cooperate than compete, and avoid classifying people—including yourself—as superior and inferior, better and worse, and prefer to enhance yourself by expanding your experiences rather than your victories.

Source: Yee, Min S., and Donald K. Wright, *The Sports Book,* (New York, NY: Holt, Rinehart and Winston, 1975), pp. 216-217. Reprinted with permission.

To explain *socialization via sport* we reiterated the values expressed in the dominant American sport creed and considered whether or not empirical evidence bears out such grandiose claims. In general, the evidence is rather scanty that sports produce such desirable traits as "democratic citizenship," "moral character," "adjusted personality," "cultivation of discipline" (beyond the specific context), and "the ability to win and lose graciously." Research regarding the personality profiles, value orientations, and social characteristics of athletes and nonathletes is not always consistent. One recent piece of research claims, however, that athletes and nonathletes tend to be similar rather than different (at least at the college/university level). Nonetheless, athletes in comparison to nonathletes appear to value social experiences more, as evidenced by their membership in social fraternities and sororities.

Value orientations, social characteristics, and personality profiles of coaches were also considered. While coaches tend to be authoritarian and conservative, they are less conservative than other social categories (business leaders or farmers, for example). Also, it is important to consider coaches' "in-role" and "out-of-role" behavior. Case studies of Frank Kush, Woody Hayes, and Joe Paterno enabled us to shine some light on the much-criticized contemporary coach.

Finally, we included a "personality inventory" for the reader to assess his/her own sports personality.

IMPORTANT CONCEPTS DISCUSSED IN THIS CHAPTER

Socialization

Socialization into Sports

Socialization via Sports

Social Learning Theory:

  Reinforcement

  Coaching

  Observational Learning (Modeling)

Success Phobia

Authoritarianism

Anticipatory Socialization

Agents of Sport Socialization:

  Family

  Peer Group

  School

Community	**Behavioral**
Mass Media	**Affective**
Types of Involvement in Sports:	**Cognitive**
Primary	**Normative Social Influence**
Secondary	**Informational Social Influence**
	Fan

ENDNOTES

[1] Leonard Broom and Philip Selznick, *Sociology* (New York: Harper and Row, 1968), p. 84.

[2] Elton McNeil, *Human Socialization* (Belmont, Calif.: Brooks/Cole, 1969).

[3] Bil Gilbert, "Imagine Going to School to Play," *Sports Illustrated* 43 (October 13, 1975), p. 90.

[4] McNeil, *Human Socialization.*

[5] Lawrence Severy, J. C. Brigham, and Barry R. Schlenker, *A Contemporary Introduction to Social Psychology* (New York: McGraw-Hill, 1976). Material is used with permission of author and publisher.

[6] "Coaching" in this context means direct teaching.

[7] B. F. Skinner, *Contingencies of Reinforcement* (New York: Appleton-Century-Crofts, 1969).

[8] A. Strauss, *Role Theory: Concepts and Research* (New York: Wiley, 1966).

[9] Albert Bandura, *Social Learning Theory* (Morristown, N.J.: General Learning Press, 1971).

[10] Jonathan J. Brower, "The Racial Basis of the Division of Labor Among Players in the National Football Leagues as a Function of Stereotypes," (Paper presented at the annual meeting of the Pacific Sociological Association, Portland, Ore., 1972), also see note 28.

[11] Implicit in this research is the idea that the general value orientations of the larger culture are distilled into the normative structure of society and, through socialization, become imparted to and internalized by individuals. Agents and agencies of socialization are vitally important in this socialization process.

[12] Howard L. Nixon, II, "Sport, Socialization, and Youth: Some Proposed Research Directions," *Review of Sport and Leisure* 1 (Fall, 1976), pp. 45-61. Used with permission.

[13] John W. Loy, Barry D. McPherson, and Gerald Kenyon, *Sport and Social Systems.* © 1978, Addison-Wesley, Reading, MA, p. 226. Reprinted with permission.

[14] Pete Axthelm, *The City Game* (New York: Harper and Row, 1970).

[15] Loy, McPherson, and Kenyon, *Sport and Social Systems: A Guide to the Analysis, Problems and Literature,* p.238.

[16] Ibid., p. 229.

[17] Ibid., p. 241.

[18] Gerald S. Kenyon and Barry D. McPherson, "Becoming Involved in Physical Activity and Sport: A Process of Socialization," *Physical Activity: Human Growth and Development,* ed. G. Laurence Rarick (New York: Academic Press, 1973), pp. 303-332; John W. Loy, Jr. and Alan Ingham, "Play, Games, and Sport in the Psychosocial Development of Children and Youth," *Physical Activity: Human Growth and Development,* ed. G. L. Rarick (New York: Academic Press, 1973), pp. 257-302; George H. Sage, "Socialization and Sport," *Sport and American Society: Selected Readings,* ed. G. Sage (Reading, Mass.: Addison-Wesley, 1974), pp. 162-172.

[19] Paul Hoch, *Rip Off: The Big Game* (Garden City, N.Y.: Anchor Books, 1972), p. 137.

[20] Eldon E. Snyder, "Athletic Dressing Room Slogans as Folklore: A Means of Socialization," *International Review of Sport Sociology* 7 (1972), pp. 89-102. Snyder has demonstrated that athletic dressing-room slogans are a means of socializing sport participants.

[21] Kenyon and McPherson, "Becoming Involved in Physical Activity and Sport: A Process of Socialization."

[22] Gerald S. Kenyon and Tom M. Grogg, *Contemporary Psychology of Sport: Proceedings of the Second International Congress of Sport Psychology* (Chicago, Ill.: The Athletic Institute, 1970).

[23] Elmer Spreitzer and Eldon E. Snyder, "Socialization into Sport: An Exploratory Analysis," *Research Quarterly* 47 (May, 1976), pp. 238-245.

[24] Robert Lynd and Helen Lynd, *Middletown* (New York: Harcourt, Brace, 1929); A. B. Hollingshead, *Elmtown's Youth* (New York: John Wiley and Sons, 1949); C. Wayne Gordon, *The Social System of the High School* (Glencoe, Ill.: Free Press, 1977); James S. Coleman, "Athletics in High School," *Annals of the American Academy of Political and Social Science* 338 (1961), pp. 33-43.

[25] A. Wohl and E. Pudelkiewics, "Theoretical and Methodological Assumptions of Research on the Processes of Involvement in Sport and Sport Socialization," *International Review of Sport Sociology* 7 (1972), pp. 69-84; Kenyon and McPherson, "An Approach to the Study of Sport Socialization."

[26] Kenyon and McPherson, "An Approach to the Study of Sport Socialization."

[27] Eldon E. Snyder and Elmer A. Spreitzer, "Family Influence and Involvement in Sports," *Research Quarterly* 44 (1973), pp. 249-255.

[28] Barry D. McPherson, "Minority Group Socialization: An Alternative Explanation for the Segregation by Playing Position Hypothesis," *International Symposium on the Sociology of Sport* (Waterloo, Ontario, Canada, 1971).

[29] Gerald S. Kenyon, "Sport Involvement: A Conceptual Go and Some Consequences Thereof," *Aspects of Contemporary Sport Sociology*, ed. G. S. Kenyon (Chicago, Ill.: The Athletic Institute, 1969); Harry Edwards, *Sociology of Sport* (Homewood, Ill.: Dorsey Press, 1973); Nixon, "Sport, Socialization, and Youth: Some Proposed Research Directions."

[30] Kenyon, "Sport Involvement: A Conceptual Go and Some Consequences Thereof."

[31] Snyder and Spreitzer, "Orientations Toward Work and Leisure as Predictors of Sports Involvement," *Research Quarterly* 45 (1974), pp. 398-406. Snyder and Spreitzer used three items to measure *affective* involvement: (1) "Sports are a way for me to relax"; (2) "Sports are a waste of time"; and (3) "I receive little satisfaction from sports."

[32] Snyder and Spreitzer, Ibid., measured this variable by having respondents match sport personalities with their appropriate sport. The twelve personalities were: Wilt Chamberlin, John Unitas, Billie Jean King, Avery Brundage, Barbara Cochran, Roberto Clemente, Phil Esposito, Pat Sullivan, John Wooden, Joe Frazier, Lee Travino, and Peggy Fleming.

[33] The word "fan" first appeared in 1682 and was spelled "fan" or "phann." Originally, it was short for "fanatic" and meant a person with an extreme or unreasoning enthusiasm or zeal. In 1899 it first appeared in an American dictionary with the meaning "an enthusiast, originally of sport." "Sportnik" has also been used.

[34] Edwards, *Sociology of Sport*, pp. 238-239.

[35] Arnold Beisser, *The Madness in Sports* (New York: Appleton-Century-Crofts, 1967), p. 126.

[36] Walter E. Schafer, "Some Sources and Consequences of Interscholastic Athletics," *Sociology of Sport*, ed. G. S. Kenyon (Chicago, Ill.: The Athletic Institute, 1969), p. 33.

[37] Edwards, *Sociology of Sport*, pp. 243-247.

[38] Harry Webb, "Professionalization of Attitudes Toward Play Among Adolescents," *Aspects of Contemporary Sport Sociology*, ed. G. S. Kenyon (Chicago, Ill.: The Athletic Institute, 1969).

[39] Richard C. Mantel and Lee Vander Velden, "The Relationship Between the Professionalization of Attitude Toward Play of Preadolescent Boys and Participation in Organized Sport," *Sport and American Society: Selected Readings*, ed. G. Sage (Reading, Mass.: Addison-Wesley, 1974), pp. 172-178.

[40] Deane E. Richardson, "Ethical Conduct in Sport Situations," *National College Physical Education Association for Men Proceedings* 66 (1962), pp. 98-103.

[41] Edwards, *Sociology of Sport*, pp. 218-220.

[42] Jay J. Coakley, *Sport in Society: Issues and Controversies* (St. Louis, Mo.: C. V. Mosby, 1978), p. 107.

[43] Bruce C. Ogilvie and Thomas A. Tutko, "Sport: If You Want to Build Character, Try Something Else," *Psychology Today* (October 1971), pp. 61-63.

[44] Ibid., p. 62.

[45] Ibid.

[46] Terry Orlick, "The Sports Environment, A Capacity to Enhance, A Capacity to Destroy" (Paper presented at the Sixth Canadian Symposium of Psycho-Motor Learning and Sports Psychology, 1974).

[47] H. Kelley, "Two Functions of Reference Groups," *Readings in Social Psychology*, ed. G. Swanson, T. Newcomb, and E. Hartley (New York: Holt, Rinehart and Winston, 1952).

[48] Eldon E. Snyder, "Aspects of Socialization in Sports and Physical Education," *Quest* XIV (June, 1970), pp. 1-7. The discussion on pp. 97-98 is used with permission.

[49] Leon Festinger, *A Theory of Cognitive Dissonance* (New York: Harper and Row, 1957).

[50] Jack Schendel, "Psychological Differences Between Athletes and Nonparticipants in Athletics at Three Educational Levels," *Research Quarterly* 36 (March 1965), pp. 52-67.

[51] R. A. Rehberg and M. Cohen, "Athletes and Scholars: An Analysis of the Compositional Characteristics and Image of These Two Youth Culture Categories," *International Review of Sport Sociology* 10 (1975), pp. 91-107.

[52] Eldon E. Snyder and Elmer Spreitzer, *Social Aspects of Sport* (Englewood Cliffs, N.J.: Prentice-Hall, 1978).

[53] Ibid., p. 96.

[54] Derrick J. Norton, "A Comparison of Political Attitudes and Political Participation of Athletes and Nonathletes" (Master's thesis, University of Oregon, 1971).

[55] Brian Petrie and Elizabeth Reid, "The Political Attitudes of Canadian Athletes," *Proceedings of the Fourth Canadian Psycho-Motor Learning and Sports Psychology Symposium* (Waterloo, Ontario: University of Waterloo, 1972), pp. 514-530.

[56] Bruce C. Ogilvie, "Psychological Consistencies Within the Personalities of High Level Competitors," *Journal of the American Medical Association* 5 (September-October, 1968), pp. 32-43.

[57] George Sage, "An Assessment of Personality Profiles Between and Within Intercollegiate Athletes From Eight Different Sports," *Sportwissenschaft* 2 (West Germany: Jahrgang) (1972/74), pp. 408-415.

[58] Coaches have always been characterized this way. Beisser, *The Madness in Sports,* p. 201, observed: "The coach has historically been perceived by his athletes as a good father to the team, protecting his boys, advising them, encouraging them . . ."

[59] James A. Mishener, *Sports in America* (New York: Random House, 1976), pp. 259-260.

[60] Gary Shaw, *Meat on the Hoof* (New York: St. Martins, 1972), pp. 63, 79.

[61] John D. Massengale, "Coaching as an Occupational Subculture," *Phi Delta Kappan* 56 (October, 1974), pp. 140-142.

[62] Ogilvie and Tutko, "Sport: If You Want to Build Character, Try Something Else," p. 63.

[63] Jerry Bronfield, "Explosive Woody Hayes," *Reader's Digest* (September, 1977), pp. 98-102.

[64] George H. Sage, "Value Orientations of American College Coaches Compared to Those of Male College Students and Businessmen," *75th Annual Proceedings of the National College Physical Education Association for Men* (1972), pp. 174-186.

[65] George H. Sage, "Machiavellianism Among College and High School Coaches," ref. 24, pp. 45-60.

[66] Eldon E. Snyder, "Aspects of Social and Political Values of High School Coaches," *International Review of Sport Sociology* 8 (1973), pp. 73-87.

[67] Penman, Hastad, and Cords, *Psychology and Social Behavior* (New York: Harper and Row, 1974).

[68] John W. Loy and George H. Sage, "Social Origins, Academic Achievement, Athletic Achievement, and Career Mobility Patterns of College Coaches" (Paper presented at the Annual Meetings of the American Sociological Association, 1972); Eitzen and Sage, *Sociology of American Sport*, pp. 155-59.

[69] Urie Bronfenbrenner, "Socialization and Social Class Through Time and Space," *Readings in Social Psychology,* ed. E. Maccoby, T. Newcomb, and E. Hartley (New York: Holt, Rinehart and Winston, 1958); Melvin Kohn, "Social Class and Parental Values," *American Journal of Sociology* 64 (January, 1959), pp. 337-351; Eitzen and Sage, *Sociology of American Sport.*

[70] Massengale, "Coaching as an Occupational Subculture."

[71] D. Stanley Eitzen and George H. Sage, *Sociology of American Sport* (Dubuque, Iowa: William C. Brown Co., 1978), p. 160.

6
Sport and Social Deviance

INTRODUCTION

The goal of socialization is to produce conforming individuals, individuals who abide by society's rules or norms. In any society, in any realm, there are persons who deviate from the expected guidelines. *Deviance* may be defined as thinking, acting, and feeling contrary to the standards of conduct or social expectations of a given group or society. It is *rule-breaking behavior,* although there is a range of tolerable behaviors. *Deviants* are individuals who engage in the rule-breaking behavior. Deviance is a generic term encompassed in such conventional expressions as cheating, crime, addiction, alcoholism, immorality, deceit, perversion, genius, and saintliness. Note that deviance refers to both "positive" and negative" departures from the norms (*Encyclopedia of Sociology,* 1974).

A positive feature of deviance in sport is the innovative eponymous "Fosbury Flop" in which a high jumper goes over the bar backwards and headfirst and lands on his back. As we will see, the roots of deviance may be either individual (pathological) or societal (social organizational or disorganizational) or both. Consider the following incidents of deviance in sport:

The recent controversy over the sex of females in international competition is a case in point. One type of sex test takes the form of *cell sampling.* This is a chromosome test in which cells from the inside cheek are scraped and examined under the microscope. In a "normal" woman about 20 cells in every 100 contain Barr bodies (collections of chromatins). At the 1968 Olympics women whose tests showed fewer than 10 cells per 100 were barred from competition. Since all females are required to submit to a series of sex tests prior to international competition, a number of renowned "female" athletes from behind the "iron curtain" have disappeared from the scene. One is led to believe that the defectors may not have passed the physical exam for one reason or another. The most fascinating and polemical case is that of the great Polish athlete Ewa Klobkowska who passed the exam but was later disqualified when the study of "her" chromosomes revealed the presence of "masculine," Y chromosomes. Is "she" male or female?[1]

In the 1976 Montreal Olympics a Russian fencer was discovered to have ingeniously wired his épée—the scoring being recorded by electronic means—so he could score points, at his own volition.[2]

GUATEMALA CITY, Guatemala—Local soccer fans, angered after their hometown club lost to an army team, attacked the winning players with machetes Friday, the army said. Five persons were killed in the melee.

The slaying occurred as the army team was boarding a bus in Santa Barbara, 170 miles from the capital, after downing the local squad 6-3, a spokesman said.

About 30 men attacked the soldiers and tried to disarm Cpl. Sebastian Espinosa, the army said.

Two hundred other villagers, armed with machetes, knives and clubs, waded into the attack as Espinosa fired his pistol into the air to try to force them away.

The army said Espinosa was hacked to death. Four villagers also were killed in the fighting.[3]

The use of drugs has become so prevalent that the apothegm "it is not how you prepare for the game but who your pharmacist is" sometimes provides the athlete with the "victory edge." The use of anabolic steroids has become so rampant and widespread that the International Olympic Committee has abolished them.[4]

Every year American colleges and universities—amateur sports—end up being disqualified or suspended for recruitment irregularities. In 1978, for example, Kansas State University was penalized by the Big Eight Conference for violations that occurred over a three year period, ending in the fall of 1977. The university had awarded 13 more football scholarships than allowed by the NCAA and had awarded seven extra scholarships in other sports.[5]

In 1975 a nineteen year old negress named Roxie Ann Rice was caught delivering quotas of marijuana to NFL players throughout the country. After presenting an unacceptable alibi for her actions, she confessed to servicing the basketball teams of Pan American University and the St. Louis Spirits, and was considering extending her services into baseball.[6]

Blood doping is another questionable practice. This procedure entails giving blood prior to a match and shortly before the event having it returned via injection on the belief that extra blood, particularly a surfeit of red blood cells, will increase oxygen transport and enhance stamina.[7]

An investigation of the thirty-sixth annual Soap Box Derby (in Akron, Ohio, 1973) revealed that one of the young participants was driving a vehicle that carried a strong electric magnet hidden in the nose of the "car." When activated, the magnet would follow the backward fall of the iron plate, making the car spring forward just a little faster than his competitors'.[8]

Offensive linemen in football frequently break the charge of on-rushing linemen during pass plays by grabbing on to their shirt and forearms.[9]

Similarly, in baseball there are occasions when illegal pitches (spitball, throwing at a batter, or the brushback pitch) become very questionable.[10]

In the 1960 Olympic Games Danish cyclist Knud Jensen collapsed during the 100 kilometer race and died later. It was established that he had taken a drug Ronicol which stimulates the circulatory system by dilating the blood vessels.[11]

In 1920 eight players of the Chicago White Sox baseball team were suspended for alleged dealings with gamblers during the 1919 World Series. The "Black Sox" scandal led to the appointment of Judge Kenesaw Mountain Landis as commissioner of baseball in 1921.[12]

In 1951 some 32 college basketball players were accused of fixing the point spread in some 86 games. Despite precautions that included removing college games from the big-city arenas, a similar scandal erupted in the late 1950s.[13]

On the surface, all these acts are *deviant*. Sociologically speaking, "deviance" (particularly that which applies to violence) may be classified as *crowd nonnormative* and *individual normative* behavior. In chapter 13 we discuss collective behavior in sport. It nicely represents the nonnormative approach since actions depart from what is considered normal and appropriate. On the other hand, individual normative behavior often appears to blend in with the nonnormative variety. However, it is frequently considered different because certain behavior patterns (such as aggression and violence) are learned and enacted by occupants of certain social positions in various sports. But there are some other prominent features that must be explored in understanding their manifestations. One issue at the root of these social problems is the "winning at any cost" syndrome. Winning is tied in with the so-called root of all evil—money. The consequences of winning, economically speaking, are particularly great at big-time universities and in the professional ranks. This winning means winning seasons, "big games," tournaments, conferences, championships, etc. For example, when the Ohio State football team plummeted from a 7-2 record in 1965 to a 4-5 record in 1966, their alumni support declined by nearly half a million dollars.

Conversely, a winning team can greatly enhance a school financially. After North Carolina State won the 1974 NCAA basketball championship, they received more than a million dollars for their athletic scholarship fund. After Duke's stellar 1978 basketball season sixty individuals and corporations contributed $100,000 each toward endowed athletic scholarships.

Similarly, when "Big Ten" coach Alex Agase was fired after his fourth consecutive losing season, the president of the university cited financial strains associated with maintaining a competitive program in intercollegiate athletics as a major reason. This means that rules will often be violated, particularly when the deviant act may not be suspect or caught. On the other hand, even when the risk of being caught is high, there are those who are willing to make this gamble because the payoffs for winning—happy fans, television money, and full stadium—are so great.

Even at the high school level—not just the collegiate big time and pros—there is evidence that winning is all. Sabock reported that high school coaches are primarily hired and fired for the following reasons:

1. To reorganize the athletic program toward a reemphasis of the "major" sports.
2. To win.
3. To gain state ranking with the team.
4. To bring new recognition to the school and community through winning and state ranking.

5. To work for all-star and all-state recognition for some of the boys on the team.
6. To satisfy the Booster Club.
7. To win championships.
8. To appease unhappy "barbershop quarterbacks."[14]

This means, as we indicated in chapters 3 and 5, that coaches frequently experience *role strain* because there are conflicting and incompatible social expectations on the person occupying that position. This strain and tension is rooted in their *limited control* with nearly complete responsibility for the game's outcome. Hence, as we will shortly see, coaches frequently employ unethical practices to circumvent such problems.

In studying deviance in sport, and other institutions as well, one must ask *what* norms and *whose* norms are being violated. For example, among football players there are many tactics (holding, spear blocking, clipping) that are not only condoned but even encouraged under certain circumstances even though the official rules explicitly forbid them. In basketball it is common for the defensive player to place his hand on the lower body of the shooter since this disrupts the latter's concentration while the official is watching the area around the ball. Similarly, basketball players often fake being fouled. Even the suspect recruiting practices of university personnel are justified on the grounds that "everybody does it" and "I must do it to remain competitive."

A THEORY OF SOCIAL DEVIANCE: MERTON'S ANOMIE THEORY

While there are a variety of theories of deviance *(psychoanalytic, social and biological pathology, differential association, social disorganizational,* and *labeling),* one provocative explanation that "fits" sport is that of Robert K. Merton.[15] He argued that our society prescribes norms of success for all persons. For many roles in sport—athlete, coach, trainer—this "success" means winning. Society also establishes channels or means through which these goals can be achieved. However, since most sporting contests result in winners and losers, various personnel are likely to be frustrated in this mutually exclusive quest. Hence, people will employ various means—proscribed as well as prescribed—to achieve the goal of success. One form of sport deviance, *cheating*—the breaking of rules to gain an unfair advantage over competitors—exists at all levels of sport and is engaged in by individuals (players and coaches), teams, and organizations. Figure 6.1 contains Merton's typology highlighting modes of individual adaptation to the gap between culturally prescribed goals and the means of obtaining them. When the goals are not easily achieved, social pressures for engaging in nonconforming behavior rather than conforming behavior exist.

Note that there are five adaptation modes: (1) *conformity,* (2) *innovation,* (3) *ritualism,* (4) *retreatism,* and (5) *rebellion.* The "+" and "–" signs in Figure 6.1 refer to acceptance and rejection, respectively, of the goals and means. While not all types of adaptation are directly relevant to sport, several are.

Conformity

"Conformists" are those who accept both the culturally prescribed success goals and the culturally prescribed means for achieving those goals. In studying dressing room slogans Snyder uncovered two—"Live by the code or get out" and "discipline"— that, superficially, would seem to

Mode or Adaptation	Cultural Goals	Cultural Means
Conformity	+	+
Innovation	+	−
Ritualism	−	+
Retreatism	−	−
Rebellion	±	±

Key: + = acceptance; − = rejection

Figure 6.1
Modes of Individual Adaptation
(Robert K. Merton, *Social Theory and Social Structure,* Glencoe, Ill., Free Press, 1957)

suggest that both coaches and players are emersed in a social environment encouraging obedience to the rules.[16] Undoubtedly, some players, coaches, and other personnel abide by these dictates; however, few persons who play for any period of time escape committing, knowingly or unknowingly, rule infractions. Rule violations, for example, have been incorporated into game strategies such as intentional pass interference to prevent a touchdown, a deliberate trip to prevent a breakaway score in football, roller derby, basketball, hockey, and soccer, belting into the second baseman to break up a double play, pushing and shoving in basketball, and taking a technical foul to stop a game's momentum. These forms of deviance are generally not serious and are subsumed under the titles of "patterned evasion of the norms" or "normal fakery."[17]

Innovation

"Innovators" are those who accept the goals but alter the means for obtaining them. In this author's mind, this form of individual adaptation most clearly reflects the nature of deviance in sport, particularly that deviance which is considered to be more serious and unethical. Recent NCAA recruiting scandals demonstrate this pattern and the roots of it.

Recruitment Violations

Recruitment irregularities are not a recent discovery. As early as 1929 the Carnegie Foundation reported dismay with illegal recruiting practices of American institutions of higher learning.[18] One of the conclusions of this massive report was that "college sports have been developed from games played by boys for pleasure into systematic, professionalized contests." That year, Iowa was expelled by Big Ten officials for improper financial assistance to athletes. Furthermore, several Big Ten universities suggested it was time for the NCAA to become more of a regulatory (vs. advisory) board. Let us begin with a case study of a relatively recent controversial recruitment incident and then trace the reasons why such deviant practices are so pervasive.

Wolf's account of recruiting irregularities regarding Connie Hawkins provides an interesting and revealing case study of the processes of illegally recruiting a star athlete.[19] Hawkins, a blue chip high school basketball player, was contacted by 250 colleges. Twelve schools brought him to their campuses and in excess of fifty sent special emissaries to speak to him on their school's behalf. He was the recipient of all the frills of high-powered recruiting—"wined and dined" at lavish restaurants, given cash, given gratis tickets, and even told by some that he would receive a financial rebate for enrolling in addition to free clothing and plane trips. Ironically, despite the fact that he was only capable of reading at the elementary school level, he said no recruiter ever asked him about his scholastic interests or future plans. Hawkins' collegiate career ended when his name was associated with the gambling scandals of the early 1960s. It was reported that his Iowa coaches pressured him to lie, in writing, absolving them and the university of any "irregularities." Wolf's comment on the Hawkins case is worth repeating:

> The Iowa coaches were not evil men. Hundreds of other coaches were also after Hawkins. The Iowa people were simply acting in the only manner it is possible to act—and still survive—in the big-time profit oriented college sports system. They had to win basketball games to keep their jobs, and to win they needed kids like Connie Hawkins. To get kids like Hawkins, they had to cheat.[20]

Larry Klein worked eight years (1964-1972) for the NCAA Enforcement Department and during that period sixty-two colleges/universities—less than 10 percent of total—were caught breaking its rules.[21] The rule most often violated was the one regarding recruiting: You can't offer anyone anything more than a scholarship before an athlete matriculates and you can't give him (historically males have been the recipients of such awards) anything more than the scholarship after he does so. NCAA rules stipulate that a male college student-athlete may receive a grant-in-aid in the form of books, tuition, board, and room.[22] However, it is not rare for potential professional athletes to illegally sign a professional contract before their careers have terminated. Professional scouts indicate that this practice is common among college football players and one college cage coach thinks 50 percent of "blue chippers" (in basketball) are paid by agents. Vignette 6.1 discusses the role of the *agent* in such transactions. While this may increase the athletes' financial support, it is clearly in violation of the NCAA rule that prohibits such transactions until the completion of the player's eligibility.

If only 10 percent of NCAA affiliates have been caught, does this imply that most schools—90 percent—conduct their recruiting honestly? Although Walter Byers, executive director of the NCAA since 1951, has said there is no more cheating in college sports than in other areas of life, this allegation doesn't tell us very much.[23] Consider this: The NCAA Enforcement Department has a total of eight investigators to catch rule violators among its 800-plus member schools! Denlinger and Shapiro reported that:

> A 1974 survey by the National Association of Basketball Coaches said that one of every eight major colleges made illegal offers to prospects, that all the cheaters were offering money, 80 percent were offering cars, and more than one-half were offering clothing. The survey was conducted among 25 recently graduated college players, 25 current high school standouts, 25 sets of parents, and 25 athletic directors of major college basketball programs. Of the 50 players interviewed, 40 percent said they had received illegal offers.[24]

Monetary incentives are not the only illegal procedures for luring athletes to particular schools. Athletes' transcripts have been tampered with, parents have been provided with jobs, housing, and money, athletes have been paid for nonexistent jobs, government monies have been illegally used to pay student-athletes, under-the-table payments have been made, and athletes of marginal ability have had substitutes take tests for them.[25] Whether these rule violations are deliberately taken by athletes or coaches, the fact remains that deviance is widespread and pervasive.

Let's assume that the 10 percent figure is the top of the iceberg and raise several other queries. If many players are taking illicit money and material objects, *who* is giving them? The NCAA says "representatives of the university's athletic interests." These "representatives" include wealthy boosters in addition to head and assistant coaches. Klein said: "The system works because every assistant coach, at least in basketball, wants to be a head coach, and he usually reaches his goal after making his boss look good."[26]

Why is money passed so freely? Because winning is the goal, fans don't flock to see losers play, and there are more seats to fill today. All these reasons add up to the quest for the pot of gold—dollars—as measured by filled stadiums and lucrative bowl and TV appearances. A survey by the NCAA revealed that in the past decade eighty-two colleges built new basketball arenas and thirty-nine of them had seating capacities in excess of 10,000.[27] Similarly, in the past ten years seating capacities in the Southeastern Conference (SEC) and Big Eight Conference were increased by 15 and 21 percent, respectively. Klein wrote:

> Take football on television: Last fall ABC-TV paid more than $17 million to NCAA member colleges for the rights to televise 13 national and 28 regional games. That covered only the regular season. Each team appearing on a national telecast collected $250,769. A regional appearance earned each team $190,000. Three universities (Ohio State, Texas, and UCLA) each appeared on one regional and two national telecasts for a take of $691,538 apiece.
>
> Football's four biggest bowls—the Rose, Orange, Cotton, and Sugar—pay around $1,000,000 a team.
>
> College basketball is catching up fast. Take the NCAA Championship tournament. Teams earned $4,350 each for playing a first-round game in 1966, and tournament winner Texas Western earned $26,102. In 1976 a first-round game alone earned each team $23,943; the four teams reaching the semifinals earned $143,657 apiece. This year's figure soared to about $40,000 and $200,000 because NBC-TV paid $4 million for tournament television rights.[28]

Hence, athletic and nonathletic personnel must innovate to achieve the elusive pot of gold at the end of the rainbow.

Relative deprivation appears to be another explanatory principle in such deviant tactics. Relative deprivation is not a scarcity of valued cultural objects (money and prestige) in absolute terms, but in terms of comparisons with others more well-off. Tom Hansen, assistant executive director of the NCAA, hypothesized that top teams—the Ohio State's, Notre Dame's, USC's, Texas'—are less likely to cheat than those pursuing this elite category,[29] this because schools with successful programs attract aspiring athletes without offering them anything but the potential of continued success. Although the charges against Oklahoma (found guilty of improper inducements, improper aid, and fringe benefits), an elite football power, is an exception, less successful schools like Canisius, Michigan

VIGNETTE 6.1
TODAY'S BIGGEST MAN ON CAMPUS IS AN AGENT

*North Carolina basketball coach Dean Smith said he was offered a bribe of 2½ per cent of a player's contract by a New York agent who wanted to sign one of his players.

*New York agent Norman Blass secured former Morgan State basketball star Marvin Webster as his client, then arranged for Webster's coach to be paid by the Denver Nuggets as a scout.

*Pat Thomas and Jackie Williams, football players at Texas A&M a year ago, say a Houston agent told them they could sign a contract with him before A&M's appearance in the 1975 Liberty Bowl, which they did. Their signatures had made them ineligible. Eventually, Thomas signed with five agents and Williams three before going to the pros.

They are there because there is money. Lots of money to be banked and invested and secured and insured. And, with some of them money to be diverted and swindled and stolen and rolled in.

They are the agents of sport.

They do not like that word—agents—though. The lawyers among them usually remind you that they are attorneys. The ones who are not prefer to be called sports representatives. No matter.

Agent, sports representative, whatever, they are on outgrowth of the industry of sport, and they are everywhere. They befriend 13-year-olds who already can jump up and see themselves in glass backboards. At that age, in the ghettos of the country, a pair of sneakers and occasional subway fare are all it costs to buy a player.

By the time the 13-year-old is 19 or 20, the agent might have to send the player a couple of hundred a month, or an advance of $5,000 or a new Eldorado before the draft.

But even a $5,000 advance is nothing if the player is a first-rounder. The agent can make that much back in an hour of negotiation. And, if the player is a Julius Erving, all the agent has to do is guard the player with his life and he can retire with him.

So, to secure someone like a Julius Erving some agents will say anything, promise anything, do anything. Money, cars, anything. Just sign.

Many of the players do sign, ensnaring themselves in levels of wheeling and dealing that they are not prepared to handle. Those players are white and black, poor and not, but a preponderance of those who suffer are black.

The reasons are simple; the percentage of blacks in football and basketball is high.

When a white All-American halfback graduates from college some sophisticated white businessman is often there to help him. If the halfback is black, a businessman is seldom around.

It's not just players who become involved. Northwestern basketball coach Tex Winter says most coaches who have coached first-round draft choices have been subjected to "offers." Even John Wooden, whose priestly image would seem to make him beyond approach, said he once was offered money and the promise of great high school prospects to influence his players to sign with one agent.

No one is beyond question. Not agents, not players, not coaches, not owners, not leagues. "It's gone on so long," said retiring Marquette basketball coach Al McGuire, "that everyone is soiled."

Hardly any of this is known publicly because it is a business that operates under the table. Not all agents are devious or dishonest, of course. Maybe not even most of them. But the world of sports agentry teems with the contemptible.

Marvin Webster was a valued commodity at Morgan State. He was 7-1 and 240 pounds and known as "The Human Eraser." He was averaging 20 rebounds a game and seven blocked shots. He was about to become the second choice in the 1975 NBA draft when a New York agent, who asked that his name not be used, went to see Webster about representing him. Webster took the agent to meet his coach, Nat Frazier. "Frazier was really nice and polite. Then he asks Marvin to wait out in the gym. All of a sudden he (Frazier) begins screaming at me about 'Where do you get the nerve to talk to my players without talking to me?' "

"He talked about how much he had helped him, how he wasn't much of a player until he got ahold of him, and he talked about all the hours he'd spent working with Marvin. That's when he came onto this thing that he (Frazier) should receive something. I said, 'Cause you worked so hard with him?' And he said yeah.

I told him, 'If the kid believes that you deserve it, fine. I'll tell him to put it in (the deal).'

"And then Frazier came right out and said, 'The only way you can get the kids is if you come across.' He just said it right out."

The agent walked out.

"That's not true at all," Frazier said. "Those guys put out a lot of lies." Frazier does agree, though, that the man he eventually recommended to Marvin Webster was Norman Blass, one of basketball's big-name agents.

And when the contract between Webster and the Denver Nuggets was signed, the Nuggets included some money for Frazier at Blass' urging, Blass said. It was set up so that Frazier would be on Denver's scouting payroll—a fact which Blass concedes.

Frazier himself admitted after some questioning that the job had been arranged, but he said it fell through.

But Nuggets owner Carl Scheer said Frazier had been paid. "We paid him a sum of money as part of Webster's contract," he said. "That was just part of the negotiations."

Such arrangements by Blass are not unusual. Dean Smith, the basketball coach at North Carolina and the 1976 U.S. Olympic coach, said he was offered a 2½ per cent of a player's contract in the spring of 1972 by Blass.

"He tried to pass it off as a finder's fee," Smith said. "He tried to put it in a nice way."

Smith didn't take it that way: Blass was asking Smith to push his player to Blass. Smith said he ushered him out.

Blass denied Smith's story. "I've never been in Dean Smith's office," he said. "That was Chuck Kaufman (Blass' business partner at the time)."

Smith is certain. "I know who Chuck Kaufman is. It was Blass." And Chuck Kaufman is certain, too. He said he never went to North Carolina.

Source: Dan Lauck, Copyright 1977, *Newsday,* Inc. Reprinted by permission.

State, Minnesota, Mississippi State, Kentucky, and Clemson have more often, in recent years, been found guilty of recruiting violations. Vignette 6.2 highlights the specific infractions for 1975 and 1976.

Others have said "bunk" to the relative deprivation explanation and have asserted that for various reasons some high-powered schools appear to be beyond reproach. For example, Ohio State University was "publicly reprimanded and censured" during the late spring of 1978 for football rule violations from 1973 to 1975. Although the typical penalties for such infractions committed by Ohio State—an assistant coach lent an automobile to an athlete, free meals were given to boosters who

VIGNETTE 6.2
THE STRONGEST NCAA ACTIONS

1975

CANISIUS: *Violations:* Gave players and prospects extra transportation and summer room and board on campus. Entertained prospects and friends excessively and paid expenses of talent scouts. Also gave a player excessive aid, bought a player furniture, bought a player clothes, paid a player's car-service bill, another's phone bill. *Penalties:* Two-year probation. No TV or postseason basketball play for two years, limit of five basketball scholarships for two years.*

MISSISSIPPI STATE: *Violations:* Offered one prospect a cash bonus for signing SEC letter of intent and then a cash payment each semester he attended. Gave prospects cash, improper transportation and entertainment and extra paid visits. *Penalties:* Two-year probation. No TV football or bowl games for two years, limit of 25 football scholarships for one year and sever all relations with three boosters.

CLEMSON: *Violations:* Offered to buy a house for a prospect's mother and to pay all the house's utility bills while the son was enrolled. Offered to buy a prospect a new car, furniture for his home and give his father substantial cash. Gave a prospect cash and offered him a substantial cash payment and additional cash each month of attendance. Gave a prospect and his friends cash at least six times on recruiting visits. Also conducted tryouts. *Penalties:* Three-year probation. No TV or postseason basketball play for three years, limit of two basketball scholarships for one year and three scholarships the next year and sever all relations with certain boosters.

1976

MICHIGAN STATE: *Violations:* Offered a prospect cash, a car, vacation transportation home, and an apartment and scholarship aid for his girlfriend. Gave other prospects improper transportation and entertainment, cash and clothes. Gave players clothes, free use of a car and helped them set up special credit accounts at a travel agency. Also failed to provide relevant materials for NCAA investigation, used an ineligible player in five games. *Penalties:* Three-year probation. No TV football or bowl games for three years, limit of 20 football scholarships for one year and 25 the next, no recruiting by one coach for three years and sever all relations with two boosters.

MINNESOTA: *Violations:* Offered a prospect a full scholarship, apartment rent, a car, cash, free plane transportation for his parents twice a season and additional financial aid for his family when necessary. Gave prospects such gifts as cash, a salary supplement for four months, extra plane transportation, a bicycle and an engraved rod and reel. Gave players cash, plane tickets, entertainment tickets, dental services, meals, long-distance phone calls, transportation for wives to tournaments, a pair of glasses, a bed and free use of cars and refrigerator. One player's parents and sister twice received free plane tickets and lodging to see home games. One player's parents, brother and girlfriend received five days free lodging. Also used four ineligibles in NCAA tournament, charged expenses on a booster's credit card, and conducted tryouts and out-of-season conditioning drills. *Penalties:* Three-year probation. No TV or postseason basketball play for two years, limit of three basketball scholarships for two years, no recruiting by one coach for two years and sever all relations with seven boosters.

*Normal limit on scholarships allowed per year is six in basketball, 30 in football.

KENTUCKY: *Violations:* Offered one prospect a racehorse and substantial cash. Offered a prospect's father diesel tractors. Gave prospects cash, betting tickets at a racetrack, dress shirts, T-shirts, jerseys and free use of a car for three weeks. Gave one player a free trip to Las Vegas, with three free days in a hotel and several cash gifts there. Gave a player drinks in a local bar for two years. Gave a player an apartment. Gave others movie admissions, meals, auto repair and $5 and $10 bonuses for such things as recovering a fumble, making a key tackle or directing a touchdown drive. Also provided improper transportation and improper entertainment and conducted out-of-season football practices and conditioning programs. *Penalties:* Two-year probation. No TV football or bowl games for one year and limit of 25 football scholarships for one year. Basketball scholarships limited to three for two years.

Source: Larry Klein, "The NCAA Enforcement Sham." *Sport* (June, 1977) pp. 42-43. Reprinted by permission.

---

brought high school prospects to the campus, and gifts of cash and transportation from boosters—include no TV appearances or postseason bowl games, the reprimand did not include such sanctions. Why? NCAA officials said because OSU disclosed the violations and a one-year investigation by the association found no additional infractions.[30] Others have countered this rationale by declaring that the NCAA does not want to lose the revenues generated from Ohio State appearing on national television. Still others have insinuated that Woody Hayes may also have been beyond reproach.

A recent book by Jack Scott described UCLA basketball violations during the tenure of Coach Johnny Wooden and superstars Kareem Abdul-Jabbar and Bill Walton. Scott said in the book that he has a letter from a former UCLA basketball star, unnamed, but obviously Bill Walton, stating that he is repaying a $4,500 "loan" that was given to him while he was at the Pac-8 school. The following tape recording between Scott and Sam Gilbert, a wealthy Los Angeles businessman who has long been portrayed as doing "favors" for and giving free financial advice to UCLA basketball players, is of interest:

Scott: "Let's skip the bull—Sam . . . I have a copy of a letter before me that was sent to you by a UCLA basketball star after he signed a lucrative pro basketball contract. The letter states the athlete was paying over $4,500 back to you that you had given him while he played basketball for UCLA."

Gilbert: "Are you going to use that letter? UCLA would have to return four NCAA championships. What I did is a total violation of NCAA rules."[31]

Scott, who lived with Walton during his first three years with the Portland Trail Blazers, said Walton believes the book to be an honest portrayal and has offered to make personal appearances that would help promote it. Scott said that his intent is not to have UCLA investigated but to point out the selective and unfair methods employed by the NCAA investigatory committee. Walton said: "I hate to say anything that would hurt UCLA but I can't be quiet when I see what the NCAA is doing to Jerry Tarkanian only because he had a reputation for giving a second chance to many black athletes other coaches have branded as troublemakers. . . . No one from the NCAA ever questioned me during my four years at UCLA."[32]

Jerry Tarkanian, former coach at Long Beach State (California) and now coach at the University of Nevada, Las Vegas (UNLV), makes an interesting case study of deviance and counterclaims in collegiate sport. Shortly after Tarkanian departed for UNLV, Long Beach was placed on probation by the NCAA for violating its rules. The university was placed on indefinite probation for not less than three years, excluded from postseason games and NCAA TV packages, had its scholarship allotment cut back for lending money to athletes, having a football player enrolled at four schools but attending none, using fraudulent test scores, and permitting a basketball player to take part in illegal tryouts.[33]

In August of 1977, the UNLV basketball program was placed on probation for alleged infractions of NCAA rules and the university was ordered to suspend Tarkanian from his coaching duties for two years. Tarkanian did not accept the declaration and won a court order, which is being appealed, to prevent his suspension. Tarkanian's run-in with the NCAA led Rep. James Santini, a Nevada Democrat, to push for a Congressional investigation of the NCAA's "double-standard" enforcement practices. Hearings by the House Committee on Oversight and Investigations are now past the eighteen month mark. The upshot of all this may be a much needed and long overdue housecleaning of NCAA practices. James E. Moss, for example, has warned the NCAA that if it retaliated against the institutions that testified before his subcommittee, the Justice Department will be asked to step in and investigate.[34]

Ritualism

Ritualists are those who reject the cultural goal—winning at any cost—but accept the means. The ritualistic approach would emphasize participation rather than winning and is summarized in the adage "it's not whether you won or lost but how you played the game." George Leonard, in *The Ultimate Athlete,* captured the ritualistic pattern in the New Games Tournament slogan: "Play hard, Play fair, Nobody hurt."[35] In projecting future scenarios, Leonard talked of "athletic" contests which eliminated dehumanization, ruthless competition, and excessive violence. The emphasis in such new games as Earth Ball, Le Mans Tug-of-War, Infinity Volleyball, Yogi Tag, New Frisbee, Boffing, and Slaughter is to go beyond exercise per se and communicate with self, others, and nature. The "new games" concept is geared to facilitate better students, happier and healthier adults, and more useful citizens.

Johnson described two future sport scenarios:[36] (1) *technosport* (sport being the product of machines and technicians), and (2) *escosport.* Escosport is more germane to the present discussion. Ecosport (usually played outdoors and stressing the relationship between sport and the environment) consists of play that is natural, unstructured, and free blown. Its goal is virtually identical to that of the "New Games" play hard, play fair, nobody hurt.

Retreatism

"Retreatists" are those who reject both the means and goals of sport. Some athletes who initially fit the "ritualistic" pattern eventually adopt this orientation. Joe Don Looney, former college and professional football player, joined a religious sect in India and denounced "worldliness." Many persons horrified and disgusted at the direction athletics has taken have entirely rejected its emphasis upon competition, violence, commercialism, and dehumanization. Merton used the term retreatism to describe "giving up." Individuals who have had *aversive* or *negative sport socialization* experiences also represent this type. Since sports are such a pervasive phenomenon, it is critical that initial sport experiences do not leave a "foul taste" in the participant's mouth. Orlick and Botterill wrote:

> The most important thing you can do to insure that the child gets the right start is to see that the child's participation is fun and enjoyable over above everything else. The simple fact is that if children are not receiving some sort of positive rewards from their participation, they will not continue. Having fun, playing, and being part of the action can be extremely rewarding for kids.[37]

Sociologists have referred to such aversive socialization experiences as "degradation ceremonies"—activities designed to "turn off" participants. Gary Shaw described such "run-offs" at the University of Texas:

> Royal . . . had all injured players (if below the first four teams) wear a jersey with a big red cross stenciled on both sides. And if at all able to walk, the injured were to continually jog around the practice field the complete workout. The red crosses were to be signs of humiliation. And throughout the spring, Royal would refer to the guys that would do anything to get out of workout and "couldn't take it." It may sound silly, but it was really an embarrassing stigma to be on your jersey. . . . It was never explained to us why only those injured below a certain team were "fake injuries." There were always several members on the first teams who were injured, yet they wore only solid jerseys.[38]

Rebellion

"Rebels" are those who not only reject the means-ends nexus but attempt to actively substitute new forms of sport. The social movements known as "shamateur activism" and the "humanitarian counter creed" (see chapter 13) illustrate this thesis quite well . . . rejecting the means-ends nexus but attempting to actively substitute new forms of sport.

In summary, *deviance* in sports, like deviance in other realms of social life, stems from several sources. Sometimes deviance emerges for unintentional reasons—role incumbents are not knowledgeable of the rules, the rules themselves are ambiguous and conflicting, or the rules may be misinterpreted. However, when the norms are known deviation from them is often a reflection of strains and pressures experienced by the actors in various social settings. In sports there are several *structural* roots of social deviance.[39]

Incompatible Value Orientations

The overriding value atmosphere of sport is ironic. Just the same, these paradoxes are not unique to sport, as Williams' delineation of American value orientations (pp. 66-67) vividly denoted. On the one hand, the values of sportsmanship and fair play are given verbal homage but, on the other, winning at any cost has gained ascendancy. Frequently, both values cannot be realized since they contain antagonistic claims. Consider the "Ten Commandments of Sport:"[40]

1. Thou shalt not quit.
2. Thou shalt not alibi.

3. Thou shalt not gloat over winning.
4. Thou shalt not sulk over losing.
5. Thou shalt not take unfair advantage.
6. Thou shalt not ask odds thou are unwilling to give.
7. Thou shalt always be willing to give thine opponent the benefit of the doubt.
8. Thou shalt not underestimate an opponent or overestimate thyself.
9. Remember that the game is the thing and he who thinks otherwise is no true sportsman.
10. Honor the game thou playest, for he who plays the game straight and hard wins even when he loses.

The realities of sport, and not just those of the big-time college and professional, make conformity to these "commandments" most difficult since winning has become such a preoccupation.

Inconsistency Between Values/Norms and Built-In Constraints

Given the priority of winning and the restrictions on the amount of practice time allowed—especially to high school and collegiate teams—it is not surprising that deception will be used to gain advantages over the opposition. Many a high school or college team will have "unofficial" practices, what are sometimes called "informal, pick-up games," prior to the official practice date. On this matter Jim Murray, a sport columnist, related the following comment sent to him by an embittered ex-high school teacher:

> I was disgusted by the deceit practiced in the athletic department—men to whom our boys look for leadership. For example, our league had a rule against having more than a certain number of practices during the summer months preparatory to the beginning of the football season. But—by pure coincidence—the whole football team would show up in full uniform on unscheduled days. Also, the coaching staff would miraculously appear. I would say that, in some cases, the coaches and team did not come in direct contact, that is, they were separated by, probably, 20 yards, but this infuriated me as an educator. As far as I was concerned, the only thing we were teaching those kids was how to cheat. And what seemed even more ridiculous was that these coaches were breaking their own rules—rules they themselves had made.[41]

Inconsistencies Within and Between the Expectations of Different Roles

Coaches are expected to cultivate discipline, yet they are increasingly expected to be sensitive to players as individuals and players as "representatives" of different ethnic, racial, and social class backgrounds. Several years ago Sandy Koufax refused to pitch a World Series game because the date conflicted with a traditional Jewish holiday. Similarly, Muhammad Ali has had to deal with conflicts between his preacher (Black Muslim) and prizefighting role. He refused military conscription and was stripped of his crown by the World Boxing Association (WBA).

While this triad does not exhaust all sources of *structural* strain, they do represent some of the more typical issues faced by occupants of sport positions. Several forms of deviance in athletics can be subsumed under these headings.

DRUGS IN SPORT

To realize the maximum social and economic benefits enjoyed by stellar performers, athletes (particularly professional ones) are under pressure to perform at consistently high levels. Over long, grueling, and injury-laden seasons some athletes have turned to drugs for assistance. Drug use has become a widespread and questionable social practice from the official culture's stance. Vignette 6.3 describes drug use among athletes.

Berkeley (University of California at Berkeley) football player Mike Mohler interviewed all players on the squad and found that 48 percent used speed and 28 percent used anabolic steroids.[42] Mohler speculated that drug usage at other big west coast schools was even more prevalent than at academically-oriented Berkeley.

Drug usage in professional sport is even more commonplace. Scott reported that Paul Lowe, a San Diego Charger running back, said: "We had to take them (anabolic steroids) at lunch time. He (the trainer) would put them on a little saucer and prescribed for us to take them and if not he would suggest there might be a fine."[43] Meggyesy (1971) noted that the St. Louis Cardinal trainer had what amounted to a drugstore in the training room.[44] The drug cabinets contained such drugs as cortisone, xylocaine, and novocain that were apparently extensively used. Bernie Parrish, former professional football player, reported that he typically ingested 70 milligrams of dexedrine before every game.[45] Further, he said he never played another college or professional game without the assistance of either dexadrine or benzedrine after his initial "trip."

Bouton said that many baseball players could not function without pep pills.[46] Oliver described the *stepping-stone* nature of drug usage when he wrote: . . . "At first they might just take them before a big game. Then it was before every game. Then they had to take them just to practice. As the players get older, they forget about how to get energy naturally and start getting it from amphetamine pills. . . ."[47]

Hoch reported that:

Ken Gray filed a $3.5 million lawsuit against the St. Louis Cardinals, their team physician, and their trainer charging he was administered "potent, illegal, and dangerous drugs . . . so that he would perform more violently." The drugs were dextroamphetamine sulfate, chlorpromazine hydrochloride, and sodium pentobarbital. Gray's suit alleges they were given to him "deceptively and without consent either expressed or implied," and as a result he sustained "injuries, nervousness, restlessness, and sleeplessness, and severe and persistent headaches, and his general health and body integrity was diminished." A similar $1.25 million medical suit was filed by defensive lineman Houston Ridge against the San Diego Chargers.[48]

The pervasiveness of drug usage is further documented in the following quotations: "It is far from excessive to conclude that the increasing use of drugs by athletes poses a significant menace to sport, one that the athletic establishment is assiduously trying to ignore."[49] And, "My experience tells me that an athlete will use any aid to improve his performance short of killing himself."[50] In 1970, nine of the first twelve medalists in the world weight lifting championships were disqualified when urine tests revealed the presence of amphetamines.

Finally, Jack Scott reported that when he was covering the 1968 Olympics, the track and field athletes were not discussing whether or not drugs should be used but which drugs were most effective

VIGNETTE 6.3

DRUG USE AMONG ATHLETES

Over the years we have read reports about athletes who have taken pep pills and burned themselves out within a short time.

Most of the cases involved professional football players who popped the "uppers" prior to games. It may have been an aging veteran who was trying to slow down the advance of time or the young recruit who was trying to improve his performance.

For let's face it: Performance is the name of the game in professional sports. It also talks big during salary negotiations.

A recent story in the Reader's Digest points up the ever-increasing use of drugs among both the professional and amateur athletes.

A case in point was the Olympic weight-lifting performance by the Russian competitor Vasily Alexeyev.

It has been hinted that the Russian weight-lifter had been using body-building steroids to improve his performance.

It was pointed out that Vasily did not appear for a precompetition medical test before the International Olympic Committee in Montreal. Some officials and competitors believed that he was out of the city having his system flushed of traces of the hormones. However, after he won the gold medal, the Russian passed his medical test.

United States hammer thrower George Frenn believed that Alexeyev was on hormones. He said the Russian had all the signs: Face blown out of proportion and he had little cholesterol globules that collect under the eyeball from too large a dose of steroids.

Frenn and other concerned athletes believe that the real danger is not only from the unfair improved performances turned in by the drug users but that one day an Olympic contestant or a football lineman might collapse during competition from being too hyped-up.

It has been reported that one track star was so "high" on pills that after a meet he practically demolished his motel room.

Among the drugs being used indiscriminately by athletes are the amphetemines, cocaine, speed, adrenalin, the tranquilizer Quaalude, anabolic steroids, to name the most commonly used.

Prolonged use of these drugs, according to medical experts, can result in medical complications ranging from cerebral hemorrhage to nutritional problems. Coming down from large doses of stimulants often leads to the use of tranquilizers, trapping an athlete into a regular merry-go-round of pill popping.

Stimulants are most widely used by participants in track meets, but it has been reported that two out of every front four offensive and defensive linemen in the NFL are on steroids.

We don't know whether the use of pep pills has filtered down to the high school level or not. No doubt it has.

Parents should be alerted to the possibility that their young athletic sons and daughters may be victimized by unscrupulous trainers and coaches who feel that winning at any price is the ultimate aim and who press their proteges into using drugs to improve their performances.

Source: *The Barnesboro Star*, May 24, 1978, p. 4B. Reprinted by permission.

---

and which drugs one "could get away with." Scott went on to say that "it is widely recognized in track and field circles that it is next to impossible to get to the top in most weight events and the decathlon without the use of these drugs since most of the top athletes are using them."[51]

Two different types of drugs are widely used in sport. The first, *restorative* drugs, are those ingested to alleviate injury, pain, nervousness, illness, and dissipation and include painkillers (aspirin, darvon), tranquilizers (valium), barbiturates, anti-inflamitants, enzymes, and muscle relaxants. These drugs are those typically found in household medicine cabinets. The second, *additive* drugs, are more controversial and questionable since they are chemical substances aimed at enhancing performance. The additive substances include amphetamines (benzedrine, dexedrine, dexamyl, methamphetamine (commonly called "speed")), and anabolic steroids. Amphetamines are central nervous system stimulants while steroids are fat-soluble organic compounds which tend to increase muscle size, change fat distribution, and produce male secondary sex characteristics (increase facial and body hair and lower voice pitch).

Both types of drugs have negative side effects in addition to the ethical problem they pose. Additive drugs, the more controversial of the two, artifically stimulate performance and have been known to produce physical and psychological dependence and damage. Scott indicates that prolonged use or excessive dosages of amphetamines can cause ulcers, cerebral hemorrhage, paronoia, cardiovascular collapse, nutritional deficiencies, aggressive behavior and irritability.[52] Anabolic steroids have been linked to prostate cancer, atrophying of the testicles, liver damage, and swelling (edema).

When examining sport deviance, however, one must tread cautiously. For example, (1) drug usage among athletes is probably not deviant from the contemporary youth's cultural values. As we said earlier, when studying deviance, it is important to ask *whose* norms—the official culture's or the youth culture's—are being broken; also, (2) an important consideration when focusing upon deviance is recognition of the fact that sociologists have been stuck on studying "nuts, sluts, and perverts"—*individual* deviants—while ignoring *collectivities* such as formal organizations and bureaucracies.[53] When we consider such machinations as Watergate, Koreagate, and similar deceit in corporate structures, we can expect such values—or lack of them—to be reflected in sport as well.

THE "FIX" OR "DUMP"

There have been occasions where the uncertain outcome of a sporting contest has been "fixed" in advance by paying off key participants in the event itself. Schecter suggested that the first "fix" in America involved a horse race in 1674.[54] This is probably the first *corroborated* fix since it would be highly improbable that some facsimile did not exist prior to that date given the long history of sport competition. Organized gambling (see Vignette 6.4) has undoubtedly been a stimulus and a response to sport deviance.

The "Black Sox" Scandal

In the World Series of 1919 the Cincinnati Reds defeated the Chicago White Sox in a controversial series. Rumors of a "fix" circulated and continued to persist until a grand jury was appointed to investigate the allegations. The jury did, indeed, find cheating and illegal tactics employed in the baseball series. Eight players were indicted for having agreed to lose the series in return for a lofty sum of money to be paid in installments (the only payment was after the Sox lost the first game, however). Gamblers had used a go-between to contact the players but the conspiracy nearly backfired when one of the Sox players, who was not in collusion, pitched and won the third game. The eight conspirators were indicted, tried, but acquitted when the confessions of three players disappeared. The "Black Sox" scandal, as it was labeled by the press and general populace alike, led to the establishment of a baseball commissioner. Judge Kenesaw Mountain Landis was named the first commissioner of baseball and declared, upon his appointment:

> It came like a flash to me, thinking of my boy, what baseball meant to him when he was young; what it means to him today. And I knew that is what baseball means to every kid in America. And then I realized that I could not refuse the responsibility and decided that if there was anything I could do to keep that game clean and honest, and to make it so that the kids of the United States never shall lose their ideals of the sport, it was a bit more than my duty to do it.[55]

Landis followed through with his promise by banning, for life, the eight White Sox players who had been implicated and involved in the 1919 "fix."

VIGNETTE 6.4
WHO IS THE TYPICAL GAMBLER?

Would you bet you know the right answer? Chances are high you might lay a bet on it if you're a man living in suburbia, reasonably well-off and well educated. Why? Because more than any other American, the affluent male suburbanite is likely to bet money, especially if he's young and a bachelor. When the Institute for Social Research of the University of Michigan conducted an "exhaustive study" of U.S. gambling for a Congressional commission in 1975, it discovered that 61 percent of all adult Americans placed some kind of money bet only with friends or co-workers, 11 percent bet with bookies, on the numbers or in unlicensed casinos, etc., and 44 percent wagered legal bets on games in various states.

People give lots of reasons for gambling their hard-earned money: to have a good time, pass the time, be challenged and make money. Bettors don't worry about losing. One stunning discovery of the survey: in states with legal lotteries and where parimutuel betting is available, there are both more illegal numbers betting and more business done with bookies than in states where these activities are illegal.

—Shirley Sloan Fader

Source: Bloomington-Normal *Pantagraph,* Jan. 16, 1977. Reprinted by permission.

The College Basketball Scandal

College basketball had a similar scandal in 1951. Point shaving and other "irregularities" began to surface. When these allegations emerged from Manhattan College in 1951, two players and three gamblers were arrested. However, more was to come. After the incidents were probed, it was eventually discovered that between 1947 and 1950, eighty-six games had been "fixed" in twenty-three cities in seventeen states by thirty-two players from seven colleges. Seven colleges were guilty of such infractions—Long Island University, New York University, Manhattan College, Kentucky, Toledo, Bradley and City College of New York.[56] Interestingly, the year following the censure Kentucky posted a 25-0 basketball season and Bradley was runner-up in the NCAA tournament.

CRIME AND THE ATHLETE

Crime is a traditional topic within the deviance literature. Until recently, athletes who ran afoul of the law seemed to escape the workings of the criminal justice system. For example, one sportswriter has quoted another as saying: "Babe Ruth could have been charged with rape on any number of his escapades."[57] Whether or not there was a conspiracy of silence to protect athletes in earlier periods is a hotly contested matter. Today, however, it *appears* that more and more athletes (although sociologists contend that the proportion of athletes getting into scrapes with the law is no greater than other segments of society) are breaking the laws, and newspapers—unlike those of former times—are devoting more coverage to these social problems.

It was Jim Bouton's iconoclastic *Ball Four* (1970) that was among the recent books to break the "conspiracy of silence" and to expose athletes (baseball players in particular) for what they were: mortal human beings with frailties. According to Youngman, athletes' "deviant behavior"—while variable—displays three patterns: (1) drugs are often involved; (2) athletes who get into repeated scrapes with the law often receive light sentences or get off altogether; and (3) charges against athletes even involve homicide.[58]

A perusal of Table 6.1 reveals the prevalence of drug-related criminal acts. Whether drug usage among athletes is more prevalent than it is among other groups (youth subcultures and deviant gangs for example) is debatable. So too is the question regarding drug arrests and convictions among athletes in comparison to other segments of American society. As we have seen, the use of drugs—both restorative and additive—is a common modus operandi among athletes in many sports. Lefkowitz concedes that the athletes may get involved in drugs because they are narcissistic individuals. He said:

> Athletes are people who are very much into their bodies—their bodies earn them their keep. . . . The drug experience is a sensual experience—it magnifies or enhances the senses for a period of time—and being involved in sports is a sensual experience. Because of this, athletes may be more prone to drug experiences.[59]

Table 6.1 also contains a list of the punishments (sentence and time served/fine paid) for a sample of athletes who have been guilty of law infractions. Take two extreme cases. Tom Payne, charged with a series of sexual offenses (rape and aggravated sodomy) is serving a life sentence (although he comes up for parole in 1983). Cesar Cedeno was charged with involuntary manslaughter and paid $100 for his behavior. The various professional leagues have similar policies concerning drugs, gambling, and associating with known criminals. However, they have not enforced them in the same way.

Athletes who have been arrested are not always convicted. Sometimes they are not even brought to trial. Leon Spinks, during his short reign as heavyweight boxing champion, was charged with reckless driving and possession of drugs. These charges were dropped shortly thereafter. Similarly, Jim Brown, former running back for the Cleveland Browns, shows four acquittals, three dropped charges, and no convictions on his record.

Some athletes—Sonny Liston (arrested for impersonating a police officer and resisting arrest in Philadelphia in 1961), Bernard King (once arrested for second degree burgulary), and Mack Herron (three different cocaine possession charges)—have had brushes with the law which did not result in convictions before they were eventually convicted. The table (6.1) does not reveal the fact that there has been a tendency for the charges to be reduced before the athlete is brought to trial. For example, Marvin Barnes was originally charged with carrying a concealed weapon, not attempting to conceal one; Bobby Lee Hunter had a murder charge reduced to manslaughter; Ron Lyle's second-degree murder charge was first-degree murder initially; and Don Murdoch was arrested for cocaine trafficking, but convicted of the lesser charge of possession.

Table 6.1 also reveals that some athletes—Cesar Cedeno, Rubin "Hurricane" Carter—have been charged with some "degree" of murder. Cedeno was charged with involuntary manslaughter in the 1974 slaying of a 19-year old woman. He spent 20 days in jail and eventually paid $100 fine. Carter was convicted of a triple murder and is currently serving a life sentence.

Crime, in general, is frequently explained in one of two ways. Some opt for the *catharsis theory*. Accordingly, aggression defuses further aggression. By venting hostilities, vengeances, and frustrations, people are less likely to commit violent acts. Consequently, athletes are less likely to commit violent crimes because sport competition provides a constructive outlet for pent-up frustration, hostility, and aggression.

Table 6.1
A Sample of Athletes' Crimes and Punishments

Name, sport	Charge(s), year	Sentence	Time served/fine paid
Marvin Barnes, basketball	Assault, 1974	1 year suspended, 3 years probation	
	Attempting to conceal weapon, 1976	2 years probation	5 months
	Violation of probation, 1976	1 year	21 months
Gates Brown, baseball	Breaking and entering, 1958	5 years	Since 1967
Rubin Carter, boxing	3 counts, first-degree murder, 1966	Life	
Cesar Cedeno, baseball	Involuntary manslaughter, 1974	$100 fine	$100
Orlando Cepeda, baseball	Cocaine smuggling and possession, 1975	Concurrent 5-year terms, $10,000	Since June 1978
Randy Crowder, football	Cocaine: 2 counts sale and delivery, 2 counts possession, 1 count conspiracy to sell, 1977	1 year, 5 years probation (3 concurrent sentences)	1 year
Joe Gilliam, football	Marijuana possession, 1976	30 days suspended, 2 years probation	
	Carrying concealed weapon, 1976	15 days suspended, $50 fine	$50
Dick Gordon, football	Failure to file tax returns, 1972	15 days, $5,000 fine	
Mack Herron, football	Marijuana possession, 1973 (Canada)	$1,000 fine	Not paid
	Cocaine possession, 1978	5 years, (1 year suspended)	Since May 1978
	Improper use of altered car title, 1978	Concurrent	
Bobby Lee Hunter, boxing	Manslaughter, 1966	18 years	6 years
	Aggravated assault and battery, 1977	3 years	Since March 1978
Shelby Jordan, football	Cocaine possession for resale, 1975	2 years	13 months
Bernard King, basketball	Marijuana possession, 1977	60 days suspended, $50 fine	$50
	Resisting arrest, 1977	60 days suspended, $50 fine	$50
Ron LeFlore, baseball	Robbery, 1965	2-5 years	2 years
	Armed robbery, 1970	5-15 years	38 months
Sonny Liston, boxing	2 counts, first-degree robbery; 2 counts, larceny from a person, 1950	5 years (concurrent)	2 years
	Assaulting a police officer, 1956	9 months	9 months

Athlete, sport	Crime	Sentence	Served
Joe Don Looney, football	Assault, 1964	1 year probation, $150 fine	$150
Rommie Loudd, football	Cocaine delivery, 1975 Cocaine delivery, 1976	14 years 2 years (concurrent)	3 years
Ron Lyle, boxing	Second-degree murder, 1962	15-25 years	7½ years
Don Murdoch, hockey	Cocaine possession, 1977	$400 fine	$400
Tom Payne, basketball	Rape, 1972 (Atlanta) Rape, 1971 (Louisville) Rape, 1972 (Marietta, Ga.) Aggravated sodomy, 1972 Detaining female against will, 1972	2 years Life 10 years 5 years (concurrent) 5 years (concurrent)	Since September 1977
Don Reese, football	Cocaine: 2 counts sale and delivery, 2 counts possession, 1 count conspiracy to sell, 1977	1 year, 5 years probation (3 concurrent sentences)	1 year
Lance Rentzel, football	Indecent exposure, 1970 Marijuana possession, 1972	5 years probation 90 days, $2,000, 3 years probation	90 days
Jim Rivera, baseball	Attempted rape, 1950	Court martial, 5 years	1 year
Elmore Stephens, football	Kidnapping, reckless homicide, 1975	20 years, 2 years (concurrent)	Since February 1976
Bill Tilden, tennis	Contributing to delinquency of minor, 1949	2 years (1 for probation violation)	18 months
Warren Wells, football	Attempted rape, 1969 Probation violation, 1971	3 years probation 1 year, 3 years probation	5 months
Norm Van Lier, basketball	Obstructing a police officer, 1972	1 year probation, $500 fine	$500
Cleveland Williams, boxing	Aggravated assault, 1964	30 days, $50 fine	30 days, $50

Source: Randy Youngman, "Crime and the Athlete," *Chicago Tribune* (October 22, 1978), p. 2. Reprinted, courtesy of the *Chicago Tribune*.

Other social scientists *(social learning theorists)* disagree with the cartharsis explanation. To them, if violence is rewarded (positively reinforced) it may continue to be manifest outside the initial setting in which it was reinforced. In short, when athletes are conditioned to behave a certain way on the field (and are rewarded for this behavior), they may be more prone to repeat this behavior off the field.

In summary, no one theoretical yardstick can adequately explain why people in general and athletes in particular deviate from societal norms. But social scientists continue to formulate theories to explain such behaviors. It may be that when athletes are no longer lionized we will no longer consider their behavior—deviant and otherwise—any more unique than that of those engaged in nonathletic pursuits.

SUMMARY

In this chapter we have considered *sport* and *social deviance.* The goal of socialization is to produce conforming individuals, individuals who abide by society's rules or norms. However, in any society, in any realm, there are persons who deviate from the expected guidelines. *Deviance* is thinking, acting, and feeling contrary to the standards of conduct or social expectations of a given group or society. It is rule-breaking behavior. *Deviants* are individuals who engage in rule-breaking behavior. Deviance in various forms pervades sport at all levels.

A theory of social deviance was advanced for its heuristic nature in explaining deviance in sport. According to this conceptual framework, our society prescribes for all persons norms of success and it also prescribes the means by which success can be achieved. However, not all individuals, groups, or organizations subscribe to the accepted means and/or goals. Therefore, in addition to *conformists,* there are also *innovators, ritualists, retreatists,* and *rebels* who alter in some fashion the cultural goals and/or the cultural means for achieving success.

We argue that innovation is a pervasive form of deviance in sport. It facilitates understanding the recurring violations that continue to exist in amateur and professional sport. In this context three *structural* roots of social deviance were considered and illustrated: (1) incompatible goal orientations, (2) inconsistency between values/norms and built-in constraints, and (3) inconsistencies between the expectation of different roles.

Special attention was paid to the use of *drugs* in sport. Of two types of drugs used—*restorative* and *additive*—it is the latter that appear to be more controversial and of questionable longterm value.

Throughout the chapter we illustrated deviance in sport by drawing upon both historical and contemporary incidents which, in light of the values advanced in the dominant American sport creed, exhibited a somewhat paradoxical nature.

Finally, we called attention to the fact that when studying deviance it is important to ask *whose* norms are being broken. This is important since drug usage in sport, to take one example, is deviant from the point of view of mainstream culture but probably not deviant from the point of view of youth.

IMPORTANT CONCEPTS DISCUSSED IN THIS CHAPTER

Deviance
Deviants
Role Strain
Cheating
Conformity
Innovation
Ritualism

Retreatism
Rebellion
Relative Deprivation
Restorative Drugs
Additive Drugs
"Fix" or "Dump"

ENDNOTES

[1] Marie Hart, "Women Sit in the Back of the Bus," *Psychology Today* 5 (1971), pp. 64-66.

[2] Wilbert M. Leonard, II, "A Sociological View of International and Olympic Sports," *Journal of Sport Behavior* (forthcoming).

[3] *Vidette*, Illinois State University (March 12, 1978), p. 8.

[4] Leonard, "A Sociological View of International and Olympic Sports."

[5] Fred Rothenberg, "Recruiting" (Bloomington-Normal, Ill.: Pantagraph), p. 84.

[6] Eldon Snyder and Elmer Spreitzer, *Social Aspects of Sport* (Englewood Cliffs, N.J.: Prentice-Hall, 1978).

[7] Leonard, "A Sociological View of International and Olympic Sports."

[8] Richard Woodley, "How to Win the Soap Box Derby: in Which Craftsmanship Abets the Passion for Success to Produce a Tale of Moral Confusion," *Harper's Magazine* (August, 1974), pp. 62-69.

[9] Howard L. Nixon, II, *Sport and Social Organization* (Indianapolis: Bobbs-Merrill, 1976).

[10] Min S. Yee and Donald K. Wright, *The Sports Book* (New York: Holt, Rinehart, and Winston, 1975).

[11] Betty Spears and Richard A. Swanson, *History of Sport and Physical Activity in the United States* (Dubuque, Iowa: Wm. C. Brown, 1978).

[12] Ibid.

[13] Yee and Wright, *The Sports Book.*

[14] Ralph Sabock, *The Coach* (Philadelphia: W. B. Saunders, 1973), p. 95.

[15] Robert K. Merton, "Social Structure and Anomie," *American Sociological Review* 3 (October, 1938), pp. 672-682.

[16] Eldon E. Snyder, "Athletic Dressing Room Slogans as Folklore: A Means of Socialization," *International Review of Sport Sociology* 7 (1972), pp. 89-102.

[17] Nixon, *Sport and Social Organization*, p. 23.

[18] Howard J. Savage, *American College Athletics* (New York: The Carnegie Foundation, 1929).

[19] David Wolf, *Foul!* (New York: Holt, Rinehart, and Winston, 1972).

[20] Ibid., p. 91.

[21] Larry Klein, "The NCAA Enforcement Sham," *Sport* (June, 1977), pp. 42-48. Used with permission.

[22] The AIAW (Association for Intercollegiate Athletics for Women), founded in 1972, is a women's counterpart of the NCAA. Their regulations regarding financial aid, recruiting, and transfers differ from those of the men's programs.

[23] Larry Klein, "The NCAA Enforcement Sham," pp. 42-48.

[24] Kenneth Denlinger and Leonard Shapiro, *Athletes for Sale* (New York: Thomas Y. Crowell, 1975), p. 42.

[25] James A. Michener, *Sports in America* (New York: Random House, 1976); Eldon E. Snyder and Elmer Spreitzer, *Social Aspects of Sport* (Englewood Cliffs, N.J.: Prentice-Hall, 1978); Nixon, *Sport and Social Organization;* Eitzen and Sage, *Sociology of American Sport.*

[26] Klein, "The NCAA Enforcement Sham," p. 43.

[27] Ibid.

[28] Ibid, p. 44.

[29]There are 3,130 colleges/universities and branch campuses in the United States. Of these, 561 (18%) are public four-year colleges, 1,395 (44%) are private four-year colleges, 925 (30%) are public two-year colleges and 249 (8%) are private two-year colleges. Relatively few schools have self-supporting sport programs. The schools with successful football programs have the best potential for generating revenues (although at some schools basketball and ice hockey have also generated revenues). A survey by the Associate Press (AP) discovered that about fifteen teams since 1945 have been consistently able to remain at the top. These institutions include Notre Dame, Oklahoma, Texas, Ohio State, Michigan, Alabama (Tuscaloosa), Tennessee, California (Los Angeles), University of Southern California, Louisiana State, Penn State, Mississippi, Nebraska (Lincoln), Michigan State, and Arkansas. See D. Crase, "The Inner Circles of Intercollegiate Football," *Sport Sociology Bulletin* 1 (1972), pp. 7-11.

[30]Steve Smith, "Tarkanian Denounces NCAA Before House Committee," *The Chronicle of Higher Education* (June 19, 1978), p. 5.

[31]Jack Scott, *Bill Walton—On The Road With the Portland Trail Blazers* (New York: Thomas Y. Crowell, 1978), Ron Rapoport, *Chicago Sun Times.*

[32]Ibid.

[33]Ray Kennedy, "A Case in Point," *Sports Illustrated* 40 (June 10, 1974), pp. 87-100; June 17, 1974, pp. 24-30.

[34]Smith, "Tarkanian Denounces NCAA Before House Committee."

[35]George Leonard, *The Ultimate Athlete* (New York: Avon Books, 1975).

[36]William O. Johnson, "From Here to 2000," *Sports Illustrated* (December 23, 1974), pp. 78-83.

[37]Terry Orlick and Cal Botterill, *Every Kid Can Win* (Chicago, Ill.: Nelson Hall, 1975), p. 7.

[38]Gary Shaw, *Meat on the Hoof* (New York: St. Martin's Press, 1972), p. 166.

[39]Nixon, *Sport and Social Organization*, pp. 20-21.

[40]Rudolph Brasch, *How Did Sports Begin?* (New York: David McKay, 1970), p. 7.

[41]Jim Murray, syndicated columnist (March 10, 1972).

[42]Paul Hoch, *Rip Off: The Big Game* (Garden City, N.Y.: Anchor Books, 1972), p. 124.

[43]Jack Scott, *The Athletic Revolution* (New York: The Free Press, 1971), pp. 144-145.

[44]Dave Meggyesy, *Out of Their League* (Berkeley: Ramparts Press, 1971).

[45]Bernie Parrish, *They Call It a Game* (New York: The Dial Press, 1971).

[46]Jim Bouton, *Ball Four* (New York: World, 1970).

[47]Chip Oliver, *High For the Game* (New York: William Morrow, 1971), pp. 44, 65.

[48]Hoch, *Rip Off: The Big Game*, p. 123.

[49]Bil Gilbert, "Three Part Series on Drugs in Sports" (July 7, 1969), p. 30.

[50]Bil Gilbert, "Three Part Series on Drugs in Sports" (June 23, 1969), p. 70.

[51]Scott, *The Athletic Revolution*, p. 150.

[52]Ibid.

[53]Alexander Liazos, "The Poverty of the Sociology of Deviance: Nuts, Sluts, and Perverts," *Social Problems* 20 (Summer, 1972), pp. 103-120.

[54]Leonard Schecter, *The Jocks* (Indianapolis: Bobbs Merrill, 1969).

[55]H. S. Fullerton, "Baseball—The Business and the Sport," *American Review of Reviews* 63 (April, 1921), p. 420; Betty Spears and Richard A. Swanson, *History of Sport and Physical Activity in the United States* (Dubuque, Iowa: Wm. C. Brown, 1978), pp. 194-196.

[56]Yee and Wright, *The Sports Book*, pp. 102-103.

[57]Randy Youngman, "Crime and the Athlete," *Chicago Tribune* (October 22-25, 1978). Used with permission.

[58]Ibid.

[59]Ibid.

7
Sport and Social Stratification

INTRODUCTION

Social stratification is the hierarchal arrangement of social groups (such as race and ethnic groups) or a society into strata (social classes) that are unequal in power, privilege, prestige, and wealth. Social stratification is a euphemism for *social inequality*. Of the myriad explanatory sociological variables, it is not too much an exaggeration to say that social class is probably the major one. The reason is simply that so many attitudinal and behavioral dimensions of social life are correlated with it. On this matter Berger wrote:

> A sociologist worth his salt, if given two basic indices of class such as income and occupation, can make a long list of predictions about the individual in question even if no further information has been given. Like all sociological predictions, these will be statistical in character. That is, they will be probability statements and will have a margin of error. . . . Given these two items of information about a particular individual, the sociologist will be able to make intelligent guesses about the part of town in which the individual lives, as well as about the size and style of his house. He will also be able to give a general description of the interior decorating of the house and make a guess about the types of pictures on the wall and books or magazines likely to be found on the shelves of the living room. Moreover, he will be able to guess what kind of music the individual in question likes to listen to, and whether he does so at concerts, on a phonograph, or on the radio. . . . He can predict which voluntary associations the individual has joined and where he has church membership. He can estimate the individual's vocabulary, lay down some rough rules for his syntax and other uses of language. He can guess the individual's political affiliation and his views on a number of public issues. He can predict the number of children sired by his subject and also whether the latter has sexual relations with his wife with the lights turned on or off. He will be able to make some statements about the liklihood that his subject will come down with a number of diseases, physical as well as mental. . . . He will be able to place the man on an actuary's table of life expectancies. Finally, if the sociologist should decide to verify all these guesses and ask the individual in question for an interview, he can estimate the chance that the interview will be refused.[1]

To Berger's list of predictions we can add two others—we can predict persons' preferences for spectator or participation sports and the particular types of spectator and participation sports they will probably enjoy. All these statements serve to underscore the manner in which one's socioeconomic status conditions one's life style.

It is the consequential nature of social class that has such importance in sport. For example, the type of *leisure*[2] activity in which one engages is very much conditioned by one's social class moorings. Historically (see chapter 2) two patterns of sport interest have predominated:[3] (1) *elite sports* such as riding to the hounds, polo, boar hunting, falconry, fencing, tennis, golf, and cricket were reserved for the upper crust who had the financial wherewithal and time available; and (2) *folk sports* such as footracing, fisticuffs, wrestling, and eye gouging, were participated in by the rank and file. The explanation for the elite/folk dichotomy merely reflects the economic and practical aspects associated with sport participation.

SPORT STRATIFICATION

According to Tumin's analysis of social stratification systems, five characteristics can be identified:[4] (1) *social,* (2) *ancient,* (3) *ubiquitous,* (4) *diverse,* and (5) *consequential.* We will use these features of social stratification to organize the subsequent discussion.

Sport Stratification Is Social

The adjective "social" before stratification signifies the root of social inequality. Social stratification cannot be explained by biological, psychological, or physiological inequalities per se among people. While these are sometimes undoubtedly important, they are not sufficient to explain social inequality. *Why then does social stratification exist?* Two sociological interpretations have been forwarded: (1) *functional* and (2) *conflict* explanations.

A Functional Explanation

In a classic *functional* interpretation of social stratification, Davis and Moore stipulated that in societies with a complex division of labor, stratification is necessary because certain roles must be performed and society must encourage and motivate members to perform these roles.[5] Accordingly, all social roles are not equally important to a society (the surgeon role is more important than that of the orderly, and the quarterback role is more important than that of an interior lineman). Society ensures that these vitally important roles will be performed by differentially rewarding their occupants. The differential rewards may be monetary in nature and/or have prestige and power differentials as well. In general, functionalists argue that those positions which are most important to a society and those which require the greatest talent and training will receive the most lucrative rewards.

Take football positions for example. It is widely held that certain positions are more important than others. According to the functionalist explanation, occupants will be remunerated in terms of the position's importance. Football, more than any other sport, appears to pay by position. The average salary of several positions in 1978 was as follows:[6]

Quarterbacks	$89,354
Running Backs	60,414
Defensive Linemen	59,644
Receivers	53,760
Offensive Linemen	52,250
Linebackers	50,416
Defensive Backs	47,403
Kickers	41,506

A Conflict Explanation

According to *conflict* theorists, social stratification exists because inequalities in power, privilege, prestige, and wealth pervade societies.[7] So long as private property exists, there will be social inequality since those in advantageous positions will guard their positions and fight any change in the status quo that would be contrary to their vested interests. When workers become conscious of their exploitation by the elite, conflict between social classes becomes inevitable. Recent conflicts between union-like players' associations (the proletariat) and team owners (the bourgeoisie) have led to boycotts and strikes (the 1972 baseball players' strike; the 1974 football players' strike; and the 1978 and '79 umpires's walkout).

Consider the case of professional baseball. From the late 1890s to the middle 1940s, blacks were barred from participating in professional baseball although they did have their own leagues.[8] Was this due to their "inferior" physical/motor skills or their "weak" biological/physiological make-up? These possible explanations are very quickly dismissed when we closely examine their performances since Jackie Robinson, the first black in professional baseball,[9] broke the "color line" in ascending from the Montreal minor league club to the Brooklyn Dodgers in 1947.

The accounts in Table 7.1 should put to rest any thought of black biological inferiority in baseball. Prohibition of blacks in pro sports was essentially the result of a *racist ideology* on the part of the larger white society in general and professional baseball executives in particular.

In December, 1867, two and one-half years after the Civil War, the National Association of Baseball Players, the executive body, met in Philadelphia to decide what to do with blacks. This organization unanimously called for exclusion "of any club which may be composed of one or more colored persons." According to Peterson, simple *prejudice* brought baseball's first color line.[10] Although the Association's members were all Northerners, most shared with Southerners the belief that the Negro was inferior and not fit company for white gentlemen.

Obviously, in light of blacks' contemporary dominance in sport (baseball, basketball, football, and boxing), physical deficiency could not be the reason for denying them participation roles. *Time* magazine reported:

Blacks have come to dominate major U.S. sports as no other minority group ever has. . . . Nearly 65% of National Basketball Association players are black. . . . In the National Football League, 42% of the players are black. Twenty of the 44 first-line offensive and defensive players in this year's Super Bowl game were black. Nineteen percent of baseball

Table 7.1
Some Observations on Blacks' Sport Performances

- Blacks have led the National League (NL) in slugging for the past 25 consecutive years. (Blacks entered the majors in 1947.)
- Blacks have won 16 of the past MVP awards in the NL (for the past 28 years); 5 in the American League (AL).
- Blacks led in home runs 16 times (of the past 30 years) in the NL; 9 in the AL.
- Blacks have led in batting average 17 times (of the past 30 years) in the NL; 6 in the AL.
- In the past five years, four black players (Willie Mays, Hank Aaron, Roberto Clemente, and Lou Brock) have reached the 3,000 hit mark. Before this, only two players (Stan Musial and Paul Waner) reached this mark in the previous 40 years.
- No white player has led in stolen bases in either league in the past 20 years.
- In the past 19 years, only two white players, Johnny Bench, and Mike Schmidt, have led the NL in home runs.
- In the entire history of major league baseball, only three men have hit for 6,000 or more total bases. Two of them—Hank Aaron and Willie Mays—are black.
- Three of the four top home run hitters of all time are black. The ranking is: Hank Aaron (755), Babe Ruth (714), Willie Mays (660), and Frank Robinson (586).
- Another black star, Lou Brock, became the first man to steal 750-plus bases since Ty Cobb retired in 1928. No white player who started playing baseball after 1919 is among the lifetime leaders in stolen bases (350 or more); five black players joined that list in the past five years.
- The statistics clearly show that the black hitter has produced more hits, more home runs, more doubles, more triples, and more stolen bases than the average white batter.
- Black pitchers have a lower earned-run average (ERA) than whites. Black pitchers also lead in strikeouts, less walks, and less hits per inning.
- Blacks have led in runs batted in (RBI's) 16 of the past 30 years in the NL; 8 in the AL.
- Blacks have received rookie of the year awards 12 of the past 30 years in the NL; 5 in the AL.
- Blacks have been NBA (National Basketball Association) scoring leaders 16 of the past 30 years.
- Blacks have won the Podoloff Cup (MVP award named after Maurice Podoloff, former NBA league commissioner) 18 of the past 23 years.
- Blacks have won the NBA rookie of the year awards 17 of the past 25 years.
- Blacks have won the ABA rookie of the year awards 8 of the 9 years between 1968 and 1976.
- Blacks have won the NBA rookie of the year awards 6 of the 9 years between 1968 and 1976.
- Blacks have won the Bert Bell Memorial Trophy (named after former NFL—National Football League—commissioner and awarded to the outstanding rookie) 12 times since 1964.
- Blacks have won the George Halas Trophy (named after former football coach George Halas and awarded to the outstanding defensive player in pro football) 7 times since 1966.
- Blacks have won the Jim Thorpe Trophy (named after the former athletic great and awarded to the most valuable player—MVP—NFL player) 7 times since 1958.
- Blacks are abundantly represented among the all time pro football players in pass receiving, scoring, and rushing.
- Since Joe Louis won the heavyweight boxing championship (over 175 pounds) from J. J. Braddock in 1937 only two whites—Rocky Marciano (1952-1956) and Ingemar Johansson (1959-1960) have been ring leaders.
- In the other boxing divisions (light leavyweight—not over 175 pounds; middle weight—not over 160 pounds; welterweight—not over 147 pounds; light weight—not over 135 pounds, feather weight—not over 126 pounds; bantam weight—not over 118 pounds; and fly weight—not over 112 pounds) blacks and Latin Americans have been well represented.

Sources: Yee, Min S., and Donald K. Wright, *The Sports Book* (New York: Holt, Rinehart and Winston, 1975); *The World Almanac* (1979); and various mass media publications.

major leaguers are black. The National League's Most Valuable Player award has been won by blacks 16 times in the past 28 seasons. The growing dominance in sports is evident in college athletics too. During the recent NCAA play-offs, for example, champion Marquette and contenders Michigan and the University of Nevada at Las Vegas each had only one white in their starting lineups. In NCAA football most of 1976's top-ranked teams were loaded with black stars—in numbers far out of proportion to the percentage of black students on campus. Of 30 medals won by American track and field athletes in the Montreal Olympic Games, 24 were garnered by black athletes. Blacks won all the U.S. medals in boxing. Most of the records in major sports—rushing, slugging, and scoring marks once held by such legendary figures as Grange, Ruth and Pettit—have been bested by Tony Dorsett, Henry Aaron, and Wilt Chamberlain.[11]

Instead, the historical reasons for such inequality stemmed from *social* sources. The unequal opportunity for blacks arose from the fact that whites have been in positions of power and influence, and blacks' initial sport ban reflected this sociopolitical fact. In short, *prejudice* and *discrimination* in the form of racism appear to have been the real culprits. In chapter 9 we will consider some of the social reasons why *females* have appeared on the sport scene only in recent years.

Sport Stratification Is Ancient

Social inequality in sport participation and spectatorship has existed from the dawn of recorded history and probably existed even before written records were kept. The ancient Olympic Games commenced (formally, circa 776 B.C.) in 1453 B.C. Certain social groups were categorically denied the privilege of taking part or even spectating. Females were not permitted to participate and formed their own games, the Herae Games, in honor of Zeus's wife, Hera. Similarly, only Greek citizens were permitted to take part. Slaves, of which there were many in the Greek city states, were also prohibited from participating.

While our knowledge regarding ancient sport participation and spectatorship is sketchy, we do know that sporting feats were sufficiently prominent during the Roman Empire that people worked every other day and that the Circus Maximus stadium in Rome had a seating capacity of 260,000.[12] Jousts and other equestrian events were popular during the Middle Ages (11th and 12th centuries) but between the 15th and 18th centuries there was relatively little recreation time and this undoubtedly stifled participation, particularly among the rank-and-file workers.

The privilege of participating in sport has, historically, varied by social class. During the Middle Ages only the aristocrats and nobles were "free" to engage in sport activities. Similarly, during the Victorian Era (1837-1901) sport became a mainstay of "polite" English society. It was incorporated into the elite "public schools" and sport-regulating agencies were developed by the graduates of such prestigious schools as Oxford and Cambridge. In the United States the exclusive New York Athletic Club (see p. 27) was composed of such occupational elites as bankers, lawyers, stock brokers, corporation officers, and business owners. Likewise, in Canada, sporting clubs were composed of and regulated by the aristocracy (Loy, McPherson, and Kenyon, 1978, pp. 341, 343).

Three observations regarding the historical nature of sport stratification are notable: (1) The status of athletes has varied. For example, in ancient Greece and Rome and in the Eastern European countries and in America today the athlete was and is held in high esteem. In contrast, in the post Greco-Roman period and in China during the early part of this century athletes had low social status. (2) Often the elites who initiated a sport discarded it when it was "taken up" by the masses. This occurred during the Middle Ages. (3) Competition between classes and ethnic groups has been discouraged or prohibited until recently. In England the working class soccer clubs did not compete against higher class opponents until the 1880s. Similarly, it wasn't until the 1970s that the different ethnic groups in South Africa engaged in competition with each other (Loy, McPherson, and Kenyon 1978).

Sport Stratification Is Ubiquitous

"Ubiquity," an unfamiliar term, means existing everywhere. It refers to something—in this case sport stratification—that is omnipresent or that is found everywhere. One way in which we can think of the universality of sport is to consider it in an international perspective.

As in so many facets of cross-cultural comparisons, nations of the world exhibit variability in their degree of sport emphasis. Table 7.2 provides a rough ordering of sixteen selected countries in terms of the degree of governmental intervention and guidance (circa 1970). One of Michener's purposes in presenting this figure was to dispel the notion that the United States' sportsmania surpasses that in other countries. He denied this myth and asserted that its emphasis was "average." Alastair Reid, a Scotsman, agreed with this assessment when he said:

> I have never felt that in the United States there is the same total immersion on the part of sport fans as in other countries—they are more critics than followers. In Europe or South America, crucial games so dominate the public attention as to affect everybody; but only on extreme occasions like the World Series does anything like that universal goggling occur in the United States. It may be because sport is more specialized, or it may be because the United States does not lock horns with other countries as frequently as do the European national teams.[13]

Table 7.2
Sport Emphasis in Sixteen Countries in 1970

Excessive	Above Average	Average	Below Average
E. Germany	Japan	Great Britain	Mexico
U.S.S.R.	Australia	U.S.	Ireland
S. Africa	Italy	Belgium	Sweden
Brazil	Hungary	Spain	India

Source: James A. Michener, *Sports in America* (New York, N.Y.: Random House, 1976), p. 375. Reprinted by permission.

In light of the collective violence and fanaticism characteristic of many sporting events (see chapter 13), we would tend to agree with the thrust of Michener's and Reid's observations. Just the same, there is growing evidence that American sports and fans' worshipping of sports are becoming increasingly aggressive and violent.

Stratification in sport and leisure is an ever-present social/cultural phenomenon. Observers have noted that sport is like fashion: its influence is propagated downward. School sports, for example, began in England and were anything but democratic. The schools were explicitly designated to educate children of genteel upper class families and were private and exclusive in nature.

Social stratification is evident both *between* and *within* sports. Some sports are classified as "major" (baseball, basketball, football) while others are considered "minor" (lacrosse, gymnastics, crew) (see Vignette 7.1). Even within a given sport there are status distinctions (judo has its hierarchy of "belts," boxing is stratified into prestige levels based upon weight classifications, and, in football, offensive backs are generally more "visible" than linemen.[14] Some athletic contests award recognition and symbolic rewards[15] in rank order of the participants' finish (gold, silver, bronze medals in Olympic competition; blue, red, and white ribbons).

Though we have so far confined our consideration of sport stratification to the United States, even in the purported "classless" Soviet sport system, stratification is manifest. Athletes in the U.S.S.R. are classified into echelons with the highest being "Honored Master of Sport." Standards of performance have been established in numerous sporting events, and those that meet these standards are differentially rewarded, both materially and nonmaterially (see Vignette 7.2).

Sport Stratification Is Diverse

Stratification takes three principal forms: (1) *class,* (2) *estate,* and (3) *caste.* In the United States the most familiar form is *class,* a system of social inequality based upon social, economic and political factors. *Caste,* in contradistinction, is a rigid system of differential privilege that is premised on traditional beliefs, particularly religion. In India, the Hindu religion has traditionally operated to solidify one's social position in terms of birth, while the South African *apartheid* (racial segregation) policy is founded on a racial basis. The third genre is that of *estate,* a legally codified feudal system found in Medieval Europe and based on a relationship to land. There were three estates: (1) the nobility, (2) the clergy, and (3) the peasantry. These social positions were largely ascribed.

In class-based societies, one's position or lot in life is said to be *achieved.* The Horatio Alger "rags to riches" stories fit nicely into this ideology. Additionally, such social forms are said to encourage upward social mobility. *Mobility* refers to movement across (*horizontal mobility*) or up or down (*vertical mobility*) the social class ladder. Additionally, vertical mobility may be assessed *intragenerationally* (comparing jobs and/or salaries within—"intra"—one's own lifetime) or *intergenerationally* (comparing jobs and/or salaries between—"inter"—father/mother and son/daughter).

Sorokin colorfully described upward mobility as "social climbing" and downward mobility as "social sinking."[16] Social descent or *downward mobility* is richly illustrated in the following case studies:

> In 1977 Joe Caldwell, a 10-year NBA and ABA veteran who once earned $210,000 a season, sat alone and destitute in his furnitureless apartment in Greensboro, N.C. His wife and children had left him, and the former All-Star forward spent much of his time watching films of his biggest plays. A movie projector was one of the few items not seized by his creditors.[17]

> In 1972 Duane Thomas led the Dallas Cowboys to victory in the Super Bowl. Five years later, almost to the day, the erstwhile $100,000-a-year running back and his pregnant wife appeared in a Dallas Court to file a voluntary bankruptcy petition, stating their assets at $4.66 and their debts at $26,979. "It was just one of those things that happen," said Thomas, who is now out of football.[18]

VIGNETTE 7.1

Claims Football Getting More than it Should

By Glen Latimer
Assistant Soccer Coach

"All animals are equal—but some animals are more equal than others."

The above quotation from George Orwell's ANIMAL FARM can be applied to Illinois State athletic programs.

Which sport is "more equal" than others? Which has the most expenses in terms of training equipment, players' personal equipment and uniforms? Which has the most coaches? Which has the highest costs for travelling and meals? Which receives the most scholarships?

Did you guess? Well done!

Football is part of the traditional American way of life. As a "foreigner," I do not share this tradition through heritage. However, I enjoy watching football on T.V. and have seen ISU play. (I thought the Marching Band was excellent!) What does mystify me is why so much money is poured into one sport, when it does not pay for itself. Gate receipts plus advertising do not equal expenditure.

You can work out your own figures and try to work out the cost of just one football player for one season. Scholarship, uniforms, training, facilities and equipment, travel, meals, coaches, tape, hospitalization, etc.

All animals are equal but football players are more equal than others. Why? Why should they receive the lion's share in preference to any other sport or in preference to the Women's Athletics program? Are they special by tradition? Or because of the entertainment they provide? Irrespective of results, one could still make a case for deficit spending on this one sport if people felt they derived pleasure, entertainment, a social occasion, tradition or whatever from the games.

It is a fact of life, though, that attitudes change when times are hard. I am reliably informed that this is not ISU's most successful season. "They are building

for the future", ... "we are a young team", ... "we need to get our offense and defense to play well together", ... "the big plays really hurt us", (taken from the Coach's Manual of Excuses to be Given to the Press).

I find it strange to see football continuing to take the lion's share of available funds, when on a cost-benefit analysis using whatever variables you care to employ, it does not warrant it!

Each year in Men's Athletics there are 120 full-ride scholarships available (worth $2,226 per person) to all sports. Football has 73 of these. The next highest sport is basketball which receives 15. You do not need a Ph.D. in mathematics to see the difference! Basketball operates nearly on a balanced budget and has a successful schedule.

Without being at all facetious, what would happen to ISU football if we only allocated 30 full-rides and redistributed the other 43 full-ride scholarships to other sports like track and field, cross country, golf, tennis, wrestling, swimming, baseball, soccer, etc. I venture to suggest that the football results would approximate to this season's results. However, the improvements in the other sports would be very noticeable.

For example, with eleven free rides in soccer it would be possible to produce a team of truly "national" standing within two years. No doubt coaches in other "minority" sports could make similar claims. (I use the term "minority" only because that is how the allocation of funds treats them.) But if the regulations could be changed and we could give 200 football scholarships, do you think our football program would be equal to the top college teams nationally?

Of course, what I am leading to involves a "mini-revolution"—especially in thinking. Why not spend the money at present going to football on the "minority" sports and make them "major" sports here at ISU? Then students would be able to see high-class national level competition and ISU could quickly gain a national reputation for producing top sportsmen and sportswomen in a variety of sports.

It really is a feasible idea but (there's always a "but," isn't there?) it would mean a big reduction in the football program, or no football at all here! (Okay, cut out the wails of anguish!)

Is that thought really too awful to contemplate? Or is it just an idea that would take a little bit of getting used to?

It could be the choice between mediocrity and high-class performance and entertainment.

Source: *Daily Vidette*, Illinois State University, October 12, 1978, p. 20. Reprinted by permission.

When he played for the Cowboys, Craig Morton was known as the Prince of Greenville Avenue, a Dallas disco area. He lived from day to day, spent freely—and went bankrupt. Now that Morton is happily remarried and resettled in Denver where he quarterbacks the Broncos, friends say he has gotten a grip on life—but he also has debts. Ten days before the 1978 Super Bowl he was tackled by a $34,635 Federal income tax lien and a $38,000 debt to a New York bank.[19]

VIGNETTE 7.2
ATHLETES' REWARDS IN COMMUNISTIC COUNTRIES

Confidential intelligence reports explain how the athletes from the communist bloc made such a spectacular showing at the recent Olympics.

The documents claim that communist countries have been force-training athletes for the Olympics since at least 1960. The star performers not only are subsidized but are pampered with luxuries in flagrant violation of Olympic rules, the documents allege.

This supports the frequent charge that communist governments develop professional athletes to compete against amateurs. One intelligence report quotes a past defector from the Cuban gymnastics team, Zulema Bregado Gutierrez, as stating: "All the athletes are professionals since athletics is their main employment."

She explained that Cuban athletes draw no salary but "receive other privileges which are tantamount to salary." She cited "free room and board and clothing." They get "much better food," and clothing "of the best materials available in Cuba," she said. These special advantages, she told U.S. intelligence men, "are not available to the rest of the population."

Another Cuban defector, Hector Rodriguez Cordoso, told about being sent to Russia to study physical education. Summarizes an intelligence report:

"For a classless society, Rodriguez said, Soviet athletes not only enjoy special class privileges, but they are actually segregated into categories according to their performance in competition.

"Most Soviet athletes who have won medals in competition of world significance, such as the Olympic Games, rank as first class athletes and receive a monthly stipend of 400 rubles in addition to other privileges such as automobiles, housing and the opportunity to travel abroad . . . .

"For every new world record a Soviet athlete sets," continues the intelligence report, "he receives a bonus of 1,000 rubles and other benefits." The document adds that lesser athletes also "receive considerable recognition, monetary and otherwise, above and beyond what an ordinary worker would receive in the Soviet Union."

According to the document, "Rodriguez was emphatic in stating that the Soviet athletes with whom he came in contact made no secret of the fact that their efforts to excel were spurred primarily by the promise of material gain."

For communist athletes, the political indoctrination is as intensive as the physical training. The Cuban gymnast, Zulema Bregado, reported that "at least 30 minutes of political indoctrination is mandatory before every daily training session." Thereafter, she was required to train for four hours "every day of the week except Sunday, year round."

The athletes are carefully coached on how to react at the Olympics. States an intelligence document: "The Cubans make a special effort to orient their athletes so that once they come in contact with foreigners, they have a preconceived party line which they are to use.

"Every effort made by the members of the team, individually and collectively, is oriented to put the communist regime of Cuba under the most favorable light. For this reason, the Cuban athletes are considered one of the best means of conveying that message."

Some of these confidential documents date back to the 1960s. Yet they accurately forecast the behavior of the Cuban athletes who performed at the 1976 Olympics in Montreal.

The indefatigable Cuban runner, Albert Juantorena, dutifully dedicated his racing triumphs to Fidel Castro and the revolution. The formidable Teofilo Stevenson, the gold-medal heavyweight boxer, also always said exactly what Castro would want to hear.

Indeed, all of Castro's athletes arrived in Montreal with a full repertoire of Cuban revolutionary slogans. Not one of them expressed a thought of his own.

There could be no denying, however, that the Cuban athletes put on a tremendous performance. Hector Rodriguez told in an intelligence interview how they were groomed for their triumph. Relates the report:

"Rodriguez revealed that every Cuban province had a training center for athletic initiation in the schools. The main purpose of these centers is to recruit promising youths as young as 11 years of age . . . (and) train them politically and technically until they reach the age and necessary capability to enter another similarly specialized school.

"The latter is at the university level and is known as Superior School of Athletic Preparation . . . . The school is located in the former Cubanacan Country Club, one of the most luxurious of Havana, and the students receive privileged treatment with regard to food, clothing and housing."

The athletic triumphs are used, according to the intelligence documents, to divert public attention from "other failures" and to demonstrate "the superiority of Marxist-Leninism ideology in sports."

The Castro regime also inflates its triumphs by counting separately all the medals awarded to team members instead of the single award to the team.

The Cubans also divided "the number of medals gained by the number of the population of each participating country," states an intelligence report. "The main purpose of this statistical manipulation is to show that percentage-wise, the Cubans can field better athletes than any other country."

Source: *The Barnesboro Star,* August 18, 1976. (Report by Jack Anderson). Reprinted by permission.

On the other hand, the personal biographies of Willie Mays, Hank Aaron, Bill Russell, Althea Gibson, Mickey Mantle, Bob Cousey, Johnny Unitas, Joe Louis, Muhammad Ali, and Jackie Robinson, among others, are evidence of the social and economic success—"social climbing"—afforded to persons of humble origins in the world of sports. Other means of fostering mobility, besides sports, include education, aggressiveness, intelligence, hard work, and luck. Refer to chapter 3, pp. 50-60, for a discussion of mobility in sport.

In case-based societies one's position is said to be *ascribed.* This implies that little or no mobility is possible and one remains in the same stratum "from the cradle to the grave." In practice, however, even in India through sanskritization some modicum of social mobility has been witnessed.

Favorite Sports by Social Class

Like so many aspects of the social universe, sport roles and *preferences* are affected by social class considerations. Consider Table 7.3 which distinguishes between spectator and participation sports by members of different social classes. Social class is trichotomized into upper (n = 188), middle (n = 175), and lower (n = 172) and cross-classified with favorite sport which is dichotomized into spectator and participant. The pattern of responses revealed that upper class persons (64.4%) preferred *participation* sports, whereas the modal response for both middle (57.1%) and lower class persons

(54.7%) was for *spectator* sports. Hodges' statement made more than a decade and a half ago continues to be valid:

> The evidence relating to social class differences in the passive-active sphere is fairly emphatic. It amounts, in essence, to this: the higher an American's social-class position, the likelier he is to be a sports "doer" than a sports "viewer."[20]

Table 7.3
Socioeconomic Differences in the Designation of Spectator or
Participant Sports as Favorites by Metropolitan Residents

Favorite Sport	Socioeconomic Strata			
	Upper (percent)	Middle (percent)	Lower (percent)	Total (percent)
Spectator	35.6	57.1	54.7	48.8
Participant	64.4	42.9	45.3	51.2
Totals	100.0 (n = 188)	100.0 (n = 175)	100.0 (n = 172)	100.0 (n = 535)

Source: Gregory P. Stone, "Some Meanings of American Sport: An Extended View," *Sociology of Sport: Proceedings of the C.I.C. Symposium on the Sociology of Sport*, ed. Gerald S. Kenyon (Chicago: Athletic Institute, 1969), p. 10. Reprinted by permission.

Despite the general popularity of sports, the list of favorite sports is relatively small and is differentiated by age, sex, resistance, and socioeconomic factors. Among an adult sample (n ≈ 540) of Minneapolis residents, Stone discovered only ten sports mentioned as "favorites" by three or more percent of the total sample.[21] The last column in Table 7.4 presents the percentage of the total sample mentioning each particular sport, as well as their implicit rank ordering. Notice that football and, to some extent, baseball stand out. Notice, too, that age, sex, residence, and socioeconomic status affect the choices of favorite sports.

Since social stratification is our present concern, notice the socioeconomic strata column. The designations in the table—"L," "M," and "U"—are statistically significant (not likely to result from chance) and provide the reader with an appreciation of the "direction" of the differences. For example, the favorite sports of lower class persons are baseball, bowling, and boxing; the favorites for middle class individuals are football, swimming, and basketball; and golf and tennis occupy the attention of upper class individuals. No social class differences were revealed in fishing and hunting. These empirical generalizations appear logical since, historically, accessibility to the facilities for golf and tennis has been limited to the upper class. The historical emphasis on physical aggression among lower class persons helps explain their designation of boxing.[22] These differences might also be explained by differential cultural values with upper class persons leaning toward participation sports and middle and lower class individuals toward spectator sports (as underscored in Table 7.3).

Table 7.4
Social Differences in Sports Designated as Favorites
by Metropolitan Residents

Favorite Sports	Selected Social Characteristics*				Percent of Respondents Selecting a Favorite Sport (n = 540)
	Age	Sex	Residence	Socioeconomic Strata	
Football			U-S	M-U-L	24.4
Baseball		M-F		L-M-U	15.4
Golf				U-M-L	11.3
Fishing		M-F			9.6
Swimming	Y-O	F-M	U-S	M-U-L	7.6
Basketball				M-L-U	6.8
Bowling		F-M		L-M-U	6.3
Tennis				U-M-L	3.7
Hunting		M-F			3.7
Boxing		M-F		L-M-U	3.3
Others too diverse to analyze					7.8

Source: Gregory P. Stone, "Some Meanings of American Sport: An Extended View," in *Sociology of Sport: Proceedings of the C.I.C. Symposium on the Sociology of Sport,* ed. Gerald S. Kenyon (Chicago: Athletic Institute, 1969), p. 11. Reprinted by permission.

*Categories of informants making most mentions of any specified activity are listed first, those making fewest mentions are listed last, reading from left to right. In the age category those less than forty years of age are designated "Y," those forty years of age or more are designated "O." In the sex category, men are designated "M" and women "F." In the residence category, "U" designates respondents living in the Minneapolis city limits; "S" those living in the suburbs. In the socioeconomic category those in the highest category are designated "U," those in the middle, "M," and those in the lowest, "L." Only significant associations (p < 0.05) are presented.

Despite the differences reported above, sports qualify as dominant preoccupations in American culture. Seventy-five percent of the males and almost 50 percent of the females in Stone's study reported discussing sports "frequently" or "very frequently."[23] According to a national survey conducted by Yankelovich, nearly 75 percent of Americans classify themselves as sport fans, although the average or "interested" (47%) outnumber the avid (25%). Further, they prefer professional sport (62%) to amateur (24%) sport and favor spectating at a live event (46%) to watching it on TV (41%).[24]

Active Participation in Sports

The extent of *active participation* in sport can be documented in a number of ways. *Newsweek* magazine reported that 87.5 million U.S. adults participated in one or more sports (sports were defined rather broadly and included activities that sport sociologists would consider debatable).[25]

Similarly, the Bureau of Census (1976) compiled estimates of the number of participants and percent of the population participating in various activities. Table 7.5 reports these findings. But does this participation apply equally across the board or is socioeconomic status related to it? Evidence seems to suggest that, indeed, social class and sport participation correlate.

Table 7.5
Relative Ranking of Outdoor Activities by Number of Participants

Activity	Participants in Millions	Percent of Population
Picnicking	74.4	47
Driving for pleasure	54.5	34
Walking for pleasure	54.2	34
Fishing	38.0	24
Playing outdoor sports and games	35.0	22
Swimming in outdoor pools	28.5	18
Nature walks	26.7	17
Boating (other than sailing)	23.3	15
Hunting	22.2	14
Attending outdoor sport events	18.9	12
Bicycling	16.7	10
Backpacking	8.6	5
Tennis	8.6	5
Water skiing	8.5	5
Golf	7.7	5
Snow skiing	7.2	5
Snowmobiling	7.2	5
Sailing	4.1	3

Source: U. S. Bureau of the Census (1976).

Burdge examined the relationship between social class (operationalized via the North-Hatt scale of occupational prestige) and involvement in leisure activities.[26] Although the concept of leisure includes activities other than sport, a great deal of leisure activity is sport related. The increasing prominence of sport can be seen in Table 7.6. Notice that, whereas the amount of monies spent on recreation has only slightly increased over the years (1930 to 1970), the amount spent on spectator sports has increased remarkably.

Burdge sampled 1,635 individuals in Allegheny County (including Pittsburgh) and designated leisure activities (of which sport is a major component and will occupy our attention) as the dependent variable. Occupational prestige, partitioned into: I—professional and high level management; II—other white collar workers; III—skilled workers; and IV—unskilled workers, was the independent variable. From his analysis we will focus exclusively on "sports activity" which is roughly equivalent to participation sports and "attending sports events" which is equivalent to spectator sports.

Table 7.6
The Growth in Sport and Recreation

	1930	1940	1950	1960	1970
Percent of consumer income spent on recreation	5.6	5.2	5.1	5.3	6.6
Spectator sports (millions of $)	NA	98	222	290	516
Outboard Motors (millions of units)	NA	NA	2.8	5.8	7.2

NA = Figures not available

Source: Data from *Information Please Almanac,* ed. Ann Golenpaul (New York: Simon & Schuster, 1976), pp. 875, 876, 63; and Max Kaplan, *Leisure* (New York: Wiley, 1975), pp. 117, 371.

Sports Activity

For the sixteen sporting activities appearing in Table 7.7, note that the highest levels of *participation* were found in the two highest occupational levels (I and II). Although most of the outcomes were not statistically significant (due to small *n*'s or numbers in many cases), there appears to be a certain clustering of sport activities around different levels of occupational prestige. For example, sports classified as "individual" (tennis, badminton, croquet, chess) appear to be popular among persons of the highest prestige level. "Team sports" (softball, basketball, and touch football) on the other hand, seem to appeal to prestige level III individuals. Prestige level II persons seem to engage in a mixture of individual sports (archery, miniature golf, wrestling) and team sports (baseball and volleyball). No participation sports were common to level IV.

Several probable explanations for the participation of the affluent in individual sports can be advanced. All of them revolve around money and the consequences of money. First, many individual sports (golf, tennis, sailing, sports car racing) are sufficiently costly to preclude or make it most difficult for certain segments of society to become involved.[27] Second, community facilities like country clubs have historically restricted those without the means to purchase membership from cultivating certain sport skills. Third, time spent away from work has been symbolic of wealth and conspicuous consumption.[28] Members of the lower social classes have neither the time nor money to engage in such exclusive activities.

Attending Sports Events

Burdge also compared *attendance* at various sporting events by occupational prestige levels (Table 7.8). As can be seen in the table, attendance was more likely (as well as statistically significant) for persons of the highest prestige level.

These data confirm and disconfirm some popular conceptions about sport attendance. For example, high prestige persons were not likely to "turn out" for stockcar, boxing, and wrestling matches, while lower prestige persons were. Level I persons were frequenters of football, baseball,

Table 7.7
Sports Activity by Prestige Level Participating Most Frequently

Activity	Prestige Level Participating Most Frequently				Level of Significance
	I	II	III	IV	
Played soccer	X				NS
Played tennis	X				.01
Played badminton	X				.01
Played croquet	X				.01
Played chess	X				.01
Played checkers	X				NS
Target shooting or vacation	X				NS
Played baseball		X			NS
Played volleyball		X			NS
Played archery		X			NS
Played miniature golf		X			.01
Played at the driving range		X			.01
Played wrestling		X			NS
Played softball			X		NS
Played basketball			X		NS
Played touch football			X		NS

Source: Rabel J. Burdge, "Levels of Occupational Prestige and Leisure Activity," *Journal of Leisure Research* (1969) pp. 262-274. The *Journal* is a publication of the National Recreation and Park Association. Reprinted by permission.

Table 7.8
Attendance at Sporting Events by Prestige Level
Participating Most Frequently

Sporting Event	Prestige Level Participating Most Frequently				Level of Significance
	I	II	III	IV	
Football games	X				.01
Baseball games	X				.01
Hockey games	X				.01
Zoo	X				.01
Soccer matches	X				NS
Golf matches	X				.01
Horse races	X				.01
Go-cart races	X				NS
Basketball games		X			.01
Stock car races			X		NS
Boxing matches			X		NS
Wrestling matches				X	NS

Source: Rabel J. Burdge, "Levels of Occupational Prestige and Leisure Activity," *Journal of Leisure Research* (1969) pp. 262-274. The *Journal* is a publication of the National Recreation and Park Association. Reprinted by permission.

hockey, golf, horse races, and zoo "events." Basketball attendance was common among level II persons, although such attendance must have been at amateur events since no pro basketball team was franchised in the Pittsburgh vicinity. Baseball, often considered to be a working-class sport, runs counter to that image. As can be seen in Table 7.8, level I persons exhibited the most frequent attendance. Although Burdge did not collect information on the number of times baseball (and other sporting events) were attended, it appears plausible that relatively few working class persons attended a great deal and many higher prestige persons attended infrequently. The outcomes of this investigation with respect to baseball and zoo attendance were diametrically opposed to those of Clarke who found these two events most frequently attended by the lowest prestige level persons.[29]

Spectator preferences for particular sports is correlated with social class just like participation preferences are correlated with social class. Gruneau indicated that the rich lean toward such sports as polo, yachting, training race horses, and sports car racing.[30] Middle class persons enjoy watching tennis, golf, sailing, and skiing. Finally, lower class persons prefer such sports as bowling, pool, boxing, auto racing, arm wrestling, figure eight skating, motocross racing, demolition derbys, and pseudo-sports like professional wrestling and roller derby. According to Eitzen and Sage, sports which appeal to working class individuals have the following characteristics:

1. The necessary equipment (such as automobiles or muscles) and skills (driving, mechanical aptitude, or self-defense) are part of working class life.
2. The sports emphasize physical prowess and manhood (machismo).
3. They are exciting and, therefore, serve as an emotional outlet. Some focus on the danger of high speed and powerful machines. Others stress violence to machines or human beings. Still others contrive events to excite the crowds (e.g., in wrestling events such as tag teams, Texas Death Matches, and the Battle Royales).
4. There is strong identification with heroes who are like the spectators in ethnicity, language, or behavior.
5. The sports are *not* school related.
6. With few exceptions, the sports they watch are individual rather than team-oriented (which is opposite their tendency to participate in team sports).[31]

No matter what the explanation, the present data strongly reveal that persons in the higher prestige levels are the greatest attenders of spectator sports. In fact, combining Stone's and Burdge's conclusions, we find that higher prestige level persons are *both* the most frequent participators and spectators in various American sporting events.

Sport as a Mechanism of Social Mobility

In what ways can sport provide a ladder for upward social mobility? Loy, after reviewing the literature on sport and mobility, advanced four ways in which *direct* involvement in athletics could facilitate vertical movement:[32]

1. Early athletic participation could lead to the high development of selected physical skills and abilities which permit direct entry into pro sports with a minimal amount of formal education. Historically, boxers, jockeys, and professional baseball players fit this mold.

2. Athletic participation may directly or indirectly enhance educational attainment. Participation in scholastic sports may foster better grades (either through the "spill-over" of desirable traits from the athletic arena or through the necessity of maintaining minimum eligibility requirements), increase the probability of graduating, and/or lead to the granting of an athletic scholarship from an institution of higher learning. Participation in intercollegiate sports may affect the attainment of an academic degree and/or the marketing of sport skills. Numerous sport participants have received these benefits in a wide range of sports (hockey, baseball, football, golf, gymnastics, soccer, swimming).

3. Athletic participation may lead to various forms of "occupational sponsorship." Boxers have frequently been supported by wealthy sponsors, and summer jobs have been provided for college athletes. More recently, steps have been taken by major U.S. employers to provide facilities, time, and money for athletes to train for Olympic and other international sporting events (see Vignette 7.3).

4. Sports involvement may lead to the development of attitudes and behaviors that are valued in the larger occupational sphere. Many ex-athletes, upon retirement, have been provided a direct channel to other occupational nooks such as sports broadcasting.

While many persons have undoubtedly profited from sport in one or more of these ways, other salient questions need answering: How much mobiliy via sports is *generally* achieved? Is it long-lived or merely short term? (See pp. 50-53). Is sports a *more* effective mobility mechanism than other avenues in our society like music, the military, and education? In *what ways* does sport participation enhance mobility? *Which sports* are the most effective mobilizers? Are professional team sports more effective than individual sports? And, assuming mobility via sports, *how long* does it last after the career has terminated? Arthur Ashe wrote this provocative statement to black parents:

> There must be some way to assure that the 999 who try but don't make it to pro sports don't wind up on the street corners or in the unemployment lines. Unfortunately, our most widely recognized role models are athletes and entertainers—"runnin'" and "jumpin'" and "singin'" and "dancin'." While we are 60 percent of the National Basketball Association, we are less than 4 percent of the doctors and lawyers. While we are about 35 percent of major league baseball, we are less than 2 percent of the engineers. While we are about 40 percent of the National Football League, we are less than 11 percent of construction workers such as carpenters and bricklayers.
>
> Our greatest heroes of the century have been athletes—Jack Johnson, Joe Louis, and Muhammad Ali. Racial and economic discrimination forced us to channel our energies into athletics and entertainment. These were the ways out of the ghetto, the ways to get that Cadillac, those alligator shoes, the cashmere sport coat.
>
> Somehow, parents must instill a desire for learning alongside the desire to be Walt Frazier. Why not start by sending black professional athletes into high schools to explain the facts of life.
>
> I have often addressed high school audiences and my message is always the same. For every hour you spend on the athletic field spend two in the library. Even if you make it as a pro athlete, your career will be over by the time you are thirty-five. So you will need this diploma. . . .

VIGNETTE 7.3
CORPORATE PLAN TO AID OLYMPIC ATHLETES

Howard Miller, a Chicago businessman, has kicked off a plan designed to enable U.S. athletes to close the competitive gap on the Soviet Union and East Germany before the 1980 Olympic Games in Lake Placid, N.Y., and Moscow ("Corporate Plan to Aid Olympic Athletes, *Chicago Tribune* (August 29, 1976), Section 3, p. 2.)

"One of the great handicaps in our system," continued Col. Miller, "has been that when our athletes leave school, they cannot continue regular training. This plan can provide that continuity."

"This plan falls within the amateur framework," said Col. Miller, "because these jobs are not tied to athletic abilities. These athletes are often college-trained men and women. They can be of real service to the companies."

Each of more than 100 giant U.S. companies would hire one or more prospective Olympic athletes of post-college age, according to the plan. The athletes would receive full pay, yet work only part time. They would train for part of each "work" day for two years or more prior to the 1980 Games.

Firms would place employee-athletes in plants or offices located near the best facilities, coaching and competition for each man's or woman's sport.

The plan, Miller realizes, is going to be criticized. Yet he feels he has answers for its critics:
* Athletes obviously do not have to work for one of the participating firms in order to make the Olympic team.
* The idea is neither charity nor welfare. The employee-athlete would have to do a day's work . . . or half a day's.
* The stopwatch and measuring tape—not big business—still determine who makes the team.
* Company presidents, Miller said, will not meddle in coaching or team-selection areas.
* An athlete would not be "black-balled" from employment by all participating companies, Miller said, if he or she did not get along in the job at one of the firms. (Courtesy of the *Chicago Tribune.*)

I'll never forget how proud my grandmother was when I graduated from UCLA in 1966. Never mind the Davis Cup in 1968, 1969, and 1970. Never mind the Wimbledon title, Forest Hills, etc. To this day, she still doesn't know what these names mean.

What mattered to her was that of her more than thirty grandchildren and children, I was the first to be graduated from college, and a famous college at that. Somehow, that made up for all those floors she scrubbed all those years.[33]

Two final observations are noteworthy.[34] First, unlike the sharp elite/folk dichotomy that once described social distinctions in sport, we have begun to see a *democratization* of sport in the United States. With increasing affluence, leisure time and mass media exposure, we can expect a continuing homogenization in the participant and spectator preferences of Americans, regardless of class.

The *embourgeoisement* of professional athletes is a second observation. This implies that as sport roles become increasingly professionalized and sports become increasingly commercialized, the occupational status of athletes has approached and even exceeded the social and material rewards received by occupants of other professional roles in American society. Salary for many skilled athletes, in particular, is considerably greater in their sport role than could be received in realms outside of sports (see chapter 11).

Sport Stratification Is Consequential

The most desirable things in life constitute the basic materials which are distributed unequally. Opportunities and chances are not equal for all athletes; instead, *institutionalized discrimination* appears to operate in sport, contrary to popular conceptions.

One of the persistent myths in American society holds that organized athletics has escaped *racism.*[35] The large number of successful and prominent black athletes—Muhammad Ali, O. J. Simpson, Hank Aaron, Frank Robinson, Kareem Abdul-Jabbar, Jim Rice, Vida Blue, Larry Doby, Lee Elder—has led many to infer that collegiate and professional sports have provided an unprecedented ladder of mobility for minority group members. Sport, then, has appeared to have "done something" for blacks. Much of this thinking has, however, been anecdotal, journalistic, and unsystematic since the sociology of sport literature contains empirical substantiation of the existence of discriminatory practices (such as recruitment policies, position assignments, performance expectations, reward and authority structures, and salary) in collegiate and professional athletics.[36] Some of the discrimination claims are more or less directly demonstrable; others are more subtle, requiring inferential leaps.

The entrance of non-white players in the major sports of baseball, basketball, and football is testimony to the changing social organization of collegiate and professional athletics.[37] In terms of *numbers,* the Afro-American athletes in pro sports are a case study. Totally excluded at one time from several pro sports, they now comprise 75 percent of pro basketball rosters, 19 percent of pro baseball rosters, and 42 percent of pro football rosters.[38] These figures are significantly higher than the blacks' proportionate 11-12 percent makeup of the American population and say nothing of black athletes' record-breaking performances as measured by points scored, batting averages, yardage gained, and "All Star" accolades.

Regarding other ethnic minorities—Latins, Asian-Americans, Mexican-Americans, and Native Americans (Indians)—there is relatively little knowledge, although this research hiatus has begun to be filled.

A brief chronology complemented by tabular representation of these trends is helpful. Blacks have made substantial progress since the Second World War in filling playing ranks in select sports. Since sport is generally considered the first institution to integrate,[39] let us examine the change in racial composition of players here, then in other arenas. After Robinson's debut in 1947, the hiring policy for blacks moved slowly but by 1953 the trend in hiring black baseball players was established. Nevertheless, a decade after Robinson's entry there were only about one dozen blacks and five Latin players in *professional baseball.*[40] Table 7.9 (second column) reveals the increasing black makeup of pro baseball.

Blacks were excluded from *pro basketball* until about 1950, although black amateurs (in collegiate circles) were on the rosters before then. Of all major sports, excluding boxing, pro basketball has made the greatest strides in fielding black players. Table 7.10 reveals the percentage of blacks in both college and pro basketball teams from 1948 to 1975.

Table 7.9
Racial Composition of Professional Teams

	Black Players as a Percent of the Total		
Year	Baseball	Basketball	Football
1954	7.5	4.6	—
1958	12.5	11.8	—
1962	17.0	30.4	16.0
1966	24.0	50.9	25.1
1970	24.5	54.3	33.7
1975	21.0	63.3	42.0

Source: Gerald W. Scully, "Economic Discrimination in Professional Sport," *Law and Contemporary Problems* 38 (Winter-Spring, 1973), p. 68. D. Stanley Eitzen and Norman R. Yetman, "Immune from Racism," *Civil Rights Digest* 9 (Winter, 1977), p. 3. Reprinted by permission.

Table 7.10
Racial Composition of College and Professional Basketball Teams, 1948-1975

Year	College			Professional
	% of teams with blacks	Black players as % of total	Average no. of blacks on integrated squads	Black players as % of total
1948	9.8	1.4	1.4	0
1954	28.3	4.5	1.6	4.6
1958	44.3	9.1	2.0	11.8
1962	45.2	10.1	2.2	30.4
1966	58.3	16.2	2.8	50.9
1970	79.8	27.1	3.4	55.6
1975	92.3	33.4	5.0	63.3

Source: D. Stanley Eitzen and Norman R. Yetman, "Immune from Racism," *Civil Rights Digest* 9 (1977), p 11. Reprinted by permission.

During the first quarter of the twentieth century blacks did play *professional football* but were excluded from that domain from the early 1930s to the late 1940s and early 1950s. Table 7.11 shows the racial composition of professional football between 1950 and 1975.

Only since the early 1960s have blacks in the professional sports of baseball, basketball, and football exceeded their proportionate 11-12 percent makeup of the U.S. population. The "watershed"

Table 7.11
Percentage of Blacks in Professional Football

Year	Percentage of Black Players
1950	0
1954	5
1958	9
1962	16
1966	26
1970	34
1975	42

Source: D. Stanley and Norman R. Yetman, "Immune from Racism," *Civil Rights Digest* 9 (1977), p. 11. Reprinted by permission.

years for these accomplishments were 1957-58, 1960, and 1958 for baseball, football, and basketball, respectively.

These statistical data, in themselves, seem auspicious for black athletes. However, within the sport milieu we find subtle and even overt acts of prejudice, segregation, discrimination, and racism when we look deeper. In the next chapter, we will more fully examine minority group participation (particularly blacks).

SUMMARY

Sport and social stratification have occupied our attention in this chapter. *Social stratification* is the hierarchal arrangement of social groups or a society into strata (social classes) that are unequal in power, privilege, prestige, and wealth. *Social class* is a major explanatory variable in sociological analysis. By knowing a person's social class, we can make probability statements about that person's preference for spectator or participation sports and the particular types of spectator and participation sports he/she will probably enjoy.

In discussing stratification in sport, we considered five features: (1) is is *social*, i.e., often results from prejudice and discrimination on the part of the dominant group and/or the economic lot of certain segments of society. (2) it is *ancient*, i.e., has existed since recorded history, (3) it is *ubiquitous*, i.e., is omnipresent or exists everywhere, (4) it is *diverse*, i.e., may foster upward mobility as in a class-based society or stifle it as in a caste-based society, and (5) it is *consequential*, i.e., enables certain segments of society to enjoy scarce resources while others do not.

To illustrate the social nature of stratification, we demonstrated that blacks' exclusion from pro baseball from the late 1890s to the middle 1940s was due to *prejudice* and *discrimination* rather than to their biological inferiority. Blacks' contemporary dominance in many major sports is testimony to the social nature of stratification.

Social stratification in sport existed as early as 776 B.C. when certain social groups in Greek society, namely females and slaves, were systematically denied the right to participate (and in some cases to even spectate). Furthermore, it existed during the middle Ages right up to today.

Stratification in sport is ever-present. It exists both between and within sports as evidenced by classifications of sports into "major" and "minor" categories and differential prestige attached to weight classes as in boxing and wrestling.

Social stratification in sport is diverse. In Western societies sport has provided a channel of upward mobility for blacks and other ethnic minority groups as well as individuals from the lower rungs of the social class ladder. Within American society there is evidence that higher prestige level persons are both the most frequent participators and spectators in various sporting events.

Finally, the consequential nature of sport stratification can be gleaned from case studies of successful black athletes like Ali, Simpson, Aaron, Robinson, Doby, Jabbar, Blue, Elder, and others. Despite the success achieved by black athletes (and other minority group members), the next chapter considers the manner in which racist practices continue to be manifest in American sport.

IMPORTANT CONCEPTS DISCUSSED IN THIS CHAPTER

Social Stratification
Elite Sports
Folk Sports
Sport Stratification is Social
Sport Stratification is Ancient
Sport Stratification is Ubiquitous
Ascribed Positions
Achieved Positions
Democratization of Sport
Sport Stratification is Diverse

Class
Estate
Caste
Horizontal Mobility
Vertical Mobility
Intragenerational Mobility
Intergenerational Mobility
Embourgeoisement of Sport
Sport Stratification is Consequential

ENDNOTES

[1] Peter L. Berger, *Invitation to Sociology* (Garden City, N.Y.: Doubleday, 1963), pp. 80-81.

[2] Leisure is popularly defined as the time we are free from the more obvious and formal duties which a paid job or other obligatory occupations impose upon us. See Max Kaplan, *Leisure* (New York: John Wiley, 1975).

[3] John T. Talamini and Charles H. Page, *Sport and Society: An Anthology* (Boston, Mass.: Little, Brown, 1973), p. 4.

[4] Melvin Tumin, *Social Stratification* (Englewood Cliffs, N.J.: Prentice Hall, 1967).

[5] Kingsley Davis and Wilbert T. Moore, "Some Principles of Stratification," *American Sociological Review* 10 (April, 1945), pp. 242-249.

[6] Ray Kennedy and Nancy Williamson, "Money in Sports," *Sports Illustrated* 49 (June 17, 1978), p. 51.

[7] R. Bendix and S. Lipset, "Karl Marx's Theory of Social Class," *Class, Status, and Power,* ed. R. Bendix and S. Lipset (New York: The Free Press, 1953), pp. 26-35; Ralf Dahrendorf, "Toward a Theory of Social Conflict," *Social Change,* ed. E. Etzioni-Halevy and A. Etzioni (New York: Basic Books, 1973).

[8] Robert W. Peterson, *Only the Ball Was White* (Englewood Cliffs, N.J.: Prentice-Hall, 1970).

[9] The first paid Negro ballplayer was John W. ("Bud") Fowler who played for a white team in New Castle, PA, in 1872. Prior to the turn of the century (circa 1883) two blacks, Weldy and Fleetwood Walker, were members of the professional Toledo baseball club. Some regard them as the first blacks in pro baseball. Moreover, a few weeks after the signing of Jackie Robinson, Rickey announced the signing of four more blacks: John Wright, Don Newcombe, Roy Campanella, and Roy Partlow. Although the policy for hiring blacks moved

cautiously, by 1953 it had become firmly entrenched. See Leonard Broom and Philip Selznick, *Sociology* (New York: Harper and Row, 1963); A. S. Young, *Negro Firsts in Sports,* (Chicago, Ill.: Johnson Publishing, 1963).

[10] Peterson, *Only the Ball Was White,* p. 17.

[11] "The Black Dominance," *Time* (May 9, 1977), pp. 57-60.

[12] Beverly Wilson, personal communication, Spring, 1978.

[13] Alastair Reid, "The Sport Scene: Heavy Going," *The New Yorker* (February 21, 1977), pp. 85-86.

[14] The famed Heisman Trophy, named after John Heisman, football coach and athletic director of the New York Downtown Athletic Club, is awarded to the most outstanding college athlete. Only twice since its inception in 1935 has the accolade been received by a non-back (Larry Kelley, Yale, end, 1936; Leon Hart, Notre Dame, end, 1949). The granting of the Outland Award, given to the outstanding interior lineman, was introduced in 1946 to give proper recognition to stellar lineman. George H. Sage, Sport and American Society, p. 231.

[15] We say symbolic because the monetary value of Olympic medals is nominal. An Olympic gold medal (which is basically silver coated with six grams of fine gold) is worth $110. The silver medal (which is pure silver) is worth $66; and the bronze medal (pure bronze) is worth $16. (*The World Almanac,* 1977).

[16] Pitirim A. Sorokin, *Social and Cultural Mobility* (New York: Free Press, 1959).

[17] Kennedy and Williams, "Money in Sports," (July 24, 1978), p. 48.

[18] Ibid.

[19] Ibid.

[20] Harold M. Hodges, Jr., *Social Stratification: Class in America* (Cambridge, Mass. Schenkman, 1964), p. 166.

[21] Gregory P. Stone, "Some Meanings of American Sport: An Extended View," *Aspects of Contemporary Sport Sociology,* ed. G. S. Kenyon (Chicago, Ill.: The Athletic Institute, 1969).

[22] Ronald W. Smith and Frederick W. Preston, *Sociology: An Introduction* (New York: St. Martin's Press, 1977), p. 428.

[23] Stone, "Some Meanings of American Sport: An Extended View."

[24] Kennedy and Williamson, "Money in Sports," (July 31, 1978).

[25] "Keeping Fit: America Tries to Shape Up," *Newsweek* (November 23, 1977), pp. 78-86.

[26] Rabel J. Burdge, "Levels of Occupational Prestige and Leisure Activity," *Journal of Leisure Research* 1 (1969), pp. 262-274. Used with permission.

[27] It is interesting to note that it was not until 1975 that Lee Elder became the first black to play in the Master's Golf Tournament.

[28] Thorstein Veblen, *Theory of the Leisure Class* (New York: Macmillan, 1899).

[29] Alfred C. Clarke, "The Use of Leisure and Its Relation to Levels of Occupational Prestige," *American Sociological Review* 21 (1956), pp. 301-307.

[30] Richard S. Gruneau, "Sport, Social Differentiation and Social Inequality," *Sport and Social Order,* ed. D. W. Ball and J. W. Loy (Reading, Mass.: Addison-Wesley, 1975), pp. 121-184.

[31] D. Stanley Eitzen and George H. Sage, *Sociology of American Sport* (Dubuque, Iowa: Wm. C. Brown, 1978), p. 216.

[32] John W. Loy, "The Study of Sport and Social Mobility," *Aspects of Contemporary Sport,* ed. Gerald S. Kenyon (Chicago, Ill.: The Athletic Institute, 1969), pp. 101-119.

[33] Arthur Ashe, "An Open Letter to Black Parents: Send Your Children to the Libraries," *New York Times* (February 6, 1977), Section 5, p. 2.

[34] Howard L. Nixon, II, *Sport and Social Organization* (Indianapolis, Ind.: Bobbs-Merrill, 1976), p. 36.

[35] In chapter 9 we will explore charges of *sexism* in sport.

[36] Paul Hoch, *Rip Off: The Big Game* (Garden City, N.Y.: Anchor Books, 1972). Norman R. Yetman and D. Stanley Eitzen, "'Black Americans in Sports:: Unequal Opportunity for Equal Ability," *Civil Rights Digest* 5 (August, 1972), pp. 20-34; John W. Loy and Joseph F. McElvogue, "Racial Segregation in American Sport," *International Review of Sport Sociology* 5 (1970), pp. 5-23; Norris R. Johnson and David P. Marple, "Racial Discrimination in Professional Basketball," *Sociological Focus* 6 (Fall, 1973), pp. 6-18; Anthony Pascal and Leonard A. Rapping, "The Economics of Racial Discrimination in Organized Baseball," *Racial Discrimination in Economic Life* (Lexington, Mass.: Heath, 1972); Aaron Rosenblatt, "Negroes in Baseball: The Failure of Success," *Transaction* 4 (September, 1967), pp. 51-53; Gerald Scully, "Economic Discrimination in Professional Sports," *Law and Contemporary Problems* 38 (Winter-Spring, 1973), pp. 67-84.

[37]These team sports are those where blacks are found in greatest abundance (boxing, too, could be added to this list but it is an individual sport) and neglects those in which there is a dearth of blacks (tennis, golf, swimming, and hockey, among others).

[38]"The Black Dominance," *Time*, pp. 57-60.

[39]One of the reasons sport is seen as a sphere of minimal segregation and discrimination stems from the fact that it was the first institution to integrate. Even the landmark 1954 Supreme Court decision (Brown vs. Board of Education of Topeka) declaring segregated educational facilities unconstitutional came later.

[40]Loy and McElvogue, "Racial Segregation in American Sport."

8

Blacks in Sport:
Prejudice and Discrimination

INTRODUCTION

Prejudice, an unfavorable feeling or attitude toward a person or group, and *discrimination,* the unfavorable treatment of a person or group, are not new phenomena. These social processes have existed in most societies, and in American society, *minority groups,* a term limited here to racial and ethnic groups (principally blacks and Spanish-speaking), have occupied socially subordinate positions. Sport, being a mirror of the larger society, tends to perpetuate these same patterns despite wishful thinking to the contrary. In this chapter we will consider the manner in which prejudice and discrimination have existed and continue to exist in the world of sport. Our focus will be upon blacks— the most visible and discriminated-against ethnic group in sport—although reference will also be made to Latin[1] professional baseball players.

A Brief History of Blacks' Involvement in Professional and Amateur Sport

Boxing was one of the first sports in which blacks participated and excelled. Tom Molyneux became the first recognized heavyweight boxing champion around 1800. A black jockey won three Kentucky Derbies in the last quarter of the nineteenth century.[2] Prior to the turn of the twentieth century (circa 1883) two blacks, Weldy and Moses Fleetwood Walker, were members of the professional Toledo baseball club.[3] Toward the end of the 1800s blacks were forced out of pro baseball (and were excluded from other sports as well) and formed their own baseball league in 1920.[4] From the late 1800s to the mid-1940s there was only a handful of black professional athletes. Henry McDonald was the first black professional football player in 1911 although it was not until 1946 that Marion Motley became the first black in the All-American Football Conference when he played for the Cleveland Browns.[5]

In 1950 three blacks broke the racial barrier in the National Basketball Association. Other black firsts include: Althea Gibson became the first black female professional tennis player in 1959; Bill Russell became the first black head coach of pro basketball's Boston Celtics in 1966; Emmit Ashford became the first black umpire (in the American League) in 1968; Wayne Embry became the first black NBA general manager in 1971; and James Harris became the first black starting quarterback (for the season) in 1975. In short, blacks' participation in professional sport was virtually nonexistent during the first half of the present century.

On the amateur level blacks' involvement tended to parallel their professional involvement. A spate of blacks who attended Eastern schools (Rutgers, Brown, Harvard, and Amherst) early in this century did participate in football, baseball, and track and field.[6] With the emergence of black colleges, blacks were also afforded an opportunity for playing sports. Fletcher reported that blacks enjoyed opportunities to participate in athletics in the U.S. Army between 1890 and 1916.[7] In Olympic competition blacks won bronze and gold medals in 1904 and 1908, respectively.

Paul Robeson of Rutgers was one of the most celebrated black athletes in the first quarter of the twentieth century and was elected to Walter Camp's All-American team in 1918. Historically, blacks played at black colleges until fairly recently. Among football conferences, it was the South Eastern Conference (SEC) that was the last one to integrate when Tennessee signed a black defensive back in 1966.[8]

In summarizing the history of black involvement in sport, McPherson wrote:

> . . . black athletes were excluded from most professional sports until the "color bar" was broken by Jackie Robinson. From the early 1900s until 1947 the color line was prevalent in most professional sports just as it was in most other social institutions. Thus, except for the few amateur athletes who competed in track and field in the Olympics or who competed in college or in the Army, integrated organized sport was not available to most blacks until the late 1940s.[9]

DISCRIMINATION IN SPORT

One of the first blatant forms of overt discrimination in sport began as early as the late 1800s. Boyle suggested the "feet-first" slide was a deliberate ploy to injure black second basemen.[10] In a similar vein, Fleischer reported that editorials in papers during the late 1800s and early 1900s warned of black supremacy in sports.[11] Vignette 8.1 demonstrates the strategy Branch Rickey employed in signing Jackie Robinson to a professional baseball contract. Today, however, the form of racism appears to have taken a more subtle cast, and even sportscasting has been judged to be racially prejudiced (see Vignette 8.2). Three aspects of sport that appear to be racially biased are: (1) *position allocation*, (2) *performance differentials*, and (3) *rewards and authority structures*.[12] Each of these will be considered.

Position Allocation

One of the recurring patterns of discrimination in collegiate and professional athletics is known as *stacking*, a term coined by Harry Edwards in 1967. It is a common form of *spatial segregation* and refers to the disproportionate concentration (i.e., stacking) of ethnic minorities—particularly blacks—in specific team positions. In effect, it denies them access to other team roles.[13] Consequently, intra-team competition is between members of the same ethnic status. For example, in baseball those competing for starting pitching positions tend to be white while those vying for the outfield slots tend to be black; in football, players competing for quarterback positions tend to be white while those competing for running back positions tend to be black.

VIGNETTE 8.1
BRANCH RICKEY'S STRATEGY FOR SIGNING JACKIE
ROBINSON TO A PROFESSIONAL BASEBALL CONTRACT

Branch Rickey, the president of the Brooklyn Dodgers, worked out deliberate tactics to see that the first black baseball player had special personal qualities as well as outstanding baseball ability. Rickey saw his task as a long-term campaign to

1. secure the backing and sympathy of the Dodgers' directors and stockholders;
2. select a Negro who would be the right man *off* the field;
3. select a Negro who would be the right man *on* the field;
4. elicit good press and public reaction;
5. secure backing and understanding from Negroes in order to avoid misinterpretation and abuse of the project; and
6. gain acceptance of the player by his teammates.

(Leonard Broom and Philip Selznick, *Sociology*, New York, NY: Harper and Row, 1963 pp. 529-532.)

Like any social action program this one met with social friction. For example, ex-baseball star Rogers Hornsby stated flatly, "Ball players on the road live (close) together. It won't work . . . ." Furthermore, the National League executives issued a report which included this statement: "However well-intentioned, the use of Negro players would hazard all the physical proprieties of baseball." (Seven club owners tacitly accepted this statement.)

Rosenblatt was among the first to notice this form of discrimination in the social organization of baseball when he observed that between 1953 and 1965 the distribution of positions on a team varied for whites and blacks.[14] For example, he pointed out that there were twice as many pitchers on a team as outfielders but there were three times as many black outfielders as black pitchers.

A more theoretical formulation of this social phenomenon combines the organizational principles of Grusky and Blalock. What is significant to the present discussion is that:

All else being equal, the more central one's spatial location: (1) the greater the likelihood dependent or coordinative tasks will be performed, (2) the greater the rate of interaction with the occupants of other positions . . ., (3) performance of dependent tasks is positively related to frequency of interaction.[15]

Blalock maintained:

(1) The lower the degree of purely social interaction on the job . . ., the lower the degree of racial discrimination. (2) To the extent that performance is relatively independent of skill in interpersonal relations, the lower the degree of racial discrimination. (3) To the extent that an individual's success depends primarily on his own performance, rather than on limiting or restricting the performance of specific other individuals, the lower the degree of discrimination by group menbers.[16]

The thrust of this formulation according to sport sociologists Loy and McElvogue is that central positions increase the likelihood that coordinating and dependent tasks will be performed, as

VIGNETTE 8.2
ARE WHITE ANNOUNCERS PREJUDICED AGAINST BLACKS?

Howard Cosell is steaming at claims that white football announcers like himself are unconsciously prejudiced against black football players. The charges came from a blind psychologist, Raymond Rainville of the State University of New York. Rainville taped NFL games on all three TV networks, featuring sportscasters like Cosell, Don Meredith, Curt Gowdy, Frank Gifford, Pat Summerall. Rainville compared their remarks about black and white players. He concluded blacks received much less praise than whites for doing the same thing. He feels the announcers are unaware of their biased attitudes. Here's Cosell's reaction: "It's garbage," said Cosell of Rainville's survey. "My whole life has been spent fighting for minority causes. I spent 3½ years fighting all alone for Muhammad Ali when he was stripped of his title. Who started the Jackie Robinson Foundation in America? . . . I go out of my way the other way when it comes to black athletes because of my beliefs. And now some guy picks out a phrase here or there, which goes against the whole fabric of one's life."

Source: *Chicago Daily News*, November 11, 1977.

---

well as increase the likelihood of social interaction with other position incumbents. Loy and McElvogue forwarded the concept of *centrality*. To them it "designates how close a member is to the 'center' of the group's interaction network and thus refers simultaneously to the frequency with which a member participates in interaction with other members and the number and range of other members with whom he interacts and the degree to which he must coordinate his tasks and activities with other members."[17] They hypothesized that "racial segregation in professional team sports is positively related to centrality."

Hence, one of the hypothesized forms of discrimination in organized athletics is spatial segregation, or what is called "stacking" in the sport literature. In brief, the hypothesis that "racial segregation in professional team sports is positively related to centrality" has been advanced. Loy and McElvogue noted that:

. . . baseball teams have a well-defined social structure consisting of the repetitive and regulated interaction among a set of nine positions combined into three major substructures or interaction units: (1) the battery, consisting of pitcher and catcher; (2) the infield, consisting of 1st base, 2nd base, shortstop, and 3rd base; and (3) the outfield, consisting of leftfield, centerfield, and rightfield positions.[18]

Baseball

Table 8.1 (column labeled "L&M") shows the distribution of white and black players by position in major league baseball between 1956 and 1967. Notice that the percentage of blacks was very small at the catcher position (5½%), moderate at the infield positions (ranging between 9 and 19%), and greatest in the outfield (32%). Since blacks comprised 19 percent of the total, those percentages (at the various positions) less than 19 percent reveal an under-representation of blacks, while those equal to and greater than 19 percent show an equal proportion or greater proportion, respectively.

Table 8.1
Distribution of White, Black, and Latin Starters by Position
in Major League Baseball 1956-1967 and 1977

Position	L&M***	White**	Black**	Latin**	Total	White	Black	Latin	Rank Order of Whites
	%	N (%)	N (%)	N (%)		% (55)	% (32)	% (12)	
Catcher	.056	25(18)	0(0)	1(3½)	26	96	0	4	1
Pitcher		22(16)	3(4)	1(3½)	26	84½	11½	4	3
1B	.194	11(8)	12(16)	3(10)	26	42	46	11½	5.5
2B	.103	11(8)	7(9)	8(27½)	26	42	27	31	5.5
3B	.180	22(16)	3(4)	1(3½)	26	85	11½	4	2
SS	.093	19(14)	2(2½)	5(17)	26	73	8	19	4
LF	.321	9(6½)	16(21)	1(3½)	26	35	61½	4	8.5
*CF	.321	5(4)	15(19)	5(17)	25	19	58	19	10
*RF	.321	9(6½)	13(17)	2(7)	24	35	50	8	8.5
DH		5(4)	6(8)	2(7)	13	38½	46	15	7
*Totals	N=99	N=138	N=77	N=29	N=244				

*% does not total 100 because all players' ethnicity was not determined.
**This column represents the % of the ethnic group's occupancy of the particular position, e.g., 16% of all white starters were pitchers.
***This column represents the proportion of blacks found by Loy and McElvogue at the designated positions. The .321 figure represents the observation that 32.1% of all blacks were outfielders.

$$\chi^2 \text{ (total table)} = 84.41, 18d_f: p < .001; V = .42$$
$$\chi^2 \text{ (white vs. black)} = 64.21, 9d_f: p < .001; V = .36$$
$$\chi^2 \text{ (white vs. Latin)} = 25.63, 9d_f: p < .01; V = .23$$
$$\chi^2 \text{ (black vs. Latin)} = 20.53, 9d_f: p < .02; V = .20$$

Source: Wilbert M. Leonard II, "Stacking and Performance Differentials of Whites, Blacks, and Latins in Professional Baseball," paper presented at the annual meeting of American Sociological Association, Chicago, Ill. (September, 1977).

When the positions were classified for a single year, 1967, Loy and McElvogue found that 83 percent of the infielders were white and 49 percent of the outfielders were black. The largest percentages of whites were reported in the catcher (96%) and pitcher (94%) positions. Eitzen and Yetman found little change in these figures for 1975.[19] The percentage of infielders who were white dropped from 83 to 76 percent, but the outfield positions held by blacks remained at 49 percent. Furthermore, pitchers (96%) and catchers (95%) remained predominantly white.

Leonard examined the distribution of starters, not all players on the roster, for the 1977 season. Table 8.1 presents the results. Of all the starters, 55 percent were white, 32 percent were black, and 12 percent were Latin. The number and percentage of whites, blacks, and Latins can be garnered from examining Table 8.1. When the individual positions were grouped into central (catcher and infield) and noncentral (outfield) positions—see Table 8.2—it was discovered that 79 percent of white players occupied central positions in contrast to 69 percent of Latins and 35 percent of blacks who did the same. Furthermore, all comparisons revealed statistically significant differences as determined by the chi square statistic.

Table 8.2
Position of Players by Ethnicity (Excluding Pitchers and Designated Hitters)

		White		Black		Latin	
		N	%	N	%	N	%
Central	Catcher	25	22	0	0	1	4
	Infield	63	57 }79%	24	35 }35%	17	65 }69%
		23	21	44	65	8	31
Noncentral	Outfield	111	100%	68	100%	26	100%

χ^2 (total table) = 46.36, d_f = 4, $p<.001$; V = .34, G = .52
χ^2 (white vs. black) = 9.78, d_f = 2, $p<.01$; V = .21
χ^2 (white vs. Latin) = 5.08, d_f = 2, $p<.10$; V = .15
χ^2 (black vs. Latin) = 10.44, 2d_f, $p<.01$; V = .22

Source: Wilbert M. Leonard, II, "Stacking and Performance Differentials of Whites, Blacks, and Latins in Professional Baseball," paper presented at the annual meeting of American Sociological Association, Chicago, Ill. (September, 1977).

Football

Turning from baseball to football, we also note a well-defined social organization. Whereas the position alignments in baseball are for defensive categories, football possesses both an offensive and a defensive alignment. The central positions for the offensive formation include center, right and left guard, and quarterback; the central defensive positions include the linebacker slots. Loy and McElvogue studied the distribution of white and black athletes in the American and National Football Leagues in 1968.[20] They discovered the majority of black athletes occupied defensive slots (59%) rather than offensive ones (41%). More specifically, blacks within the offensive alignments comprised 4 percent of the players at central positions and 34 percent at the non-central ones. For the defensive alignments blacks occupied 8 percent of the playing personnel at central positions and 42 percent at peripheral ones.

Dougherty replicated Loy and McElvogue's study using 1974 data.[21] He found a continuation, for the most part, of the earlier patterns. On offensive teams, 9 and 42 percent of central and non-central positions, respectively, were manned by blacks. Defensively, 10 and 56 percent of the central and peripheral positions, respectively, were manned by blacks. Hence, several years later a similar position distribution was generally found, although there were some changes.

Brower also found that the situation in pro football resembled that of pro baseball.[22] He found that blacks were statistically more likely than whites to be on starting teams. More specifically, for 1970, 63 percent of black players started in comparison to 51 percent of white players. These findings lead Brower to write: "Black . . . players must be superior in athletic performance to their white counterparts if they are to be accepted into professional football. . . . mediocrity is a white luxury."[23]

Brower also provided longitudinal data for examining stacking in football.[24] Table 8.3 shows the distribution of white and black athletes by position for 1960 and 1975. Several observations are noteworthy. First, blacks' contribution, numerically speaking, has risen from 12.3 to 41.6 percent. Second, central positions continued to be disproportionately occupied by whites. Third, blacks have increasingly replaced whites at non-central positions.

Table 8.3
Distribution of White and Black Players in Major League Football
1960 and 1975 (in percentages)

Playing position	1960*			1975		
	% of all whites	% of all blacks	Percent black by position**	% of whites	% of blacks	Percent black by position
Kicker/Punter	1.2	0	0	9.0	.2	1.3
Quarterback	6.3	0	0	9.7	.5	3.5
Center	5.3	0	0	6.7	.5	4.9
Linebacker	11.5	3.6	4.2	17.4	8.6	26.0
Off. Guard	8.0	1.8	3.0	8.7	4.5	26.9
Off. Tackle	8.3	23.2	28.3	8.6	5.7	31.8
Def. Front Four	11.0	14.3	15.4	12.3	15.7	47.6
End/Flanker	22.6	7.1	4.6	11.6	20.2	55.3
Running Back	16.5	25.0	17.5	8.1	21.1	65.2
Def. Back	9.3	25.0	27.5	8.1	23.2	67.3
	100.0	100.0		100.2	100.2	
Total number	(199½)	(27)	12.3	(870)	(620)	41.6

*The 1960 data were compiled by Jonathan Brower, who obtained them from the media guides published annually by each team. Whenever a player was listed at two positions, Brower credited him as one-half at each position. 1975 data are taken from 1975 *Football Register* published annually by *The Sporting News.* Since both the media guides and the *Football Register* are published before each season, they include only information on veterans. The total N for 1960 is smaller than one would expect, presumably because Brower was unable to obtain media guides for all teams.

**Since blacks were 12.3 percent of the player population in 1960, those playing positions with a black percentage less than 12.3 were under-represented. In 1975 those positions less than 41.6 percent black were under-represented.

Source: D. Stanley Eitzen and Norman R. Yetman, "Immune from Racism," *Civil Rights Digest* IX (Winter, 1977), p. 5. Reprinted by permission.

In interpreting these data Eitzen and Yetman wrote:

> Blacks appear to have made some inroads in the central offensive positions—for example, a shift from 97 percent white to 87 percent white from 1960 to 1975. But when length of time in the league is held constant, the overwhelming proportion of whites in these positions remains. Among those players in the league 1 to 3 years, 79 percent were white in 1975; 4-6 years, 80 percent white; and 10 or more years, 96 percent white. (The latter may be a consequence of the league's having a small proportion of blacks in the past.)[25]

Basketball

Research on stacking in basketball has been somewhat neglected. This is due, in part, to Edwards' declaration:

> In basketball there is no positional centrality as in the case in football and baseball, because there are no fixed zones of role responsibility attached to specific positions. . . . Nevertheless, one does find evidence of discrimination against black athletes on integrated basketball teams. Rather than stacking black athletes in positions involving relatively less control, since this is a logistical impossibility, the number of black athletes directly involved in the action at any one time is simply limited.[26]

Eitzen and Tessendorf reasoned differently.[27] The astute basketball observer knows that basketball positions vary in responsibility, leadership, and in such mental abilities as judgment and decision making, and outcome control. To substantiate this the researchers content-analyzed instruction manuals to determine whether specific responsibilities were associated with guard, forward, and center positions. They found general consensus regarding the requirements for these different positions. Guards were seen as the team's quarterback or "floor general" and were to have such characteristics as good judgment, leadership, and dependability. The center was viewed as possessing the greatest amount of outcome control because of his location relative to the basket and his serving as the team's pivot man. Forwards' desired traits included speed, quickness, physical strength, and rebounding ability, the latter two characteristics give credence to the notion of "glass eater."

On the basis of this information Eitzen and Tessendorf hypothesized that blacks would be disproportionately found—*stacked*—at forward and under-represented at center and guard. Their empirical findings were mixed. For 274 NCAA basketball teams (1970-71 season) they confirmed their hypothesis. Whereas 32 percent of the entire sample was black, 41 percent of the forwards were black, but 26 and 25 percent of guards and centers, respectively, were black. This distributional pattern held for starters as well as the "bench" and for Division I and II teams. On the other hand, their hypothesis was not substantiated in professional basketball. Nearly two-thirds of pro basketball players were black, and in professional basketball, unlike football and baseball, stacking did not appear to be operative.

CONSEQUENCES OF STACKING AND THEORETICAL EXPLANATIONS

In the three major team sports alluded to above (with the exception of *pro* basketball), stacking exists. What are its consequences? There appear to be several ramifications of stacking:[28]

1. Nearly 75 percent of radio, TV, and newspaper advertising slots were allotted to players from central positions (as a result of surveying 65 percent of pro football teams).

2. Because non-central playing positions in baseball and football depend to a considerable extent on speed and quickness (attributes which diminish with age), playing careers appear to be shorter for those occupying these positions than for those occupying central positions. This is supported by noting that in 1975, 4.1 percent of the players listed in the *Football Register* in the predominately black positions—defensive back, running back, and wide receiver (65 percent of all black players)—had been playing professionally for 10 or more years, in contrast to nearly 15 percent of whites in their predominant positions of quarterback, center, and offensive guard.

3. Shortened careers are a harbinger of less lifetime earnings.

4. Shorter careers reduce players' pension benefits since remuneration from these problems is dependent upon the duration of one's career.

5. The paucity of black coaches and managers can be traced to earlier position occupancy.[29] In baseball between 1871 and 1958, 75+ percent of all managers had been former infielders or catchers. Since blacks are "stacked" in the outfield, it may be that they do not acquire and cultivate the necessary skills required for these "executive" positions.

We have presented the theoretical rationales advanced by Grusky, Blalock, and Loy and McElvogue to account for stacking. A host of other explanations exist. For convenience's sake, we will subsume the various accounts under three categories: (1) *sociological/social psychological*, (2) *psychological*, and (3) *biological.*[30]

Sociological/Social Psychological Explanations

Since most investigations of stacking have been undertaken by sociologists, it should not be surprising that their explanations predominate. These include the following (Curtis and Loy, 1979):

1. The Stereotyping Hypothesis

According to this school of thought, stacking is a consequence of management's perceptions regarding the physical, social, and personality skills of minority and majority group members coupled with their perceptions of the different physical, social, and personality skills required for occupants of different playing positions. Our earlier example whereby coaching manuals indicated agreement regarding the skills of basketball guards, centers, and forwards dovetails with this contention. In football, too, we have seen that central positions call for certain traits and non-central positions demand others, and the fact that blacks and whites are disproportionately distributed among these positions further supports this hypothesis. On the matter Brower wrote:

> The combined function of centrality in terms of responsibility and interaction provides a frame for exclusion of blacks and constitutes a definition of the situation for coaches and management. People in the world of professional football believe that various football positions require specific types of physically- and intellectually-endowed athletes. When these beliefs are combined with the stereotypes of blacks and whites, blacks are excluded from certain positions. Normal organizational processes when interlaced with racist conceptions of the world spell out an important consequence, namely, the racial basis of the division of labor in professional football.[31]

While Brower wrote exclusively for football, the same *stereotyping* process applies to other sports as well.

Tutko provided some evidence for the stereotyping hypothesis.[32] He presented 300 coaches—those persons who should be able to identify characteristics of black and white athletes because of their direct personal experience with them—with a list of traits or characteristics and asked them, "would you expect black or white athletes to be high or low on each of these items?": (1) orderliness, (2) exhibitionism, (3) impulsivity, (4) understanding, and (5) abasement (humility). The majority of the coaches expected blacks to be "low" on orderliness, understanding, and abasement and "high" on exhibitionism and impulsivity. In terms of the actual results on a scale of items measuring these traits, blacks scored "high" on orderliness, understanding, and abasement and "low" on exhibitionism and impulsivity. In short, expectations and empirical results were polar opposites. The moral is simple: coaches held conceptions of black athletes that were not scientifically verified. The unfortunate side effect is that people think and act toward social categories in terms of their conceptions even when their expectations are fallacious.

2. The Interaction and Discrimination Hypothesis

This explanatory notion is premised on the idea that management and players perceive intimate interaction between minority and majority members in negative terms and, consequently, work to exclude the minority members from central (with high interaction potential) positions. Underlying this hypothesis is probably the majority group's belief that minority group members possess undesirable characteristics.

3. The Outcome Control Hypothesis

This account views management and players as preferring to keep minority members out of positions of control, leadership, and authority because of prejudice cr the belief that ethnic minorities are not capable of adequately executing such responsibilities. Edwards has argued for this interpretation:

> Centrality of position is an *incidental* factor in the explanation of positional segregation of race in sports. The factors which really should be considered have to do with the degree of relative outcome control or leadership responsibilities institutionalized into the various positions. . . . Centrality . . . is significant only in so far as greater outcome control and leadership . . . are typically invested in centrally located positions since actors holding these positions have a better perspective on the total field of activity.[33]

To Edwards, this explanation coupled with the myth of black intellectual incompetence is the real culprit.

4. The Prohibitive Cost Hypothesis

Medoff advanced an economic argument for stacking.[34] To him, the high cost of training athletes for certain positions coupled with the low socioeconomic standing of minorities is responsible for differential position occupancy. Due to their "inferior" socioeconomic status, blacks will be relegated to non-central positions because they lack access to training, instruction, equipment, facilities, and coaching. Under such situational contingencies blacks choose those positions with relatively little "cost." Medoff provided a modicum of support by showing a positive correlation between the rising socioeconomic status of blacks and their increase in central positions between 1960 and 1968. Such a conclusion assumes all other conditions (such as prejudice and discrimination) have remained constant, an assumption not empirically verified.

5. The Differential Attractiveness of Positions Hypothesis

This explanation assumes minority members perceive positions differently and make choices on the basis of these perceptions. There are, however, two variants of this hypothesis. *First,* minority group athletes select those playing positions that provide the greatest opportunity for individual success, recognition, achievement, popularity, prestige, and monetary rewards. When former all-pro wide receiver Gene Washington was at Stanford, he played quarterback his first two years and switched to flanker his junior year. Washington himself, not his coaches, desired the change. "It was strictly a matter of economics. I knew a black quarterback would have little chance in pro ball unless he was absolutely superb."[35] Outfield positions in baseball and wide receivers, cornerbacks, and running backs in football require independent task activity and receive much visibility and publicity; generally these positions are correlated with high salaries. This formulation does not, however, account for blacks' under-representation at other lucrative and socially significant positions, such as quarterbacks, pitchers, and catchers, as well as their absence from professional sports like hockey, tennis, golf, auto racing, and horse racing (see pp. 180-181).

The *second* variation of this hypothesis contends that blacks shy away from those positions that are perceived to be unattainable at higher levels of sport competition. Eitzen and Sanford found a significant shift by blacks from central to non-central positions for a sample of 387 pro football players who formerly played in high school and college.[36] Eitzen and Yetman wrote:

> . . . given discrimination in the allocation of playing positions (or at least the belief in its existence), young blacks will consciously avoid those positions for which opportunities appear to be low (pitcher, quarterback), and will select instead those positions where they are most likely to succeed (the outfield, running and defensive back).[37]

6. The Role Modeling Hypothesis

According to this thesis young blacks emulate and seek to play the positions in which black stars have been successful. In other words, black youths *model* themselves after those blacks who have attained success and recognition, and those visible blacks have played at non-central positions. McPherson argued that the first black baseball players were predominately outfielders, and the first black football players were in the offensive and defensive backfield and the defensive line.[38] It is precisely in these non-central slots that blacks are over-represented today.

There has been a spate of indirect evidence supporting this hypothesis. Brower interviewed 23 white and 20 black athletes and found that 70 percent of the black athletes had only black role models (while white athletes had role models from both races) and the majority of these role models played traditional black positions.[39] Castine and Roberts reported that, among black college players, 57 percent had a black idol and played the same position as the idol when they were in high school, and 48 percent played the same position as the idol while in college.

The present hypothesis does not explain the initial playing positions of blacks when the "color bar" was lifted nor the fact that blacks shift from central high school and college playing positions to non-central ones in the pros. This formulation implies the operation of irrationality, too. "It assumes that as black athletes become older and are in more keenly competitive conditions, they will be more likely to seek positions because of their identification with a black star rather than because of a rational assessment of their own athletic skills."[40]

In summarizing these sociological/social psychological explanations, we find the first three—the *stereotyping hypothesis,* the *interaction and discrimination hypothesis,* and the *outcome control hypothesis*—maintaining that prejudicial and discriminatory social processes are operating. The principal discriminatory agents are majority group players and management. Each of these hypotheses also implies the operation of social psychological mechanisms; that is, they involve assumptions about differential perceptions regarding minority and majority players by both players and management. The remaining four are to some extent premised on early socialization experiences whereby minority and majority group members self-select themselves out of certain positions and into others. Then, the perceptions and subsequent actions based upon these definitions channel their behavior accordingly.

Psychological Explanations

There are currently two "psychological" interpretations for the stacking phenomenon.

1. The Hypothesis That Blacks Excel at Reactive Tasks

Worthy and Markle contend that blacks excel at *reactive* activities (those in which the individual must respond appropriately at the right time to changes in the stimulus situation) whereas whites excel at *self-paced* ones (those in which the individual responds whenever he chooses to a relatively static and unchanging stimulus).[41] To test their hypothesis, they reasoned that blacks should excel at hitting, a reactive task, whereas whites should excel at pitching, a self-paced task. As support for this claim, they demonstrated that whereas 7 percent of pitchers were black, 24 percent of non-pitchers were black. Another test of their contention applied to basketball. They suggested free throw shooting is essentially self-paced while field goal shooting is reactive. They found that whites excelled at free throw shooting (a self-paced activity) and blacks at field goal shooting (a reactive activity).

Worthy and Markle's data were criticized by Jones and Hochner on methodological grounds.[42] The latter researchers claimed that the former's data were frequency counts and not performance factors, and that the data analysis did not demonstrate white superiority at free throws and black excellence at field goals. In re-analyzing and replicating Worthy and Markle's study, Jones and Hochner found support for superior black performance at hitting and superior white performance at free throw shooting. The other contentions—racial differences in field goal percentages and white superiority at pitching—were not upheld.

Dunn and Lupfer studied 55 white and 122 black fourth-grade boys playing a modified game of soccer and discovered that, consistent with Worthy and Markle's hypothesis, self-paced activities were superior for whites and reactive activities were superior for blacks.[43]

The present hypothesis may account for blacks' over-representation at "reactive" playing positions, e.g., outfield (baseball), wide receivers, cornerback, running back (football), and their under-representation in such "self-paced" sports as bowling, golf, and swimming. Just the same, the hypothesis does not explain blacks' under-representation in such reactive individual sports as auto racing, fencing, skiing, squash, and tennis (see pp. 180-181).

2. The Hypothesis That Blacks and Whites Have Personality Differences

Jones and Hochner wrote:

> The manner in which an individual is socialized into sports activities will have a significant effect on his sports personality. . . . Further, this sports personality will have a significant effect on sports preference and performance.[44]

According to them, black athletes in comparison to whites "(1) emphasize an individualistic rather than a team orientation, (2) stress style or expressive performance over success or technical performance, and (3) reflect a personalized power orientation associated with individual winning instead of a power orientation correlated with team winning." The researchers cite evidence in support of their hypothesis, but the overall evidence is at present quite meager.

Biological Explanations

Several investigators have discovered statistically significant differences between select samples of white and black athletes on a variety of *anthropometric* (measurements of the body) measures.[45] These studies have shown that blacks have (1) longer arms and lower legs, (2) greater hand and forearm length, (3) less body fat, (4) shorter trunks, (5) narrower hips, (6) greater muscle mass, (7) greater skeletal weight, (8) wider bones in the upper arm, (9) more muscle tissue in the upper arm and thigh, (10) less muscle mass in the calf, (11) a higher degree of mesomorphy, (12) a lower vital lung capacity, (13), a different heel structure, (14) more muscle fibers needed for speed and power and fewer of those needed for endurance, and (15) a higher specific gravity. Additionally, there is evidence that black bodies function differently from white bodies. They mature more quickly, they are more likely to have hyper-extensibility ("double-jointedness"), dissipate heat more efficiently, become chilled more easily in cold temperatures, and possess superiority in rhythmic abilities.[46]

These biological-physiological differences have been used by some to explain blacks' dominance in numbers and performance in certain sports as well as their under- or over-representation in some sports and at particular playing positions. For example, blacks' arm and leg lengths have been cited as explanations for their outstanding performances in certain running and jumping events (track and field), over-representation in some sport niches—outfield (baseball), defensive backs, running backs, and wide receivers (football). Their greater mesomorphy, lower vital lung capacity, and higher specific gravity have been advanced as reasons for their paucity in swimming and endurance events.

Several criticisms of these bio-physiological explanations for racial variations in sport demand our attention. First, most of these differences are average (mean) differences and fail to account for variations within particular races as well as the overlap between members of different races. Second, just how such differences affect athletic performance in interaction with each other is not fully known. For example, there is little evidence that buoyancy is related to swimming ability. Third, some of the advantages of black athletes may offset one another. Malina wrote:

The greater weight and density of the Negro skeleton, might possibly offset the advantage suggested by mechanical principles relative to body proportions; . . . further, since strength of muscle is physiologically related to its cross-sectional area, it is difficult to assume that the Negro calf musculature produces more power, enabling him to excel in the sprints and jumps.[47]

Fourth, the samples of performers, particularly top-level performers, have not been randomly selected.

PERFORMANCE DIFFERENTIALS

The empirical data suggest that blacks and whites (as well as Latins in baseball) do *not* perform at the same level. It appears that blacks must perform better if they are to transit from the minor leagues to the majors, as well as to maintain their positions in a specific sport. This form of discrimination is called "unequal opportunity for equal ability" by Yetman and Eitzen (1972).

Baseball

Rosenblatt observed that between 1953 and 1957 the mean batting average for blacks was 20.6 points higher than that for whites.[48] Between 1958 and 1961 this mean difference was 20.1, while from 1962 to 1965 it was 21.2. More recent studies have discovered a continuation of this gap at around 21 percentage points.[49] It seemed that:

. . . discriminatory hiring practices are still in effect in the major leagues. The superior Negro is not subject to discrimination because he is more likely to help win games than fair to poor players. Discrimination is aimed, whether by design or not, against the sub-star Negro ball player. The findings clearly indicate that the undistinguished Negro player is less likely to play regularly in the major leagues than the generally undistinguished white player.[50]

Pascal and Rapping studied whether black minor leaguers must be better than whites to be promoted to the major leagues.[51] Based upon a sample of 784 major league players, dichotomized into veterans (n = 453) and non-veterans (n = 331), they found that regardless of position, blacks' mean lifetime average was higher than whites'.[52] Furthermore, for pitchers who appeared in 10 or more games, black pitchers won 10.2 games in comparison to 7.5 for whites. These findings led them to conclude:

On the average a black player must be better than a white player if he is to have an equal chance of transiting from the minor leagues to the major.[53]

Edwards claimed that it was generally conceded that black athletes are superior to whites.[54] To support this statement, he uses "evidence" from research in sports other than baseball. Leonard confined his study to pro baseball and made all possible *pair* comparisons among white, black, and Latin players.[55] Statistical comparisons were made in the following categories: (1) batting averages (for 1973 and 1974), (2) slugging, (3) home run averages, (4) runs batted in, (5) fielding averages,

(6) earned run averages (1973 and 1974), (7) number of strike outs, and (8) number of bases on balls. Notice that categories 6, 7, and 8 are components of pitching performance, 5 is a "defensive" category, and 1, 2, 3, and 4 are "offensive" categories.

In general, Edwards' assertion that blacks were superior athletes received empirical corroboration. For both 1973 and 1974 there were statistically significant differences between black and white batting averages. In 1973 black averages were 17 points higher and in 1974, 14 points higher. Although these batting average differentials were slightly lower than Rosenblatt's and Yetman and Eitzen's, they indicated the same trend. Also interesting was the finding that Latin averages were significantly higher than whites'. Although the black batting average was higher than Latins', the difference was not significant.

There were also significant differences—in favor of blacks—in slugging, home run production, and runs batted in. Blacks were the best performers on all these variables. White averages on these dimensions were higher than Latins', but the differences were not statistically significant. On the pitching performance factors, there were some slight differences, but none were statistically significant. The same was true of fielding averages.

When Leonard's data were compared with more extensive data,[56] the same rank ordering of performances was, in general, revealed. Neft et al. categorized ethnic groups into black, Latin, and white and compared performance differentials for three time periods: (1) 1947-60, (2) 1961-68, and (3) 1969-73. On batting, slugging, home runs, ERA's, and bases on balls, the same order of performance, generally favoring blacks and Latins over whites, was discovered.

Leonard constructed the following "ideal types" for Latin, black, and white professional baseball players on the basis of aggregate minor and major league statistics:

Latins have spent about 4½ years in the minors and during that time have played in 470 games, come to the plate nearly 1700 times, scored about 270 runs, made 470 hits, banged nearly 40 homers, driven in 220 runs, and maintained a .276 batting average.

Latin players have spent more than 6 years in the majors and during that time have participated in 775 games, come to the plate 2800 times, scored almost 350 runs, produced 760, 50, and 755-plus hits, home runs, and RBI's, respectively, while maintaining a .270 batting average. In addition, they earn about $96,000 per annum, were born outside the United States, tend to be infielders and are about 29 years old.

Blacks have spent approximately 4 years in the minors and during that time have played in slightly less than 400 games, come to the plate about 1400 times, scored 250 runs, produced 425 hits, banged a little more than 40 home runs, drove in slightly more than 200 runs, and maintained a batting average of .283.

Black players have spent about 5½ years in the majors and during that time have played in nearly 700 games, come to the plate 2400 times, scored more than 350 runs, produced 670, 77, and 400 hits, home runs, and RBI's, respectively, while maintaining a .279 batting average. They earn about $103,000 a year, tend to be outfielders and are about 29 years old.

Whites have spent about 3½ years in the minors and during that time have played in approximately 360 games, come to the plate nearly 1300 times, scored almost 200 runs, made a little more than 350 hits, banged 33 home runs, knocked in 180 runs, and maintained a .270 batting average.

White players have spent slightly more than 4½ years in the majors and during that time have played in 550 games, stood at the plate almost 1900 times, scored 240 runs, produced 500, 44, and 498 hits, home runs, and RBI's, respectively, while maintaining a

.264 batting average. They average $90,000 a year and tend to concentrate at the infield positions with a disproportionate number manning one of the battery positions and are about 28 years old.[57]

Football

Demonstrating performance differentials in football is strained by the fact that the outcome of the game is heavily based upon team performance coupled with the fact that offensive statistics are more extensive and more frequently published than defensive ones. At present, the most complete data for which comparisons between whites and blacks can be made are for running backs and wide receivers. A significant performance factor in football is average yards gained. Black runners have gained a little more than one-half yard per carry over their white counterparts, and wide receivers have gained nearly two more yards per pass reception. Black backs score nearly twice as often as white backs. Furthermore, black receivers score more than whites by a 1.78 factor. Black players were also used more than white players. Scully wrote:

> Among running backs, blacks will have about 33 more rushing attempts per season, a differential of about 56 percent over white running backs, and they will have 4.4 more pass receptions per season, a 41 percent differential. Among wide receivers blacks will complete nearly 8 more passes per season, a differential of some 50 percent in comparison to white wide receivers.[58]

Basketball

Three indices of scoring—field goal and free throw percentages and points scored—will be compared.[59] The findings are mixed with respect to race as well as statistical significance in the two professional leagues. For example, blacks had higher field goal and free throw percentages in the ABA (but not significantly higher), whereas whites had higher field goal (not significant) and free throw percentages ($p < .05$)[60] in the NBA. With regard to scoring, blacks' performance was superior to whites' in total points per season (101.41 in the ABA and 35.50 in the NBA), points per game (1.42 in the ABA and 1.15 in the NBA), and points per minute (.05 in the ABA and .03 in the NBA), but only the last variable was statistically significant.

Some researchers believe points scored per minute is the best single indicator of performance because of the fast pace of basketball. Using this indicant, blacks significantly outperformed whites by a 12.5 percent margin in the ABA and by 7.3 percent in the NBA.

Blacks out-rebounded whites in both leagues, but the data were significant only in the ABA. In both leagues whites had more assists, but these differences were not significant. In basketball, unlike football where blacks appear to be used more intensively, blacks in the ABA did play in more games and record more total "floor" time, but in neither case was the difference significant.

Leonard and Schmidt compared black/white performances (among the top 25 NBA and ABA scorers) in eight categories: (1) average point production for 1972-73, (2) games played, (3) minutes played, (4) number of field goals made, (5) number of free throws made, (6) number of rebounds, (7) number of assists and (8) total number of points scored.[61] None of the sixteen comparisons (eight in both leagues) produced statistically significant differences between blacks and whites although there were directional differences generally favoring blacks. Table 8.4 contains the summary statistical data.

Table 8.4

Summary Table of $\bar{X}$'s, S's, and t Values for Comparing White and Black Performances of Top 25 Players in the NBA and ABA for 1973

	NBA White (n = 8)		NBA Black (n = 17)			ABA White (n = 8)		ABA Black (n = 17)		
	$\bar{X}$	S	$\bar{X}$	S	t Value	$\bar{X}$	S	$\bar{X}$	S	t Value
Average Point Production	22.00	2.41	23.92	4.13	-1.21 N.S.	19.56	4.03	20.57	4.19	-0.56 N.S.
Games Played	80.00	2.00	78.52	3.46	1.10 N.S.	79.37	6.54	80.23	4.65	-0.37 N.S.
Minutes Played	3,024.25	322.21	3,152.29	208.94	1.19 N.S.	2,958.25	437.57	2,895.11	302.56	0.42 N.S.
Field Goals Made	714.00	64.69	765.82	123.58	-1.10 N.S.	610.62	152.60	604.94	135.80	0.09 N.S.
Free Throws Made	329.50	8.00	347.70	120.24	0.38 N.S.	323.75	105.50	399.88	109.93	-1.62 N.S.
Number of Rebounds	696.50	372.94	599.58	353.29	0.62 N.S.	737.00	306.21	619.58	363.32	0.78 N.S.
Number of Assists	347.87	139.50	385.00	207.34	-0.45 N.S.	304.62	173.45	305.76	129.47	-0.01 N.S.
Total Number of Points	1,757.50	176.28	1,879.35	333.43	-0.96 N.S.	1,576.12	392.10	1,641.88	294.23	-0.46 N.S.

Source: Wilbert M. Leonard, II and Susan Schmidt, "Observations on the Changing Social Organization of Collegiate and Professional Basketball," *Sport Sociology Bulletin* 4 (Fall, 1975) p. 34.

Several researchers have explored the "unequal opportunity for equal ability" notion in pro and collegiate basketball. Yetman and Eitzen analyzed the performance of players on 246 integrated NCAA basketball teams in 1970.[62] They found 67 percent of the blacks and 44 percent of the whites occupied starting positions. These results applied regardless of region of the country, size, or type of school. The researchers suggested this may be due to discriminatory recruitment practices in which only "star" blacks were granted scholarships.

In a more encompassing study, Yetman and Eitzen surveyed black participation in *college* basketball from 1954 to 1970.[63] They found blacks disproportionately under-represented in the second five (the "bench"). On *pro* teams blacks were found to be slightly over-represented in starting roles, but the differences diminished from 1958 to 1970. For the 1975 season Eitzen and Yetman discovered that while blacks continued to be over-represented as starters, a decline from 76 percent in 1962 to 61 percent in 1975 had been witnessed. Johnson and Marple, considering the first eight *pro* players on pro basketball teams, discovered 60 percent of the top eight were black in comparison to 52 percent in the lower four positions.[64]

Johnson and Marple provide evidence that in *pro* basketball less productive black players appear to be "dropped" earlier than less productive white players.[65] In testing this hypothesis the researchers trichotomized years in pro basketball into: (1) rookies, (2) 2-4 years' experience, and (3) 5 or more years' experience. They found a reduction of white players from 46.5 to 37.7 percent between the first two categories, whereas blacks increased from 53.5 to 62.3 percent between the rookie and 2-4 years' experience categories. To Johnson and Marple, this suggested that marginally skilled whites are provided with more of an opportunity to make the team than less skilled blacks. For players with five or more years' experience, there was an increase (over the percentage in the 2-4 year category) from 37.7 to 46.3 percent whites and a decline from 62.3 to 53.7 percent blacks. They interpreted this to mean that blacks are "let go" earlier (when their performances begin to become suspect) than whites. To test this contention, they examined the correspondence between race and experience while holding constant *points per game* (trichotomized into less than 10 *ppg*, 10-19 *ppg*, and 20 and more *ppg*). Regardless of experience, blacks were in the majority. For marginal players who scored less than 10 *ppg* but were at least in their fifth year of experience, 43 percent were black as opposed to 57 percent white in the same category. This cannot be attributed to the unavailability of blacks since they were in the majority among those with five or more years of experience and scoring 10-19 *ppg* (59%) and 20 or more *ppg* (63%). These data were consistent with other nonempirical contentions claiming blacks must be better to be given a chance to play in professional sport.[66]

EXPLAINING THE SUPERIORITY OF THE BLACK ATHLETE

The data reported herein generally attest to superior performances on the part of black athletes (see pp. 139-141 also). Several attempts to explain why this is the case have been advanced.

Matriarchal Explanation

One scheme for explaining superior black performance is attributed to the historically dominant *matriarchal* black family structure (a form of family organization in which power and authority are invested in the female).[67] The argument is that a black male reared in the absence of a father compensates for this "social/emotional void" by developing very positive, meaningful, and intense relationships with the coach, a surrogate father figure. As a consequence, his identification with the coach as a father figure leads him to outperform whites who have been socialized in the statistically dominant *patriarchal* (male dominated) family structure. As interesting and appealing as the matriarchal explanation seems, it does not cohere with other empirical findings. For example, about one-third of black families are structured this way, but in *absolute numbers,* there are more whites who come from matriarchal families. Further, the past and present protests of black athletes against the dominant group—even white coaches—denies the compensatory role the coach father-figure may have on athletic prowess.

Race-Linked Characteristics Explanation

Kane has invoked three major race-linked categories to explain black athletic superiority. One of these is that there exist *racially linked physical and physiological characteristics.*[68] The limitation of this approach surrounds the scientific ineptness of the concept of "race." Race seems to be more meaningfully understood as a *social* rather than a biological designation. Furthermore, the black population and the black athlete manifest significant variability in body physiques, body proportions, and other anatomical and physiological features. Coakley wrote:

> To say that Kareem Abdul-Jabbar, Julius Erving, George McGinnis, David Thompson, Lenny Wilkins, and Calvin Murphy are successful in professional basketball because of some similar physical trait is absurd. Even if they all had similar bones in their heels and double-jointed hips, such characteristics would be insignificant compared to the dramatic differences between them. Indeed Calvin Murphy and George McGinnis have more in common with white players such as Ernie DiGregorio and Dave Cowens, respectively, than with any of the other black players mentioned.[69]

A second explanation of black athletic superiority advanced by Kane is a *race-linked psychological* one. Here, black athletes are conceived to be "calm, cool, and collected," particularly under pressure. This conclusion was reached using case studies but is inconsistent with the survey data of Ogilvie.[70] On the IPAT (Institute for Personality and Ability Test), it was found that black athletes were significantly ($p < .05$) more "uptight," concerned, and serious than their white counterparts. However, on another IPAT item—"casual-controlled"—successful black athletes scored significantly ($p < .01$) higher than white athletes, suggesting a more controlled orientation. These data are attitudinal in nature, and there may exist discrepancies between responses to verbal items and actual behavior. One possibility Edwards raises is that the myth of black athletes' "coolness" may become self-fulfilling.

The third category Kane advanced to explain black athletic superiority revolved around *unique, racially specific, historical experiences* stemming from slavery. In brief, he contended that survival of blacks demanded and required an excessive degree of physical-physiological skill. Calvin Hill, a black graduate of Yale and a former stalwart on the Dallas Cowboys, summed up the essence of this position:

> I have a theory about why so many sports stars are Black. I think it boils down to the survival of the fittest. Think of what African slaves were forced to endure in this country merely to survive. Well, Black athletes are their descendents. They are the offspring of those who are physically tough enough to survive.[71]

As a consequence of this natural selection and survival of the fittest argument, the potential for superior athletic performances accrued to black athletes. As with the other explanations, this one suffers from scientifically unacceptable assumptions. The implication that blacks are a "pure" race is not supported by demographic data regarding inbreeding among human populations.

A Sociological Explanation

Our own thinking leads us to cautiously disregard these three explanations. In their place we find the ideas of Edwards[72] and Eitzen and Sage[73] most appealing. Edwards' reasoning is sociological in nature: "different *value orientations* and a *lack of opportunity to participate* offer the greatest promise as explanatory factors." We believe that the rationale applies to the historical paucity of Asian-Americans, Mexicans/Mexican-Americans, Puerto Ricans, and Native Americans (Indians) in American athletics. The fact that there are performance differentials attests not to the fact that there are inherent superiorities but that the role models available for blacks and the closed occupational doors in other areas have led minority group members to participate and excel in areas that have not been barred to them.[74] Edwards said:

> With the channeling of black males disproportionately into sports, the outcome is the same as it would be at Berkeley if we taught and studied nothing but English. Suppose that everyone who got here arrived as a result of some ruthless recruitment process where everyone who couldn't write well was eliminated at every level from age six all the way through junior college. It would only be a short time before the greatest prose—the greatest innovations in teaching, learning, and writing English—came out of Berkeley. It is the inevitable result of all this talent channeled into a single area. The white athlete who might be an O. J. Simpson is probably sitting somewhere behind a desk.[75]

Eitzen and Sage argue that black dominance in sport can be plausibly explained by *structural constraints* on blacks in American society.[76] These constraints are of two types: (1) *occupational discrimination,* and (2) *the sports opportunity structure.* Since blacks have historically been denied job opportunities in various sectors of American society, they have channeled themselves into other socially acceptable outlets, one of which is sport. However, occupational discrimination does not explain why blacks have gravitated to some sports (football, basketball, baseball, boxing, and track) and not to others (swimming, golf, tennis, skiing, and polo).

According to Phillips this selectivity can be explained by the sport *opportunity structure.*[77] This is reminiscent of Medoff's "prohibitive cost" hypothesis. Eitzen and Sage wrote:

> Blacks tend to excel in those sports where facilities, coaching, and competition are available to them (i.e., in the schools and community recreation programs). Those sports where blacks are rarely found have facilities, coaching, and competition provided in private clubs. There are few excellent black golfers, . . . and they had to overcome the disadvantages of being self-taught and being limited to play at municipal courses. Few blacks are competitive skiers for the obvious reasons that most blacks live far removed from snow and mountains, and because skiing is very expensive.[78]

It seems fair to say that, ironically, racist ideologies in the larger society are at least partially responsible for black athletic superiority. This may also prove to be the case with other ethnic minorities. The continued existence of ethnic athletic superiority may be a barometer of the lack of equal opportunity in other work-related realms in American society. As these barriers are broken—and legislation has moved in that direction—we may witness an "equalization" of ethnic performances in the sports world as well as in the occupational world at large.

REWARDS AND AUTHORITY STRUCTURES

We have seen that black performances are superior to those of whites. Is this fact a predictor of higher financial remuneration? Black athletes in professional sports have commanded gigantic yearly salaries. In 1978 football players O. J. Simpson and John Riggins were earning $733,358 and $250,000, respectively; basketball players Julius Erving ($600,000), George McGinnis ($3.2 million in six years), Kareem Abdul-Jabbar ($625,000), David Thompson ($400,000 per year for five years plus $200,000 in deferred compensation), and Bob Lanier ($350,000 per year) were also commanding huge sums; baseball players Gary Matthews and Joe Morgan were making $400,000 yearly, and Reggie Jackson was earning $580,000.

When *average* salaries (arithmetic means) of whites and blacks are compared, there is *no* evidence to support the charge of discriminatory practices. Since data for sports other than baseball are not readily available, the comments regarding financial rewards apply exclusively to this sport. Scully compiled Table 8.5 (upper tier) showing the *average* salary of whites and blacks by position for the 1968-69 season.[79] In all cases blacks earned larger salaries, exceeding those of whites from a minimum of $9,100 (outfield) to a maximum of $21,500 (pitchers).

Leonard's study of the 1977 baseball "elite" (starters) discovered mean salaries of $103,000, $96,000, and $90,000 for blacks, Latins, and white players, respectively.[80] When these mean figures were "broken down" by race and position, it was discovered that (lower tier Table 8.5) whites had the highest salaries at pitcher, 3B, CF, and RF; blacks had the highest at catcher, 2B, and designated hitter (DH); and Latins had the highest at 1B, SS, and LF.

When average salary differentials exist but performance differentials also exist, one cannot easily establish salary discrimination. To tap this dimension, it is necessary to examine the interrelationships among race, performance, and salary. Scully studied this question and concluded that, by holding performance levels constant, blacks experienced salary discrimination because they received less pay than whites for equivalent performance.[81] He argued that salary differences favoring blacks were due to equal pay for superior performance. For example, in employing regression analysis, he contended that to earn $30,000 black outfielders had to out-perform whites by about 65 points in their slugging averages.

Data on salary differentials for ethnic groups in sports besides baseball are meager. Nevertheless, Mogrell reported no significant differences in bonuses[82] and starting salaries among black and white professional *football* players. He did, however, find higher salaries for white veterans than blacks, but this difference was not significant. One important caveat is in order: namely, little can be made of the data unless adjustments for position and performance are considered in the analysis. Since Scully has demonstrated performance differentials favoring blacks, the equal black/white salaries would be indicative of salary discrimination, all other things being equal.

Another area of unequal opportunity resides in the lucrative business of endorsing or promoting commercial products. In 1968, the Equal Employment Opportunity Commission revealed that in 1966 only 5 percent of 351 commercials associated with New York sport events featured blacks.

Table 8.5
Average Racial Salary Differentials in Major League Baseball,
1968-1969*, 1977**

1968-1969

Position	Black	White	Difference
Outfield	$66,000	$56,900	$ 9,100
Infield	$53,100	$40,800	$12,300
Pitchers	$59,900	$38,400	$21,500

1977

Position	White	Black	Latin	Entire Group
Pitcher	$121,227 (n=22)	$100,000 (n=3)	$ 50,000 (n=1)	$116,038 (n=26)
Catcher	84,800 (n=25)	145,000 (n=1)	— (n=0)	87,115 (n=26)
1B	91,091 (n=11)	124,583 (n=12)	211,667 (n=3)	120,462 (n=26)
2B	48,909 (n=11)	124,857 (n=7)	62,250 (n=8)	73,462 (n=26)
SS	83,368 (n=19)	65,000 (n=2)	106,400 (n=5)	86,385 (n=26)
3B	103,409 (n=22)	101,667 (n=3)	75,000 (n=1)	102,115 (n=26)
LF	64,778 (n=9)	127,750 (n=16)	150,000 (n=1)	106,808 (n=26)
CF	131,000 (n=5)	68,267 (n=15)	88,000 (n=5)	84,760 (n=25)
RF	109,222 (n=9)	101,923 (n=13)	50,000 (n=2)	100,333 (n=24)
DH	74,400 (n=5)	84,833 (n=6)	60,000 (n=2)	77,000 (n=13)

*1968-1969 data are from Gerald W. Scully, "Economic Discrimination in Professional Sports," *Law and Contemporary Problems* 38 (Winter-Spring, 1973), p. 76.
**1977 data are from Wilbert M. Leonard, II, "Social and Performance Characteristics of the Pro Baseball Elite: A Study of the 1977 Starting Lineups, *International Review of Sport Sociology* (forthcoming).

Similarly, Yetman and Eitzen found that of the starters for one professional football team in 1971, 8 of 11 whites (73%) in comparison to 2 of 13 blacks (15%) appeared in advertising and media slots.[83] The difference may reflect the dearth of blacks in central playing positions since 75 percent of all advertising opportunities were given to football players who occupied central playing positions.

Once one's direct athletic involvement in sport has terminated, there is evidence that discrimination continues to exist. This observation is reflected in several areas:[84]

1. *Sportcasting.* No black has had a job other than providing the "color" in radio and television sport broadcasting.

2. *Officiating.* Most game officials are disproportionately white. In the history of baseball there have been only two black umpires; professional basketball has only recently broken the "color line", and most blacks in football are head linesmen.

3. *Managers and Owners.* Black ownership is nonexistent. Data for the 1976 baseball and football season showed that, in 24 baseball clubs and 26 football franchises, only one coach was black. In the black-dominated pro basketball, 5 of the 17 (29%) head NBA coaches were black. In the

college circles, again for 1976, not a single major college had a black head coach and only a spattering of colleges (Illinois State, Arizona, Georgetown, Harvard, Eastern Michigan, and Washington State) had a black head coach in basketball or track.

Leonard and Schmidt reported that black head coaches increased from 2 to 21 between 1970 and 1973, but this tabulation included both major (NCAA Division I) and smaller schools.[85] In major colleges the percentage of black head basketball coaches increased from .64 to 5.1 percent and the percentage of major colleges with blacks on their coaching staffs increased from 20 percent (1971) to 45 percent (1975) (Berghorn and Yetman, "Black American in Sport," 1976).

In the minor baseball leagues there is also a paucity of blacks. In 1973 there were only two black managers in 100-plus minor league teams. In the NFL for 1973 there were only 12 blacks—7 percent among the 180 assistant coaches.

Frank Robinson broke the "color bar" in managing a professional baseball team when he became the "field general" of the Cleveland Indians in 1974. Only three coaches in major league baseball (less than 3 percent) were black that year. Furthermore, Frank Robinson has been quoted as saying: "You hardly see any black third base or pitching coaches. And those are the most important coaching jobs. The only place you see blacks coaching is at first base, where most anybody can do the job."[86] In the summer of 1978 Larry Doby (the first black baseball player in the American League) became the second black baseball manager when he took over the helm of the Chicago White Sox.

4. *Executive Positions.* In 1976, only one major college, Southern Illinois University, had a black athletic director (Gayle Sayres). In professional circles there were no black owners of sport franchises. No black held a high executive position in baseball and there was only one black assistant to Commissioner Bowie Kuhn. In pro basketball 2 of the 17 (12%) NBA clubs had black general managers in 1971 (Wayne Embry, a former NBA star, was the first black to occupy such a position in professional sports).

SUMMARY

In this chapter we have reviewed the existence of *prejudice* and *discrimination*—forms of *racism*—in sport. *Prejudice,* an unfavorable feeling or attitude toward a person or group, and *discrimination,* the unfavorable treatment of a person or group, have been pervasive phenomena in sport from antiquity to today. However, our thrust has been to examine these social processes in *contemporary* times.

Three modern forms of racism revolve around: (1) *position allocation* ("stacking"), (2) *performance differentials* ("unequal opportunity for equal ability"), and (3) *rewards and authority structures.* *Stacking* refers to the disproportionate concentration of ethnic minorities, especially blacks, in specific team positions and is a common form of spatial segregation. For example, in baseball blacks tend to be over-represented in the outfield positions while whites tend to be over-represented at the positions of pitcher, catcher, and infield. In football, blacks tend to be disproportionately found in running back positions while whites tend to be more likely to occupy quarterback and other positions like center and guard. In basketball there is a tendency for blacks to be concentrated at the forward positions rather than at the center and guard positions (in collegiate basketball but not in pro basketball where over two-thirds of all players are black). In general, blacks tend to occupy non-central positions (in the major team sports of baseball, football, and basketball) while whites tend to occupy central positions.

Stacking appears to have important consequences as well. Advertising slots tend to go to those occupying central positions, black positions such as defensive back, running back, and wide receiver are associated with shorter careers and shorter careers mean less lifetime earnings and fewer pension benefits.

A host of *sociological/social psychological, psychological,* and *biological* reasons have been advanced for explaining these differences.

Regarding performance, empirical evidence suggests that blacks and whites (and Latins in pro baseball) do *not* perform at the same level. Generally speaking, black performance in the team sports of baseball, football, and basketball is superior on most specific indices of performance (such as batting average, home run production, field goal and free throw percentages, points scored per minute, touchdowns scored, number of pass receptions, etc.).

The author contends that the superior performance of black athletes is probably due to *occupational discrimination* in the larger society whereby blacks have been channeled into only a few socially acceptable outlets—such as sport—and the sports opportunity structure whereby blacks take to those sports which have not been barred to them for various reasons.

With respect to rewards and opportunity structures, there is evidence that while black superstars are recipients of handsome salaries and other benefits, blacks may have to outperform whites to receive such sums. Furthermore, they are not readily found in sportscasting, officiating, management, and ownership and executive positions. In short, although strides toward equality have been made, racism continues to exist in American sport.

IMPORTANT CONCEPTS DISCUSSED IN THIS CHAPTER

Prejudice

Discrimination

Racism

Stacking (Position Allocation)

Centrality

The Stereotyping Hypothesis

The Interaction and Discrimination Hypothesis

The Outcome Control Hypothesis

The Prohibitive Cost Hypothesis

The Differential Attractiveness of
   Positions Hypothesis

The Role Modeling Hypothesis

The Hypothesis that Blacks Excel at Reactive Tasks

The Hypothesis that Blacks and Whites Have
   Personality Differences

Biological Explanations

Performance Differentials

Matriarchal Explanation

Race-Linked Characteristics Explanation

A Sociological Explanation

Structural Constraints

Occupational Discrimination

Sports Opportunity Structure

Rewards and Authority Structures

ENDNOTES

[1] "Latin" refers to those parts of America colonized by the Spanish and Portugese and includes, geographically, Central and South America, Cuba, Puerto Rico, and the Dominican Republic.

[2] R. E. Clement, "Racial Integration in the Field of Sports," *Journal of Negro Education* 23 (1954), pp. 222-230; B. Quaries, *The Negro in the Making of America* (New York: Collier, 1961).

[3] Robert Boyle, *Sport–Mirror of American Life* (Boston, Mass.: Little, Brown, 1963); David Q. Voight, "Reflections on Diamonds: American Baseball and American Culture," *Journal of Sport History* 1 (May, 1974), pp. 3-25; Robert W. Peterson, *Only the Ball Was White* (Englewood Cliffs, N.J.: Prentice Hall, 1970).

[4] Peterson, *Only the Ball Was White.*

[5] D. Stanley Eitzen and George H. Sage, *Sociology of American Sport* (Dubuque, Iowa: Wm. C. Brown, 1978), p. 236.

[6] E. B. Henderson, *The Black Athlete—Emergence Arrival* (New York: Publishers Co., 1968).

[7] M. E. Fletcher, "The Black Soldier Athlete in the United States Army, 1890-1916," *Canadian Journal of History and Sport Physical Education* 3 (December, 1972), pp. 16-26.

[8] Eitzen and Sage, *Sociology of American Sport,* p. 238.

[9] Barry D. McPherson, "Minority Group Involvement in Sport: The Black Athlete," *Sport Sociology,* ed. A. Yiannakis et al. (Dubuque, Iowa: Kendall/Hunt, 1976), pp. 153-166.

[10] Boyle, *Sport—Mirror of American Life,* pp. 103-105.

[11] McPherson, "Minority Group Involvement in Sport: The Black Athlete," p. 158.

[12] Eitzen and Sage, *Sociology of American Sport,* pp. 244-255; D. S. Eitzen and N. R. Yetman, "Immune From Racism?" (see endnote 19). Used with permission.

[13] One researcher defines stacking as the assignment "to a playing position, an achieved status, on the basis of an ascribed status." See Donald W. Ball, "Ascription and Position: A Comparative Analysis of 'Stacking' in Professional Football," *Canadian Review of Sociology and Anthropology* 10 (May, 1973), pp. 97-113.

[14] Aaron Rosenblatt, "Negroes in Baseball: The Failure of Success," *Transaction* 4 (September, 1967), pp. 51-53.

[15] Oscar Grusky, "The Effects of Formal Structure on Managerial Recruitment: A Study of Baseball Organization," *Sociometry* 26 (1963), pp. 345-353.

[16] Hubert M. Blalock, Jr., "Occupational Discrimination: Some Theoretical Propositions," *Social Problems* 9 (Winter, 1962), pp. 240-247.

[17] John W. Loy and Joseph F. McElvogue, "Racial Segregation in American Sport," *International Review of Sport Sociology* 5 (1970), pp. 5-23.

[18] Ibid., p. 8.

[19] D. Stanley Eitzen and Norman R. Yetman, "Immune From Racism?" *Civil Rights Digest* 9 (Winter, 1977), pp. 3-13.

[20] Loy and McElvogue, "Racial Segregation in American Sport."

[21] Joseph Dougherty, "Race and Sport: A Follow-up Study," *Sport Sociology Bulletin* 5 (Spring, 1976), pp. 1-12.

[22] Jonathan J. Brower, "The Quota System: The White Gatekeeper's Regulation of Professional Football's Black Community" (Paper presented at the Annual Meeting of the American Sociological Association, New York, August, 1973).

[23] Ibid., p. 3.

[24] Eitzen and Sage, *Sociology of American Sport.*

[25] Eitzen and Yetman, "Immune From Racism?" p. 4.

[26] Harry Edwards, *Sociology of Sport* (Homewood, Ill.: The Dorsey Press, 1973), p. 213.

[27] Eitzen and Irl Tessendorf (cited in Eitzen and Sage, *Sociology of American Sport*).

[28] Eitzen and Yetman, "Immune From Racism?"

[29] Another possible reason for their paucity in these circles could be overt discrimination on the owners' parts, whereby competent blacks are eschewed because of owners' prejudices and/or because they fear the negative reaction of fans to having blacks in leadership positions.

[30] James E. Curtis and John W. Loy, "Race/Ethnicity and Relative Centrality of Playing Positions in Team Sport," *Exercise and Sport Sciences Reviews* 6 (1978), pp. 285-313, Philadelphia, Penn.: The Franklin Institute Press, 1979. Used with permission.

[31] Jonathan J. Brower, "The Racial Basis of the Division of Labor Among Players in the National Football League as a Function of Stereotypes" (Paper presented at the Annual Meeting of the Pacific Sociological Association, Portland, Ore., 1972).

[32] Tutko (cited in Edwards, *Sociology of Sport*).

[33] Edwards, *Sociology of Sport,* p. 209.

[34] M. H. Medoff, "Positional Segregation and Professional Baseball," *International Review of Sport Sociology* 12 (1977), pp. 49-54.

[35] Jack Olsen, "The Black Athlete—A Shameful Story," *Time* (August 8, 1968).

[36] D. Stanley Eitzen and David C. Sanford, "The Segregation of Blacks by Playing Position in Football: Accident or Design?" *Social Science Quarterly* 55 (March, 1975), pp. 948-959.

[37] Eitzen and Yetman, "Immune From Racism?", p. 6.

[38]McPherson, "Minority Group Involvement in Sport: The Black Athlete."

[39]S. Castine and G. C. Roberts, "Modeling in the Socialization Process of the Black Athlete," *International Review of Sport Sociology* 3-4 (1974), pp. 59-73.

[40]Eitzen and Yetman, "Immune From Racism?", p. 6.

[41]M. Worthy and A. Markle, "Racial Differences in Reactive versus Self-Paced Sports Activities," *Journal of Personality and Social Psychology* 16 (1970), pp. 439-443.

[42]J. Jones and A. Hochner, "Racial Differences in Sports Activities: A Look at the Self-Paced versus Reactive Hypothesis," *Journal of Personality and Social Psychology* 27 (1973), pp. 86-95.

[43]J. Dunn and M. Lupfer, "A Comparison of Black and White Boys' Performance in Self-Paced and Reactive Sports Activities," *Journal of Applied Social Psychology* 4 (1974), pp. 24-35.

[44]Jones and Hochner, "Racial Differences in Sport Activities: A Look at the Self-Paced versus Reactive Hypothesis," p. 92.

[45]S. L. Norman, "Collation of Anthropmetric Research Comparing American Males: Negro and Caucasian" (Master's thesis, University of Oregon, 1968). J. Jordon, "Physiological and Anthropometrical Comparisons of Negroes and Whites," *Journal of Health, Physical Education and Recreation* 40 (November/December, 1969), pp. 93-99. R. M. Malina, "Anthropology, Growth and Physical Education," *Physical Education: An Interdisciplinary Approach*, ed. R. Singer et al. (New York: Macmillan, 1972), pp. 237-309.

[46]Jay J. Coakley, *Sport in Society: Issues and Controversies* (St. Louis, Mo.: The C. V. Mosby Co., 1978), p. 304.

[47]Malina, "Anthropology, Growth and Physical Education," p. 300.

[48]Rosenblatt, "Negroes in Baseball: The Failure of Success."

[49]Eitzen and Yetman, "Immune From Racism?"

[50]Rosenblatt, "Negroes in Baseball: The Failure of Success," p. 53.

[51]Anthony Pascal and Leonard A. Rapping, *Racial Discrimination in Organized Baseball* (Santa Monica, Calif.: The Rand Corporation, 1970).

[52]This study has been criticized on the grounds that other factors besides hitting average are important (such as bunting ability and defensive skills).

[53]Pascal and Rapping, *Racial Discrimination in Organized Baseball*, p. 36.

[54]Edwards, *Sociology of Sport*, pp. 190-191.

[55]Wilbert M. Leonard, II, "Spatial Separation and Performance Differentials of White, Black, and Latin Pro Baseball Players" (Paper presented at the Annual Meeting of the American Sociological Association, Chicago, Ill., September, 1977).

[56]David S. Neft, Roland T. Johnson, Richard M. Cohen, and Jordan A. Deutsch, "The Black, Latin, White, Report," *The Sports Encyclopedia: Baseball* (New York: Grosset and Dunlap, 1974).

[57]Wilbert M. Leonard, II, "Social and Performance Characteristics of the Pro Baseball Elite: A Study of the 1977 Starting Lineups," *International Review of Sport Sociology* (forthcoming).

[58]Gerald W. Scully, "Economic Discrimination in Professional Sports," *Law and Contemporary Problems* 38 (Winter-Spring, 1973), p. 73.

[59]Ibid., pp. 73-75.

[60]Designations like "$p < .05$" mean that less than 5 times in 100 could chance produce the outcomes. Hence, the reader can be reasonably confident that these differences are "real" and not "spurious."

[61]Wilbert M. Leonard, II and Susan Schmidt, "Observations on the Changing Social Organization of Collegiate and Professional Basketball," *Sport Sociology Bulletin* 4 (Fall, 1975), pp. 13-35.

[62]Norman R. Yetman and D. Stanley Eitzen, "Black Americans in Sports: Unequal Opportunity for Equal Ability," *Civil Rights Digest* 5 (August, 1972), pp. 20-34.

[63]Ibid.

[64]Norris R. Johnson and David P. Marple, "Racial Discrimination in Professional Basketball," *Sociological Focus* 6 (Fall, 1973), pp. 6-18.

[65]Ibid.

[66]Boyle, *Sport—Mirror of American Life;* Jim Bouton, *Ball Four* (New York: World, 1970); Harry Edwards, *The Revolt of the Black Athlete* (New York: Free Press, 1969); D. C. Boulding, "Participation of the Negro in Selected Amateur and Professional Athletics from 1935 to 1955" (Master's thesis, University of Wisconsin-Madison, 1957); Johnny Sample, *Confessions of a Dirty Ballplayer* (New York: Dial, 1970).

[67]Edwards, *Sociology of Sport*, pp. 191-192.

[68] Martin Kane, "An Assessment of Black is Best," *Sports Illustrated* 34 (January 18, 1971), pp. 72-83.

[69] Coakley, *Sport in Society: Issues and Controversies*, p. 305.

[70] Bruce C. Ogilvie, *Problem Athletes and How to Handle Them* (London, England: Pelham Books, Ltd., 1966).

[71] Edwards, *Sociology of Sport*, p. 197.

[72] Ibid., pp. 175-176.

[73] Eitzen and Sage, *Sociology of American Sport*, pp. 241-243.

[74] Terry Bledsoe, "Black Dominance of Sports: Strictly from Hunger," *The Progressive* 37 (June, 1973), pp. 16-19.

[75] "The Black Dominance," *Time* (May 9, 1977), pp. 58-59.

[76] Eitzen and Sage, *Sociology of American Sport*.

[77] John C. Phillips, "Toward an Explanation of Racial Variations in Top-Level Sports Participation," *International Review of Sport Sociology* (November, 1976), pp. 39-55.

[78] Eitzen and Sage, *Sociology of American Sport*, p. 242.

[79] Scully, "Economic Discrimination in Professsional Sports," p. 76.

[80] Leonard, "Social and Performance Characteristics of the Pro Baseball Elite: A Study of the 1977 Starting Lineups."

[81] Scully, "Economic Discrimination in Professional Sports."

[82] Robert Mogrell, *Wall Street Journal* (May 1, 1973). Pascal and Rapping, "The Economics of Racial Discrimination in Organized Baseball," found significant differences in bonuses for whites and blacks *prior* to 1958. This difference decreased over the years so that by 1965-67 it was virtually eliminated.

[83] Yetman and Eitzen, "Black Americans in Sports: Unequal Opportunity for Equal Ability."

[84] Eitzen and Yetman, "Immune from Racism?", p. 8.

[85] Leonard and Schmidt, "Observations on the Changing Social Organization of Collegiate and Professional Basketball."

[86] Pete Axthelm, "Black Out," *Newsweek* (July 15, 1974), p. 57.

Women in Sport

INTRODUCTION

Women's contemporary involvement in sport is not new. Historically, women have been both spectators and participants, and their activities now range from simple recreation pastimes to serious college, international, and professional competition. Nonetheless, *sex role expectations* of women have perennially provided major obstacles to the full realization of their sport potential. Though women's roles in sport now encompass an enormous variety of activities, *sexism*—an unfair attitude toward or the partial treatment of individuals on the basis of their sex—continues to linger on. In this chapter we will trace the emergence of the female role in sport from ancient Greece to the present. See Vignette 9.1 for a synopsis of significant events in female sport.

HISTORICAL BACKGROUND OF WOMEN IN SPORT

A chronology of women in sport is important for two reasons: (1) it provides a perspective from which to understand and assess their contemporary sport experience, and (2) it establishes a basis for many of the ideas, especially the myths, that have worked to the disadvantage of females who have aspired to compete in athletics.

Certainly one of the earliest civilizations to have specific prescriptions for the role of the female in sport was Greece. The Greeks embodied their cultural values and ideals in their gods and goddesses and by doing so laid the foundations for many of our contemporary images of women athletes. Greek goddesses were known to participate in such activities as horseback riding, hunting, swimming, and running. The mythical Amazons (literally, "without breasts") were a group of supernatural women who lived apart from men (except for the purpose of procreation) and developed a completely matriarchal society. They were described as "... shining young women in shining armor, with a horse between their legs and arrogantly scrawling the supremacy of their sex on the unending scroll of the wind."[1]

The Greek goddesses, however, were not totally characterized by traits of independence and power. Athena, Artemis, and Atalanta were goddesses who personified ideas of excellence for females but who, nevertheless, suffered certain weaknesses. Athena, the goddess of wisdom who led

VIGNETTE 9.1
SIGNIFICANT EVENTS IN FEMALE SPORT

Pre 776 B.C.   Herae Games
1831   Catherine Beecher's *Course of Calisthenics for Young Ladies* published.
1837   Mt. Holyoke, a female institution, opened with exercise required.
1865   First college women's physical education program, Vassar College.
1870   Middie Morgan became first female sportswriter.
1887   First national women's singles tennis championship.
1900   Women made their Olympic debut in golf and tennis.
1923   White House Conference on women's athletics.
1925   Gertrude Ederle became the first female to swim the English Channel.
1928   Females permitted to participate in Olympic track and field events for the first time.
1932   Babe Didrikson starred in Olympics.
1949   Ladies Professional Golf Association (LPGA) formed.
1959   Althea Gibson became first black professional tennis player.
1968   Katherine Switzer suspended by AAU for participating in 26-mile Boston Marathon.
1969   Tuesdee Testa became first female jockey at Santa Anita.
1971   Billie Jean King (tennis player) became first professional female athlete to earn $100,000.
1972   Title IX program passed by Congress.
1973   Publication of *The Sportswoman.* Billie Jean King–Bobby Riggs tennis match in Astro-dome.
1974   Publication of first issue of *WomenSports.* Little League charter amended to allow girls.
1975   *Title IX* regulations take effect.
1977   Women's basketball doubleheader in Madison Square Garden drew 15,000 spectators. Chris Evert (tennis player) earned $500,000.
1978   Formation of Women's Professional Basketball League.

men into battle, and Artemis, the goddess of the hunt who excelled in the use of the bow and arrow, were both rejected by men. Atlanta had so much speed she was allowed to marry only the male who could outrun her. She was duped by Hippomenes who rolled three golden apples in front of her and then passed her as she bent down to pick them up. And finally Hera (for whom the Herae Games were named) fulfilled the role of helpmate, submitting her will to her husband, Zeus.[2] Thus, although the Greeks gave some positive characteristics to their goddesses, they still relegated them to a subordinate positions when compared to their gods. The societal ideals of what was "good" and desirable were invested in the male gods.

Ancient Rome also played a critical role in the casting of female roles. The Roman family was *patriarchal,* and virtually all the power was invested in the male. The female was often under the rule of the male—her father, brother, husband, and son. Females were forbidden to be physically active and were restricted to spectatorship at chariot races, gladiatorial combat, and athletics.

Even the early Christian church provided no relief from this firmly entrenched sexism. St. Paul wrote: "For man . . . is the image and glory of God; but the woman is the glory of man. For the man is not of the woman, but the woman of the man. Neither was the man created for the woman, but the woman for the man."[3]

The *medieval period* (circa 400-1500 A.D.) also helped to shape the attitudes toward women. By the end of the 14th century sport was an acceptable endeavor for noble women who participated in such pastimes as ice-skating and jousting. This was short-lived, however, since the later medieval period brought about a change in the concept of women's roles. The Age of Chivalry put women back on a pedestal where they were to be worshipped, protected, and, in essence, "de-womanized." Thomas Aquinas provided a prevailing viewpoint: "The woman is subject to the man on account of the weakness of her nature, both of mind and body . . .Woman is subjection according to the laws of nature, but a slave is not."[4] By the end of the 16th century one saw female sport accepted only by the nobility, and then only in such approved activities as shuttle cock, riding, and dancing. These notions continued to hold their sway until the era of sport expansion in the middle 1800s.

THE FEMALE ROLE IN SOCIETY AND SPORT

Societal Expectations of Females

In Western society women have long been cast under the image of the "weaker" sex. The traditional roles of males have attempted to combine husband, father and occupation while females have been wives and mothers. Eventually women rebelled against these restrictive cultural scripts. The women's liberation movement of the 1960s has been one of the most influential and far reaching social movements for women's rights. The impetus for this new feminism was Betty Friedan's *The Feminine Mystique* (1963).[5] Women began to question why they should be forced to give up careers or other goals to play the wife/mother role. They began to rebel against traditional views of females as weak and subservient. Up to this point sexism permeated our society and sharply restricted females from achieving goals other than that of wife and mother. In time the feminist movement turned its eyes to one of the most exclusively male bastions, sport. As Marie Hart said: "When the role of female is no longer limited to mother, secretary, or Miss America, isn't it about time that women were given not only freedom but respect for being successful in sport?"[6]

The women's movement became particularly effective with the formation of two bodies: (1) the Women's Action Group (WAG), and (2) the National Organization of Women (NOW). The purpose of these organizations was to eliminate sexism and bring women into full participation in the mainstream of American society. Just the same, the sexist practices of sport were apparently not recognized until the early 1970s. For example, it wasn't until 1973 that NOW passed a resolution to the effect:

> NOW opposes and actively works to eliminate all forms of discrimination against women and girls in recreation and sports, including school, college, community physical education, and recreation programs and facilities.[7]

Task forces for NOW were organized with the avowed purpose of implementing the thrust of this proposal.

Male Ideals Embodied in Sport

> "The flag bearer ought to be a man, a strong man, a warrior. A woman's place is in the home."—Russell Knipp's reaction to Olga Connolly carrying the U.S. flag in the Munich Olympic parade.

Sport in the United States has served as a masculine *rite of passage*. A rite of passage is a "ceremony" that facilitates movement from one status in life to another. It is a vehicle for *socialization* into adulthood. Males have traditionally participated in sports to affirm their masculinity. Through Little League Baseball, Pop Warner Football, and the like, boys were afforded an opportunity to establish their sex-role identity. However, sport programs for girls were in very short supply.

Pierre de Coubertin, the founder of the present-day Olympics, issued the following sexist statement:

> Respect of individual liberty requires that one should not interfere in private acts . . . but in public competitions, (women's) participation must be absolutely prohibited. It is indecent that the spectators should be exposed to the risk of seeing the body of a woman being smashed before their eyes. Besides, no matter how toughened a sportswoman may be, her organism is not cut out to sustain certain shocks. Her nerves rule her muscles, nature wanted it that way. Finally, the egalitarian discipline that is brought to bear on the male contenders for the good order and good appearance of the meeting risks being affected and rendered inapplicable by female participation. For all these practical reasons as well as sentimental ones, it is extremely desirable that a drastic rule be established very soon.[8]

The concept of masculinity in sport is one that has been constantly reinforced by parents, coaches, the media, and others involved directly and indirectly in sport. Sport was the setting where a man could test his manliness against another man. "Here's where we separate the men from the boys" is a favorite phrase of coaches during a tense moment of a contest. A player who gives his all in a losing effort is applauded because "he stood there and took it like a man." Announcers describe players as "tough" and "aggressive," descriptions which fit well with societal definitions of males. Much of this is a carryover from the work ethic that built the country. If hard-working men made this country great, then men proving themselves in sporting contests reinforced the ethic.

Jack Scott, for one, has been a leading critic of sport as a proving ground for masculinity. He described a condescending comment about Micki King, former American Olympic diver, by her coach: "That's how I knew she was going to be good, because the very first time I saw her she dove like a man."[9] Here we see the crux of the problem for females in athletics. The statement implies that males are the standard for success and it assumes that males will dive better than females. In analyzing this comment, Scott says he (the coach) should have said she dives correctly, for surely she dives better than all but a handful of American males. With a grasp on the background of women in sport and some of the problems they face, we can move into a more intensive discussion of the female role in sport.

Sport as an Anomaly for Females

Jan Felshin, a prominent writer on the social aspects of women in sport, uses the term *social anomaly* in describing the role of females in sport.[10] Sport, as has been shown, is defined in masculine terms. Women, as traditionally defined, have no place in sport. The women who do choose to participate in sport either have had to take measures to enhance and reinforce their femininity, i.e. wear cute hairdos, frilly uniforms, etc., or face the consequences of being labelled *deviant* for entering this male realm. Consequently, the female in sport is often forced to become apologetic.[11]

It seems that the circumstances surrounding the debut of women in the world of sport appears to be somewhat unique. The young boy who goes into sport is constantly told it is good for him; sport is an integral and compatible part of society's and his self-definition. When blacks began to enter the professional sport ranks they encountered various forms of discrimination (see chapters 7 and 8). But they, too, felt that sport was good for them. It was others' prejudices that were the real culprits. Females, on the other hand, seemingly have to go through a whole process of *social-psychological redefinition* to participate in sport. In a sense they are forced to prove their femininity, which illustrates that femininity is not a characteristic inherent in womanhood, but rather a function of social and psychological definition.

The traditional role of women in sport is *not* that of competitor. Rather, women have been forced off to the sidelines to fill some kind of supportive-affective role. This parallels the societal expectations of females. Although not necessarily typical, one has only to look at the recent rise in popularity of the NFL cheerleaders. Spurred on by the adoration for the Dallas Cowboy cheerleaders, it seems the entire league has gone to cheerleading squads which feature not cheers but long, silky hair, revealing halter tops, and very short shorts. Perhaps it is fitting that football, one of the most "masculine" professional sports, gives us another image of the female in sport performing a supportive activity. Every fall and winter columnists in newspapers and magazines churn out a column on the poor "football widow."

When a female does attempt to enter sports in a central, participatory role, she does so at some risk. Because of the nature of the contests, sports reward the aggressive, the dominant, and the victor. Hard work and determination are two of the building blocks. For a female to play sports and play them well, she must enter into a world where this aggressiveness is positively reinforced. According to traditional cultural stereotypes, however, females are not to be aggressive. Thus the female in sport "breaks" society's rules for her and sets up a conflict between societal, self, and sport expectations. Sometimes she is labelled *deviant* for not conforming to society's expectations.

An even more severe accusation than the questioning of one's femininity is a questioning of the female competitor's sexual preferences. Often these women are unfairly labelled as lesbians. The line of reasoning goes something like this: If they want to play sports, which incorporate male ideals, then they must be frustrated males. Then if they're that frustrated about not being male, they will never want to have sex with a man. Hardly is this line of thinking very logical but it has endured for quite awhile. In fact, because of it women are forced to take measures to enhance their femininity and demonstrably prove their sex identity (see p. 195). This lesbianism attack has been most prevalent in the Ladies Professional Golf Association. The Association along with the media tend to play up the better looking players such as Laura Baugh and Jan Stephenson. The former was once described in a *Sports Illustrated* report as follows:

> A cool braided California blond named Laura Baugh made quite a splash . . . her perfectly tanned, well-formed legs swinging jauntily. The hair on her tapered arms was bleached absolutely white against a milk-chocolate tan. Her platinum hair was pulled smartly back in a Viking-maiden braid.[13]

Such commentary might well describe a fashion show or a beauty pageant rather than a golf match. The admiration was more for her looks than her skill. This, however, helps serve as an explanation for the recent popularity of Nancy Lopez. Lopez combined both: she was attractive and able to play the game with great skill.[14]

Golf is one sport where females have been sanctioned to participate. According to cultural norms, however, there are certain activities which, historically, have not been acceptable for females. These include: bodily contact, application of body force to some heavy object, projection of the body into or through space for long distances, and cooperative face-to-face opposition in situations in which some body contact may occur.[15] Any sports which have these characteristics have frequently been deemed socially unacceptable. They seem to include the three major professional sports of football, baseball, and basketball as well as wrestling, judo, boxing, weightlifting, hammer throw, pole vaulting, long foot races, high hurdles, and many types of team sports.

Sports which are deemed acceptable have the characteristics of being scaled down in terms of force to be applied in performing the desired tasks. "Force is applied to weightless objects with lightweight implements and velocity is attained by the use of manufactured devices."[16] Tennis, golf, swimming, diving, skiing, figure skating, gymnastics, archery, fencing, badminton, squash, volleyball, and bowling are sports in which women are heavily represented.

The Olympics, the competitive grounds for all that is supposedly good in sport, provide an example for the application of these notions of acceptability. Women are not allowed to lift heavy weights, throw the hammer, pole vault, run the high hurdles, or run long distances. They are permitted to run the low hurdles, however. The ban on long distance racing seems slightly ridiculous when one looks at some of the marathon times women have been recently turning in. (See Vignette 9.2 for a case study of one female marathon runner.) The list of approved events do require skill although sheer strength is not essential.

MYTHS VERSUS REALITIES

Discrimination against women in sport can be easily linked to a "spill-over" effect of discrimination against women in general. Three particular arguments which have been enlisted historically to justify discrimination against women in sport and which have now been thoroughly exposed as myths are worth examining:[17]

1. Athletics are physically harmful.
2. Women don't play sports well enough to deserve equality.
3. Girls are not really interested in sport.

Sports Are Physically Dangerous for Females

"I love to see myself getting strong, being competent, and taking care of myself. That's probably the most motivating part of being an athlete."[18]

This quote by Kate Schmidt, an American javelin thrower, runs counter to the notion that sports are harmful to women, particularly their physical development. Gilbert and Williamson in a series of articles on women in sport list two notions which form the basis for the idea that sports are dangerous for females.[19] The *first* is a traditional view of women as physically fragile and weak. The *second* is that the physical activity required in sport will cause females to become overly muscular.

These myths have thwarted the attempts of women to enter the sport realm. When the sport expansion began in the middle to late 19th century, women naturally joined in. This increased participation brought two reactions from physical educators. One progressive reaction was to greet

VIGNETTE 9.2
A FEMALE SOCIAL CHANGE AGENT: KATHERINE SWITZER

Katherine Switzer was the first female to run in the Boston Marathon (in 1968) and received a suspension from the AAU for her efforts. Ms. Switzer commented: "I didn't know it was illegal for women to run. I had not even heard of anything called 'women's liberation'. I had been running up to 10 miles a day with men, and had actually run 31 to prepare for the event. It all sounds so odd today. Then I was a freak. But now I'm chic." Since her feat the number of women competing in marathons has increased and the finishing times have decreased. In 1978 Bill Rodgers won the Boston Marathon in 2:10:13. Fifteen women broke three hours, an accomplishment that was thought impossible for women five years ago. An even better indication of the improvement of women is the world record time of 2:32:30 turned in by Grete Waitz, of Norway, in the New York Marathon, her first. Although the Olympic committee has been reluctant to permit females into long distance races, the International Amateur Olympic Federation—the track and field governing body—has sanctioned a 3000 meter world championship for females in 1980. Furthermore, some authorities believe females may be running the 10,000 meter race in the 1988 Olympics. Katherine Switzer, in short, has become an important *social change agent,* a role model if you will, for significant alterations in women's sport.

Source: Karen Peterson, Features and News Service, 1978.

---

the movement with enthusiasm, emphasizing the physical benefits of exercise. A second, more prevalent, reaction was concern for the health of females. Many physical educators took the lead in pointing out what they felt to be the detrimental effects of exercise.[20] Their efforts resulted in a lack of quality athletic programs for women long into the 20th century.

The allegation that sports are physically harmful to females pivots around the possible injury to their reproductive organs and breasts and the effects on the menstrual cycle and pregnancy. Consider the female reproductive organs first. The female uterus is one of the best protected and shock resistant organs of the human anatomy. Contrary to popular "male" belief, it is considerably more protected than the male genitalia.[21] Furthermore, studies have shown that female athletes have shorter and easier deliveries during pregnancy.[22] Similarly, there is as yet no conclusive evidence that women who participate in sport develop breast cancer disproportionately; hence, there appear to be no rational medical reasons for women to disengage from physical activity. Finally, since males wear protective gear covering their genitalia, there is no reason why females could not wear protective chest apparatus as well. There is also agreement among medical researchers and gynecologists that sports have little effect on menstruation and there is no need to restrict physical activity during any phase of the menses. In fact, women have won gold medals in the Olympic track and swimming events while menstruating.[23]

Another argument for restricting females to certain types of physical activity is that males are, in most cases, bigger and stronger. The mature male skeleton is more rugged, the bones are more massive and have greater density, and the joints are larger. In addition, at maturity the female weighs 5 pounds less and gives up an average of 5 to 6 inches in height. Women do have an advantage lower center of weight and a wider knee joint which combine to give them greater stability in relation to size. Many other physical factors give the male an advantage in strength, leverage, and arc of movement.[24] Although males may have a physical advantage, that should not serve to keep females from competing against (at least) each other.

It is during the formative years of youth that most females are socialized *away* from sport, yet it is precisely at these times that females often are physically mature, and capable of serious athletic competition. Klafs and Lyon state that at any age, a growing girl has reached greater maturity than a boy of the same age.[25] Females reach their maximum strength at age 12½, or one year before the onset of the menarche.[26] Consider the Olympics. One sees pre-teen and early-teen girls constantly breaking records in swimming and gymnastics competition. Gymnastics seems rarely to have a woman beyond the age of eighteen competing; yet their male contemporaries often don't come into their prime until college age or later.

Information compiled to date shows that females are taking no great physical risks by participating in sports (see Vignette 9.3). Wyrick argues there is more performance overlap than difference and the lower performance is due to cultural restrictions on females.[27] The empirical foundation for this conclusion, however, is not certain. Much research contains an "elitist" basis in that most physiological studies have been done on Olympic-caliber athletes. Nonetheless, the evidence clearly refutes the notion that females are physically unsuited for vigorous athletic competition.

The second myth surrounding the denial of females' full participation insinuates that they will develop overly muscular bodies. Medical research yields two reasons why females won't gain bulging muscles. Harmon Brown, an endocrinologist, wrote: (1) the amount of body fat females have (22 to 14 percent on the average male) masks muscular development, and (2) females only produce 5 to 10 percent of the amount of androgen, the male sex hormone of males.[28] Klafs and Lyon conclude: "It is inherent endocrinological and morphological factors that are responsible for femininity and not vigorous physical activity, which too often is held to blame."[29] Thus we see the notion that physical activity will masculinize the female is also rejected by medical science.

An important (although some would say insidious) consequence of this problem is the Olympic procedure of "sex testing" female competitors. The stated intent of these tests is to ensure there are no male impersonators competing as women, since this has happened in the past. Hitler set up a "woman" at the 1936 Olympics who set a world high-jump record and then, several years later, admitted "she" had been forced to compete as a woman for the glory of the Third Reich. There were also two French women who won medals in 1952 in Oslo who turned out to be males. Another intent of the test is to screen out the one woman in 1000 who could be a genetic male, a condition called pseudo-hermaphroditism. The test was first used at Budapest at the European track and field championships in 1966. Of the 243 athletes tested, no one failed, but six world class athletes skipped the competition after it was announced there would be tests. The test involves a microscopic examination of cells from the inside of the cheek or a hair follicle for identifying the typical XX female chromosome pattern. In the history of the test only one woman has failed. Ewa Klobkowska, a 21-year-old Polish sprinter, in 1967 failed the test for having a male chromosome pattern. Apparently she had internal testicles that produced male hormones without her knowledge. The test is not a popular subject among women competitors. A standing joke is the certificate they receive after passing the test which certifies they are, in fact, females. Jane Frederick, an American pentathlete, is one of its most outspoken critics: "The official explanation of this test is to protect us from imposters and from women who are really men, whatever that means. No, I don't really believe it. I think they're really saying, 'You're so good, we just can't believe you're a woman. So prove it.' "[30]

VIGNETTE 9.3

WOMEN ATHLETES HURT differently, NOT MORE

MINNEAPOLIS (UPI)—Woman athletes usually manage to keep their heads intact better than their male counterparts but have a tendency to hurt their knees and develop anemia, say University of Minnesota experts.

A century ago, doctors warned women against certain forms of strenuous exercise. Although an additional 10,000 women now take part in college athletics each year, many old attitudes persist.

Roger Hallin, UM team physician for women's athletics, said there is nothing particularly delicate about a woman athlete's body; it's just different.

For many years, doctors perpetuated the notion that a blow to the breast can cause cancer. Yet, no studies support this theory, he said.

In an interview, Hallin said he sees fewer head and neck injuries among women athletes than among men. "They just don't bang their heads at each other like the men do," he said.

He said knee injuries are more common among women athletes because of the width of the female pelvis and the resulting oblique angle of the thigh bone. The female knee has a painful tendency to slip out of place under stress.

Leah Wollenburg, UM's women's trainer, said women no longer do deep-knee squats.

"It was discovered a few years ago that they were really tough on the female knee," she said, adding that they had already caused a lot of damage.

Miss Wollenburg said anemia is a serious and common hidden problem.

"Women in general have a tendency to be anemic," she said. "The demands a woman athlete puts on her body make the problem worse."

This fall, for the first time, UM is requiring blood tests of all female athletes to check for anemia.

Hallin says menstruation and its effects on women are another myth.

Generations of mothers have warned their daughters not to swim, ride a horse, or undertake other strenuous exercise during menstruation.

Most doctors now believe exercise actually helps relieve normal menstrual cramps, Hallin said. He also said sweating from heavy exercise alleviates swelling caused by excess water retention and reduces the need for diuretics that sometimes are prescribed for menstrual problems.

Tests do show athletic performance is adversely affected by menstruation, especially among swimmers, but the more fit a female athlete is, the less menstruation affects performance.

The UM experts concluded the female body is just as tough and durable as the male body, although women respond differently to the stress of physical exertion.

"Women athletes do not have more injuries just because they're female," Hallin said.

Women Don't Play Sports Well Enough to Deserve Equality

This argument, in perspective, is illogical and irrational. For example, if college athletic directors were to determine whether or not male teams were to be fielded based on the quality of play, one might well see a dramatic cutback in many athletic programs. This argument assumes any sports for males are good, but the only sports for females should be ones where they have developed considerable proficiency. The argument becomes a vicious circle when one asks the next logical question. If they don't have legitimate programs, how can they develop the necessary skills? There are data to refute this argument.

Wyrick cites a study of Olympic female athletes in track and field and swimming.[31] These events were chosen because they: (1) require maximum utilization of physical skills, (2) use objective measurement, and (3) demand that both sexes perform the same events. In each Olympics, the study found women were improving, especially in the field events where women showed the most improvement. Possible explanations for this include larger size for each successive generation and a loosening of cultural restrictions on events which require the moving of heavy weights. In fact, statistics show that by the 1976 Olympics women swimmers were competing at a level 93 percent that of the males. Moreover, Don Schollander's 1964 Olympic record in the 400-meter free-style swimming event was surpassed by almost three seconds by a 15-year-old East German girl at the 1976 Montreal Olympics.

In conclusion, this argument is based on an elitist model of sport. Should participation in and enjoyment of sport be limited only to the most skillful? Perhaps Simone de Beauvoir, in an oft-quoted passage from *The Second Sex*, best answers this question for women:

> And in sports the end in view is not success independent of physical equipment; it is rather the attainment of perfection within the limitations of each physical type: the featherweight boxing champion is as much a champion as is the heavyweight; the woman skiing champion is not the inferior of the faster male champion: they belong to two different classes. It is precisely the female athletes who, being positively interested in their own game, feel themselves least handicapped in comparison with the male. . . . Let her swim, climb mountain peaks, pilot an airplane, battle against the elements, take risks, go out for adventure, and she will not feel before the world that timidity. . .[32]

Women Are Not Really Interested in Sports

This, too, has more basis in fiction than in fact. Toward the end of the chapter (in the section "Current Trends"), an analysis of current sport trends will show that where "quality" programs are offered, the response has been very good.

SPORT SOCIALIZATION FOR FEMALES

As touched on earlier, one of the main features of American sport is that young boys are socialized *into* sport and girls are socialized *away* from sport. But just how does this happen? There have been many studies on the effects of sport socialization but they have mostly concentrated on males, reflecting the historical reality that sports have been monopolized by them. Recently, though, this trend has begun to reverse itself and there have been studies which help explain why females are entering sports.

Socialization into Sport

In studying socialization *into* sport there are three classes of variables to be considered: (1) personal attributes, (2) socializing agents, and (3) the social structure. Most studies on women in sport have been directed at the personal attribute category, involving attributes such as attitudes, femininity concepts such as self-image and self-concept, and personality.[33] Most of the data are fragmented and provide no real insight into female sport socialization. The intent of studies on this level is reflective of the social bias against female participation in its inference that the only reason for them to enter sport is for some kind of personal reason. It ignores the possible effect the agents of socialization and structure of the community might have.

As has been stated earlier in the book (chapter 5), two main socializing agents are *significant others* and *reference groups*. Important among these two categories are the family, peers, school, teachers, and other members of the community. These agents, by teaching and reinforcing specific behaviors, exert a profound influence on the learning process. A manifestation of this is the learning of appropriate *sex-role behaviors*. Studies have shown that sex-role differentiation is learned very early in life. Greendorfer cites studies which suggest sex differences in play behavior at age one.[34]

Greendorfer examined the question of how females learn to participate in sport.[35] Her investigation grew out of a lack of research on the effect of significant others. She checked to see if differences existed among three social agents: (1) family, (2) peers, and (3) schools during three different life stages: (1) childhood, (2) adolescence, and (3) young adulthood. She found that during the first stage females were more influenced by peers and family than teachers and coaches. A possible explanation for this pattern might be a lack of involvement in organized sporting activities and greater involvement in family and friendship-oriented activities. During adolescence, peers, teachers, and coaches emerged as significant agents of socialization. This probably reflects their increased involvement in school activities. By the period of young adulthood the family's influence declined and the peer group remained dominant. Thus, over time, one sees the decline in importance of the family as an agent of sport socialization and the emergence of the peer group as dominant.

In a study conducted along similar lines, Koehler set out to find the dominant socializing agent in three different areas of influence on sport involvement: (1) early encouragement, (2) first teaching of fundamentals, and (3) teaching of strategies.[36] She then divided her college subjects into six groups: state or private schools, early or late starters, and individual or team sports. Her findings showed that early starters depended on family agents for their initial encouragement and teaching of fundamentals, while late starters depended on non-family agents. Among those family agents, the father dominated. She did uncover one very important trend which supports the contention that women in sport have tended to do things of their own volition. She found that self-motivation was a more significant influence on sport involvement than family or non-family agents.

In studying the correlates of female sport participation, Snyder and Spreitzer[37] concocted two groups of subjects: (1) female participants in high school gymnastics, basketball and track (the "experimental group") and (2) female nonparticipants (the "control group"). Two findings were noteworthy. First, there was little difference in mothers' and fathers' sport interest between the two groups. Second, the most marked contrast between female participants and nonparticipants resided in the time at which their athletic participation began. More specifically, the participants began their active sport experience earlier than did the nonparticipants. Although the sample of subjects was representative among Ohio high schools, we do not know how generalizable they would be across the nation as a whole.

Another means of socialization investigated by Greendorfer was the *role theory model*.[38] She hypothesized that males would be the most influential role model given the predominance of male sports in our society. The scarcity of role models has been advanced as a reason for the scarcity of females in sport. Her investigation found males provided the most influential role model in childhood, both sexes influential during adolescence, and the female role model significant as adult. There is one qualification to the data, however. Although the influence of the male role model decreased over time its effect never totally diminished and was still significant at the adult level.

The experience of black women in sport seems to be an exception to the general socialization of females away from sport. Some authors believe it might be easier for the black female to be accepted in the world of sport.[39] Hart has written:

There is a startling contrast between the Black and White female athlete. In the Black community it seems that a woman can be strong and competent in sport and still not deny her womanliness. She can even win respect and high status; Wilma Rudolph, Wyomia Tyus, Elaine Brown, for example.[40]

One of the arguments is that given the great number of black female-headed families and these accompanying images of strength, it is possible for them to be strong in sport and still not have to deny their femininity. Thus they can enter sport without facing the role conflict white females do.

SOCIALIZATION VIA SPORT

There is also a scarcity of empirical data regarding female socialization *via* sport. Most of the information isn't the result of rigorously conducted scientific investigation but, instead, speculation. Perhaps time will tell if women become more dominant and aggressive as a result of sport participation.

Much of the commentary in this area concerns the view that as women developed their own athletic programs they would learn from the scandals which have periodically besieged their male counterparts. The hope was for a more humane model which would operate for the benefit of all and urge cooperation and enjoyment over the sole emphasis on victory.[41] Some recent findings show this might not be the case. In the spring of 1978 a report on women's intercollegiate basketball showed evidence of severe recruiting violations and a sport structure moving closer to that of the males.[42] To conclude from these findings that females are being socialized by sports to view them in traditionally male terms is premature. Future research will clear up what is only conjecture at this time.

Achievement Motivation

The concept of *achievement motivation* is more of a psychological than sociological concept, but it does have a high degree of relevance when one investigates the circumstances surrounding female sport involvement. David McClelland and John Atkinson define a need to achieve as "a relatively stable disposition to strive for achievement or success."[43] Birrell lists two general *myths* concerning women: (1) they do not have a high need to achieve and (2) achievement motivations are developed solely as a result of early child training and that level is irreversibly fixed at an early age. Definitive conclusions on the relationship between achievement motivation and the tendency to become involved in sport is yet to be established not only for females but also for males. Data do, however, refute the two myths listed above.

THE MEDIA

A significant characteristic of our modern, industrialized, technological society is the tremendous impact of the *mass media*. Their ability to shape and manufacture opinions and ideas is extremely potent. As noted in chapter 2 (and most fully considered in chapter 12) the rising influence of the media is almost concurrent with the rise of sport. Their influence (or lack of it) on women's sport is an area that needs to be considered. In 1973, NBC televised 366 hours of live sports of which one hour, the Wimbledon finals, was devoted to women.[44] Until recently, the media have cast the female into two negative images: (1) as a sex object, and (2) as a wife-mother. Rarely has she been projected as a physically active and autonomous individual.

The early sport magazines, under the control of female physical educators, reinforced the traditional images of women as weak and inferior to men physically and emotionally. Their editorials urged a de-emphasis of collegiate sport for women. A study of advertisements showing women participating in sport from 1900-1968 in the *Ladies Home Journal* showed in no year did the total exceed 20 out of an average total of 1400 advertisements.[45] One might well contrast these statistics with the current trend in advertising toward women joggers and golf and tennis players.

It seems that the media's full acceptance of female athletes is slow. In the 1920s as women entered the Olympics and began to form national sport organizations, the Florida real estate boom started. This bonanza was built on exploitative ads employing photographs of females in clinging swimsuits. In the 1970s with the further acceptance of females competing in sports, one seemingly cannot watch a Sunday afternoon football game without an occasional dwelling of the cameras on various portions of the female anatomy while being subjected to some inane comment by the announcer. Such "honey shots" have been commonplace in amateur and professional sport. When females are accepted physically exerting themselves in events which require strength, the American media portrayed Kornelia Ender, winner of four gold medals and a silver one in the 1976 Olympics, as a "bionic beast."[46] John Naber went home with the same winnings but was, curiously, not given the same pejorative label. For contrast, the 1970s have seen the emergence of two magazines, *The Sportswoman* (1973) and *WomenSports* (1974), which take a rather progressive view of women in sport.

A curious turning point for women in their struggles to gain entry into the world of sport was part sport and part farce. The Billie Jean King-Bobby Riggs 1973 tennis match marks a significant episode for women. A black educator commented: "I think women felt about Billie Jean beating Riggs the way blacks felt after Joe Louis beat Jim Braddock—pure pride."[47] She won the $100,000 winner take all event 6-4, 6-3, 6-3, before 30,492 people in the Astrodome. This event, mainly contrived for television and all those advertising dollars, provides a link (although some would deny it) between the media and the current trends of increased female participation.

CURRENT TRENDS

In recent years there has been an increase in female participation in sport. This growth has occurred across the sport spectrum. Females are now playing in Little Leagues and high schools, and colleges are establishing full athletic programs.

Little League baseball had previously been one of the exclusive bastions of male sports. It even had a charter from the United States Congress which stated the purpose of the league was to instill "manhood."[48] In 1972 in Hoboken, New Jersey, a 12-year-old named Maria Pepe proved in the tryouts she was capable of making the team. When she was assigned to a team, the national headquarters revoked the charter of the local team for violating the "boys only" policy. Eventually she went to court to challenge these restrictions. Meanwhile, in Ypsilanti, Michigan, another young girl, Carolyn King, made the team. The league refused to let her play but when the city council ordered them to let her play, they did and had their charter revoked also. Finally on January 30, 1974, Maria Pepe's case reached Gilbert H. Francis, director of the New Jersey Civil Rights Commission, who held that Little League must be open to all children and had the decision upheld by the State Supreme Court.[49] Thus Congress was forced to revise the charter to permit girls to play and changed the stated purpose of the league to be the promotion of citizenship and sportsmanship (avoiding the sexist terminology).

A second area which has seen an increase in participation has been high school athletic programs. From the 1970-71 school year to 1977-78, statistics show the number of participants increased from 294,000 to 2,083,040, or an increase of 608.5 percent (National Federation of State High School Association Statistics). As the statistics indicate (see Tables 9.1 and 9.2) these increases have been across the board covering all types of sports. Of particular interest is not only the increased number of participants but also the rise in schools offering additional programs.

Table 9.1
Girls' Total Participation in High School Sports

Year	Total Participants	Change	+ Percent
1977-78	2,083,040	+438,040	+26.6
1976-77	1,645,000	+345,000	+26.5
1974-75	1,300,000	+483,000	+59.1
1972-73	317,000	+523,000	+177.9
1970-71	294,000	—	—
From 1970	—	+1,789,040	+608.5%

Source: Statistics by National Federation of State High School Associations, 1978.

Table 9.2
Fastest Growing Sports and Sponsoring Schools

Sport	No. of Schools	Increase over 1976-77	% Growth
1. Cross Country	3,892	1,261	47.9
2. Basketball	17,053	2,122	14.2
3. Tennis	7,197	926	13.2
4. Softball	7,266	770	11.8
5. Volleyball	11,690	1,083	10.2
6. Track (outdoor)	13,798	1,162	9.2
7. Gymnastics	3,655	276	8.2
8. Swimming & Diving	3,420	135	4.1

Source: Statistics by National Federation of State High School Associations, 1978.

The third area of increased participation, and arguably the most important, is intercollegiate athletics. In fact, using the term intercollegiate athletics when talking about women in sport is, itself, a sign of progress. For it was at this level that female physical educators in the early part of the 20th century warned of the dangerous effects of exercise and were effective in keeping any sports in which interest was shown on a non-serious, non-competitive basis. Two examples of this idea are the *play day* and the *telegraphic meet*. On a *play day*, women from several schools would gather and be mixed together and form teams which had members from each of the schools. They would then play a variety of sports or recreational activities. The *telegraphic meet* involved participation in the events at one's own school (for instance, swimming) and then telegraphing the results to a designated official. This resulted not only in a saving of money but also prevented females from engaging in face-to-face competition.

One of the main controlling groups in women's sports in the 20th century has been the Division of Girl's and Women's Sports (DGWS) of the American Association for Health, Physical Education and Recreation. They set the rules and standards for women's sport from the 1920s until the early 1970s. Their main philosophy was to keep women's programs on a small scale, stressing the opportunity to participate. They have been roundly criticized for this stand, but in their defense, perhaps this is a more sensible approach to sport, rather than the elitist view that often prevails in this country. Still their policies placed severe restrictions on the more highly skilled female who could not find adequate challenges on the collegiate level and was forced to go outside the educational institution. DGWS adhered to this position even until the mid-1960s by forbidding an athlete to compete on the intercollegiate level while also a member of a team in the same sport outside her institution.[50] This particularly affected women who wished to compete with track clubs in non-college meets. By now the winds of change were beginning to blow and the dissatisfaction accompanied by new realizations resulted in the formation in 1971-72 of the Association for Intercollegiate Athletics for Women (AIAW).

The establishment of AIAW is another one of those watershed decisions. It marked a shift in power from the physical educators to those who placed more emphasis on athletic programs. This is one of the main distinctions between men's intercollegiate athletics and women's. In the pre-1960 era, physical educators were most vocal in discussing women in sport. On the other hand, one rarely heard of a male physical educator planning directions for the men's sport programs. In men's programs there appears to be more of a fissure between physical education and athletics than in women's.

AIAW started out with 278 members and has grown to 825-plus today. Offering 7 national championships in 1972-73, that number has risen to 17 at the present time. Their estimates show approximately 100,000 women in intercollegiate sports compared to approximately 170,000 men. A particularly sticky issue has been their regulations on scholarships and recruiting. Recruiting has been problematic. The Association allegedly forbids outright recruiting, requiring the prospective athlete to make an inquiry to the school about the program. Hannon points out that this rule is often laughed at by college basketball coaches.[51] The other issue, scholarships, was resolved in 1973 when they repealed their prohibition. Once they have the right to give scholarships, they have another matter— money—to clear up before they determine how many they can give out.

The discussion of money and women's intercollegiate athletics brings us to *Title IX*. The disparity in athletic budgets was such that women could never really hope to establish any kind of quality program without some kind of financial aid. For example, at the University of Washington, in the 1973-74 academic year, the women's budget was $18,000 or 7/10 of 1 percent of the $2.6 million men's athletic budget.[52] Ironically, *Title IX*, which has been labelled the savior for the women, was not passed with the intent of aiding athletics. It was passed along with several other of the Educational Amendments of 1972, and reads:

> No person in the United States shall, on the basis of sex, be excluded from participation in, be denied the benefits of, or be subjected to discrimination under any education program or activity receiving Federal financial assistance.[53]

Collegiate sports fell under the amendment via the implementing regulations HEW used in enforcing *Title IX*. HEW is given the power to deny the use of federal funds to any institution that doesn't conform to their standards, but has not yet done so since the regulations went into effect in 1975.

Understandably, *Title IX* is not viewed very kindly by many men's athletic directors. Given the financial squeeze most educational institutions face today, the only place money could be found for the women was to slice off a chunk of the men's budget. A particularly sore spot concerns revenue-producing sports, such as football and basketball. Quite often the revenue from these sports provides the money for the rest of the men's programs. The HEW regulations didn't contain any reference to revenue-producing sports, which the NCAA claims they don't want to exempt. Their plan was to apply their revenues to men's programs before turning over any money to the women. They filed suit, *NCAA v. Matthews,* in 1976 seeking a declaratory judgment to keep them from having to comply with *Title IX*. They eventually dropped the suit and it seems men's programs have not suffered all that much, but there is still quite a bit of tension over money for athletic budgets. Margot Polivy, an attorney for AIAW, estimates the best women's programs run about 15 to 18 percent of the level of the men's, and on the average about 10 percent.[54] Funding at various schools for male and female programs appears in Figure 9.1.

The NCAA's need for cost-cutting measures has been exacerbated by the rising demand of women's intercollegiate athletics for increased funding, if not outright equality in funding. At the University of Texas, the budget for women's intercollegiate athletics rose from $27,000 to $128,000 in three years.[55] The coverage of *Title IX* explicitly includes women's intercollegiate athletics. Directors of Men's Intercollegiate Athletics at "big-time" universities shudder to think that gate revenues from men's football will pay for the operation and travel of the women's field hockey team. John A. Fuzak of Michigan State University has labelled financial equality for men and women in intercollegiate athletics as "economic insanity."[56]

The impact of *Title IX* on both men's and women's intercollegiate athletics is typified by the situation at the University of Illinois. Eighty-two percent of the total budget for men's intercollegiate athletics of all types at the University is derived from gate revenues in men's football and men's basketball.[57] Cecil Coleman, former Director of Men's Intercollegiate Athletics at the University, argued that such revenues belong to men's intercollegiate athletics and therefore cannot justifiably be disbursed to support women's intercollegiate athletics under the guise of equal treatment. In response to this dilemma, Senator John Tower has proposed amendments to *Title IX* regulations which would allow individual revenue-generating sports to retain all or most of the revenues directly attributable to those sports.[58] The future of these amendments is in doubt at this juncture although the NCAA has made impassioned pleas in their support (see Vignette 9.4).

Sage puts forth a hypothesis on this matter that runs counter to the sentiment of most males.[59] He believes women's sports are still a tool of the males in control. He theorizes that men aren't really that upset about women entering into their ranks, because once they start trying to establish major programs, they won't so readily complain about the big dollars men are spending as they will be spending the large sums, too. His second suggestion is that women will begin to support the men's programs, especially the revenue-producing sports, because the health of their programs depends in part on the health of the men's.

This finally brings us to the ranks of professional sports. For quite a while women have had their own golf and tennis tours, but it was a female jockey who first broke the sex barrier. In February 1969 Tuesdee Testa was the first female rider at Santa Anita. The jockeys boycotted her

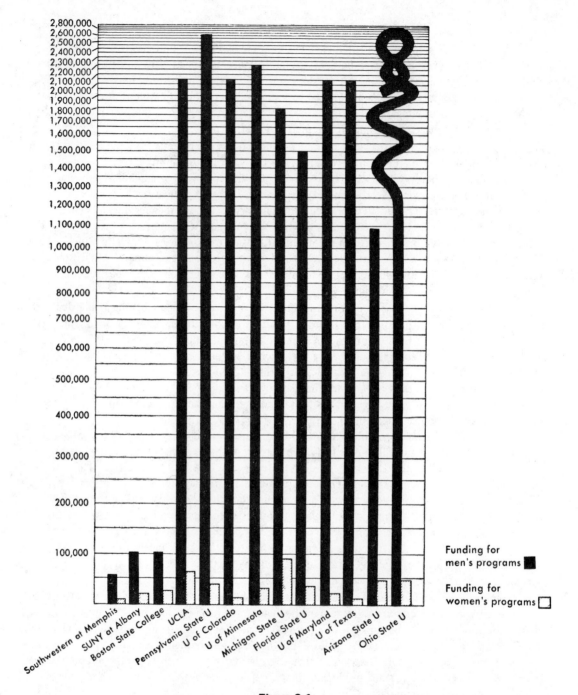

Figure 9.1
Funding of Select Men's and Women's Intercollegiate Sports in 1974
(Reprinted by permission of Charter Publishing Company)

VIGNETTE 9.4

Sports guidelines stiffened

WASHINGTON (UPI)—The government Wednesday proposed strict new guidelines that will require the nation's colleges and universities to spend millions of dollars upgrading their sports programs for women.

Allowances would be made for the expensive and lucrative bastion of men's football, which supports much of the athletic programs at some big schools.

But the guidelines, expected to go into effect next fall, advise that colleges could lose federal funds if they fail to provide more scholarships and equal opportunities for women to participate in basketball, tennis, swimming and other intercollegiate and club sports.

The required average equal spending on individual male and female athletes at most schools would also include equal playing facilities, food, coaching staffs and other areas.

"They are designed to ensure that women's intercollegiate athletic programs receive the resources and commitments to which they are entitled," said the Department of Health, Education and Welfare.

The proposed guidelines, announced by HEW Secretary Joseph Califano at a news conference, will be sent to colleges and civil rights groups. They will have 60 days to comment and offer advice on changes.

The rules will toughen the Title IX amendments to the Equal Education Act passed by Congress in 1972. HEW put out Title IX sports compliance regulations in 1975 but gave colleges three years to comply.

appearance but went back when fines against them were levied. Although the situation is improving, the professional tours are not equally funded. In 1971 Billie Jean King became the first female to win $100,000. That same year, however, the leading men's winner, Rod Laver, won $290,000 by playing in one-third the tournaments. The women's golf situation was even worse. In 1972 Kathy Whitworth led the LPGA with $65,063 in winnings in 29 tournaments, while Jack Nicklaus won $320,542 in only 19 tournaments. The situation, however, has been improving. LPGA and tennis earnings were up 30 percent in 1973 and 5 women tennis players made over $100,000. In 1977 Chris Evert became the third highest paid tennis player, winning $503,134, and 1978 estimates are that Nancy Lopez's combined income from golf purses and endorsements will approach $500,000.[60] The situation for women's professional sports improves slowly, but for the average player the income disparity (in comparison to men) continues to be quite a handicap.

SUMMARY

To summarize the status of women in sport is a complicated task. In western society the traditional *social definition* for females was one of subservience and subordination to men. Given this view, women were not expected or encouraged to compete in sports that demand competitiveness and self-exertion. The notion that sport is the exclusive realm of the males has carried through from the days of the ancient Greeks to present times. The recent past has seen an increase in athletic participation by women, but these women have had to deal with traditional expectations by reconciling them with the expectations of self, society, and sport. This struggle has resulted in the labelling of women in sport as "social anomalies."

The idea that women shouldn't compete in sport is based on three *myths*: (1) Athletics are physically dangerous for women. (2) Women don't play sports well enough to deserve quality. (3) Women aren't really interested in sports. Medical evidence has proven the falsity of the first myth. The second and third myths are slowly being refuted by the results of increased participation and enhanced performance. The skill levels of women have been consistently improving and where programs are being offered, more and more women are participating.

One of the main culprits in perpetuating the idea that women shouldn't compete in sport has been the media. Their presentations have dwelled on the efforts of men, often ignoring any female competition which may have occurred. When they have broadcast "female" events, the reports have sometimes been exploitative and biased.

In response to the *women's liberation movement* which began in the 1960s, women have increased their participation in sport. Girls now have gained entry into Little Leagues, and as they progress through school, opportunities arise for them as educators offer more extensive programs. Even in the professional ranks women have made progress in terms of size of purses and playing conditions.

What all of this holds for the future remains to be seen. Some feel women are capable of developing athletic programs which avoid the evils of the men's, while others feel they will fall prey to the temptations of big money. Some advocate separate programs while other propose combining the two sexes. Whichever path is chosen, it is sure to bring about even more participation by women. Perhaps the "Golden Age" of sport has already passed, but that was an age without women. If there is another such age to come, it will surely include women.

IMPORTANT CONCEPTS DISCUSSED IN THIS CHAPTER

Female Role	Female Socialization Into Sport
Sexism	Sex Role Behavior
Title IX	Opportunity Set
Women's Movement	Socialization Via Sport
Women's Action Group	Achievement Motivation
National Organization for Women (NOW)	Patriarchal
Rite of Passage	Deviant
Social Anomaly	Role Model Theory
Supportive Role	Play Day
Myths	Telegraphic Meet
Association for Intercollegiate Athletics for Women (AIAW)	Division of Girl's and Women's Sports (DGWS)

ENDNOTES

[1] Betty Spears and Richard A. Swanson, *History of Sport and Physical Activity in the United States* (Dubuque, Iowa: Wm. C. Brown Publishers, 1978).

[2] Eleanor Metheny, "Symbolic Forms of Movement: The Female Image in Sports," *Sport and American Society*, ed. G. Sage (Reading, Mass.: Addison-Wesley, 1974), pp. 289-301.

[3] S. L. Bem and D. J. Bem, "We're All NonConscious Sexists," *Beliefs, Attitudes, and Human Affairs* (Belmont, Calif.: Brooks, Cole, 1970).

[4] St. Thomas Aquinas, *Summa Theologica,* trans. Fathers of the English Dominican Province (London, England: Burns, Oates, and Washbourne, 1914-1942).

[5] Betty Friedan, *The Feminine Mystique* (New York, NY: W. N. Norton & Co., 1963).

[6] Marie Hart, "On Being a Female in Sport," *Sport in the Sociocultural Process,* ed. M. Hart (Dubuque, Iowa: Wm. C. Brown Publishers, 1976), p. 444.

[7] The National Organization for Women, *Statement of Purpose* (Washington, D.C.: 1966), p. 1.

[8] Gerber et al., reference 20, p. 137.

[9] Jack Scott, "The Masculine Obsession in Sports," *Women's Athletics: Coping With Controversy,* ed. Barbara J. Hoepner (Washington, D.C.: AAHPER, 1974), p. 85.

[10] Jan Felshin, "The Triple Option for Woman in Sport," *Quest* 21 (January, 1974), pp. 36-40.

[11] Ibid.

[12] Bil Gilbert and Nancy Williamson, "Women in Sport: A Progress Report," *Sports Illustrated* 38 (May 28, June 4, and July 11, 1973).

[13] Harold Peterson, "Formful Win in a Most Formful Affair," *Sports Illustrated* 35 (August 23, 1971), p. 48.

[14] Frank Deford, "Nancy With the Laughing Face," *Sports Illustrated* 49 (July 10, 1978), pp. 24-31.

[15] Betty Menzie, "Sociological Aspects of Women in Sports," *Women's Athletics: Coping With Controversy,* ed. Barbara J. Hoepner (Washington, D.C.): AAHPER, 1974), pp. 105-106.

[16] Metheny, "Symbolic Forms of Movement: The Female Image in Sports," p. 301.

[17] Gilbert and Williamson, "Women in Sport: A Progress Report."

[18] "Comes the Revolution," *Time* (June 26, 1978), p. 55.

[19] Gilbert and Williamson, "Women in Sport: A Progress Report."

[20] Ellen W. Gerber, Jan Felshin, Pearl Berlin and Waneen Wyrick, *The American Woman in Sport* (Reading, Mass.: Addison-Wesley, 1974).

[21] M. C. Dunkle, "What Constitutes Equality for Women in Sport," *Newsletter* for the Project on the Status and Education of Women (Washington, D.C.: Association of American Colleges, 1974).

[22] Gerber, Felshin, Berlin, and Wyrick, *The American Woman in Sport.*

[23] Ibid.

[24] Carle Klafs and M. Joan Lyon, *The Female Athlete* (St. Louis, Mo.: The C. V. Mosby Co., 1973).

[25] Ibid.

[26] Gerber, Felshin, Berlin, and Wyrick, *The American Woman in Sport.*

[27] Ibid.

[28] Gilbert and Williamson, "Women in Sport: A Progress Report."

[29] Klafs and Lyon, *The Female Athlete,* p. 56.

[30] Deborah Larned, "The Femininity Test," *WomenSports* (July 1976), p. 9.

[31] Gerber, Felshin, Berlin, and Wyrick, *The American Woman in Sport.*

[32] Simone de Beauvoir, *The Second Sex* (New York: Knopf, 1952), p. 373.

[33] Susan L. Greendorfer, "Socialization Into Sport," *Women and Sport: From Myth to Reality,* ed. S. L. Greendorfer (Philadelphia, Penna.: Lea and Febiger, 1978), pp. 115-140.

[34] Ibid.

[35] Ibid.

[36] Gretchen Koehler, "Agents Who Have Influenced Women to Participate in Intercollegiate Sport," *HPRIC* (Brigham Young University, 1973).

[37] E. Snyder and E. Spreitzer, "Correlates of Sport Participation Among Adolescent Girls," *Research Quarterly* 47 (December), pp. 804-809.

[38] Greendorfer, "Socialization Into Sport."

[39] Hart, "On Being Female in Sport," Harry Edwards, *Sociology of Sport* (Homewood, Ill.: Dorsey Press, 1973).

[40] Marie Hart, "Women Sit in the Back of the Bus," *Psychology Today* 5 (1971), pp. 64-65.

[41] George H. Sage, "Women in Sport: Cooptation or Liberation?," *Colorado Journal of Health, Physical Education, and Recreation,* 1 (March, 1975). Menzie, "Sociological Aspects of Women in Sports."

[42] Kent Hannon, "Too Far, Too Fast," *Sports Illustrated* 48 (March 20, 1978), pp. 34-45.

[43] Susan Birrell, "Achievement Related Motives and the Woman Athlete," *Women and Sport: From Myth to Reality,* ed. S. L. Greendorfer (Philadelphia, Penna.: Lea and Febiger, 1978), pp. 153-171.

[44] Gilbert and Williamson, "Women in Sport: A Progress Report," p. 96.

[45] Gerber, Felshin, Berlin, and Wyrick, *The American Woman in Sport.*

[46] Cheryl McCall, "Who's Afraid of Bulging Biceps: A Call to Arms for Woman Athletes," *Ms* (May, 1977), p. 26.

[47] Gilbert and Williamson, "Women in Sports: A Progress Report," p. 29.

[48] James A. Michener, *Sports in America* (New York: Random House, 1976).

[49] Ibid.

[50] Gerber, Felshin, Berlin, and Wyrick, *The American Woman in Sport.*

[51] Hannon, "Too Far, Too Fast."

[52] Gilbert and Williamson, "Women in Sport," p. 28.

[53] *Title IX*, Educational Amendments, 1972.

[54] "Comes the Revolution."

[55] *NCAA News* (October 1, 1975).

[56] Ibid.

[57] *NCAA News* (September 15, 1975).

[58] *NCAA News*.

[59] Sage, "Women in Sport: Cooptation or Liberation?"

[60] Gilbert and Williamson, "Women in Sport: A Progress Report."

Sport and Small Groups

INTRODUCTION

In the sport arena the most basic social group is the *team*. It is both intriguing and surprising that this natural micro social system has not more often been studied in natural, experimental, and field situations by social scientists. Mills wrote:

> Not only are they (small groups) micro-systems, they are essentially microcosms of larger societies. They present, in miniature, societal features, such as division of labor, a code of ethics, a government, media of exchange, prestige rankings, ideologies, myths, and religious practices. Through careful examination of these micro-systems, theoretical models can be constructed and then applied to less accessible societies for further test and modification. Small group research is thus a means of developing ways of thinking about social systems in general.[1]

It would seem that *small groups* in sport would provide a natural testing ground, an *in vivo* laboratory, for many conceptual schemes in sociology. Among the substantive topics to be investigated could be small *group processes* (cooperation, competition, conflict), collective behavior, personal influence, leadership, morale, socialization, group structural properties (communication, power, affect networks, division of labor), prestige and cohesion (Snyder and Spreitzer, 1974).

GROUP DYNAMICS

The empirical study of small groups did not begin until shortly after the Second World War. Kurt Lewin (1890-1947), generally considered to be the father of this social psychological tradition, did much to encourage such research by establishing the Research Center for Group Dynamics at the Massachusetts Institute of Technology (MIT).[2] His seminal ideas were influential in creating what is known as the *group dynamics* tradition in social psychology. Group dynamics is the study of the *structure* (stable patterns of social positions and role relationships) and *functioning* (the social processes that occur) of small groups. What is a "small" group is difficult to define precisely. Generally, however, it consists of from three or more to fifteen or fewer persons congregated together.

The essential feature of a group is *organization*. It is a set of organized parts which: (1) performs some function as a unit (*common goal*). Sometimes this feature is referred to as purposive performance; (2) has "system" components that are interrelated; it has a *structure* (a stabilized pattern of statuses and roles including the very important role of leadership; and (3) contains mechanisms that regulate the group members' behavior. In other words, small groups have *normative features* that exert a certain amount of pressure on the members to conform.[3]

The *common goal* orientation of the small group seems to be easy enough to understand. It refers to the collectively agreed upon process or end result of the group's interaction. It can vary from a specific material creation to something as elusive as sociability. The *structure* of the group is a bit more difficult to conceptualize because of its abstractness. *Group structure* is the orderly and stable pattern of position and role relationships that emerge. There are several varieties of group structure (affect, power, task, and communication). A *role,* as we said earlier, is a behavior pattern considered to be appropriate and acceptable to the individual actor as well as to the other group members. For example, the role relationship between leader and follower is a clear-cut one. But there exists role relationships other than leader and follower, as will be illustrated in "The Football Team as a Small Group." A system of sanctions—rewards and punishments—that channel behavior along certain lines comprises the *normative* feature.

Athletic teams nicely meet the criteria for small groups which are typically characterized by a common collective goal (winning): rules and guidelines ("norms") governing participants' conduct; a network of positions, interpersonal relations, and interaction patterns (the "social structure"). Many studies of small groups in sport have concentrated upon individual, interpersonal, and structural correlates of team success. In methodological terms, the former triad have comprised the independent or causal variables in the analyses and the latter the dependent or criterion variable. For the moment let us consider the football team as a small group.

The Football Team as a Small Group

Dobriner provides an excellent example of a football team as a small group.[4] "The 'game' is primarily a relationship between two teams in competition for 'points' (the goal) on a fixed and determined locality (the field) over a period of time (playing-time 60 minutes) according to normative definitions establishing the nature of the game (the rules)."[5]

Consider the *common goal* orientation first. Each team attempts to coordinate its efforts to produce a victory; all players on each team seek to produce a win for their side.

The *structure* or stable pattern of statuses and positions consist of the eleven specific and formal positions occupied by the players. These positions include the offensive positions of center, quarterback, end, guard, tackle, etc., and the defensive positions of free safety, noseguard, linebacker, etc.

Norms define the appropriate and inappropriate behavior for the game in general (players of opposing teams must wear jerseys of contrasting colors, no offensive player on the scrimmage line may receive the snap from center) and the occupants of different positions (an offensive lineman may not receive a forward pass, and an offensive player may not illegally use his hands to hold a defensive player). When the rules are broken the referee may sanction (penalize) the violating team.

In summary, a football team—and other sport teams as well—can be conceptualized in terms of a small group with its characteristics of purposive performance, social structure, and normative features.

LEADERSHIP

In discussing the essence of the "group," we noted the importance of the structure (stable pattern of position and role relationships) of a social collectivity. What is certainly one of the most important positions in a group—if not the single most important one—is that of *leader*.

In several studies two basic functions of leaders, neither of which is particularly surprising, have emerged. One classic investigation was undertaken by A. W. Halpin and B. J. Winer.[6] Their objective was to empirically uncover the *basic functions of leaders*. To accomplish this objective, they devised and administered a questionnaire to a large number of different groups. Through a statistical procedure known as factor analysis,[7] they identified four functions of leaders, although only two of these four factors were relevant. These two factors were labeled: (1) *consideration* and (2) *initiating structure*. *Consideration* refers to the leader's social skills in interpersonal relationships. Consideration includes such social competencies as empathy, understanding, cooperation, respect, and warmth which take place as leader and "followers" interact. This is called a *socio-emotional* role. *Initiating structure*, on the other hand, is the dimension of leadership conducive to accomplishing the task or goal before the group. In small groups, someone "takes on" what is called the *task-specialist* role. To be assured that the group doesn't become just a goal-less social gathering, someone has to keep the group moving toward its objective. Usually, but not always, the two roles—*socio-emotional* and *task*—are played by different individuals. However, to the extent that a single person is able to perform both effectively, the group is frequently productive, cohesive, and efficient.

Effectiveness of Different Leadership Styles

In a classic study of the effectiveness of different leadership styles, Lewin, Lippitt, and White studied the *performance* and *morale* of ten-year-old-boys' play groups that were convened to engage in various arts and crafts activities.[8] Three "social climates" or "group atmospheres" were deliberately manipulated. One group had an *autocratic* leader who "took matters into his own hands" by deciding policies, assignments, and procedures. In addition, his personal style was characterized by aloofness. In contrast, the *democratic* leader made suggestions, served as a repository of advice, and pleasantly interacted with the group members. He, as well as the group's members, participated in the decision-making processes. Finally, the *laissez-faire* leader simply presented the materials and gave no direction or guidance to the boys, remained aloof, and permitted them to make all of their own decisions. Subsequent examination of both *performance* and *satisfaction* suggested significantly different outcomes of the three leadership styles. The least work, as well as the poorest quality products, occurred in the *laissez-faire* group. It is reported that boys in this treatment condition frequently became discouraged and quarreled with each other. The autocratic group seemed to be most productive, but not the most content, of the three groups. Boys in this treatment condition frequently vented their hostilities toward the authoritarian leader. In almost a paradoxical fashion, the members of the autocratic group were highly dependent upon the leader and, upon his leaving the room for any extended period of time, would find it most difficult to continue working in his absence. Morale was highest in the democratic setting and productivity was about equal to that of the autocratic atmosphere. This group appeared to be most adaptable and was able to continue with the tasks when the leader was in abstention.

Leadership Behavior of Coaches

Studies of coaches' behavior have not produced a consistent set of findings regarding which styles are most effective. For example, Swartz compared seventy-two successful (won more than 50 percent of their games) and unsuccessful (lost more than 50 percent of their games) college coaches and found no significant differences among their leadership styles.[9] Lenk compared "authoritarian" and "democratic" rowing crew coaches and found that neither tended to be more effective than the other.[10]

The highly successful ex-UCLA cage coach, Johnny Wooden, was subjected to observational analysis. Tharp and Gallimore observed his behaviors during practice and categorized them into ten categories of leadership behavior.[11] They discovered that slightly more than 50 percent of his behaviors were instructions regarding *what* to do and *when* and *how* to do it. A study by Danielson dittoed these findings.[12] He concluded that "commonly perceived behaviors in hockey coaching are mainly of a communicative nature with surprisingly little emphasis on domination."

Finally, in Mudra's investigation, small college and big time coaches' leadership styles were compared.[13] He concluded that leadership behaviors were likely to be situation specific. Whereas big-time coaches exercised greater control and authority, small college coaches stressed insight and problem-solving behavior.

Fiedler's Contingency Model of Leadership

Probably the best explanation of the interaction between the relevant variables involved in leadership, satisfaction, and productivity is summarized in Fred Fiedler's *contingency model*.[14] The model is fairly elegant in attempting to interrelate the interaction among four variables: (1) the *situation*, (2) the *activity* or *task* before the group, (3) the *leader*, and (4) the *characteristics* of the group. The first stage in developing the model was to determine whether the leader was task-oriented (what was earlier called "initiating structure") or person-oriented (what was previously termed "consideration"). To assess this feature, the leader was asked to execute a test called the Least Preferred Co-Worker (LPC) inventory. Specifically, leaders were asked to think of the most incompetent (i.e., least preferred co-worker) person they had ever worked with and to describe that individual by such criteria as pleasantness, helpfulness, cooperativeness, and the like. According to Fiedler, leaders who were reluctant to describe the LPC in negative terms were probably people-centered (as opposed to task-centered) leaders. On the other hand, leaders who felt free to describe the LPC in negative terms were more likely to be task-oriented.

Once the basic leadership orientation was determined ("people-centered" or "task-centered"), the next chore Fiedler set for himself was to study different kinds of groups to see if one kind of leadership style was consistently more effective in maximizing productivity. These investigations led him to conclude that there were *no* consistent differences. Since there was no consistent pattern, Fiedler then devised a scheme for classifying different situations or contexts in which groups operated. One way of categorizing situations was in terms of a group's favorable or unfavorable reaction to the leader. According to Fiedler, three factors were primarily responsible for determining how favorable a group was toward the leader: (1) the leader's personal relationship with the group members, (2) the extent to which the task of the group was structured or unstructured, and (3) the leader's legitimate power (the ability with which rewards and punishments could be meted out).

Fiedler hypothesized that in situations where the group was favorable toward the leader, the task was fairly clear-cut and the leader had legitimate power, a task-centered leader would be more effective than a people-centered one. Similarly, if the group were unfavorable toward the leader, the leader had little legitimate power, and the task were somewhat ambiguous, then a task-oriented leader would also be more effective. In this latter situation, if anything were to be accomplished, the leader had to be quite directive. Between these two extremes would lie a leader who was moderately favorable. Now, if the task were clear-cut and the leader possessed official power—but was only moderately favorably perceived—a people-centered leader would prove most effective.

With this as a backdrop, Fiedler investigated the relationships between leadership and team effectiveness of high school basketball teams. Contrary to expectations, he found that teams in which the members selected their friends as co-workers had poorer winning records than those in which their best friend and best co-worker were not necessarily the same person. Again, contrary to his hypothesis, he found that leaders who were accepting of their less preferred co-workers were generally less successful than those who focused upon performance and task objectives. In short, members of successful basketball teams preferred task-oriented individuals as co-workers whereas members of less successful teams preferred more socially oriented co-workers.

Have Fiedler's hypothetical assertions been confirmed in actual research? Sometimes they have. More specifically, when leaders are perceived in either favorable or unfavorable terms, the task-centered leader has been more effective. When leaders are moderately favorably perceived, a people-oriented leader has been more effective. What this line of research suggests is that *there is no single kind of leadership that is best under all circumstances.* Instead, it behooves "management" to "match" leadership styles with the situation, group, and nature of the task rather than to employ one absolute standard. This matching is why the paradigm is called the *contingency* model of leadership. The most effective leadership style is contingent—that is, dependent—upon other variables in the specific context. Table 10.1 summarizes these interrelationships.

Bird investigated the relationships among leadership style, cohesion, skill, and success of women's intercollegiate volleyball teams in Division I and Division II.[15] Interestingly, for winning teams in Division I the players' coach was perceived as relationship-oriented whereas players on losing teams perceived the coach as task-oriented. These results were reversed in the perceptions of Division II players. Bird suggested:

> Some explanation for these results might be within structural changes which may occur owing to the skill level of players. Perhaps on less highly skilled teams, effective coaching strategy demands greater use of designated positions such as hitters or setters, whereas on highly skilled teams, such as Division I, positions are more flexible because of the type of playing strategy employed. If this is so, then the prediction which was generated from Fiedler's contingency model for highly structured team groups would indeed be applicable to less highly skilled teams such as those in Division II. An alternative explanation might be that players on more highly skilled teams may be sufficiently motivated and, therefore, respond more to a supportive, socio-emotional coach. In either case, the results strongly suggest that effective leadership or coaching style is somewhat related to situational factors such as player skill.[16]

Figure 10.1
The Relationships Between Situational Factors, Leadership Styles, and the Effectiveness of the Task Performance of the Group As Predicted by Fiedler's Contingency Model of Leadership

Leadership Style	Situational Factors*		
	Very Favorable	Intermediate Favorable	Very Unfavorable
Relationship-Oriented Leader (High LPC)	Ineffective	Effective	Ineffective
Task-Oriented Leader (Low LPC)	Effective	Ineffective	Effective

*Situational factors include: (1) leader-follower relations, (2) task structure, and (3) power position of leader.
Source: Adapted from Fred E. Fiedler, *Leadership* (New York, NY: General Learning Press, 1971)

GROUP PROCESS AND PERFORMANCE

Group Cohesiveness and Team Success

Following Festinger's lead, cohesiveness may be *conceptually* defined as "the resultant of all the forces acting on the members to remain in the group."[17] A moment's reflection should lead you to acknowledge the global nature of this definition.[18] Just the same, it provides us with a starting point from which to explore the relationships between team esprit de corps and task performance. *Operationally*, cohesiveness has been measured using players' ratings of: (1) value of team membership, (2) teamwork, and (3) comradship among players (Nixon, 1976).

Many persons glibly assume that cohesiveness and success go hand in hand. For example, it is not uncommon to hear coaches or managers of winning teams attributing success to the team's morale (a component of cohesiveness). However, the scientific research regarding this correlation is not definitive; in fact, much of it is contradictory and inconclusive. As an aside, do you recall the squabbling that characterized the World Series Champion New York Yankees in 1977 and 1978, the Oakland Athletics in 1972 and 1973, and the N.L. pennant winning L.A. Dodgers in 1978?

A few studies have concentrated on interpersonal perceptions of team members and team effectiveness. Fiedler, as we've seen, found that successful teams were characterized by task rather than affective interpersonal relationships.[19] On the other hand, Klein and Christiansen discovered positive correlations between cohesiveness as measured by interpersonal attractiveness and performance basketball teams.[20] Their study also revealed that the consensus regarding the leader was a favorable one. Heinicke and Bales also found positive associations between agreement on leader and successful task-oriented teams.[21]

Studies of successful basketball teams (Fiedler; Grace; Melnick and Chemers), rifle teams (McGrath), Olympic rowing teams (Lenk), soccer teams (Veit), and bowling squads (Landers and Luschen) have discovered *inverse* (or no) associations between cohesiveness and team success.[22] This means that winning and not-so-cohesive teams go together and losing and cohesive teams are correlated. On the other hand, investigations of successful rifle teams (Myers, Chapman and Campbell), football teams (McIntyre), baseball teams (Landers and Crum), basketball teams (Arnold and Straub; Nixon; Widmeyer), and volleyball teams (Bird; Slepicka) have found *positive* associations between success and cohesiveness.[23] Of course, these latter studies have discovered just the opposite relationship between the two variables.

These ironic findings may stem from different operationalizations of cohesiveness and/or its conceptual nebulousness.[24] Additionally, the *types* of teams examined have not been synonymous. Introducing two social-psychological concepts serves as a partial remedy to this muddle: (1) *interacting groups*—those in which the participants are engaged simultaneously in a task requiring continuous adjustment and coordination, and (2) *coacting groups*—those in which the participants perform a task independently of the other members. Contrasting rugby, hockey, baseball, soccer, lacrosse, basketball, football, and volleyball teams (interacting groups) with skiing, bowling, wrestling, boxing, golf, gymnastics, track and field, tennis (singles), swimming and rifle teams (coacting groups) serves to distinguish groups which require interdependent activity from those that demand similar or identical activities but not in a concerted and coordinated manner. Thus, the distinction between the two concepts resides in the degree of *interdependence* required as well as the *division of labor* within the team.

On this foundation Landers and Luschen forwarded the following two hypotheses:[25] (1) for interacting teams, successful performance produces more cohesiveness; and (2) for coacting teams, unsuccessful performance produces more cohesiveness. Although Landers and Luschen's own research on bowling teams is consistent with these formulations, other investigations are not.

Social-psychologically speaking, even though some research is not supportive of these two hypotheses, the conceptual framework is valuable since it calls our attention to reasons why and qualifications for apparently dissimilar scientific findings. More specifically, it attunes us to the importance (or lack of) the coordination dimensions (i.e., performance structure) in achieving success in sport activities. Particularly challenging is the implication that interacting teams rely on interpersonal coordination and a good deal of interaction to achieve success, while for coacting teams these same conditions do not contribute so favorably and, in fact, rivalries among team participants may be conducive to success.[26]

GROUP COMPOSITION AND STRUCTURE

Group Composition

Group composition refers to the various characteristics of the people who belong to it.[27] Properties of group composition include, among other things, social characteristics, personality characteristics, abilities, aptitudes, and physical factors.

Social Homogeneity

Eitzen studied the relationship between social homogeneity/heterogeneity of players (similarities/differences among members in such variables as social class and religion) and team success.[28]

He found among Kansas high school basketball teams that heterogeneity fostered clique formation and the development of with-in group factions that was not conducive to victory. As an aside, he excluded the social category of race from the analysis. Cliques on a racial basis often emerge, and furthermore, athletics—particularly collegiate and professional team sports—are arenas where ethnic minorities are increasingly discovered.

Group Structure

Group structure is "the overall system of integrated position, role, and status relationships."[29] Let us first consider the relationship between group structure and team success.

Essing studied soccer teams in the German Federal League and scrutinized the correlation between stability of team line-ups and achievement.[30] His results confirmed the following: (1) stable team line-ups were directly associated with team success, (2) the higher and more consistent each player's performance, the more successful was the team, and (3) the more turnover in personnel, the more likely was the team to be unsuccessful (a corollary of 1). Essing's orientation proposed line-ups as the independent variable and team success as the dependent factor. However, it is important to realize that the independent/dependent variable arrangement could be just the reverse (stable line-ups may be a consequence of—not a cause of—task success).

The correspondence between *leadership* longevity and team success has also been investigated. In other words, what is the relationship between a manager or coach's tenure and the team's overall win-loss record? Eitzen and Yetman reviewed the basketball records of some 129 college basketball teams over a forty-year (1930-1970) time span.[31] Their data tabulations found that 657 coaching changes had occurred during this period and that coaching turnovers were *negatively* associated with victory, but this relationship was dependent upon the teams' records *before* the role replacement. Coaching changes were much more prone to occur after an unsuccessful season than after a successful season. Consequently, new coaches will generally be more successful than their predecessors. But, and importantly, unsuccessful teams will tend to do better the next year regardless of a coaching change. In other words, when you're "down," there's only one way to go: up! The sociologists' major conclusion was that managerial succession does *not* have much influence on team success. One final observation emerging from their research was the correspondence between a coach's tenure and the team's success. Interestingly, this relationship was curvilinear. Up to a point (13 years was the maximum), the longer the tenure the greater the team's success. However, this pattern reversed itself after reaching the apex. Again, this may very well be due to the fact that after one has been successful (if you are not successful, you find your job in jeopardy) there is only one way to go: down!

Leonard compared the 1977 opening day starting lineups with the starting lineups the last week of the professional baseball season and discovered a "turnover" rate—the percentage (and number) of players no longer with the team they "started" with—to be about 7.5 percent.[32] Of the 140 American League players, there were eleven "turnovers," 8 percent. Of the 108 National League players, there were eight "turnovers," 7 percent. Nineteen of 248 players (7.5%; mode = 0; arithmetic mean = 0.75) were with a different team than that with which they started. There was less than one "turnover" per major league club. The 1977 World Series teams, Los Angeles and New York, had zero and one "turnover," respectively. The two teams competing in divisional championships—Philadelphia and Kansas City—did not have any.

In this section we have focused upon sport teams as mini-social systems and have analyzed them using some social-psychological concepts. Despite the specific (athletics) applied character of small group analysis presented here, it is worth repeating that many of the same dynamics apply to numerous other small groups like committees, clubs, crews, and organizations. Much of our country's business—civic and industrial—is conducted within small groups. Therefore, the effectiveness of group functioning is of practical as well as theoretical concern.

FORMAL STRUCTURE AND ORGANIZATIONAL LEADERSHIP

Grusky advanced a theory of *formal structure* to explain the recruitment of *baseball* managers.[33] It provides an excellent illustration of how sociological theory can be adapted to studying sport phenomena. Grusky maintained that "the formal structure of an organization consists of a set of norms which define the system's official objectives, its major offices or positions, and the primary responsibilities of the position occupants."[34] This formal structure, he added, patterns behavior along three lines: (1) spatial location, (2) nature of task, and (3) frequency of interaction. Spatial location may be divided into central and non-central positions; tasks may be dichotomized into independent and dependent categories; and interaction subsumed under two headings, frequent and infrequent. Combining these three criteria he defined two types of positions in a formal structure, those with high ("high" interactors) and low ("low" interactors) interaction potential. The general hypothesis was that position in the formal structure of an organization contributes to the development of role skills essential to career movement. Grusky wrote:

> As interaction is positively related to liking, high interactors should be selected more often than low interactors as the most respected and popular members of the organization. Also, high interactors should be more likely to learn cooperative social skills and develop a strong commitment to the welfare of the organization. Low interactors should be more likely to focus on individualistic rather than team values and tend to be psychologically distant or aloof. In formal organizations which utilize these or related characteristics as official or unofficial criteria for managerial selection, high interactors should be selected for exclusive positons more often than low interactors.[35]

Let us examine Grusky's model in baseball, football, hockey, and basketball.

Baseball's Social Structure

The defensive social organization of a baseball team is composed of three interaction units: (1) outfield (left, center and right fielders), (2) infield (shortstop and first, second, and third basemen), and (3) battery (pitcher and catcher). The specific positions which constitute these "units" differ with respect to spatial location, type of task, and frequency of interaction. The spatial location and type of task components should be fairly obvious. Frequency of interaction may not be so intuitive. Loy and McElvogue's data add empirical support for the differential interaction potential of baseball positions.[36] They operationally defined interaction potential in terms of the total number of *assists*[37] made by position incumbents. Assists appear to be meaningful in the present discussion in several ways. They provide an indication of: "(1) the rate of interaction, (2) the number and range of other group members with whom a position occupant interacts, and (3) the degree to which dependent tasks are associated with given positions."

Loy and McElvogue found the rank order of field positions with respect to number of annual assists remained identical for all years scrutinized. Catchers and shortstops ranked first and second, respectively, in the number of assists followed by second, third, and first basemen and outfielders.

Grusky selected a systematic random sample of 465 players from *The Official Encyclopedia of Baseball*.[38] The publication contained every player who appeared in a regularly scheduled major league game from 1871 to 1958. Of the 465 players, thirteen had gone on to manage professionally. The major group of field managers consisted of the total population (N = 107) of managers of the sixteen professional baseball teams between 1921-41 and 1951-58. He found that in excess of 75 percent of baseball managers were recruited from high interaction positions and less than 25 percent were recruited from low interaction positions. More particularly, managers were most often former catchers (26.2%), shortstops (14.0%), and third basemen (13.1%). Furthermore, virtually all baseball managers were recruited from former baseball players.

Professional Baseball Umpires

Using the same theoretical framework, Breglio hypothesized that umpires would be recruited from low interaction positions because of the requirements of officiating; that is, since umpires need to be somewhat aloof and independent, they will tend to come from positions of low interaction.[39] Out of a total population of 1257 umpires, 52 percent (N = 656) had formerly played in the major leagues. Of these former players, almost 68 percent had occupied low interaction positions, i.e., the outfield. A duplication of this research by Mitchell failed to confirm the Hypothesis.[40] Questionnaires were sent to active baseball officials and, of those returned (approximately 50%), 59 percent formerly held high interaction positions and 41 percent were former occupants of low interaction positions.

Baseball Coaches

Loy, Sage, and Ingham sent postcard questionnaires to college coaches at schools in which there were 1000 or more males in the student body.[41] They discovered that 72 percent of all college coaches were recruited from high interaction positions and that 69 percent of all team captains and co-captains were selected from high interaction positions.

Football Coaches

Because of the "social structure" of football teams, it is more difficult to classify positions into "high" and "low" interaction categories. Nevertheless, Grusky's formal structure theory has been used with some success in studying the recruitment of collegiate and professional coaches. With respect to spatial location, the positions of center, guard, quarterback, and linebacker are considered central (i.e., high interaction ones) while all other positions are considered non-central (i.e., low interaction ones).

Roland assessed the playing positions (in both the colleges and pros) of all coaches (N = 366) in the NFL between 1970 and 1976.[42] Of these 366, 196 (54%) had both college and pro playing experience, 170 (46%) had only college experience, and 9 (2%) had neither experiences. Roland found that almost 50 percent were recruited from high interaction positions.

Massengale and Farrington studied college football coaches' (Division I, N = 136) former positions.[43] They found that 65 percent of all head coaches, 63 percent of assistant head coaches (including offensive and defensive coordinators), and 49 percent of assistant coaches were recruited from high interaction positions. Hence, there appears to be a greater likelihood for former high interactors to become head coaches than for former low interactors to do so.

Hockey

In hockey, the positions of center and defense are defined as central ones while the positions of goal-tender and wing are defined as peripheral ones. Roy discovered that nearly 67 percent of the managers and 74½ percent of the coaches were recruited from high interaction positions.[44] Additionally, he found that 76 percent of the captains and 78 percent of the co-captains of hockey teams were selected from central playing positions.

Basketball

Klonsky studied 67 coaches who had played professionally between 1946 and 1975.[45] He defined the position of forward as a peripheral position and guard (because of the high rate of interaction and the performance of dependent and coordinative tasks) as most central, with center as the pivotal position. He discovered that among his sample of coaches 63½ percent had had previous playing experience at guard, nearly 29 percent had been forwards, and 8 percent had been centers.

In summary, Grusky's theory of formal structure as it relates to recruitment patterns has been a fruitful scheme for testing many sociological propositions in the world of sport. In general, in the team sports of baseball, football, hockey, and basketball there is empirical substantiation that leadership tends to emerge from those having had experience at central (high interaction) positions.

SPORT GROUPS AS SUBCULTURES

So far we have examined small groups in sport as miniature social systems. Small groups, however, can be studied as subcultures. A *subculture* can be defined in a number of ways but Wolfgang and Ferracuti's definition is sufficient in the present context.[46] It is "a central theme, a sub-ethos, or a cluster of values that is differentiated from those in the total culture." Members of a subculture share a common set of norms, values, beliefs, and symbols that give them a distinct identity within the dominant culture. In the larger society familiar subcultures include those of occupational (graduate students share common experiences, goals, problems), age (the adolescent subculture has been written about extensively), ethnic (black, Chicano), religious (Jewish), and socioeconomic (upper class, working class, lower class) groups.

The study of sport subcultures has received little attention until recently. Like other subcultures, sport subcultures may be viewed as a subsystem of the dominant culture, and characterized by a distinct set of norms, values, beliefs, and symbols. Phillips and Schafer have suggested that *all* athletes comprise a subculture.[47] Since the scientific data regarding the distinct differences (personality, life style, educational aspirations and achievements, etc.) between athletes (in various sports) and nonathletes is not definitive,[48] it is probably more accurate to talk of *specific* sport subcultures than a *general* sport subculture.

Loy, McPherson, and Kenyon suggested that there are three types of sport subcultures: (1) *occupational,* (2) *avocational,* and (3) *deviant.*[49]

Occupational Subcultures

When professional sport became increasingly professionalized, commercialized, and bureaucratized, *occupational subcultures* emerged within the sport world. When this occurred, participation in sport became a work rather than leisure role and was characterized by socialization, formalization, and role differentiation. Some of the sport subcultures that have been examined include boxing (Weinberg and Arond; Hare, as cited in chapter 3), professional wrestling (Stone; Rosenberg and Turowetz), baseball (Andreano; Bouton; Charnofsky; Haerle), horse racing (Scott), football (Kramer; Meggesey; Shaw), hockey (Faulkner; Smith and Diamond), and college coaching (Massengale; Sage).[50]

These studies, wrote Loy, McPherson, and Kenyon:

> . . . have described and to varying degrees attempted to explain anticipatory socialization; the prerequisite technical and social skills; recruitment patterns; the informal and formal occupational socialization process; the behavioral norms, value components, and expectations concerning interaction with those inside (the team) and outside (owners, media, fans, officials) the sub-cultural system; the argot (language) of the sport system; the social structure, social organization, social status, and social mobility within the sport; and the process of coping with failure, demotion, dismissal, and retirement, and the subsequent adjustment to the dominant culture.[51]

Avocational Subcultures

Contrasted with the occupational subculture in which the work role is paramount is the *avocational subculture* in which the leisure role is predominant. In recent years there has been a dramatic rise in both active and passive sport participation (see pp. 2-3). Such rapidly growing participation sports as tennis, snow skiing, jogging, platform tennis, and racketball have a strong physical fitness component to them. Some of the avocational subcultures that have been studied include tennis (Hyman), rock climbing (Donnelly), karate (Jacobs), parachuting (Arnold), surfing (Pearson), and motocross (Martin and Berry).[52] In summarizing avocational subcultures, Loy, McPherson, and Kenyon wrote:

> While having many of the same characteristics and processes as an occupational subculture, an avocational subculture is unique in a variety of ways. For example, the meaning of the activity is normally more expressive than instrumental; there is normally less time commitment, at least in the initial stages; the recruitment and socialization process is less formalized; the social organization is less bureaucratic; there is less status differentiation and mobility within the system, although prestige rankings based on skill evolve; and the activity is more likely to occur without an audience in a non-urban environment. Furthermore, . . . many avocational subcultures are organized around a technological

device such as a parachute, hot rod, dune buggy, or glider. Thus, as society becomes increasingly technocratic, we can expect to see the emergence of new avocational sub-cultures that will reflect the new technology.[53]

Deviant Subcultures

Rather than repeat what is presented in chapter 6 on deviance, let it suffice to say that in sport *deviant subcultures* include the practices of hustling in pool (Polsky),[54] gambling and cheating in many sports, and institutionalized violence (in football, boxing, and hockey). Rather than label these sports as unique deviant subcultures, it should be reckoned that deviant behavior is probably present in some form in most sport subcultures.

SUMMARY

Sport and small groups have occupied our attention in this chapter. The essential feature of a *small group* (roughly from three to fifteen persons congregated together) is *organization*. A small group is a set of organized parts which perform some function as a unit, that is, has a *common goal*; has system components—a *structure*—that are interrelated; and has *normative* features that exert pressure on the members to conform.

One of the most significant components of a group is the structure or stable patterns of position and role relationships. One of the most important positions in the group is that of *leader*. Studies of *leadership* have discovered that leaders perform two important functions: (1) *consideration*—or the social skills used in interpersonal transactions, and (2) *initiating structure*—or the skills employed to accomplish the task or goal before the group. In children's play groups, it has been discovered that certain types of leadership—*autocratic, democratic,* and *laissez-faire*—have a differential impact on the group's productivity and morale. Similarly, studies of leadership behavior among coaches suggest differences between small-time and big-time coaches with the former engaging in more insight and problem solving behavior and the latter tending to exhibit greater control and authority. However, inconsistencies in the research regarding coaches' leadership style is abundant.

Fiedler's *contingency model of leadership* has proven somewhat successful in predicting effective leadership in different contexts. According to this formulation, there is no single kind of leadership that is best under all circumstances. Instead, leadership is contingent—dependent upon other variables in the specific context.

In reviewing the relationship between *group process* and *performance*, it was shown that not always does group cohesiveness lead to team success. Some research has discovered a positive relationship between cohesiveness and team success; others have discovered the opposite. Part of the problem lies in the failure to distinguish between *interacting groups* (those in which the participants engage in a task requiring continuous adjustment and coordination) and *coacting groups* (those in which the participants perform a task independently of other members).

Group composition and *group structure* were also considered. The empirical evidence suggests that *social homogeneity* bodes well for success and stable group structure (as measured by consistent team lineups) is conducive to success. On the other hand, the relationship between leadership (i.e., coaches') longevity and team success appears to be curvilinear in nature.

A theory of *formal structure* as it relates to recruitment patterns has been a fruitful scheme for testing many sociological propositions in the team sports of baseball, football, hockey, and basketball.

In addition to studying small groups as miniature social systems, they can also be studied as subcultures. A *subculture* is a cultural theme, a sub-ethos, or a cluster of values that is differentiated from those in the total culture. Members of a subculture share a common set of norms, values, beliefs, and symbols that give them a distinct identity within the dominant culture. Subcultures in sport have been classified as *occupational* (e.g., boxing, wrestling, baseball, horse racing, football, hockey, and college coaching), *avocational* (e.g., tennis, karate, surfing, motocross, rock climbing, and parachuting), and *deviant* (e.g., hustling, gambling, and institutionalized violence).

IMPORTANT CONCEPTS DISCUSSED IN THIS CHAPTER

Group Dynamics	Fiedler's Contingency Model
Purposive Performance	Group Cohesiveness
Group Structure	Interacting Group
Normative Features	Coacting Group
Leadership:	Group Composition
Initiating Structure	Social Homogeneity
Consideration	Formal Structure
Leadership Styles:	Subcultures:
Autocratic	Occupational
Democratic	Avocational
Laissez Faire	Deviant

ENDNOTES

[1] Theodore M. Mills, *The Sociology of Small Groups* (Englewood Cliffs, NJ: Prentice-Hall, 1967), p. 3.

[2] Kurt Lewin, "Field Theory and Experiment in Social Psychology: Concepts and Methods," *American Journal of Sociology* 44 (1939), pp. 868-897.

[3] John W. McDavid and Herbert Harari, *Psychology and Social Behavior* (New York. Harper and Row, 1974), pp. 251-252.

[4] William M. Dobriner, *Social Structures and Systems* (Pacific Palisades, Calif: Goodyear Publishing Co., 1969), pp. 116-120. Used with permission.

[5] Ibid., p. 117.

[6] A. Halpin and B. Winer, "The Leadership Behavior of the Airplane Commander" (Ohio State University Research Foundation, 1952).

[7] *Factor analysis* is a statistical procedure by which one takes a set of empirical variables, examines their intercorrelations, and reduces them to a smaller number of conceptual factors that are more or less common to the variables with which one began. Factor analysis helps identify the common threads underlying a host of variables.

[8] K. Lewin, R. Lippitt, and R. White, "Patterns of Aggressive Behavior in Experimentally Created 'Social Climates', *Journal of Social Psychology* 10 (1939), pp. 271-299.

[9] J. L. Swartz, "Analysis of Leadership Styles of College Level Head Football Coaches From Five Midwestern States" (Ph.D. dissertation, University of Northern Colorado, 1973; cited in Loy, McPherson, and Kenyon, 1978).

[10] H. Lenk, "Authoritarian or Democratic Styles of Coaching?", *Team Dynamics*, ed. H. Lenk (Champaign, Ill. Stipes, 1977), pp. 81-89.

[11] R. G. Tharp and R. Gallimore, "What a Coach Can Teach a Teacher," *Psychology Today* 9 (January, 1976), pp. 75-78.

[12] R. R. Danielson, "Multidimensional Scaling and Factor Analysis of Coaching Behavior as Perceived by High School Hockey Players," *Research Quarterly* 46 (October, 1975), pp. 323-334.

[13] D. E. Mudra, "A Critical Analysis of Football Coaching Practices in Light of a Selected Group of Learning Principles" (Ph.D. dissertation, University of Northern Colorado, 1965).

[14] Fred E. Fiedler, "A Contingency Model of Leadership Effectiveness," *Advances in Experimental Social Psychology*, ed. by Leonard Berkowitz (New York: Academic Press, 1964), pp. 149-190.

[15] A. M. Bird, "Development of a Model for Predicting Team Performance," *Research Quarterly* 48 (March, 1977), pp. 24-32.

[16] Ibid., p. 31.

[17] Leon Festinger, "Informal Social Communication," *Psychological Review* 57 (1950), p. 274.

[18] At least three different definitions of "cohesiveness" have been used: (1) attraction (and resistance) of individuals to a group, (2) morale or motivational level of individual group members, and (3) coordination of individual group members' efforts. See M.E. Shaw, *Group Dynamics* (New York: McGraw-Hill, 1971).

[19] Fred E. Fiedler, "Assumed Similarity Measures as Predictors of Team Effectiveness," *Journal of Abnormal and Social Psychology* 49 (1954), pp. 381-388.

[20] Michael Klein and Gerd Christiansen, "Group Composition, Group Structure, and Group Effectiveness of Basketball Teams," *Sport, Culture, and Society*, ed. John Loy and Gerald Kenyon (New York: Macmillan, 1969), pp. 397-408.

[21] C. Heinicke and R. F. Bales, "Developmental Trends in the Structure of Groups," *Sociometry* 16 (1953), pp. 7-38.

[22] Fiedler, "Assumed Similarity Measures as Predictors of Team Effectiveness," and H. Grace, "Conformance and Performance," *Journal of Social Psychology* 40 (1954), pp. 233-237. M. J. Melnick and M. M. Chemers, "Effects of Group Structure on the Success of Basketball Teams," *Research Quarterly* 45 (March, 1974), pp. 1-8; Joseph F. McGrath, "The Influence of Positive Interpersonal Relations on Adjustment Effectiveness in Rifle Teams," *Journal of Abnormal and Social Psychology* 65 (1962), pp. 365-375. Hans Lenk, "Top Performance Despite Internal Conflict," *Sport, Culture and Society*, ed. John Loy and Gerald Kenyon (New York: Macmillan, 1969), pp. 393-397. Hans Veit, "Some Remarks Upon the Elementary Interpersonal Relations Within Ball Game Teams," *Contemporary Psychology of Sport*, ed. Gerald Kenyon (Chicago, Ill. The Athletic Institute, 1970). Daniel M. Landers and Gunther Luschen, "Team Performance Outcome and the Cohesiveness of Competitive Coacting Groups," *International Review of Sport Sociology* 2 (1974), pp. 57-69.

[23] Albert Myers, "Team Competition, Success, and the Adjustment of Group Members," *Journal of Abnormal and Social Psychology* 65 (1962), pp. 325-332; L. J. Chapman and D. T. Campbell, "An Attempt to Predict the Performance of Three-Men Teams from Attitude Measurements," *Journal of Social Psychology* 46 (1957), pp. 277-286; Thomas D. McIntyre, "A Field Experimental Study of Attitude Change in Four Bi-Racial Small Groups" (Ph.D. dissertation, Pennsylvania State University, 1970); D. Landers and T. Crum, "The Effect of Team Success and Formal Structure on Interpersonal Relations and Cohesiveness of Baseball Teams," *International Journal of Sport Psychology* 2 (1971), pp. 88-95; G. Arnold and W. Straub, "Personality and Group Cohesiveness as Determinants of Success Among Interscholastic Basketball Teams," *Proceedings of the Fourth Canadian Psycho-Motor Learning and Sport Symposium*, ed. I. Williams and L. Wankel (Ottawa, Canada: Department of National Health and Welfare, 1973), pp. 346-353; Howard L. Nixon, II, "Team Orientations, Interpersonal Relations and Team Success," *Research Quarterly* 47 (October, 1976), pp. 429-435; W. N. Widmeyer, "When Cohesiveness Predicts Performance Outcome in Sport," (Ph.D. dissertation, University of Illinois, 1977); Bird, "Development of a Model for Predicting Team Performance," and P. Slepicka, "Interpersonal Behavior and Sports Group Effectiveness," *International Journal of Sport Psychology* 6 (1975), pp. 14-27.

[24] In addition, one must be cognizant of: (1) the possible effects of the group's task performance structure and related general group structural factors (see, for example, the distinctions between interacting and coacting groups), and (2) whether cohesiveness is treated as an independent or dependent variable (Nixon, 1976).

[25] Landers and Luschen, "Team Performance Outcome and the Cohesiveness of Competitive Coacting Groups."

[26] Hans Lenk, "Maximum Performance Despite Internal Conflict," *Kolner Zeitschrift fur Soziologies und Sozial-psychologies* 10 (1966), pp. 168-172; Nixon, *Sport and Social Organization* (1976), pp. 28-32.

[27] *Social Psychology*, CRM Books (Del Mar, Calif.: Ziff-Davis, 1974), p. 426.

[28] D. Stanley Eitzen, "The Effect of Group Structure on the Success of Athletic Teams" (Paper presented at the Seventh World Congress of Sociology, Varna, Bulgaria, 1970).

[29] McDavid and Harari, *Psychology and Social Behavior*, p. 305.

[30] W. Essing, "Team Line-up and Team Achievement in European Football," *Contemporary Psychology of Sport*, ed. Gerald Kenyon (Chicago, Ill. Athletic Institute, 1970).

[31] D. Stanley Eitzen and Norman R. Yetman, "Managerial Succession, Longevity, and Organizational Effectiveness," *Administrative Science Quarterly* 7 (1972), pp. 110-116.

[32] Wibert M. Leonard, II, "Social and Performance Characteristics of the Pro Baseball Elite: A Study of the 1977 Starting Lineups," *International Review of Sport Sociology* (forthcoming).

[33] Oscar Grusky, "The Effects of Formal Structure on Managerial Recruitment: A Study of Baseball Organization," *Sociometry* 26 (1963), pp. 345-353.

[34] Ibid., p. 345.

[35] Ibid., p. 346.

[36] John W. Loy and Joseph F. McElvogue, "Racial Segregation in American Sport," *International Review of Sport Sociology* 5 (1970), pp. 5-23.

[37] An *assist* is the official credit awarded in the scoring of a game to a player who throws a ball in such a way that it results in a putout. In the scoring, the strikeouts made by the pitcher which are caught by the catcher are considered to be putouts or "assists" for the catcher. Obviously, the catcher assists in calling the signals as well as catching the ball in strikeouts (Loy and McElvogue, 1970).

[38] Hy Turkin and S. C. Thompson, *The Official Encyclopedia of Baseball* (New York. A. S. Barnes and Co., 1959). pp. 554-586.

[39] Jefferey Breglio, "Formal Structure and the Recruitment of Umpires in Baseball Organization" (Paper presented at the American Sociological Association Annual Meeting, New York, August, 1976).

[40] John Mitchell, "The Professional Official: Toughest Role in Sport" (Master's thesis, Illinois State University, 1978).

[41] John Loy, J. Sage, and A. Ingham, "The Effects of Formal Structure on Organizational Leadership: An Investigation of Varsity Baseball Teams," (cited in Loy, McPherson, and Kenyon, 1978, p. 134).

[42] P. Roland, "Ascription and Position: A Comparative Analysis of Playing Position on the Careers of Professional Football Coaches," (cited in Loy, McPherson, and Kenyon, 1978, p. 135).

[43] John Massengale and F. Farrington, "The Influence of Playing Position Centrality on the Careers of College Football Coaches," *Review of Sport and Leisure* 2 (June, 1977), pp. 107-115.

[44] G. Roy, "The Relationship Between Centrality and Mobility: The Case of the National Hockey League," (cited in Loy, McPherson, and Kenyon, 1978, p. 135).

[45] Bruce Klonsky, "The Effects of Formal Structure and Role Skills on Coaching Recruitment and Longevity: A Study of Professional Basketball Teams" (Paper for Department of Psychology, Fordham University, 1975).

[46] Marvin E. Wolfgang and F. Ferracuti, *The Subculture of Violence* (London, England: Tavistock, 1967).

[47] John C. Phillips and Walter E. Schafer, "Subcultures in Sport—A Conceptual and Methodological Approach," *Sport Sociology*, ed. A. Yiannakis et al (Dubuque, Iowa: Kendall/Hunt Publishing, 1976), pp. 129-134.

[48] Eldon E. Synder and Elmer Spreitzer, *Social Aspects of Sport* (Englewood Cliffs, NJ: Prentice-Hall, 1978).

[49] John W. Loy, Barry D. McPherson, and Gerald Kenyon, *Sport and Social Systems: A Guide to the Analysis, Problems and Liberature* (Reading, Mass.: Addison-Wesley, 1978), pp. 185-190; copyright © 1978, Addison-Wesley, Reading, Mass. Reprinted with permission.

[50] S. Kirson Weinberg and Henry Arond, "The Occupational Culture of the Boxer," *American Journal of Sociology* 57 (1952), pp. 460-469; Nathan Hare, "A Study of the Black Fighter," *The Black Scholar* 3 (November, 1971), pp. 2-9; Gregory P. Stone, "Wrestling: The Great American Passion Play," *Sport:Readings From a Sociological Perspective*, ed. E. Dunning (Toronto, Canada: University of Toronto Press, 1972), pp. 301-335; M. Rosenberg and A. Turowetz, "The Wrestler and the Physician: Identity Workup and Organizational Arrangements," *Sport and Social Order*, ed. D. W. Ball and J. W. Loy (Reading, Mass. Addison-Wesley, 1975), pp. 563-574; Ralph Andreano, *No Joy in Mudville* (Cambridge, Mass. Schenkman, 1965); Jim Bouton, *Ball Four* (New York: World, 1970); Harold Charnofsky, "The Major League Professional Baseball Player: Self-Conceptions versus the Popular Image," *International Review of Sport Sociology* 3 (1968),

pp. 39-53; Rudolf K. Haerle, Jr., "Career Patterns and Career Contingencies of Professional Baseball Players: An Occupational Analysis," *Sport and Social Order,* ed. D. W. Ball and J. W. Loy (Reading, Mass.: Addison-Wesley, 1975), pp. 461-519; Marvin Scott, *The Racing Game* (Chicago, Ill. Aldine, 1968). Jerry Kramer, *Farewell to Football* (New York: Thomas Y. Crowell, 1970); Dave Meggyesy, *Out of Their League* (Berkeley, Calif.: Ramparts Press, 1970); Gray Shaw, *Meat on the Hoof* (New York. St. Martin's, 1972); R. Faulkner, "Coming of Age in Organizations: A Comparative Study of Career Contingencies of Musicians and Hockey Players," *Sport and Social Order,* ed. D. W. Ball and J. W. Loy (Reading, Mass. Addison-Wesley, 1975), pp. 525-558; Michael Smith and F. Diamond, "Career Mobility in Professional Hockey," *Canadian Sport: Sociological Perspectives,* ed. R. Gruneau and J. Albinson (Don Mills, Ontario, Canada: Addison-Wesley, 1976), pp. 275-293; E. Vaz, "The Culture of Young Hockey Players: Some Initial Observations," *Training: A Scientific Basis,* ed. E. Taylor (Springfield, Ill.: Charles C. Thomas, 1972), pp. 222-234; John Massengale, "Coaching as an Occupational Subculture," *Phi Delta Kappan* 56 (October, 1974), pp. 140-142; George Sage, "An Occupational Analysis of the College Coach, *Sport and Social Order*, ed. D. W. Ball and J. W. Loy (Reading, Mass. Addison-Wesley, 1975), pp. 395-455.

[51] Loy, McPherson, and Kenyon, *Sport and Social Systems: A Guide to the Analysis, Problems and Literature,* p. 196; copyright © 1978, Addison-Wesley, Reading, Mass. Reprinted with permission.

[52] Harvey Hyman, "A Sociological Analysis of a Tennis Court," *World Tennis* (February 1971), pp. 60-61; P. Donnelly, "Outsiders—The Climber as a Deviant: A Reply to Grietbauer and Kingsley," *Climbing* (January-February, 1976), pp. 31-33. G. Jacobs, "Urban Samurai: The Karate Dojo," *Sport Sociology*, ed. A. Yiannakis, et al (Dubuque, Iowa. Kendall/Hunt, 1976), pp. 134-142; D. Arnold, "The Social Organization of Sky Diving: A Study of Vertical Mobility" (Paper presented at the Pacific Sociological Association Annual Meeting, Portland, Ore., April, 1972); K. Pearson, "The Symbol of the Revolution: A Surfboard," (Paper presented at the Sociological Association of Australia and New Zealand, 1974); Thomas W. Martin and Kenneth J. Berry, "Competitive Sport in Post-Industrial Society: The Case of the Motocross Racer, *Sport Sociology*, ed. A. Yiannakis et al (Dubuque, Iowa: Kendall/Hunt, 1976), pp. 28-34.

[53] Loy, McPherson, and Kenyon, p. 188.

[54] N. Polsky, "Of Pool Playing and Poolrooms," *Games, Sport and Power*, ed. G. P. Stone (New Brunswick, N.J.: Transaction Books, 1972), pp. 19-54.

Sport, Economics, and Politics

INTRODUCTION

In chapter 1 we introduced the sociological concept of "social system." This notion implies that the institutions of a society are interconnected and that changes in one reverberate into others. In other chapters we have examined the systemic relation between the institutions of sport and the family, religion, and education. In this chapter, we will demonstrate the interrelationships between the institutions of sport, politics, and the economy.

To begin with, it is useful to distinguish three levels of sport:[1] (1) *informal sport,* (2) *organized sport,* and (3) *corporate sport. Informal sport* is that which many of us engaged in during the early years of our life and in some of our adult discretionary time. Our primary motivation was to participate in spontaneous, playful activity from which we gained a sense of enjoyment, fulfillment, and satisfaction. These physical activities often included using makeshift bats, goals, and balls, and were played under somewhat ambiguous rules.

Organized sport is often an accompaniment of extracurricular activities during grade school, high school, and college but also includes certain types ("low key") of interscholastic, amateur (YMCAs, youth programs), and intercollegiate programs. The distinguishing characteristics of organized sport include formal teams, leagues, codified rules, officials, equipment, and organizations.

Corporate sport contains elements of informal and organized sport but with additional components. The additional elements are those of *economics* and *politics* (see Vignette 1.1, p. 6)—sport as big business and power politics. The corporate level of sport—that characterized by the subordination of the players' participation for their own intrinsic interests to extrinsically-motivated features such as to please fans, owners, alumni, and powerful pressure groups—is the foundation for most of the discussion in this chapter. This level of sport has led to the saying, "It's no longer a game, it's a business."

Emergence of Corporate Sport

No single event is responsible for the "corporatizing" of sport. However, economic and political factors have contributed to its development. According to Hoch,[2] "The character and scale of sports today is the child of monopoly capitalism."[3] Sport began to take on its present appearance when the economy began to recover from the Depression during the 1930s. Further, the bureaucratic administration of contemporary sport became well-entrenched around the early 1950s. Nixon wrote:

> This was a time when those in control of professional sport were forced to confront the dual dilemma of decreasing attendance and the unknown impact of television. In this context, a new sports entrepreneur stepped into the picture, one with less concern for the esthetic aspects of sports and more for sound business practices and the maximization of profits. These organization persons have fundamentally transformed the character of sports during the past two and one-half decades.[4]

Ties between Industry and Sport

Throughout this century sports and industry have been intertwined. Hoch reported that as early as 1926 the owners of boxing arenas in major American cities were dismayed by the under-utilization of property and facilities between boxing matches and circuses.[5] To make their capital more cost efficient, they lured a number of Canadian hockey teams to play their games in the vacant arenas. Similarly, after the Second World War, the owners realized that they could make even greater use of their facilities if basketball games could also be scheduled there. Hence, such material conditions as sport arenas, initially poorly utilized, created a demand for sport production and consumption.

The sport of auto racing was largely the creation of automobile manufacturers to promote, advertise, and sell their products. Since then, companies that produce automobile accessories—tires, gasoline, oil, brake linings, shock absorbers, batteries, or whatever—have helped sponsor events and drivers for the publicity gained through such endorsements. Looney reported that in 1974 A.J. Foyt received nearly $250,000 for using Goodyear tires and twenty other Indy 500 drivers received payments ranging from $10,000 to $300,000 from either the Goodyear or Firestone rubber companies.[6] These two leading tire producers had budgets of $8 million (Goodyear) and $3 million (Firestone) for automobile racing.

Other ways in which corporations "subtly" broadcast their products is to sponsor a sporting event or even underwrite the cost of constructing stadiums (Schaefer Stadium in Foxboro, Busch Stadium in St. Louis, and Rich Stadium in Buffalo). Additionally, manufacturers of numerous products have co-opted stellar athletes such as Joe Dimaggio, Mark Spitz, Hank Aaron, Bruce Jenner, O. J. Simpson, Peggy Flemming, Joe Namath, and Johnny Bench, to name a few, to promote and endorse their products. Bjorn Borg, the famous tennis player, epitomizes this theme. According to Kennedy and Williamson:

> Taking it from the top in 1977, he received $50,000 a year to wear a headband advertising Tuborg, a Danish beer. The Scandinavian Airlines System patch on Borg's left shoulder was good for $25,000. He got $200,000 for donning Fila shorts, socks and warmup suits, $100,000 for using Bancroft rackets—plus $2,000 for having them strung with VS gut—and $50,000 for wearing Tretorn tennis shoes. By also lending his name to cars, cereals, games, comic books, statues, bed linen, jeans and towels, Borg earned from $1.5 to $2 million.[7]

Other total earnings for select players appear in Table 11.1.

Table 11.1
Examples of Athletes' Total Earnings 1977/1977-1978

Athlete	Sports Earnings	Outside Income	Total Earnings
Kyle Rote, Jr. NASL	$20,000	$200,000	$220,000
Arnold Palmer, PGA	21,950	3,500,000	3,521,950
Bobby Orr, NHL	600,000	500,000	1,100,000
Marty Hogan, racquetball	41,000	25,000	66,000
Laura Baugh, LPGA	46,373	300,000	346,373

Source: Ray Kennedy and Nancy Williamson, "Money in Sports," *Sports Illustrated* 49 (July 24, 1978), p. 43.

The granddaddy of all sport spectacles—the "Super Bowl"—is the most lucrative annual event in American mass culture. It has come to epitomize the systemic relationship between sport and commercial interests. According to Real, advertising occupied slightly more than 15 percent of Super Bowl VIII air time. The 1974 telecast included 65 advertisements (sponsored by some 30 different companies), of which 52 were 30- or 60-second commercials. When the products advertised were categorized, they included automobiles (7 advertisements), automobile tires (7), automobile batteries (4), beers (4), wines (3), television sets (3), insurance companies, credit cards, railroads, banks, NFL (2), and hotels, retail stores, airplanes, locks, movies, copiers, and foods (1).[8] Not to be forgotten was CBS's charges for a minute of advertising, which ranged between $200,000 and $240,000. According to Real:

> The advertisements for New York Life Insurance and Boeing were constructed on sports themes, as were notices for upcoming CBS sports programs. Tire and battery advertisements emphasized strength and dependability, virtues helpful in both winter and football. Liquor appeals included traditional glamor, gusto, and fun. The fuel shortage was evident in the emphasis of automobile advertisements on economy and efficiency. Consumer unrest was reflected by promotion of general corporate images as well as specific products. "Don't be fuelish" public service notices were included, in keeping with the Nixon administration's approach to fuel shortages, and a plug was inserted for NFL players going on a trip for the Department of Defense.[9]

According to reports, top corporate executives inundated the stands and boxes. Buckley indicated that 10,000 seats (of the 90,000 seats available for Super Bowl VII) were awarded to individuals or corporations with commercial and promotional ties to the league.[10] The Nelson Research Firm reported that 66 percent of corporation executives earned $20,000 or more per annum liked football "quite a lot" (in comparison to 42 percent who said the same for pro baseball). Carl Lindemann, Jr., then vice president of NBC sports, said "I'd be hard pressed to name a top executive who doesn't follow football avidly."[11] Chief executives Nixon, Ford, and Carter (who invited the Washington Bullets' 1978 championship basketball team to the White House) typify how "corporation managers" feel about sports.

THE ECONOMICS OF PROFESSIONAL SPORT

The Sports Owner

When typical sport fans sit in front of their televisions or attend an event in person, they can easily identify the players. They're the ones with the flashy uniforms and Simpson, Jabbar, Jackson, Rose, Havlicek, or Lafleur printed on the back. They differ in physical skill or specific task to be performed, but they are readily identified as the athletes, the performers. But ask those same fans to name the owner and the task the owner performs and it's a whole new ballgame. Is he/she a young executive with a flair for marketing a product? Perhaps the team is a subsidiary of a corporation along with amusement parks, movies, banks, oil refineries or any of a number of industries. Or might the team be owned by a woman acting as a front for her husband's fortunes? These are only a few examples of the diversified class of professional sport owners. Probably only one of the fans' perceptions of owners is correct: they have money.

Just how sports have gotten to their present stage where the sports page often seems a combination financial page and court report is a question often asked. In many ways the change in the type of ownership is symbolic of the evolution of professional sport as a whole.[12] The early owners were those who grew up with the game. Men such as George Halas in football, Eddie Gottlieb in basketball, and Clark Griffith, Connie Mack, and John McGraw in baseball involved themselves in the total operation of the franchise. Their whole business was sports, and they helped provide stability for young leagues. They made money but they promoted the game, even barnstormed for the sake of exposure.

The second stage of owners was treated initially with great trepidation. These men were business tycoons with large industrial holdings who sought both to contribute to the community and advertise their product. The beer barons August Busch, Jr., of the St. Louis Cardinals and Jacob Ruppert of the New York Yankees, and Phil Wrigley of the Chicago Cubs with his chewing gum industry were members of this class. There was fear that they would commercialize sport by using sport as a market for their product. This breed, however, has generally been rich but public-minded men who showed a great deal of concern for the game. Some believe that the era of the "sportsman owner" died with the deaths of the Red Sox's Tom Yawkey and the Cubs' Phil Wrigley in the latter 1970s.

The third stage in ownership is the corporate manager who approaches sport as a business proposition. Frequently an absentee owner, the concern often isn't for the town, team, or sport, but which team up for sale offers the best tax advantage. As will be explained later, such an owner, through the use of depreciation and capital gains tax laws, seeks to use the team to his advantage for several years and then sell it. For instance, in the American Basketball Association there were 27 changes of ownership in a decade, and in the National Basketball Association for the period 1963-75 the league added nine new teams and saw an overturn of 44 owners and principals.[13]

The easiest facts of ownership to comprehend are the costs, revenues, and profits. These are the tangibles of ownership. But still questions remain. Who are the owners? Why would someone invest in sports these days, aside from financial considerations? It is ironic that those who control sport are some of the least known people in sport. While we cannot name and identify all of the owners, we can point out some examples to answer some of the questions.

One type of ownership is represented by the New York Knicks (basketball), Rangers (hockey) and St. Louis Cardinals (baseball). They are all *subsidiaries* (companies whose controlling interests are owned by other companies) of larger corporations, Gulf-Western (Knicks and Rangers) and Anheuser-Busch (Cardinals), respectively. The team often stands on the same ground with other operations, such as movies and oil with the Knicks and beer and amusement parks with the Cardinals. Just because they are part of vast corporations, however, doesn't mean they can draw upon these vast financial reserves. The Cardinals, for example, must stand on their own feet financially, and all money for baseball operations must be generated by the franchise. There are others that can draw upon those reserves. In the present situation concerning the free agent status (see pp. 247-248), this creates the fear in some corners that the wealthiest teams will acquire the best players and dominate their sport.

It is virtually impossible for an individual owner to compete for a player when another "corporate" team is also vying for him. John Bassett, proprietor of the World Hockey Association's (WHA) Birmingham Bulls, recently said: "I lost two players . . . to the Rangers . . . I couldn't compete . . . so I called Madison Square Garden and told them if they sent me some dough, they could have them right away."[14]

Calvin Griffith of the Minnesota Twins and Walter O'Malley of the Los Angeles Dodgers are throwbacks to the old type of owner. Their sole financial concern is their team, and the operation of the team is often a family concern. Calvin Griffith, for example, inherited the team from his father. While the Twins have recently experienced trouble with free agent defections, the Dodgers are the envy of many sports owners. They own the team, stadium, concessions, parking, and even a service station on the parking lot. Combine all these income sources with an annual draw of at least 2½ million and there is little reason to see why one would not be jealous of the Dodgers.

The Milwaukee Bucks basketball team is one of nine *publicly owned* teams with 2800 shareholders. This type of ownership is clearly the exception. Often these teams are in the smaller cities and have faced financial difficulties. The only way for some of them to survive was to put shares out for public sale to raise the necessary capital.

The most prevalent type of ownership is the owner who has made large sums of money in another line of business and chooses to use some of it in the sport market. For example, Ray Kroc, owner of the San Diego Padres, is the owner of the McDonald's fast-food chain. Paul Snyder, former owner of the Buffalo Braves, owned a fast-food corporation and was the largest shareholder in Nabisco. Building his shipping business up into a $100 million a year operation, George Steinbrenner used some of his capital to buy the New York Yankees. Finally, there is the NFL oil bloc represented by Lamar Hunt of the Kansas City Chiefs, John Mecom of the New Orleans Saints, Bud Adams of the Houston Oilers, and Clint Murchison of the Dallas Cowboys.

The problem of fans' identity with the owner is perhaps best represented by Ruly Carpenter of the Philadelphia Phillies and Hugh Culverhouse of the Tampa Bay Buccaneers. Carpenter, grandson of R. R. M. Carpenter (the patriarch of Dupont) who bought the Phils in 1943, grew up on an estate which had a full-sized baseball diamond in the front yard. As part of the family fortune estimated at $100 million, Ruly inherited the team in 1972 at the age of 32.[15] A man who spends most of his time with the team, Carpenter is considered the prototype of the future owner.

The example of Hugh Culverhouse cannot be used to generalize about all sports owners, but he serves to represent the identity problem. In describing him and his wife Jay, a recent article said:

They are nice people. They have a nice life. They skip off in their private jet (they're both pilots) or yacht to the Bahamas or some other foreign climate for long weekends of golf, gambling, and dancing. Out by the pool at Los Cedros, there is a patch of Astro-Turf. Drawing on a supply of 10,000 Japanese golf balls, the Culverhouses often while away a leisurely hour or so on the Astro-Turf, teeing up and driving one ball after another into the river.[16]

Even if it cannot be conclusively proven that owners are the cause of the problems in pro sports (see Vignette 13.1 for the fans' perceptions of owners), the problems with ownership are at least symptomatic of societal-wide difficulties. If sport does survive the present stage, the ownership concept will have to change, since even now we find it infiltrated by *syndicates* ("a group of individuals or organizations combined or making a joint effort to undertake some specific duty or carry out specific transactions or negotiations"), *conglomerates* ("a company consisting of a number of subsidiary companies or divisions in a variety of unrelated industries, usually as a result of merger or acquisition"), and *shareholders* (a holder or owner of shares in a corporation). Or perhaps this will never happen. The future is very cloudy, but the present state can best be summed up by a statement by Sam Schulman of the Seattle SuperSonics, who said: "Owning a pro team is an ego trip."[17] Other reasons for ownership include "fun, excitement, ego fulfillment, power, visibility, personal satisfaction from knowing athletes ('jock sniffing'), vicarious identification as an athlete, another goal to conquer, and community service."[18]

Franchise Appreciation

Despite owners' claims that players' demands for exorbitant salaries are driving them to the poor house, the value of sport franchises has steadily increased. For example, consider the case of the Montreal Canadiens Hockey Club.[19] In 1910 it was bought for $7,500, sold in 1921 for $11,000, and sold again in 1935 for $165,000. In 1957 the club was purchased for an estimated $2.7 million and in 1971, 58 percent of the shares were sold for about $15 million. In pro basketball, the franchise value of the Boston Celtics rose from $2.8 million in 1965 to $6.2 million in 1969; the San Diego Rockets' value increased $4 million dollars in four years (worth $1.7 million in 1967 and $5.7 million in 1971). The Cleveland Browns were bought in 1953 for $600,000, sold in 1961 for $4 million, valued in 1969 at $14 million and valued again seven years later at $20 million.[20] In one year the World Football League's Florida Blazers went from an inception price of $250,000 to $3 million.[21] Other illustrations of *capital appreciation* can be seen in comparing the costs when teams entered their respective leagues with their estimated value if sold in 1978 (*Sports Illustrated*, July 17, 1978, p. 40):

Team	1966 Cost	1978 Cost
Los Angeles Kings	$2 million	$8 million
Seattle SuperSonics	$1.75 million	$12 million
New York Mets	$1.8 million	$16 million

With the opportunity for such quick gains, it is little wonder that owners are quick to get in on the ground floor and then sell out before the onslaught of problems the WFL faced. Then, in 1975 the escalation reached a peak when Hugh Culverhouse, owner of the Tampa Bay Buccaneers paid a record $16 million entrance fee just for the privilege of joining the NFL owners' fraternity. Finally, the popular business magazine *Forbes* reported that the collective value of pro baseball had increased $47.3 million for American League clubs and $114.9 million for National League clubs since their inception.[22]

In spite of these enormous franchise costs, one should not get the impression that sport ownership is a losing proposition. Surely there is some inducement to get people to fork over such sums of money to get their hand in sport. One of these inducements is profits. According to McPherson: "With few exceptions, the owner of a professional sport organization is an entrepreneur whose ultimate goal is to maximize profits directly from the sport franchise, or indirectly by using financial losses in the sport domain as a tax deduction for other interests."[23]

Profit, however, is not automatic upon ownership. For instance, in the 1977-78 season 10 of 18 (56%) of the NHL hockey teams lost money, as did 9 of 22 (41%) NBA basketball teams, 5 of 26 (19%) baseball teams, and 4 of 28 (14%) NFL football teams. Table 11.2 depicts these findings along with the gross revenue for the four sports in 1974 and 1977-78. For comparative purposes, consider that in 1974, 22 of 27 (82%) basketball teams lost money as did 12 of 24 (50%) major league baseball teams, 10 of 28 (36%) hockey teams and 2 of 26 (8%) football teams.[24] The latter figures for basketball are somewhat atypical since the sport was involved in a bidding war at the time and both leagues had franchises in very weak market areas.

The kingpin of the profit scene is the National Football League. In 1973-74, the 26 NFL teams averaged $945,000 in before-tax profits.[25] Only two teams, the San Diego Chargers and Houston Oilers turned up in the red that year. These figures are supportable although there are discrepancies according to players and owners. The NFL Players Association and their representative Ed Garvey maintained the average was $1.7 million while the owners countered that it was $800,000.[26] The example of Leonard Tose, owner of the Philadelphia Eagles, lends credence to the claims of those who say the main determinant of success isn't found in the win-loss column but on the financial balance sheet. Since he purchased them in 1969, the Eagles have had one winning season but have seen their profits rise from $412,000 in 1969 to $1,500,000 in 1975,[27] and their franchise value rise from $2,500 in 1933 to $25,000,000 in 1978.[28]

The Law of Depreciation as Applied to Sport

Due to the sometimes uncertain outlook for profits, there must be some other monetary attraction for sport investment. One incentive is depreciation. The *law of depreciation* is a mainstay of American business. Over the years tools, equipment, resources (and persons in sport) wear out. The tax laws permit a portion of the value of a commodity to be deducted because each year it wears out and becomes less valuable. This law is applicable to all businesses but takes an interesting twist when applied to sport.

Depreciation is a basic tax and business concept in which one counts *capital* (property or money accumulated) as a deductible cost of doing business. When an owner acquires a new player, he not only receives the legal right to his services, but also the legal right to depreciate that player's value for several years. On the surface this practice is sensible since athletes, much like cars, are generally not as valuable after five years as they were when "new." But there is a wrinkle for sports that makes depreciations so important in this present era of ownership. What the owner deducts for depreciation can be charged against the profits of a collateral business when the franchise doesn't turn a profit. For instance, suppose the owner of a pro sport franchise also owned a

Table 11.2
Financial Character of Baseball, Football, Hockey, and Basketball Teams, 1974, 1977-78

1974

Baseball		Football		Hockey		Basketball	
Of 24 Major-League Teams		Of 26 Major-League Teams		Of 28 Major-League Teams		Of 27 Major-League Teams	
12 made money or broke even	12 lost money	24 made money	2 lost money	18 made money	10 lost money	5 made money	22 lost money
Gross Revenues: 180 million dollars, including 46 million from sale of TV rights		Gross Revenues: 163 million dollars, including 45 million from TV		Gross Revenues: 90 million dollars, including 11 million from TV		Gross Revenues: 50 million dollars, including almost 10 million from TV	

Source: Henry G. Demmert, *The Economics of Professional Team Sports* (New York, NY: Joint Council on Economic Education 1976), p. 17. Reprinted with permission of the Joint Council on Economic Education, © JCEE 1976. All rights reserved.

1977-1978

Baseball		Football		Hockey		Basketball	
Of 26 Major-League Teams		Of 28 NFL Teams		Of 18 NHL Teams		Of 22 NBA Teams	
21 made money	5 lost money	24 made money	4 lost money	8 made money	10 lost money	13 made money	9 lost money
Gross Revenues: $230 million, including 23.2 million from national TV		Gross Revenues: $250 million, including 60 million from national TV		Gross Revenues: $65 million, including 180,000 from national TV		Gross Revenues: $95 million, including 10.5 million from national TV	

Source: Ray Kennedy and Nancy Williamson, "Money: The Monster Threatening Sports," *Sports Illustrated*, July 17, 1978, p. 58.

large trucking firm. If he had $500,000 deductible depreciation for his athletes and his franchise broke even, and his trucking firm made $750,000, he would only have a $250,000 profit to pay taxes on.

Consider the purchase of an expansion franchise. The new owner buys two assets: (1) an "intangible" license to the franchise—which is really a monopoly right—that permits the team to engage in games with other league clubs, share in the broadcast revenues of the league, and occupy an exclusive territory, and (2) a "tangible" batch of players (and their contracts) that may be selected from the rosters of established teams in an "expansion draft." For the most part, the franchise consists of a set of rights—the right to do business in a contrived scarcity, monopoly situation, and share in league broadcast revenues (which can amount to as much as $2½ million annually)—rather than some tangible product. The law of depreciation works this way. The license cannot be depreciated because, technically, it does not wear out (in fact, in recent years it has appreciated as we indicated earlier). Players, on the other hand, do wear out and their value diminishes. It is to this latter component of the franchise that the "law" applies and it is technically referred to as the *amortization* of player contracts.

Amortization of Player Contracts

Suppose that the purchase price of an expansion franchise amounts to $10 million. The new owners allocate 75 percent of that amount ($7.5 million) to the value of player contracts and, of course, the 25 percent remainder to the franchise license. The player costs can be amortized over a five-year period and treated as an annual indirect loss of $1.5 million ($7.5 million divided by 5 years equals $1.5 million per year). The problem that arises is that the buyer and seller have diametrically opposed interests—the buyer wants to allocate as much of the purchase price as possible to "tangibles" (player contracts) so he can depreciate their value, but the seller prefers to maximize the amount attributed to the "intangible" license and thereby treat the money as capital gains (profit from the sale of assets) and receive a tax break on it.

For years the federal government allowed the buyer and seller to distribute costs in each of their best interests. This meant that as soon as a new buyer secured the title to a team, he could begin the depreciation process again even though the seller had done the same before. The new buyer at a later point in time sells the club and the new owner begins the amortization again. This process has been called *depreciation recapture*. Aside from the economics of the matter, this procedure produced a very important, unanticipated consequence. Once a buyer had depreciated the cost of player contracts (usually taking about 5 years), it was no longer profitable to retain ownership of the club. In addition, other business tycoons saw the opportunity to purchase the club for their own financial interests. This helps to explain the turnover in sport club ownership and flurry of new franchises in recent years that have come and gone almost overnight. Obviously, all owners have not been caught up in this merry-go-round and retain ownership for other reasons. However, the primary motive appears to be profit maximization.

One final matter is important in sport ownership and franchise purchases. If an owner amortizes players but has no profits to charge them against, the benefit is for nought. At this juncture, the owner's other business operations become significant. If the owner owns a profitable brewery, chewing gum factory, or whatever, the amortization of contracts can be applied against the profits in the other business for tax savings. Suppose a new franchise at the end of the year shows an operating loss (revenue minus direct costs) of $1 million per year for 5 years. If the amortization of player contracts over those five years amounted to $1½ million per year, the owner may report annual losses of $2½ million for tax purposes ($1.5 million for depreciation plus $1 million for operating losses).

If the club is incorporated in such a way (part of several commercial industries) and if the new owner is in a 50 percent tax bracket (a conservative estimate since the financial assets of sports owners sometimes places them in even higher tax brackets), they can enjoy a considerable tax savings. For example, suppose the owner of a pro sport franchise also owns a large trucking firm. Suppose the trucking firm made $10 million during the same time that the owner reported $2½ million dollar losses. Instead of paying taxes on $10 million, he only has to pay taxes on $7½ million. In brief, the benefits of ownership stem from two sources: (1) the amortization of player contracts and (2) the tax bracket of the franchise owners. Or, as Noll argues, there is "no evidence that the prime motivation of the vast majority of owners is any consideration other than profits.[29] Roone Arledge, president of ABC Sports, and lawyer Tom Evans echoed Noll's contention when they said, "Sports used to be run as a hobby by team owners. Now, it's a tax shelter for a lot of them or their corporations. . . . Of all the traditional tax-shelter deals, this is clearly the best.

Recent Changes

A 1974 court decision suggests there may be a trend against allowing clubs to allocate excessive amounts of monies to player contracts, thereby reducing the tax advantages produced by amortization. E. Cody Laird, a minority owner of the Atlanta Falcons, sued for a $48,219 refund of 1967 and 1968 taxes. The Falcons were owned by a Subchapter S corporation called Five Smiths Inc. Such a corporation was treated as a partnership, so the corporation itself didn't pay taxes, but each partner paid his share of the taxes or deducted the losses which can offset taxes on a collateral business.[31] The Atlanta Falcons franchise cost $8.5 million and after various fees were paid, $50,000 was attributed to the franchise price and about $7.7 million to player price. The Internal Revenue Service disallowed all but $1 million of this depreciation. While depreciating $1.5 million in both 1967 and 1968, the club reported losses of $506,329 and $551,047. Thus, the club cleared about $1 million each year before depreciation.[32] The IRS had slashed those depreciation figures to $200,000 for each year. Thus, the refund Laird was suing for was for income taxes on profits the IRS alleged the Falcons actually made (Table 11.3 summarizes this discussion).

Table 11.3
Laird, Federal District Court, Georgia, Counterclaims and Disposition

Component	Buyer's Allocation	%	IRS Allocation	%	Judge's Award	%
Franchise value	$50,000	0.65	$6,722,914	86.42	$460,871[a]	5.96
TV Rights					4,277,043	55.04
Player Cost	$7,772,914	99.35	1,050,000	13.58	3,035,000	39.00
Total	$7,772,914[b]	100.00	$7,772,914[b]	100.00	$7,772,914[b]	100.00

a = Actual award, $410,871, to which must be added the $50,000 agreed upon by the buyers and not in contention.

b = Of the total franchise cost of $8.5 million, $727,086 was for debt service.

Source: Adapted from James A. Michener, *Sports in America* (New York, NY: Random House, 1976), p. 236.

Senior District Court Judge Frank Hooper chose the middle ground in placing the depreciable player value at slightly over $3 million. The unique item in the decision was Hooper's choice to award $4,277,043 to the value of television rights. The remaining $460,871 was ruled to be the value of the franchise. Also, the original contestant got a refund of less than half of the $48,219 he sought. The important effect of this decision is not the actual amounts awarded, but the principles they represent. No longer can the owner use the franchise just for a quick tax write-off. This decision lends strength to the IRS rule of reasonable allocation concerning depreciation. The third important effect is the judge's recognition of the importance of television rights. Certainly in this day and age professional sports are built upon television (see chapter 12). Also important was Hooper's belief that since it was impossible to determine the useful life of these rights, he could not allow them to be depreciable. While it will still take a very wealthy person to obtain a franchise, this decision means owners will probably hold on to franchises longer, possibly recapturing that disappearing bond between owner and team. More recently, in 1976, Congress passed the *Tax Reform Act* which stipulated that the portion of the purchase price that the buyer allocated to player costs could not exceed the portion allocated by the seller. Also, it set a limit for player costs at 50 percent.

In summarizing the benefits of ownership, it is crucial to comprehend the amount of a franchise's cost that is distributed to players and the license itself. In the early 1960s, it was customary to estimate the worth of a franchise at $50,000 (the cost that could not be depreciated) and 98 percent as an expense item (player costs) that could be used for tax write-offs. Bill Veeck, the Chicago White Sox owner, gives an example. When the Milwaukee Braves moved to Atlanta, the cost of the players was set at $6 million and the cost of the franchise at $50,000. A ten-year depreciation on player costs would yield an annual tax write-off of $600,000. Put differently, the Braves would pay no taxes on the first $600,000 of profit and since corporate taxes ran about 50 percent, the club would be saving about $300,000 a year or $3 million over the ten years.[33] Recent court decisions have established a precedent against the traditional allocation procedures as illustrated in Table 11.3.

THE FINANCING OF SPORTS FACILITIES

Okner found that about 70 percent of all pro stadia were publicly owned and financed (through revenue bonds) and rented to sport organizations at relatively low rates through "sweetheart" leases.[34] To take an extreme example, the *recommended* rental fee for newly refurbished Yankee stadium was set at $1 per year! In fact, in 1977 the Yankees paid the city of New York $170,681 for stadium rental from their gross earnings of $13.4 million. Similarly, the 1977 Brewers paid the county a mere $21,149 for rental of Milwaukee County Stadium when more than 1.1 million people passed through their turnstiles at an average ticket price of $3.68. To balance the ledger, the average sport team pays less than 10 percent of its home gate receipts for stadium rental. The following dollar amounts were paid by selected sport franchises:[35]

Sport	Franchise	Rental Fee
NHL Hockey	Vancouver Canucks	$508,000
	Pittsburgh Penguins	250,000
NFL Football	Kansas City Chiefs	557,633
	San Diego Chargers	300,054

Sport	Franchise	Rental Fee
NBA Basketball	Golden State Warriors	$ 300,000
	Detroit Pistons	82,000
American/National	Philadelphia Phillies	1,014,068
League Basketball	Milwaukee Brewers	21,149

Okner goes on to say that rentals are relatively low for sport organizations for the following reasons:[36]

1. to enhance the prestige of the community and thereby stimulate economic activity in non-sport enterprises.
2. to generate employment, consumer sales and tax collection from sporting events.
3. to provide recreational opportunities to community residents.
4. to improve the morale of the citizens.

In the past decade and a half many new sport facilities have been built or renovated at the tax-payers' expense. The reason is that in all too many cases the project cannot pay for itself and becomes a public liability. This is what happened in the construction of the New Orleans Superdome (at a cost of $163 million), Kansas City's Harry S. Truman sports complex (at a cost of $75 million), Philadelphia's Veterans Stadium, Hackensack Meadowlands in East Rutherford, New Jersey (at a cost of $340 million), Denver's Mile High Stadium and the rehabilitation of Yankee Stadium (at a cost of $100 million).

In addition to relatively low rental fees, other indirect tax benefits accrue to professional sport barons at the local level. Okner estimated that 82 percent (44 of 54) of publicly-owned teams had property taxes ranging between $8.8 and $13.4 million.[37] The community loses this tax assessment, but this subsidy may have the effect of keeping the cost of tickets down, providing athletes with lucrative salaries, and the owners with larger profits.[38]

The location of a major sport franchise in a community is usually an economic boon to the area since it increases the volume of business transacted by hotels, restaurants, taxis, and other business enterprises. Additionally, the city receives revenue from ticket taxes, concessions, employee taxes, and stadium rental fees. For example, the New York Yankees add $50 million annually to their bankrupt city, and the Pittsburgh Pirates generate an extra $21 million. Miami, Florida, earned some $40 million from a single event—the Super Bowl—in 1976. Finally, the Super Bowl in New Orleans added $25 to $35 million to the economy in 1977. Other major sporting events like the World Series, Indianapolis 500, Kentucky Derby, NBA playoffs, and championship boxing matches contribute to the economic bonanza of a community.

Construction of new stadia and renovation of old ones raises two serious ethical issues. *First,* should public monies be used to finance such structures? *Second,* should public monies be channeled into sports when many cities have inadequate housing, school, and medical facilities? To highlight this latter issue, consider the following situation: The cost of the 1976 Montreal Olympics was in the neighborhood of $1.5 billion. But what was so vexing were the problems already diseasing Montreal—poverty and pollution, for example, had been given inadequate attention. A study of the Montreal City Health Department of 3,400 urban school children found that more than one-half were physically ill, most of them suffering from upper respiratory and skin diseases.[39] Ten percent of these required hospitalization. "In one school, 21 percent was undernourished, 41 percent were emotionally disturbed, and 51 percent lived in houses with inadequate sanitation facilities." More than half of the houses in one sector of Montreal were either uninhabitable or substandard. Montreal's air was passing the "danger limit" and 300 million gallons of raw sewage was dumped daily into the St. Lawrence River. "The real winners: a few athletes, politicians, and construction firms."

In sum, pro sports occupy an envious position with respect to tax breaks and exemptions. Stadium and arena bonds have typically been used to build sport facilities and have been tax exempt. Okner estimated that if stadium construction bonds were taxable, a revenue of $10.2 million annually would fall into the federal government's coffers.[40] Moreover, the local and state governments do not charge interest on construction bonds. Another financial loophole is that income derived from selling players, franchises, and equipment is not taxed as capital gains. Additionally, team owners are permitted to depreciate player contracts, equipment, and facilities.

Having discussed some of the *advantages* of sport ownership, let us turn to some of the *costs* of ownership.

THE COSTS OF OWNERSHIP

The Laborer

On the cost side of the ledger are three primary categories: (1) *player compensation* (salaries, bonuses, deferred payments and fringe benefits), (2) *game expenses* (travel expenses, stadium rental), and (3) *general and administrative costs* (salaries of owners, executives, and concessionaires). While varying from one sport and team to the next, Figure 11.1 displays the distribution of income in 1974 for NFL teams. Note that the bulk of expenses surrounds player costs (45 percent of total), and the relatively small percentage profit of 3.9 percent.

Until recently the salaries of pro athletes have been relatively low; however, recent studies have shown that the average income of active male athletes is higher than for most males in the labor force. The turning point came in 1960 when the upstart American Football League bid for rookies and veterans from the entrenched National Football League. Prior to that time salaries of $100,000 or more were rare. Following the loosening of the purse strings in pro football, the ABA began competing with the NBA for players and, more recently, the WHA began challenging the NHL. Every phase of the "money warfare" since 1960 has resulted in salary increases in *all* professional sports, since pro athletes (and their players' associations and business managers) tend to consider pay raises in sports other than their own as enhancing their own worth as well.[41]

The pattern to salary escalation has been similar in virtually all cases. When a new league makes its debut, it begins to raid the established league for "top draw" athletes to bolster gate receipts and publicity. The case of basketball is instructive. Prior to the inception of the ABA in 1967, the average rookie salary in the NBA was $8,000 in 1961 and $12,500 in 1967. In 1970-71, under pressure from the ABA, the average NBA rookie salary soared to $46,000. Further, the median salary in the NBA before the establishment of the ABA was $20,000; in 1971 it rose to $43,000.[42] In 1977, when the two leagues merged, the average salary was $120,000 (this high salary was due to several activities, such as collective bargaining, wage and price inflation).

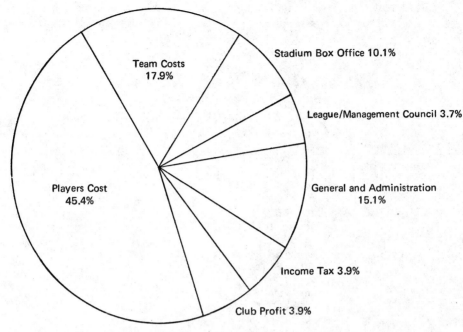

Figure 11.1
Distribution of Income 1974
(From Henry G. Demmert, *The Economics of Professional Team Sports,* New York, Joint Council
on Economic Education, 1976, p. 16. Reprinted with permission of the Joint Council on Economic
Education, from *The Economics of Professional Team Sports,* Economic Topic Series, ©JCEE 1976.
All Rights Reserved.)

The same thing happened when the NHL and WHA competed for players. Prior to the inception
of the WHA, the average NHL salary was about $24,000 during the 1971-72 season. It rose to an esti-
mated $40,000 in 1972-73 when the newly formed WHA began bidding for players.[43] In 1977-78
the average salary of professional hockey players was in the neighborhood of $96,000.

In pro football the same pattern of salary escalation occurred. When Sonny Werblin of the New
York Jets signed Joe Namath of Alabama in 1964 for $427,000, the ball began to roll with increasing
momentum. In the case of Bobby Hull, the entire fledgling WHA underwrote the signing of the superstar. The same thing happened when Rick Barry was lured away from the ABA–the league members
agreed to pay about $7,000 each for his $100,000 salary. When the now defunct World Football
League (WFL) began bidding for established players, football salaries jumped from an average of
$27,500 in 1973 to an average of $42,000 in 1975. They dropped with the demise of the WFL.[44]

In 1977-78 the *average salary or winnings* for athletes in basketball, hockey, baseball, football,
golf, NASL soccer, pro skiing, racquetball, and bowling was $143,000, $96,000, $76,349, $55,288,
$33,525, $17,500, $14,911, $3,500, and $2,649, respectively. Table 11.4 contains data for minimum
salary or lowest winnings, by sport, in addition to the average salary or winnings. Further, the estimated number of players by sport is: basketball (200), baseball (600), hockey (600), tennis (200),
football (1200), golf (300), and jockeys (2500).[45] Table 11.5 contains probable earnings for highly

paid professional athletes in 1977-78 in auto racing, baseball, basketball, bowling, boxing, football, golf, harness racing, hockey, jockeys, racquetball, pro skiing, NASL soccer, and tennis.

Table 11.4
Average Salary or Winnings and Minimum Salary
or Lowest Winnings (1977-1978)

Sport	Average Salary or Winnings	Minimum Salary or Lowest Winnings
Auto Racing	Not Available	Not Available
Baseball	$ 76,349	$21,000
Basketball	143,000	30,000
Bowling	2,649	0
Boxing	Not Available	Not Available
Football	55,288	20,000
Golf	33,525	30
Harness Racing	Not Available	546
Hockey	96,000	30,000
Jockeys	Not Available	Not Available
Racquetball	3,500	0
Pro Skiing	14,911	133
NASL Soccer	17,500	0
Tennis	Not Available	0

Source: Ray Kennedy and Nancy Williamson, "Money in Sports," *Sports Illustrated* 49 (July 24, 1978), pp. 42-43.

In the past decade average salaries in pro sport have risen considerably. The statistics below document this trend for 1967, 1972, and 1977-78 for the four major pro team sports (*Sports Illustrated*, July 17, 1978, p. 46):

Sport	1967	1972	1977-78
Basketball	$20,000	$90,000	$143,000
NHL Hockey	19,133	44,109	96,000
Baseball	19,000	34,092	76,349
Football	25,000	35,000	55,288

Salaries, particularly for superstars, are often misleading. Among the most deceptive fiscal reports was that of Catfish Hunter in 1975. His case serves to underscore the point. He apparently signed a five-year contract for $3.75 million. Hunter did *not* have a yearly take-home pay from baseball of $750,000. In fact, Hunter took home about $100,000 a year and his contract was for less than

pp. 42-43; *The Sporting News,* March 10, 1979, p. 31.

Table 11.5
Probable Earnings for Highly Paid Professional Athletes (1977-1978)

Sport	Athlete	Salary
Auto Racing (1977)	Cale Yarborough, NASCAR	$477,498
	A. J. Foyt, USAC	356,828
Baseball (1979)	Dave Parker	1,000,000*
	Rod Carew	900,000
	Pete Rose	745,000
Basketball (1977-78)	Kareem-Abdul Jabbar	625,000
	Pete Maravich	625,000
	Julius Erving	600,000
Bowling (1977)	Mark Roth	105,583
	Tommy Hudson	89,393
	Earl Anthony	72,690
Boxing (1977)	Muhammad Ali	5.75 million
	Ken Norton	2.20 million
	Roberto Duran	550,000
Football (1977)	O. J. Simpson	733,358
	Fran Tarkenton	350,000
	Joe Namath	350,000
Golf (1977)	Tom Watson	350,000
	Jack Nicklaus	310,000
	Lanny Wadkins	244,882
Harness Racing (1977)	Herve Fillion	255,000
	John Chapman	246,900
	Carmine Abbatiello	226,100
Hockey (1977-78)	Bobby Orr	600,000
	Gilbert Perreault	350,000
	Phil Esposito	325,000
Jockeys (1977)	Steve Cauthen	615,175
	Angel Cordero, Jr.	521,847
	Laffit Pincay, Jr.	438,595
Racquetball (1977)	Marty Hogan	41,000
	Charlie Brumfield	21,000
	Davey Bledsoe	7,250
Pro Skiing (1977-78)	Andre Arnold	92,883
	Josef Odermatt	73,231
	Jim Hunter	35,915
NASL Soccer (1978)	Giorgio Chinaglia	283,333
	Franz Beckenbauer	250,000
	Dennis Tueart	200,000
Tennis (1977)	Jimmy Connors	922,657
	Guillermo Vilas	800,642
	Chris Evert	503,134

*Estimated average based on payment during five-year life of contract and deferred payments, 1989-2007, which will be devalued by inflation. Actual value, depending on economic factors, could range from $775,000 to something over $1 million.

Source: Ray Kennedy and Nancy Williamson, "Money in Sports," *Sports Illustrated* 49 (July 24, 1978), pp. 42-43; *The Sporting News,* March 10, 1979, p. 31.

$3 million, more than half of which was in deferred payments. Hunter's five-year pact was broken down this way:[46]

Item	Amount
Five-years' playing salary	$ 500,000
Cash Bonus	100,000
Deferred Bonus	250,000
Insurance	500,000
Scholarships (for two children)	36,000
Buick	6,000
Deferred Salary	1,500,000
Total	$2,892,000

The Athletic Labor Market

An interesting social and economic question is: "What variables affect salary determination?" To answer this query, we need to know something about the *athletic labor market*.[47] The pool of potential professional athletes is made up of individuals with physical and mental skills which, in combination with specialized training, make them sought-after commodities of production. There are two basic sources of training for aspiring pro athletes. First, hockey and baseball have "farm systems" whereby "parent" clubs own or have a working agreement with minor league teams and bear virtually all the training costs (this amounted to about $1.5 million per team in baseball in 1978). Football and basketball, on the other hand, sign players directly out of collegiate circles and bear virtually none of their training costs (the costs that accrue to colleges and universities is one reason for the "four-year rule," see p. 298).

Regardless of an athlete's training, a key component of future financial success is the perceived or actual indispensability of the athlete as a factor of production. With highly refined skills his dollar worth will in most cases exceed the value of his services (his *opportunity cost*) in the best alternative employment (outside of sports). This difference is termed *economic rent*. In a situation of competitive bidding, a player's salary will tend toward equality with his *marginal revenue product*. Here is the way it works.

Consider a candy manufacturing company. For simplicity's sake, suppose the hiring of a new worker produces 50 new boxes of candy a day, each box selling for one dollar. As a result of the new worker being hired, the output increases—the increase of 50 boxes of candy per day is the *marginal product* accounted for by the additional worker. If the firm sells the candy for $1, the additional revenue—called the *marginal revenue product*—amounts to $50 (marginal product of 50 multiplied by price of $1). Any good business person knows the wage of the new worker cannot exceed $50 per diem; otherwise, the added worker becomes an immediate financial liability.

Suppose this worker makes $20 per day. Assuming all other conditions equal, this figure is the worker's *opportunity cost* and another candy firm would have to pay him at least that amount to entice him to work there. In a competitive market, some firm will pay him close to his marginal revenue product. While this hypothetical example focuses upon an industry producing goods rather than services, the factors in salary determination are essentially the same. The athlete is producing a service—public entertainment—among other things. Hiring professional athletes is supposed to increase outputs, i.e., wins, and successful teams, particularly those in large markets, tend to attract more paying fans. As a consequence of increased attendance, the team's revenue will rise. If a team realizes $50,000 more dollars per year for signing a player, then the athlete's salary is likely to approach this figure. Noll predicted that in a city of 3½ million a superstar may add 90,000 fans per season;[48] hence, the athlete's salary will begin to approach this added revenue. Consider, too, a superstar pitcher who is well publicized and pitches frequently. If he attracts an additional 15,000 spectators each time he goes to the mound, an additional revenue of $50,000-plus is generated (based on an admission price of $3.50). Over a season this added revenue begins to approach two million dollars.

Sport as a Monopoly

The bugaboo in this rationale is that labor markets in the sport industry have not been competitive. The professional sport industry has been unique among American industries. It is the only self-regulating monopoly. Sport owners operate as a *cartel,* an economic body in which a group of firms—teams—within the same industry—league—make decisions on matters of common interest—rules, expansion, promotion, scheduling, etc. Such a socioeconomic arrangement is illegal in other American businesses. It is this monopolistic structure upon which are built sport's financial and competitive benefits.

To understand this state of affairs, it is necessary to momentarily regress in history. On July 2, 1890, President Grover Cleveland, disturbed by the pervasive influence of the Standard Oil Trust on American society, pressured Congress to pass the *Sherman Antitrust Law.* This made illegal "every contract, combination in the form of trust or otherwise, or conspiracy in restraint of trade or commerce among the several states or with foreign nations."[49] This statute, while not directed at baseball in particular, had profound implications for the sport for several reasons: (1) there was a "combination" of twenty-four teams located in eight different states and they obviously engaged in interstate commerce, (2) they restrained trade since a team in one city could not directly hire a player in another city, and (3) the owners conspired to keep players' salaries low.

After the passing of the Sherman Antitrust legislation, the courts began to adjudicate what it meant. In 1922 Supreme Court Justice Oliver Wendell Holmes handed down a decree pronouncing, in essence, that baseball was not in violation of the federal antitrust laws. Although the courts tried other cases between 1922 and the late 1960s, professional baseball's extra-legal status remained sacrosanct. Hence, Holmes' decision meant each baseball league (football, basketball, and hockey have also enjoyed this exemption by default) controlled three activities: (1) the competition for players, (2) the location of franchises, and (3) the sale of broadcasting rights. Our concern here will be upon the manner in which players were and continue to be kept in bondage.

The Reserve Clause

Certain arrangements such as the *player reserve system* systematically eliminated interclub competition for a player's services. While the specifics of the player reserve system varied from one sport to another, the common denominator was that each club had the sole right to negotiate with players whose services were reserved exclusively to that club. Under these circumstances players' salaries were determined solely by the owner. This is termed a *monopsonist*[50] relationship—players had a single buyer to whom they could sell their services. The monopsonist system applied to veterans as well as rookies.

The player reserve clause was most restrictive in professional baseball and hockey; it was a standard feature of every player's contract. The consequence of the reserve clause was that players had no control over which team they played for during their entire careers. The team owners invoked the terms of a player's contract so that the only way players were able to change teams was for the owners to release them outright or permit another club to negotiate with them.

Consider this restrictive practice in pro baseball. Once a player contracted with a particular organization, his future was at their disposal. If his contract was sold or if he was traded to another team, the player was obligated to the new organization. To become a *free agent*—an athlete not under any contract to any club—the baseball player had to secure an outright release from his present club, and such occurrences were rare. Furthermore, most players were first placed on *waivers,*[51] thereby giving other organizations the option of purchasing their contracts at a nominal waiver fee.

Social changes have recently altered these traditional restrictive procedures. Curt Flood's court battle was the first (see p. 298). In February, 1976, a U.S. District Court Judge upheld the free agent status of L. A. Dodger Andy Messersmith and Montreal Expo Dave McNally. Both pitchers had played the 1975 season without a contract and claimed that in doing so they had satisfied an option year and were entitled to free agent status. Management disagreed, citing their (traditional) perpetual ownership of a player's services, but their litigation appeals were denied. This socio-legal ruling set a precedent so that the baseball players' legal status was like that in football and basketball, in which athletes are required to play one year beyond their contract before being eligible for free agent status. This new status permits the players to engage in negotiations with other clubs within the league.

The Option Clause

Professional football and basketball have not used the reserve clause approach; instead, they have used the *option system.* Under the *option clause,* the owners had the exclusive right to invoke the terms of a player's contract for one year following the expiration of the contract. If a player desired to go on the bidding market—become a free agent—he had to play one additional year (beyond the contract's expiration) for 90 percent of his previous year's salary. To illustrate the consequences of "playing out one's option," consider the case of Walter Payton, one of the premier running backs in the NFL. After Payton's stellar 1977 performance, he desired a contract similar to O. J. Simpson's $733,358. The Bears' management offered him something less than $400,000 for three years. Instead of accepting the contract, he played the 1978 season for $66,000 (110 percent of his 1977 salary), although on the eve of the opening game he negotiated a more lucrative three-year contract.

Football, while a bit less confining than baseball, has historically allowed athletes to become free agents after playing out their option (performing services for their club for an additional year beyond their contract).[52] But, in practice, labor conditions were not as auspicious as they might appear. For one thing, players who announced their intent to play out their option were subjected to an automatic 10 percent salary reduction during their option year. For another, the *Rozelle Rule* (named after the NFL commissioner Pete Rozelle) required the new employer to compensate the old employer (with athletes or money of equal value) and, if the two negotiating clubs could not agree, the amount was determined by the commissioner. The Rozelle Rule read as follows:

Any player, whose contract with a league club has expired, shall thereupon become a free agent and shall no longer be considered a member of the team of that club following the expiration of such contract. When a player, becoming a free agent in such manner, thereafter signs a contract with a different club in the league, then unless mutually satisfying arrangements have been concluded between the two league clubs, the commissioner may name and then award to the former club one or more players, from the active, reserve or selection (college draft) list (including future selection choices) of the acquiring club as the commissioner in his sole descretion deems fair and equitable; any such decision by the commissioner shall be final and conclusive.[53]

Prior to the 1977-78 football season, the "Rozelle Rule" was voided. Rather than compensation determined solely by the commissioner, a codified set of rules determined the nature of the compensation and did not include cash transfers from one club to another.

The Free Agent Draft

The reserve system as applied to rookie players is called the *free agent draft* and stipulated rules and regulations for players who had not previously signed major league contracts. Clubs selected athletes in the inverse order of their previous year's finish. Once a player had been chosen, the club retained exclusive bargaining rights with him and like the reserve system operating with veterans, a rookie's contract could be traded or sold.

In baseball, the drafting club owned the draftee for six months. After that period, if the player had not signed, his name was returned to the pool of eligibles, and he was able to be drafted by another club. In other sports, the drafting club retained perpetual option over the player and the player could not expect—ever—to be returned to the pool of draftees and had to play for the selecting club or not at all. The legal status of the draft system is currently being debated in the courts. Although a 1976 court decision declared that it was an infraction of the federal antitrust laws, it is still being used.

In our market economy, these confining practices are questionable. Their perpetuation is due to agreements among the clubs of a league not to tamper with another team's "property." When tampering occurs, heavy penalties are levied on the abuser. Two 1975 cases highlight the extent to which professional sports attach importance to exclusive contracts and draft rights as well as enforce them. The Atlanta Hawks had illegally signed Julius Erving and were fined $400,000 and two second-round draft picks when it was determined that his services were owned by the Milwaukee Bucks. Similarly, when the New York Knicks signed George McGinnis, who rightfully belonged to the Philadelphia 76ers, they were forced to forfeit their number one draft pick in 1976 and lost one-half million dollars (on his two million dollar contract).

How Well Does the Player Draft System Work?

The manifest purpose of the player draft system is to provide competitive balance among teams. Hence, the teams that finish at the bottom get the first picks and the teams that finish at the top get the last picks. Reason would lead us to believe that the impact of the draft is probably quite limited.

To illustrate the argument, consider this example. The Pittsburgh Steelers won the Super Bowl in 1979, while the San Francisco 49er's had the poorest record. When it came time to draft college players, theoretically (since clubs typically negotiate with each other) San Francisco would select first and Pittsburgh last. Since there are twenty-eight NFL teams, San Francisco would pick 1st, 29th, 57th, 85th, etc., until the pool of eligibles was depleted. Pittsburgh, on the other hand, would pick 28th, 56th, 84th, etc. It is obvious that the only real advantage to the last place team lies in a *single* pick per year. It would stand to reason that in a team sport like football it is unlikely that a single player could "turn the franchise around," since there are offensive, defensive and special teams.

In a team sport like basketball, it is more likely that a single superstar (a Kareem Abdul-Jabbar, David Thompson, or Bill Walton) could make a significant impact on a team.

Demmert contends that a club's scouting system probably contributes more to the overall success of a team than does the player draft.[54] This line of reasoning particularly applies to later draft rounds after the highly publicized players have been selected. Football teams like the Oakland Raiders, Miami Dolphins, and the Pittsburgh Steelers have done quite well in the draft despite picking in later rounds.

In summary, while the draft system may have some effect on maintaining competitive balance, its actual contribution is open to attack. Despite the owners' argument that the player draft and reserve system function to equalize talent, there is ample evidence that it has not. In baseball, for example, the New York Yankees dominated the American League from 1921 to 1965. The Yankees won six of eight American League pennants between 1921 and 1928, seven of eight between 1936 and 1943, and fourteen of sixteen between 1949 and 1965. The St. Louis Cardinals, New York Giants, and Brooklyn Dodgers dominated the National League from 1940 to 1960. Similarly, in pro basketball the Boston Celtics reigned supreme during the 1950s and 1960s. Between 1947 and 1972, the Boston Celtics won eleven championships and the Lakers won six. Bill Russell, the Celtics' super center, was there for all of them. The Minneapolis Lakers, led by George Mikan, won six basketball titles in three different leagues in seven years (1948-54). Similarly, the Green Bay Packers dominated pro football during the 1960s, the Miami Dolphins in the early 1970s, and most recently, the Pittsburgh Steelers. Two Dynasties in ice hockey have been those of the Montreal Canadiens and the Toronto Maple Leafs. Up to 1975, in 34 seasons, twenty-four Stanley Cups were won by either the Canadiens (14) or the Maple Leafs (10). The Canadians have won it fourteen times in the last 23 seasons. Two other clubs, the Detroit Red Wings and the Boston Bruins, have won five or more Stanley Cups in the NHL. The first expansion team to win the Cup was the Philadelphia Flyers in 1973-74. Hence, whatever else is working, team championships and player talent do not appear to have been equalized over the last half century or so.

The Legal Status of Professional Athletes

Historically, professional athletes, unlike other professionals, have not been free to offer their services to the highest bidder, choose their employers, or change jobs. Though athletes did possess this ability in the early years of baseball, well before the turn of the century it was usurped from them. Since then, the legal prerogatives of pro athletes have become hotly contested matters.

In team sports, the professional team owners argue that if players were permitted to freely negotiate contracts with various clubs, the richest clubs would end up with the best players. If this situation occurred, it would destroy the competitive balance of sports and not be in the best interests of the game. A vicious cycle would ensue in which the poorest teams would accumulate the poorest records and fans would desert their stands. Although the richest teams may end up with the best players, there is no guarantee that they will win championships. In recent years the Philadelphia 76ers were talent-laden with such superstars as Julius Erving, Doug Collins, and George McGinnis, yet they did not win the pro basketball championship. The same applied to the Los Angeles Lakers who lime-lighted Wilt Chamberlin, Jerry West, and Elgin Baylor. To balance the ledger, it is only fair to mention the New York Yankees, who seemed to be successful in "buying" the world baseball championship when they acquired Reggie Jackson to accompany their star-studded team.

Another reason offered by the owners is if players were allowed to freely negotiate, it is possible that situations would arise in which players would have "conflicting interests." For example, players might find themselves in a situation where their actions could lead to victory for their present club or the club they were contracted to for the following season. To avoid this happening (regardless of whether it would or not), the complex system of rules we have been discussing was drawn up to regulate interteam competition.

SOME RECENT CHANGES IN PROFESSIONAL SPORT

Free Agent Draft

In 1976 twenty-four major league *baseball* players—4 percent of the 600 players—stripped of the traditional reserve clause, were declared free agents by the courts. Club owners engaged in a bidding war for their services. Fourteen of these players had price tags ranging between $750,000 and $3 million, a total of $20.5 million in salaries, bonuses, and deferred payments, which was enough to buy an entire franchise. The 1976 free agent scorecard appears in Table 11.6. What will this ultimately mean to the game of baseball? Several significant questions arise: Do the exorbitant contracts set a precedent that endangers the basic structure of baseball? Can the game survive these economic pressures? Will the baseball fan, the last one in big-time sports who is able to enjoy modest family entertainment, become disenchanted with rising ticket prices, shifting of their team heroes, and the general cold-business aspects of the enterprise? Will baseball's competitive balance so necessary for fan appeal and gate receipts be altered by the ability of wealthy franchises such as the New York Yankees to outbid their rivals for talent? Opinion is mixed and only time will tell.

As in baseball, alterations in the player-owner relationship in professional *football* have occurred. The professional football owners and the National Football League Players' Association reached an agreement which included several major features: (1) minimum salary schedules were established for both rookies and veterans. Undrafted rookies' salaries started at $15,000 (would rise to $17,000 in 1980); (2) the player draft system was changed. Any player drafted must receive a minimum of $20,000 or be declared a free agent, and if the draftee refused to play for the drafting club, he entered the draft the following year, and if still unable to reach an agreement, he became a free agent; (3) the Rozelle Rule was altered, as we indicated earlier, so that no cash payments are exchanged from one club to another. Instead, a set number of draft picks are awarded to the free agent's former club depending on the player's salary; (4) if a player (after four years) decided to play out his option, he had to receive 110 percent of his previous year's salary; (5) players were not subject to arbitrary hair or dress codes; and (6) all players are required to pay membership dues to the Players' Association.[55]

Table 11.6
1976 Free Agent Scorecard

The scorecard on baseball's free-agent sweepstakes, in which nine teams paid $20.5 million for 14 leading players thrown onto the open market. Included are player, position, previous club, reported contract price:

CALIFORNIA ANGELS (AL): Bobby Grich, inf Baltimore, $1.75 million, five years; Don Baylor, of, Oakland, $1.6 million, five years; Joe Rudi, of, Oakland, $1 million, five years.

NEW YORK YANKEES (AL): Reggie Jackson, of, Baltimore, $3 million, five years; Don Gullett, p, Cincinnati, $2 million, five years.

TEXAS RANGERS (AL): Bert Campaneris, ss, Oakland, $750,000, five years; Doyle Alexander, p, New York Yankees, $800,000, six years.

SAN DIEGO PADRES (NL): Gene Tenace, 1b-c, Oakland, $1 million, five years; Rollie Fingers, p, Oakland, $1 million, five years.

BOSTON RED SOX (AL): Bill Campbell, p, Minnesota, $1.05 million, five years.

MONTREAL EXPOS (NL): Dave Cash, 2b, Philadelphia, $1.5 million, five years.

ATLANTA BRAVES (NL): Gary Matthews, of, San Francisco, $1.75 million, five years.

CLEVELAND INDIANS (AL): Wayne Garland, p, Baltimore, $2 million, 10 years.

MILWAUKEE BREWERS (AL): Sal Bando, 3b, Oakland, $1.3 million, five years.

Source: Bloomington-Normal *Pantagraph*, Dec. 5, 1976, B-8.

As in baseball and football, alterations in the player-owner relationship in professional *basketball* have occurred. The changes included: (1) the option clause was stricken from standard player contracts, meaning that basketball players did not have to play an additional year after their contracts expired; (2) the owner of a player had the right of "first refusal," that is, if the current owner equalled the contract offered to the player by another club, the owner retained the "right" to keep the player; and (3) the compensation rule (akin to football's Rozelle Rule) will be stricken in 1980.[56]

We have been discussing the economics of sport ownership and player salaries. What remains is a consideration of the entire size—economically speaking—of the sports enterprise.

THE SIZE OF THE SPORT INDUSTRY

How big is the sport industry? While figures vary depending upon what is and isn't included in the final tallies, we are sure of one thing: it is big! One source says we spend $100 billion a year on sports and recreation—more than we spend for national defense.[57] On the other hand, the *professional* sport industry comprises a very small slice of the economic pie. For example, the average gross of an NFL team is about $8.9 million, or equivalent to that of a small supermarket; the returns for a typical NBA franchise are approximately $4.3 million, or commensurate with those of a large gasoline station; the entire gross revenues for major league baseball in 1977 were $230 million, a figure exceeded by the snuff and chewing-tobacco industry. The total gross revenues for the four major pro team sports—hockey, baseball, basketball, and football—of $640 million do not begin to fare well in comparison to Exxon's gross returns of $48 billion.[58] Table 11.7 provides figures for the sporting goods industry and Table 7.6 (p. 150) highlights the dollar growth in sport and recreation.

At the outset, it is important to realize that the profits realized by professional sport are difficult to determine. Aside from this disclaimer, it is necessary to understand the political/economic

Table 11.7
Sporting Goods: A $6 Billion-Dollar Business—And Growing

Spending by Americans for most types of sporting equipment—particularly for participatory sports—is on the rise. Estimates for the 10 top activities:

	Spending in 1975 (millions of dollars)	Change in Past Two Years
Bicycles and supplies	$1,114.6	Down 6%
Firearms and hunting gear	1,063.8	Up 37%
Equipment for organized teams	689.3	Up 29%
Golf equipment	543.5	Up 23%
Tennis equipment	522.5	Up 85%
Fishing tackle	461.7	Up 13%
Snow-skiing equipment	378.0	Up 38%
Camping Gear	334.1	Down 13%
Baseball, softball equipment for individuals	169.0	Up 21%
Billiard equipment	115.5	Not Available

IN ADDITION: Another 800 million dollars will be spent on a host of other sporting activities, such as archery, hockey, basketball, bowling, and water skiing.

ALL TOLD: Americans will pay some 6.2 billion dollars this year for sporting goods, up 21 percent in just two years.

Source: National Sporting Goods Association.

system in which American sports are embedded. Under capitalism, the ultimate goal is to maximize profits. This can be accomplished through direct revenue received from box office receipts, TV, and radio rights, or less directly by using financial losses as tax deductions and through the amortization of player contracts.

As a rule, professional sport franchises are *not* publicly owned corporations. Because of this, they are not required by law to reveal the financial details and transactions of their operations. Furthermore, the finances of pro sport franchises are generally kept secret. However, it is generally agreed that pro sport clubs have two major sources of revenue: (1) the sale of tickets to persons who attend the games, and (2) the sale of television and radio broadcast rights. Figure 11.2 pictorially displays the operating income of professional football teams in 1974. While not all sports conform to this distributive pattern, it can be seen that nearly 90 percent of the revenue emerged from these two sources. Divided up further, over one-half and one-third of the income was derived from ticket sales and broadcast rights, respectively, with concessions and postseason features contributing about 10 percent (combined) to the total.

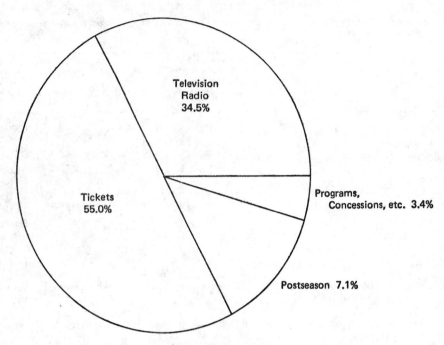

Figure 11.2
Operation Income 1974 NFL
(From Henry G. Demmert, *The Economics of Professional Team Sports,* New York, Joint Council
on Economic Education, 1976, p. 16. Reprinted with permission of the Joint Council on Economic
Education, from *The Economics of Professional Team Sports,* Economic Topic Series, ©JCEE 1976.
All Rights Reserved.)

Determinants of Attendance

Research has isolated a small number of variables that are significant in explaining attendance
at home games in the sports of baseball, basketball, football and hockey.[59] The most important
factor is the quality of the team as measured by wins and losses. Almost without exception winning
teams abet higher levels of paid attendance. However, economists maintain that limits exist as to how
much a club can enhance its paid attendance by improving team quality since other variables need
to be considered (coaches, training methods, franchise location, etc.).[60] Clearly, a league in which
one team dominated all the others for years would not be conducive to box-office success.

Another critical variable in a team's attendance is the market area in which home games are
played. All pro sports leagues enforce a system of territorial rights which assigns each club the right
to operate in a restricted geographical area, usually a metropolis. No other club within the league
may perform there, either in person or via broadcast, without the home club's permission. This
amounts to the club monopolizing a given market area.

Because of variations in the size of the *market area* as well as direct economic competition from alternate forms of entertainment and recreational activities (including other sport franchises), markets, from the start, differ with respect to potential revenues (see p. 272). Such differences generally are significant contributors to the financial welfare of pro franchises.

There are several significant consequences of market areas. First, different market areas possess differential revenue potential. This means that a star player will be worth more in some market areas, such as New York or Los Angeles, than in others, for example, Kansas City or Seattle. Quirk wrote: "Franchises in lowdrawing areas typically sell good players to franchises in highdrawing areas. . . . Thus, in baseball, a star player who is worth $500,000 in revenue potential to Kansas City would be worth $2 million in New York."[61] Because of the differential revenue potential, teams in certain areas are able to purchase highly sought players because they can make up for the player costs in gate receipts. The final 1977 standings when correlated with player payroll were almost perfect. For example, in the National League East the order of finish with player payroll in parentheses was: Philadelphia ($3,497,900), Pittsburgh ($2,485,475), St. Louis ($1,782,875), Chicago ($1,725,450), Montreal ($1,645,575), and New York Mets ($1,469,800) (*Sports Illustrated*, July 17, 1978, p.182).

In strong market areas, as opposed to weaker ones, improvement in team quality enhances attendance. Therefore, owners in stronger markets are more prone to invest (i.e., purchase players) because of the economic payoff. In weaker areas, box-office success is less likely to be realized; hence, owners there will be less motivated to purchase quality players. In the long run, therefore, competitive balance among league teams is not likely to be manifest. This is not to say that teams in weaker areas are not likely to win—such as the Portland Trail Blazers (1977)—since the outcome of a contest is the result of many unpredictable factors: injuries to key ball players, unexpected good or poor performance, or sheer luck.

Revenue Sharing

To compensate for market area differentials, many professional leagues practice *revenue sharing* in which home game receipts are divided with the visiting team. As a consequence, in the course of a season, teams will share in the income generated by both strong and weak market clubs. However, the extent of gate receipt sharing varies among the different sports. For example, visiting teams in the American League receive 20 percent of the gate receipts whereas the National League awards 10 percent. The NFL has adopted a 40 percent revenue-sharing procedure while the visting teams in the NBA and NHL receive nothing except a modicum league assessment.[62]

Broadcast Rights and Sales

The second largest source of revenue for professional team sports is the sale of broadcast rights. Historically, there has been a dramatic change in this sphere. In the mid-1950s, 15 percent of the revenues for a typical football and baseball club emanated from this source. Today, the modal football club depends upon broadcast sales for at least 35-40 percent (see Figure 11.2) of its revenues and the typical baseball club for more than 25 percent.

There are two sources of broadcast revenues for most pro sports clubs: (1) individual clubs may negotiate their own broadcast rights package with local radio and TV stations, and (2) the league may barter with national networks for all clubs within its jurisdiction. The former procedure produces major income differentials because of differences in market strength; the latter leads to a more equitable distribution of income among teams within the league. In 1961, Congress passed legislation authorizing professional sport leagues to pool the sale of broadcast rights without being subject to antitrust laws. This meant that the league could negotiate national broadcast rights for all teams within its jurisdiction. The upshot of this monopolistic practice meant more money could be generated from the sale of fewer games. According to Nader and Gruenstein, the real losers were the fans since they ultimately had less access to sports programming and paid more for it.[63]

The established leagues have a sound combination of local and nationwide contracts. The NFL operates in the second manner described above and has sold national broadcast rights, at different times, to CBS, NBC, and ABC. Major league baseball, as of 1976, had a contract with NBC and ABC and each club had its own local TV and radio package. The NBA had a nationwide contract with CBS and individual teams have their own local contracts. The NHL lost its national network contract with NBC in 1975, and the clubs rely solely on local broadcast rights. This loss of TV money is one reason why hockey is presently struggling. In general, the sport leagues that recently developed—ABA (now merged with NBA), WHA, NASL, and WFL (now defunct)—have not been successful in selling their products to the TV media since their franchises are generally located in smaller cities and/or weaker markets which are less attractive to the TV networks and advertisers.

Other Revenue Sources

Besides these two major revenue sources—paid attendance and broadcast rights—others include concessions, marketing rights to club emblems, and the sale of player contracts. For example, Sportservice, the largest concessionaire, grossed $100 million in 1972. In doing so, they helped provide hungry and thirsty fans with 20 million hot dogs, 30 million soft drinks, 25 million cups of beer, and 5 million bags of peanuts. Emprise, Sportservice's mother corporation, secured exclusive "feeding" rights to a large number of sporting events including pro football, baseball, basketball, and hockey, bowling, golf, jai-alai, horse and dog racing, and skiing. While part of these revenues go to the sport in question, there is some evidence that these exclusive rights are linked with organized crime syndicates and are in violation of antitrust statutes.[64]

Noll has conducted the most comprehensive study to date regarding the finances of major sports teams.[65] If one were to merely balance out revenues (tickets, broadcast rights, and concessions) and costs (salaries, travel expenses, facility rentals, and equipment), few franchises would show a profit. Such a bleak financial picture stems from *accounting losses* (expenses exceeding revenues). Of utmost significance in the determination of profits are less visible features of professional sport like subsidies from local, state, and federal governments in the form of tax concessions and low rentals of stadiums.

When tax advantages and other benefits of ownership are considered, Noll's data, while dated, concluded that typical teams in the NFL ($1,150,000), NHL ($1,000,000), major league baseball ($357,000), and the NBA ($217,000) realized the profit amounts in parentheses.[66] On the other hand, the ABA and WHA lost $155,000 and $225,000, respectively. Note that these are average figures per team in the respective leagues. Table 11.8 shows a breakdown of revenues, costs, and profits of "average sports clubs." The table provides one with insight regarding team profits before and after tax write-offs. Noll found that there is a pattern to these profits and losses. Clubs located in larger markets and/or fielding winning teams realized profits, while those in smaller markets and/or fielding losing teams were financially unsuccessful; i.e., showed smaller profits or even ended up in the "red."

Table 11.8
Revenues, Costs and Profits of Average Sports Clubs
(all figures in thousands of dollars)

League Year	NFL 1970	Major League Baseball 1969	NBA 1971	NHL 1973	ABA 1971	WHA 1973
Revenues	5050	5225	1815	4250	690	850
Game attendance	2700	3200	1200	3450	500	700
Broadcasts	1850	1420	360	550	20	100
Other	500	605	255	250	170	50
Direct costs	3350	4955	1815	2750	1120	1500
Player compensation	2000	1070	700	1000	400	600
Games	950	1190	600	1350	300	625
General and administrative	350	1375	340	225	330	175
Promotion	50		175	75	120	100
Player development	0	1320	0	100	0	0
Cash flow	1700	270	0	1500	-430	-650
Indirect costs	600	445	435	500	140	100
Player amortization	500	445	370	500	110	100
Interest	100	n/a	65	n/a	30	n/a
Pretax profit	1100	-175	-435	1000	-570	-750
Benefit of ownership	1150	357	217	1000	-155	-225

Note: These estimates refer to teams of average quality for each league. The "Benefit of Ownership" figures take into account the profit picture when all tax write-off possibilities are taken advantage of. Noll considers this the best gauge of the true profitability of a sports franchise.

Source: Based on "Profitability of Professional Sports Teams," Table 4-1 in "The Product Market in Sport" by Roger G. Noll, chapter 4 in *Conference on the Economics of Professional Sport Proceedings*, Washington, D.C.: The National Football League Players Association, 1974. That table was in turn a summary of tables in Roger G. Noll, "The U.S. Team Sports Industry: An Introduction" in Noll (ed.), *Government and the Sports Business*, op. cit. These latter tables supply estimates for the profitability of weak and strong teams as well as the average reported here. Reprinted with permission on the Joint Council on Economic Education, from *The Economics of Professional Team Sports*, ©JCEE 1976. All rights reserved.

Also, the extent of profits and losses is affected by the extent of revenue sharing. There is less discrepancy between profits and losses among teams in leagues that practice revenue sharing (NFL) than in leagues that do not (NBA). Table 11.2 presents more recent data regarding the financial character of the four major team sports.

SUMMARY

In this chapter we have discussed what many believe to be the driving force in sport—*economics*—and have considered the interconnections between the institutions of sport, politics, and the economy. Of the three levels of sport—*informal, organized,* and *corporate*—it is clearly the latter that is most applicable to professional sport in America. The distinguishing elements of corporate sport include big business and power politics. While no single event is responsible for the corporatizing of sport, economic and political factors—from the 1930s on—have been major contributors.

In discussing the economics of professional sport, attention was paid to the modus operandi of the sports owner. While several different types of owners have headed sport franchises, many modern-day sports owners are corporate managers. They are individuals who take advantage of federal tax laws. One federal statute that is helpful for understanding the flurry of new franchises and turnover in sport ownership is the *law of depreciation*, whereby the value of commodities can be deducted because each year they wear out and become less valuable. Here is the way it works: when a new franchise is purchased, the new owner buys essentially two things: (1) the franchise license and (2) a batch of players. The former element cannot be depreciated, but the latter can (through the *amortization* of player contracts). When the depreciation of players is combined with, say, financial losses in the sport's franchise, this amount of money can be deducted from the owner's collateral profitable business endeavors for a considerable tax savings. While many sport franchises have shown accounting losses, one must be cognizant that this is only part of the picture since these losses can be used to the owner's advantage in conjunction with other businesses.

Frequently the financing of sports facilities ultimately ends up on the public's lap since stadium construction and refurbishing projects do not pay for themselves. In addition, sport facilities are frequently rented for nominal fees and indirect tax benefits accrue to professional sport owners at the local level (publicly-owned teams do not pay property taxes).

Professional athletes' salaries are a major expense account of the owners. Historically, player salaries have been low and players' mobility has been restricted through such procedures as the *reserve system* (through which the team owning a player had perpetual rights over a player's destiny), *option clause,* and *free agent draft.* These standard operating procedures have served to keep players in bondage. Recent court cases have voided many of these traditional procedures so that players' salaries have soared and movement has become more commonplace in the past few years.

Although the size of the sport industry is difficult to accurately determine, one thing is certain: it is huge. Americans spend at least one billion dollars a year on sport and recreation. In general, professional sports are profitable (when considering tax benefits, depreciation, etc.) but perhaps less so today than a decade or two age. Profits vary from one sport to another for various reasons (revenue sharing and market area location). Complexities aside, none can deny that sport, today, is "big business."

IMPORTANT CONCEPTS DISCUSSED IN THIS CHAPTER

Informal Sport
Organized Sport
Corporate Sport
The Law of Depreciation
Amortization of Player Contracts
Opportunity Cost
Economic Rent
Marginal Product
Marginal Revenue Product
Free Agent
Monopoly

Sherman Antitrust Law
Reserve Clause
Option System
Free Agent Draft
Revenue Sharing
Capital
Waivers
Depreciation Recapture
Tax Reform Act
Cartel
Monopsony

ENDNOTES

[1] Bil Gilbert, "Gleanings from a Troubled Time," *Sports Illustrated* 37 (December 25, 1972), pp. 34-36; D. Stanley Eitzen and George H. Sage, *Sociology of American Sport* (Dubuque, Iowa: Wm. C. Brown Co., 1978). p. 18.

[2] Paul Hoch, *Rip Off: The Big Game* (Garden City, NY: Anchor Books, 1972), p. 39.

[3] *Capitalism* is an economic system in which investment in and ownership of the means of production, distribution, and exchange of goods and wealth are maintained chiefly by individuals or corporations.

[4] Howard L. Nixon, II, *Sport and Social Organization* (Indianapolis, Ind.: Bobbs-Merrill, 1976), p. 56.

[5] Hoch, *Rip Off: The Big Game*, p. 30.

[6] Douglas S. Looney, "The Salesmen Run a Costly Race at Indy," *The National Observer*, May 25, 1974, p. 18; Eitzen and Sage, *Sociology of American Sport*, p. 171.

[7] Ray Kennedy and Nancy Williamson, "Money in Sports," *Sports Illustrated* 49 (July 24, 1978), p. 49.

[8] Michael R. Real, "Super Bowl: Mythic Spectacle," *Journal of Communication* 25 (Winter, 1975), pp. 31-43.

[9] Ibid.

[10] Tom Buckley, "Business in a Front Seat for Today's Super Bowl," *New York Times* (January 14, 1973), p. 1.

[11] Frank Lalli, "And Now for the Pre-Game Scores," *Rolling Stone* (February 28, 1974), p. 40.

[12] James A. Michener, *Sports in America* (New York, Random House, 1976). Ralph Nader and Peter Gruenstein, "Blessed are the Fans, For They Shall Inherit $12 Bleacher Seats, Indigestible Hot Dogs, $2 Bottles of Beer and 100 Overpaid Superstars," *Playboy* (Spring, 1978), pp. 98.

[13] Ray Kennedy, "Who Are These Guys?", *Sports Illustrated* (January 31, 1977), pp. 50-58.

[14] Kennedy and Williamson, "Money in Sports," (July 17, 1978), 49, p. 88.

[15] Kennedy, "Who Are These Guys?"

[16] Ibid., p. 55.

[17] "Trouble in the Sports World," *U.S. News and World Report* (August 12, 1974), pp. 52-55.

[18] D. Stanley Eitzen, *Sport in American Society* (New York: St. Martins, 1979), p. 325.

[19] A substantial portion of the material in this chapter has been adapted from Economic Topic 239. Used with permission.

[20] Michener, *Sports in America*, p. 363.

[21] "Trouble in the Sports World," p. 53.

[22] "Who Says Baseball is like Ballet?" *Forbes* (April 1, 1971, p. 30.

[23] Barry D. McPherson, "Sport Consumption and the Economics of Consumerism," *Sport and Social Order*, ed. D. W. Ball and J. W. Loy (Reading, Mass.: Addison-Wesley, 1975), p. 262.

[24] Henry G. Demmert, *The Economics of Professional Team Sports* (New York: Joint Council on Economic Education, 1976).

[25] "Trouble in the Sports World," p. 52.

[26] Kennedy, "Who Are These Guys?"

[27] Ibid.

[28] Kennedy and Williamson, "Money in Sports," (July 17, 1978), 49, p. 40.

[29] Roger G. Noll, *Government and the Sports Business* (Washington, D.C.: The Brookings Institute, 1974).

[30] Ibid.

[31] *Wall Street Journal* (February 27, 2975), p. 16.

[32] Ibid.

[33] Hoch, *Rip Off: The Big Game*, pp. 51-52.

[34] Benjamin A. Okner, "Direct and Indirect Subsidies to Professional Sports" (Paper presented at the Brookings Conference on Government and Sport, Washington, D.C., December 6-7, 1971); Kennedy and Williamson.

[35] Kennedy and Williamson, "Money in Sports," p. 71.

[36] Okner, "Direct and Indirect Subsidies to Professional Sports."

[37] Ibid.

[38] It has been discovered that ticket prices and attendance were *positively* correlated. As attendance increased, so too did the cost of ducats. See Noll, *Government and the Sports Business*.

[39] J. McMurty, "A Case for Killing the Olympics," *Sport Sociology*, ed. A. Yiannakis, et al. (Dubuque, Iowa: Kendall/Hunt, 1976), pp. 51-55.

[40] Okner, "Direct and Indirect Subsidies to Professional Sports."

[41] Min S. Yee and Donald K. Wright, *The Sports Book* (New York: Holt, Rinehart and Winston, 1975), p. 40.

[42] J. G. Scoville, "Labour Aspects of Professional Sports," (Paper presented at the Brookings Conference on Government and Sport, Washington, D.C., December 6-7, 1971).

[43] Ibid.

[44] Bob Collins, "NFL Player Salaries Drop With WFL's Credibility," *Rocky Mountain News,* March 23, 1975, p. 72.

[45] John W. Loy, Barry D. McPherson, Gerald S. Kenyon, *Sport and Social Systems: A Guide to the Analysis, Problems and Literature* (Reading, Mass.: Addison-Wesley, 1978), p. 268.

[46] Kennedy and Williamson, "Money in Sports," (July 17, 1978), 49, p. 52.

[47] Denmert, *The Economics of Professional Team Sports.*

[48] Roger G. Noll, "Attendance, Prices, and Profits in Professional Sports" (Paper presented at the Brookings Conference on Government and Sport, Washington, D.C., December 6-7, 1971).

[49] Michener, *Sports in America*, p. 386.

[50] Whereas a *monopoly* means one seller, a *monopsony* means one buyer.

[51] "Professional sport organizations have a system of rules whereby other clubs in the league may claim a player before a club can drop a player from their roster or trade that player or sell his contract to a club in another league. A club can pick up a player "on waivers" by buying his contract for the stipulated waiver price. When a club places a player on waivers, it has the right to withdraw the player's name from the list a limited number of times even if a claim is made. If no other club claims the player, the player "clears waivers" and is subsequently dropped from the club or can then be traded to a club in another league." See *Sports Dictionary* (Springfield, Mass.: G. and C. Merriam Co. Publishers, 1976).

[52] Until the 1974-75 season, the NHL had a perpetual reserve system akin to that of baseball. Today, however, it implements the one-year *option system.* The commissioners in the NHL and WHA have not been as adamant in the mandatory compensation procedure as football. One of the reasons reflects the direct economic competition between the WHA and NHL. Recently, the WHA and NHL have negotiated a merger. If the merger reaches fruition, it will undoubtedly alter the league's leniency on this matter.

[53] Denmert, *The Economics of Professional Team Sports*, p. 13.

[54] Ibid., p. 8.

[55] "Behind Pro Football's Labor Peace," *New York Times* (March 6, 1977), p. 89; Eitzen and Sage, *Sociology of American Sport.*

[56] Douglas S. Looney, "The Start of a Chain Reaction," *Sports Illustrated* 44 (February 16, 1976), pp. 18-20.

[57] Michener, *Sports in America.*

[58] Kennedy and Williamson, "Money in Sports," (July 17, 1978), p. 34.

[59] Noll, "Attendance, Prices, and Profits in Professional Sports," and *Government and the Sports Business.*

[60] Demmert, *The Economics of Professional Team Sports.*

[61] James Quirk, "An Economic Analysis of Team Movements in Professional Sports," *Law and Contemporary Problems* 38 (1973), pp. 42-66.

[62] Demmert, *The Economics of Professional Team Sports,* p. 3.

[63] Nader and Gruenstein, "Blessed are the Fans, For They Shall Inherit $12 Bleacher Seats, Indigestible Hot Dogs, $2 Bottles of Beer and 100 Overpaid Superstars."

[64] John Underwood and Morton Sharnik, "Look What Louis Wrought," *Sports Illustrated* 36 (May 29, 1972). pp. 40-54; Eitzen and Sage, *Sociology of American Sport,* p. 178.

[65] Noll, "Attendance, Prices, and Profits in Professional Sports."

[66] Ibid.

12
Sport and the Mass Media

INTRODUCTION

Sociologically speaking, the development of *mass media* (the press, radio, and television) has been a basic determinant of *popular* (or *mass*) *culture. Popular culture* "involves standardized material goods, art, life styles, ideas, tastes, fashions, and values. It is the homogenized product of mass media." Sport, as we will see, has become one of the most visible and influential elements in contemporary mass culture.[1]

Mass communication, a by-product of industrial technology, refers to the transmission of a message (through a technological medium) to an audience that is geographically dispersed. The term is usually applied to the activities of radio broadcasting, telecasting, the press, and publicly screened films, and is considered to be one of the major *social processes* affecting and affected by sport. The relationship between the media and sport is genuinely symbiotic, each needing the other for survival. As we will see, however, sport appears to need more the media, particularly TV, rather than the other way around. Hoch described the symbiotic relationship between sport and the media as follows:

> One factor that made a decisive difference was the tremendous coverage of sports by the press. About the same time the first sports leagues began, there developed (not by coincidence) the sort of mass-audience-oriented newspapers needed to sell mass consumption products. A symbiosis between sports and the new media was quickly established in which sports became the decisive promotional device for selling popular newspapers, and newspapers were the decisive promotional device for selling sports spectacles. (This symbiotic relationship between sports and the media, now including radio and television, is a central feature of the political economy of both sports and the media to this day.)[2]

POPULAR CULTURE AND SPORT FANS

The Sport Consumer

Of the many *sport roles*, none is more pervasive nor widespread than that of sport consumer. To demonstrate the relationship between popular culture and sport, two types of sport consumption roles will be identified: (1) *direct consumer* and (2) *indirect consumer.*[3]

The *direct consumer* is one who attends a live sporting event, i.e., goes to the track, gridiron, ballpark, arena, fieldhouse, or court. Table 1-1 (p. 3) reveals the extent of contemporary spectatorship. Notice that the total number of sport consumers for these events was about 206 million, 273 million, and 315 million for 1965, 1974, and 1977, respectively. One source predicted that more than 300 million fans would pay almost $2 billion to attend sporting events in 1978.[4] According to another source, estimated paid admissions in 1977 included 82 million for horse racing, 49 million for auto racing, 44 million for collegiate and professional football, 44 million for baseball, 34 million for basketball, 23 million for hockey, 19 million for greyhound racing, 6 million for soccer, 5 million for professional wrestling, 4 million for tennis, 3 million for boxing, and 3 million for golf.[5] Special events like the Indy 500, World Series, Super Bowl, and Olympics draw huge throngs of sport spectators as well.

The *indirect consumer* absorbs sport through the mass media of TV, radio, books, magazines, newspapers, and discussion. Of the media, TV appears to far surpass the others as a medium of sport consumption, although 40 million people subscribe to sport magazines.[6] Table 12.1 permits a determination and comparison of the number of viewers in the audiences for various sporting contests. The 1979 NFL Super Bowl (100 million), baseball's 1977 World Series (100 million), and the 1976 Summer Olympics (800 million) attracted the largest viewing audiences. Also, college football rivalries (Oklahoma vs. Texas, Pitt vs. Penn State, Ohio State vs. Michigan) and post-season bowl games typically draw huge throngs—live and via TV—of partisan fans.

SPORT AND THE MASS MEDIA

Although it is the medium of television (see Vignette 12.1) that has so radically altered the landscape of sport, other media, notably the press and radio, have been important. We will examine the influence of these "other" media (since they occupied the social scene before the cathode ray tube) and then return to television.

The Press (Newspapers and Magazines)

The *newspaper* was the first significant medium of mass communication. Although writing was invented millennia ago, the development of the printing press by Guttenberg (1400-1468) had to await certain technological discoveries. Even upon the advent of the printing press, social conditions had to ripen before its effectiveness and utility could be realized. Prior to the 1800s there were isolated sport stories appearing in the press. The first sport reported was a boxing match in England and appeared in the *Boston Gazette* on May 5, 1733, followed by sporadic accounts of prize fights, horse and boat races in the 1700 and 1800s. It wasn't until the 1830s that two critical social conditions—*urbanization* and *literacy*—reached the point where the printed page could be financially solvent and socially appreciated.

Table 12.1
Sports on Television

	Average Ratings and Viewer Composition			Ages of Men Viewers		
	Household rating	Percent men	Percent women	18-34 (40%)	35-49 (25%)	50+ (35%)
Football:						
NFL Superbowl	47.2	57	43	39%	25%	36%
ABC-NFL	21.2	67	33	36	29	35
CBS-NFL	16.1	67	33	39	25	36
NBC-NFL	13.5	68	32	37	26	37
College bowl games						
College All-Star games	12.3	60	40	34	26	40
NCAA regular season	13.2	68	32	34	26	40
Baseball:						
World Series	29.8	58	42	30	26	44
All-Star game	24.5	60	40	34	19	47
Regular season	9.0	66	34	28	15	57
Horse racing:						
Kentucky Derby	14.9	51	49	36	21	43
Preakness	11.9	52	48	27	23	50
Basketball:						
NBA regular season	7.2	67	33	44	21	35
NBA playoffs	7.9	67	33	43	23	34
NBA All-Star game	8.6	60	40	49	21	30
NBA championships	12.7	67	33	49	17	34
Bowling:						
Pro tour	7.1	52	48	28	26	46
Auto Racing (Grand Prix)	6.0	54	46	27	23	50
Golf:						
Tournaments	5.8	60	40	28	20	52
Tennis:						
World Championship	3.0	50	50	27	33	40
World Invitational	3.2	58	42	44	24	32
Multi-sports series:						
American Sportsman	7.5	53	47	35	30	35
ABC WW Sports						
Saturday	8.8	59	41	40	25	35
Sunday	12.4	56	44	41	25	34
CBS Sports Spectacular	6.4	56	44	38	23	39

Source: Nielsen Sports, A. C. Nielsen Company (Chicago, IL: Media Research Services Group, 1977). Reprinted by permission.

VIGNETTE 12.1
TV SPORTS—THE TUBE AS A SHRINE

Since coast-to-coast television became common place 25 years ago, the American public has demonstrated an insatiable thirst for sports.

It gives weekly testimony to the thesis that sports is another religion in America. Or, as Barry Frank, CBS vice president of sports, put it recently: "Religion we do on Sunday morning; sports we do on Sunday afternoon." The ratings are better on Sunday afternoon.

This year the three major networks plan to offer more than 1,200 hours of sports on television—365 by CBS, 370 by NBC and 550 by ABC.

Add local baseball, basketball and hockey to that. We watch arm-wrestling from Petaluma, Calif., and we watch a man on a motorcycle try to fly across a pool filled with sharks in Chicago. We watch great basketball players trying to play tennis and television comedians playing touch football. We watch almost anything and we ask for more.

Whether the constant bombardment of the public with free sports events on television is causing sports to eat its young—taking the payoff today at the expense of tomorrow's health—is, the networks say, the responsibility of sports, not of television.

"Greed is a never-ending circle," Frank said. "Where does it start? It's almost a perfect circle. The players want more money, the owners want to be able to give it to them. They in turn want more money. They say expenses go up and prices are rising, so the owners want to sell their product for more money."

The money is in large amounts.

*Baseball is entering the second year of a four-year contract calling for approximately $93 million, according to baseball's director of broadcasting, Dave Meister.

*The NBA is in the first year of a four-year contract that calls for $47.9 million, if the second two-year option is picked up, CBS said.

*For college football, the NCAA has the second year remaining on its contract for $18 million a year, according to Tom Hansen of the NCAA television committee.

*The NFL, a league official said, is entering the last year of a four-year contract with the three networks calling for an estimated $200 million, which doesn't include the conference championship games or the Super Bowl.

What has resulted is a change in the fabric of American life. There was a time when businesses operated with half-interest the first week in October because the World Series was being played on the radio in the stockroom. Office pools flourished on the number of runs scored in an inning. In order for the greats of tennis to meet, they had to earn their way to the finals of the big tournaments and the Grand Slam meant winning the U.S., British, French and Australian tournaments.

Instead we now have the World Series being played at night with the fans chilled in Cincinnati's Riverfront Stadium while America watches in the comfort of home with the sponsor's beer within arm's reach. Instead, we have Jimmy Connors and Rod Laver meeting in a match for a king's ransom in Las Vegas, starting times and timeouts are stipulated by television with the acquiescence of one commissioner after another.

But is it evil? Is it immoral to depict the Tasmanian breath-holding championship as sport?

Has television no conscience? Have the programmers no fear for what over-saturation might do to the future? "I'm concerned with that," Roone Arledge, chief of ABC Sports, said. "On the other hand, it really doesn't work out that way. Anything that is successful (on television), there are 23 copies of successful television formats and they have a way of shaking themselves out. There were too many westerns, but "Bonanza" and "Gunsmoke" went along fine. The bad ones go and the good ones stay."

It's the view of Alvin Rush, senior vice president at NBC in charge of sports administration, that sports television isn't the great menace to the live gate. "It's the same as the movies," he said. "Put on a great show, you'll draw a great crowd. It's still tough to get a ticket for a good event."

The officials of professional football, basketball, baseball and golf speak of television as the great promoter of interest in their sports. Tournament golf admittedly wouldn't exist on the same scale without television. According to Steve Reid, who negotiates television contracts for the PGA television provides 38 per cent of the purses of tournaments that are not even on television. Sponsors know that golf moves merchandise. The great growth in tennis interest can be directly attributed to television, which showed world-class competition to an audience that had never seen it before.

The public away from the big cities had never seen big-league baseball or football, either, before the advent of the coaxial cable and national telecasts in 1951.

Television made the public aware of professional football, which had been the exclusive province of a few large cities. There were 12 teams in 1951; there are now 28.

America has become aware of tennis as an intensely competitive and athletic game when it was viewed, not too long ago, as an effete pastime of the wealthy. The infusion of television money has put new life into long-moribund boxing. Television of the 1972 and '76 Olympics has made gymnastics—especially women's gymnastics—a significant aspect of physical education in this country, and made Olga Korbut and Nadia Comancei household names.

Arledge, Frank and Rush, the reigning commissioners of television sports, contend that they didn't make those events and games popular; they merely gave them exposure and the games won their own popularity.

A more demonstrable criticism of television sports is that it does no social commentary or investigative reporting of any kind other than occasional editorial comment by Howard Cosell or deeper questioning by Larry Merchant on NBC's grandstand.

There are issues in sports that affect the public—the evils of recruiting, of falsified college admissions, of drug use, the threat of the agent and the use of public funds for private gains in the business of sports. But television still portrays only the fun and games.

There has been some belated attention given to the language of the broadcasters. CBS has even sent a former great quarterback (no names, please) back to freshman English because he doesn't speak the language and doesn't realize it.

But attempts to lift the pretty rug of sports and uncover the dirt get only clucking expressions of regret from network sports.

Arledge and Frank concede that television in general has been remiss in that area. Arledge says ABC may delve into it when it introduces a magazine program later in the year with a format similar to CBS's highly rated "60 Minutes," which occasionally gives a segment to critical examination of areas in sports. Rush says "Grandstand" does the same for NBC. But none of the networks gives the time or the money for a fully developed report.

All three executives present the same kind of reasoning for not probing the unsavory areas. "The public is not interested in it," Arledge said. "Look at the sale of books. Bob Lipsyte wrote a great book ("Sportsworld") that hasn't sold at all." (Note: author Lipsyte said that "Sportsworld" has sold "nowhere near" the first printing of 15,000.)

But so far the public has bought television at whatever lowest common denominator and asked for more and more. But some slight softening has been felt. Television has backed off in its tennis programming—which often matched live action on one channel against taped performances of the same players on another—when ratings dropped. Now, Arledge said, ratings for fewer tennis events have improved.

In recent years baseball has been putting fewer home games on local television and commissioner Bowie Kuhn recommends that his teams move farther along those lines. That was the nature of the NFL's blackout of home games, which both Arledge and Frank think Congress should not have interrupted.

And some NCAA officials perceive another danger in the glamor television imparts to any school it blesses with its cameras. The revenue is shared among conference schools (leaving Notre Dame, Penn State and Pitt to wax rich as independents), but the ability to promise national exposure is the most potent recruiting tool today.

Rush estimates that by the time of the 1980 Olympics in Moscow, NBC will have invested $100 million in the telecasting of 150 hours and expects to make money. The sponsors will stand in line to pay for the anticipated audience. Sponsors paid between $225,000 and $250,000 for one minute of commercial time in the last Super Bowl telecast.

So that thrusts the responsibility for protecting the interest of sport back into the hands of sports themselves.

"If people decide it's better to stay home and watch on television than it is to go to the games, I don't think anything happens to television," Arledge said. "It means the owners are in trouble."

Cozens and Stumpf provide an insightful sociological account of the emergence of the newspaper in general and the sport page in particular.[8] Sports, for the most part, were covered in the middle 1850s by weekly newspapers devoted exclusively to them. Even as early as 1835 the *Sun, Transcript,* and *Herald*—three New York newspapers—were "covering" prizefights, horse and foot races, and a few other sport events. Henry Chadwick, who some believe merits the accolade "original sportswriter" and "father of baseball," was reporting on cricket matches between the United States and Canada, but was not receiving compensation since the big New York dailies— *Times* and *Tribune*—were not giving much space to sport news. Chadwick was eventually hired by the *Herald* in 1862 to regularly cover baseball games.

William Randolph Hearst purchased the *New York Journal* in 1895 and made a concerted effort to outdo his rivals in the reporting of sporting events. The fruit of his efforts was the sporting section of the newspaper as we know it today. Hearst instituted the practice of having athletic greats —Hobart on tennis, Bald on cycling, Heffelfinger on football, and Batchelder on wheeling—write columns.

In tracing the emergence of the newspaper in general and the sport page in particular, an understanding of the changing social environment is indispensable. Cozens and Stumpf discuss three sociologically relevant features:[9]

1. *Expansion of Space and Extent of Coverage.* Prior to the First World War, sport coverage was confined to a relatively small number of athletic contests such as baseball, college football, horse racing, and boxing. In the last couple of decades, the sport page has covered the gamut of sporting activities "including basketball, bowling, billiards, golf, lacrosse, cycling, wrestling, archery, lawn

and court tennis, squash, skiing, canoeing, ice and field hockey, hunting, fishing, motorboating, rowing, swimming, diving, and water polo." The social basis of this expansion correlated with the fact that the illiteracy rate dropped by 9.3 percent between 1870 and 1900 (from 20 to 10.7%) and the percentage of children attending schools increased from 57 to 72 percent. Similarly, the number of newspapers rose from 2,226 in 1899 to 2,600 in 1909, as did the total daily circulation, from 24 million in 1909 to 33 million in 1919.[10]

During this formative period (and today as well) there was a marked improvement in the quality of sportswriting. In addition to possessing a knowledge of sport, and the vicarious enthusiasm of fans, the sportswriter must be knowledgeable about law, politics, female fashions, domestic relations, genealogy, dramatics, and war.[11]

The 1920s witnessed a boom in sport columns. Many factors were responsible for this bonanza: (1) war veterans, having been exposed in various ways to sport, returned from overseas; (2) colleges and universities across the country were building stadiums to accommodate fans' interests; and (3) a post-war economic boom was putting more money into the populace's pocketbooks. In addition, sport was coming of age and the "Golden Era" featured such colorful personalities as Babe Ruth, Johnny Weissmuller, "Red" Grange, Cliff Hagen, Knute Rockne, George Halas, Bill Tilden, Jack Dempsey, Bobby Jones, and Helen Wills, to name a few. While several sports profited from newspaper publicity, it was the "national pastime" of baseball that was the major beneficiary.

2. *Reader Interest Demands Free Sport Publicity*. Once sport became a mainstay of the newspaper, the amount of space devoted to it increased to where a disproportionate amount of space and time and energy to gather sport facts and write reports presented a problem. Newspapers were generous with the amount of space devoted to sport since it was believed that this was what readers wanted. It was believed that coverage would also maximize circulation.

3. *Sport Page Reflects the Social Scene*. The thesis that the sport section mirrors or reflects the key social issues of the time has been advanced. Brillhart reported that sport columns devoted space to the following social issues:[12] (a) *The Depression* and economic retrenchment as demonstrated through the adjustments in admission prices to accommodate lower income level persons and the staging of various benefit and charity sport events; (b) *Race Relations* reflected in opposition to banning Negroes from baseball and the anti-Semitic atmosphere of the 1936 Berlin Olympics; (c) *Public Morality* with relation to selling beer in stadia, athletic prosleytizing, and gambling in sport. There was also discussion of the participation of women in sport as well as their proper "uniforms" (skirts vs. shorts); (d) *Technological Change* as to whether or not football games should be broadcast by radio and the issue of "night" baseball; and (e) *The Basic American Proclivity to Help the Underdog* as reflected in the "Alabama" Pitts case. Pitts was convicted of second-degree murder at the age of 19 in 1930 in New York State and was offered a professional baseball contract upon his pardon, which led to battles between various judicial bodies regarding its appropriateness and legality (see pp. 130-134 for a discussion of crime and the athlete).

The sport page has always been a target of controversy. It has been extravagantly praised and unmercifully criticized for its contents. The parallels between scandals in sport and in the world at large are probably not coincidental. For example, the infamous "Black" Sox (see pp. 115, 129) and Teapot Dome scandals were coinciding events—one in sport, the other in politics. Again, it appears sport reflects the larger social atmosphere.

Despite the spectacular growth television made possible for sport, the financial success of teams, particularly professional ones, is greatly enhanced by the coverage they receive, gratuitously, in the newspaper. A favorable press—toward a player or a team—is enormously beneficial.

Magazines and Periodicals

The American Farmer, published in 1819, was the first American periodical devoted to sport. It included accounts on fishing, hunting, shooting, bicycle matches, and the philosophy of sport.[13] The *magazine industry* has undergone considerable change in response to the broadcasting media. Magazines aimed at general audiences have, with the exception of *TV Guide* (circulation about 20 million) and *Reader's Digest* (circulation approximately 18½ million), encountered fiscal difficulties (traditionally large circulation periodicals like *Look* and *Life* folded in the early 1970s). Specialized magazines, however, have thrived because of the selected readership they can offer their advertisers and patrons (*Encyclopedia of Sociology*, p. 169).

One of the first successful periodicals devoted to sport—*Sport*—today has a circulation of 1.4 million. On August 16, 1954, *Sports Illustrated* made its debut. Today, it is the most widely circulated sport magazine with a weekly circulation of 2.4 million. Other sport based magazines are popular (*Field and Stream, Sports Afield, Hot Rod, Golf Digest, Car and Driver*, and *Golf*) but the significance of *Sports Illustrated* resides in articles focusing upon the social significance of contemporary sport. Of course, other types of articles appear, but *Sports Illustrated* frequently features series of articles covering socially meaningful problems.

Broadcasting Media

Radio was pioneered in the 1920s by receiver manufacturers such as RCA, Westinghouse, and other independent entrepreneurs. The initial years of radio broadcasting strongly affected modern broadcasting and governmental policies toward it. Moreover, the radio corporations extended their purview to television and shaped this medium as well.[14] By the 1920s, live broadcasts of sporting events were being carried, first locally and then nationally. KDKA in Pittsburgh, generally recognized as the first commercial radio station, was broadcasting fights and baseball games in 1921.[15] Lee indicated that public broadcasting actually came *after* sport broadcasting.[16] On August 20, 1920, a radio station owned by the *Detroit News* broadcasted the results of the World Series. Also, the first college football broadcast came from a station located in Texas in 1920.

The Jack Dempsey/George Carpentier heavyweight boxing championship on July 21, 1921, was the first fight to be broadcast. Six years later, one department store sold $90,000 worth of radio equipment in the two weeks prior to the Dempsey/Gene Tuney championship bout.[17]

Radio ownership grew steadily from the 1920s to the present, and it is now estimated that there are more radio receivers (over 300 million in 1978) than people. This means more than one radio for every man, woman, and child in the United States. Because of the entrance of TV (98 percent of all U.S. households own at least one), radio broadcasting has altered its marketing approach. Instead of large audiences and national network programming, it now concentrates on ethnic programming, news, talk shows, or one type of music. Many local stations purchase the broadcast rights to college and professional sporting activities. Radio stations in America broadcast over 400,000 hours of sport annually (*Encyclopedia of Sociology*, pp. 169-172).

Television

The United States was the first country to introduce television to a mass audience. This occurred shortly after the Second World War, and today there are few households—about 2 percent—not plugged in to this technological medium. Television has had a dramatic impact on American leisure-time activities. There are nearly 1,000 TV stations (727 commercial; in the United States, most of them affiliated with one of the three major , and CBS).[18] Most of the mass-audience media are supported by advertis- as a consequence, influenced at least indirectly by the dictates of the adver- on results from choosing the most marketable products as measured by the (ignette 12.3), a weekly estimate of a program's audience size based on a na- seholds. The relative popularity of sport programs can be inferred from the ranking of the largest total audiences for special events: (1) "Gone With the Wind," (2) Super Bowl (1979), (3) "Roots," and (4) World Series (1975). The largest all-time audience for an event was the Apollo II Moon Flight (on 7/20/69).

Television, like no other medium, dominates sport today. In the past decade or so, America's sports have come to be a prodigal child of television, providing for the hawkers on Madison Avenue a bonanza opportunity for vast markets. Because of TV markets, the venues of the major leagues have extended into America's remotest hinterlands. Skylines and downtown areas of cities have been altered by the spectacle of stadiums, arenas, auditoriums, and amphitheatres. The geography, the economics, the schedules, the esthetics, and the ethos of sport have come to depend upon TV's cameras and advertising monies.[19]

The game which has profited most from "cyclops," is football says Michener, "Starting with a spectacle which already had the ingredients—power, speed, varied movements, choice of plays, enough pause between plays to allow the man at home to decide what strategy the quarterback will employ, plus an alluring violence—the rules' makers and Commissioner Rozelle have been un- canny in their ability to make the right decision at the right time." According to Chandler, football is a superb TV sport because of its patterned and recurring series of crises.[20] There are four downs to traverse ten yards and time between plays to permit viewing fans to guess what the next play will be and allow announcers to "set the stage" for the next play; replay and comment on the last episode via "instant replay" are squeezed in and these are followed by commercial messages.

Speaking of "instant replay" (first appearing in 1963), it is noteworthy to consider the way in which it can and has created *sport heroes*: Jerry Kramer described his success through television as follows:

> Over and over and over, perhaps twenty times, the television cameras reran Bart's touch- down and my block on Jethro Pugh. Again and again, millions of people across the country saw the hole open up and saw Bart squeeze through. Millions of people who couldn't name a single offensive lineman if their lives depended on it heard my name repeated and repeated and repeated. All I could think was, "Thank God for instant replay."[21]

HOW TELEVISION HAS AFFECTED SPORT

In what ways have the media, particularly television, influenced sport? Television has affected the economy, ownership and location of franchises, scheduling, staging, management, dynamics, and even the aesthetics of sport. Usually it has been cast in the role of villain and is frequently criticized on six grounds: (1) the avalanche of TV sports will turn the United States into a nation of viewers rather than doers, (2) TV reshapes sport to meet its own needs and whims, (3) TV is responsible for contriving artificial timeouts and excessive commercials, (4) TV at the collegiate level provides select

VIGNETTE 12.3
HOW THE NIELSEN TV RATINGS ARE ARRIVED AT

Since 1950 the A. C. Nielsen Company has been an integral part of the television industry. Its major purpose is to measure television audiences, document its growth and characteristics for advertisers, agencies, broadcasters and others involved in the medium. Since the number of televised sporting events has continued to grow it is of interest to know how the actual ratings are arrived at. The first thing we must emphasize is that the Nielsen ratings are not intended to nor do they measure program *quality*. Instead, they provide *reliable and quantitative estimates* of TV audience size and characteristics.

The rating techniques are based upon sampling theory and are scientifically valid. A *sample* (part of the total phenomenon of interest) is selected because to study the entire *population* of 71 million TV homes would be financially and practically prohibitive. Sampling is not a last resort but a highly efficient procedure for estimating characteristics of a larger population from which it is selected. Nielsen selects a probability sample—technically it is an *area probability sample*—of about 1200 households. These households are randomly selected and households cannot volunteer to be part of the sample. Each sample household's television set is installed with a device smaller than a cigar box—technically known as the Storage Instantaneous Audimeter (SIA)—which monitors and records in its computer-like memory whether or not the TV is on and what channel it is tuned to. When Nielsen's Central Office Computer in Dunedin, Florida wishes to retrieve this information it is sent along special telephone lines to the Office. This procedure enables Nielsen to determine what shows are turned on. To determine *who*—not *what*—is tuned in a separate sample of National Audience Composition (NAC) households keep a diary of their viewing habits.

Through these procedures the Nielsen organization produces a *TV rating*—a statistical estimate of the number of homes tuned to a program. Hence if a program receives a rating of 44.4 as did a recent Super Bowl, it means that nearly 44½ percent of U.S. TV homes were tuned in to that program. Since over 71 million households (98 percent of the total number of households) have TV sets, a rating of 44.4 means that an estimated 31½ million TV households tuned in. In other words:

Rating X 71 million = Number of Households Tuned In

It must be emphasized, however, that the figures are *estimates*—but accurate ones. If the Nielsen sample constructed a rating of 44.4 percent, the true rating lies somewhere between 43.1 and 45.7 sixty-seven percent of the time. One-third of the time the "error" may be larger but when repeated ratings are taken the range of error correspondingly reduces.

In summary, ratings appear to benefit the television audience—because they provide a barometer of peoples' likes and dislikes. It also provides the TV industry—advertisers, agencies, networks, TV stations, program producers—with vital information regarding the public's viewing habits and preferences.

Source: "Nielsen Television 78," A. C. Nielsen Co. (Chicago, IL: Media Research Services Group, 1978).

---

schools with an edge in recruiting, (5) TV coerces sports into altering their rules, and (6) TV distorts the nature of the game it covers.[22] Let us examine more closely some of these criticisms.

The Scheduling, Staging, Management, and Dynamics of Sport

In football, the role of linesman was established because of the need of sportcasters to know the yard line where the offensive team took over possession of the ball. This enabled them to quickly determine the distance traversed by the offensive team. Another official has been added, although this one is not dressed in the traditional referee's black and white striped uniform nor listed in the official program. It is the television network man, frequently adorned in an iridescent orange uniform whose job is to signal the real officials when arbitrary timeouts are to be called for "a word from our sponsor." Ordinarily no problem is encountered in finding time for ads; however, there are and have been occasions whereby an untimely "timeout" was necessitated to hear from the sponsors.[23] In fact, Peter Rhodes, a soccer official, once wore an electronic beeper on his shoulder so he could whistle timeouts at the request of the TV network.

There are other ways TV has dictated the course of the game. Notre Dame and Georgia were scheduled to "lock horns" on Saturday, November 9, 1974. ABC discovered that if the teams could agree to play Monday night, September 9, the network would be able to broadcast the opening game to a nationwide audience. The contest was subsequently moved up. Of course, such maneuvers are not necessarily all negative since each school received handsome revenues from the TV contract. It did prompt Bear Bryant to utter, "We think TV exposure is so important to our program and so important to this university that we will schedule ourselves to fit the medium. I'll play at midnight if that's what TV wants."[24]

Another television interference occurred in April, 1974. The New York Knicks and Boston Celtics had faced grueling competition in the NBA play offs. It had taken Boston six games to eliminate Buffalo and New York seven to down Baltimore. The Knicks series ended Friday and CBS ordered the two finalists to prepare to start the series on Sunday so the big Sunday TV audience would be caught (Michener, 1976, pp. 298-299).

On December 19, 1975, the Blue-Gray All-Star Game was scheduled to be played in Montgomery, Alabama. The Miz-Lou Television Network had arranged to have a three-hour segment blocked off for the coverage. When confusion at the start of the game indicated it might run longer than the segment alloted, the TV barons dictated that the first quarter would be 12 rather than 15 minutes long. But, as the game progressed, it appeared that there would be a block of time left over since it was moving along extraordinarily quickly. So extra minutes were addended to the third and fourth quarters and in the final 31 seconds the "Yankee" squad scored a touchdown and won 14-13. One Blue-Gray committeeman apologized to the "Confederates." tacitly admitting that they had won the game—or were robbed from winning it by television (Michener, 1976, p. 299).

Another controversial contest was the fourth game of the 1977 National League Playoffs between the Dodgers and the Phillies. The game was played during a steady rainfall much to the chagrin of the Philadelphia team and fans, particularly when it became apparent that the wet conditions were major obstacles to victory. One of the reasons the game was played under deplorable circumstances was to avoid problems in the scheduling of the opening day World Series Game. See Vignette 12.2 for two fans' and one owner's agreement on TV's intrusion into sport.

The Grand Slam of tennis was held in Boca Raton, Florida, in 1978. The starting time was set for 1 P.M., but it was necessary to push up the starting time to 12:30 P.M. to accommodate TV. A near-riot flared up when fans became angry upon finding the match well into the second set before many of them could take their seats. A few weeks following the Grand Slam, NBC refused to telecast a title fight between featherweight champion Cecilio Lastra and challenger Sean O'Grady because the World Boxing Association did not sanction the bout (Kowet, July 1, 1978, p. 3).

VIGNETTE 12.2
FANS AND AN OWNER AGREE ON TV'S ROLE

THE FAN:

TV's Role in Playoffs Draw Fire

Sports Editor, The San Diego Union:

I wish to express my dismay at the lack of integrity on the part of baseball officials who allowed television to dictate that one of the most important baseball games of the year had to be played in the rain. Conditions for the Saturday night game in Philadelphia were such that there was no way the game should have been played.

If they stretch the season as long as they do these days, they should be prepared for postponements due to weather. The World Series start could have been and should have been delayed in order to play all games in something approaching decent weather.

Most sports writers have evidently accepted television's encroachment into these important matters. I heard few complaints from the media. I will admit that conditions were the same for both teams but this is no excuse and the assumption that the decision to play the game was Chub Feeney's to make is hogwash. In the 70's it is TV money that calls the shots.

Al Benson
El Cajon

THE OWNER:

Red-Eye Series

George Steinbrenner has some thoughts on the relationship between baseball and television. "Baseball is a game that may be getting controlled too much by television," said the Yankees' owner. "They set the schedule rather than what might be best for the clubs and players. We should have more time between the playoffs and World Series."

There's nothing revolutionary about that line of thinking. What's interesting is that Steinbrenner made the comments during an interview with Barbara Walters for ABC's Evening News.

Source: *The San Diego Union,* October 14, 1977, C-4. Reprinted by permission from *The San Diego Union.*

Ways in Which Sport Rules Have Been Altered to Accommodate TV

Golf, a sport altered by TV's limelight, has been tailored for television.[25] Originally, the scoring in golf was based upon *match play* in which the number of holes won—not the total number of strokes—determined the victor. The problem for TV was twofold: (1) no one could predict the duration of the game, and (2) a game could be decided at a hole where no cameras were mounted. The result: *medal play* in which each player's total score, or strokes, is compared against all others participating in the tournament. If scores were deadlocked at the end of regulation play, the tied scorers began play at the 15th hole and played until one player outright won one hole (instead of playing 18 holes the next day as they did before TV entered the scene).

Tennis has been a good TV sport because, as Chandler said, it contains a series of patterned confrontations between server and receiver with so many points to win a game, set, and match.[26]

However, it is still not ideal for TV since its duration is indeterminate. In the wake of this dilemma, there has been talk of switching the nature of tennis to three sets with the total number of games won determining the winner. At present, there is a set-ending tie-breaker procedure. The telecast of the Billie Jean King/Bobby Riggs match in September 1973 was watched by over 37 million people. Furthermore, it was viewed by more women than men. A big upsurge in the number of people playing tennis, particularly women, followed the event.[27]

Soccer and *hockey* have been disappointing TV sports. There are several reasons for this. First, because of the constant movement (in soccer there are no time-outs and play is stopped only when the ball goes out of bounds, when there is a flagrant foul, or when someone is injured), it is difficult for cameramen to follow the ball or puck. Second, the games lack the crisis points so characteristic of football. Third, there is typically little scoring. Perhaps these sports will be modified so that they become better TV sports. At present, the NHL is seriously considering dropping its traditional three 20-minute periods for four 15-minute periods with a shorter break between each period. Apparently hockey moguls believe this will make the game more palatable to hockey TV viewers and sponsors alike.

Basketball, while somewhat monotonous, has high fan appeal because it involves considerable scoring and movement. Furthermore, the ball is large enough to follow on the screen and timeouts provide opportunities for commentary and commercials. *Baseball*, a slow game, has a number of positive characteristics as a TV sport—the personal struggle between pitcher and hitter, the cycle of mini-crises involving three strikes, four balls, three outs, and nine innings.[28] In addition, baseball permits sufficient time for advertisement, commentary, instant replay, anecdotes, and has a tradition of "America's national pastime."

Gymnastics boomed after TV made a star of gymnast Olga Korbut. Before her TV debut, there were about 100,000 gymnastic adherents. Today that figure has more than tripled. Don Ohlmeyer, NBC executive producer of sports, said: "They held (before the 1972 Munich Olympics) important gymnastics meets at high-school gyms, and couldn't sell tickets. Now they hold important meets in Madison Square Garden, and scalpers stand outside getting their price."[29]

The Location of Franchises

One of the most dramatic ways in which the media, particularly TV, affect sport is in the determination of *franchise locations*.[30] In recent years franchises have come and gone almost as quickly as dandelions appear on a summer lawn. To understand the location and probable success of a franchise, the concept of *market area* is revealing. Two criteria—*area of dominant influence* (ADI) and *designated market area* (DMA)—are critical in the location of franchises.

The Area of Dominant Influence

The *ADI* allocates every county in the United States to the metropolitan area that dominates its viewing habits. For example, McLean County in the center of Illinois shares bipartisan Chicago and St. Louis sport fans. If the bulk of the viewers in the area rely on Chicago for news and entertainment, then Chicago would be the ADI for the county. On the other hand, if the TV viewers turned south, St. Louis would be the ADI.

The Designated Market Area

The *DMA*, a more sophisticated index of TV viewers' habits, assigns geographical districts to the dominant metropolitan area during *prime time*, This latter measure is an indicator of advertising potential used by program sponsors. Table 12.2 contains a list of the populations of 32 metropolises, their ADI and DMA rank in addition to wealth per capita and percent of U.S. TV households. These figures illuminate certain critical points. The Baltimore and Milwaukee franchises have experienced problems despite populations of two million. Part of the explanation for their problem lies in the ADI and DMA ratings.

Baltimore is located between two other major sport meccas—Washington, D.C., and Philadelphia—and some of its viewing audience is siphoned off to those areas. While its population ranks 20, its ADI and DMA rank 19 and 20, respectively. Milwaukee suffers the same problem in being located between Chicago and Minneapolis. Whereas its size ranks 24, its TV potential is 26 and 23 on the television indices.

Tampa's case is the reverse. While the metropolitan area ranks 18 on population, its TV potential is greater than such major cities as Cincinnati, Buffalo, Denver, New Orleans, Kansas City, Milwaukee, and San Diego.

Finally, consider San Francisco/Oakland. Several competing pro franchises exist in the Bay Area, e.g., 49ers/Raiders and Giants/Athletics. The area is wealthy, ranks high on the TV indices, and has a large population, but has experienced difficulty in supporting two football and two baseball teams. This makes it understandable why reports of the Giants being liquidated bear some credibility.

It was because of the anticipated additional (between $½ and 1 million per year) TV-generated revenue that the Boston/Milwaukee Braves are now in Atlanta, the Minneapolis Lakers are located in Los Angeles, the NFL Chicago Cardinals are "homed" in St. Louis, the Philadelphia/Kansas City Athletics are in Oakland, the Brooklyn Dodgers are in Los Angeles, and the New York Giants are in San Francisco.

THE ECONOMIC IMPACT OF TELEVISION AND SPORTS

The economic aspect of TV and sport is probably the most significant feature in understanding their mutual needs. To appreciate the size of the TV pot, consider that in 1963 TV paid football—collegiate and pro—$13.9 million. By 1966 this figure had grown to $41.1 million, and by 1968 to $54.7 million. In 1970 it was $58 million and in 1975, $60 million. Colleges and universities, while sharing in this cornucopia, derived $5.1, $10.2, $12, and $16 million in 1963, 1968, 1970, and 1975, respectively. Of course, the difference between the total figures and these here is that siphoned off to professional football. Michener said: "The overall television expenditure for sports, counting the specials and oddball events is a staggering $200,000,000 per year."[31]

Other professional sports have joined in this bonanza. The growth of TV receipts in golf is impressive. From a mere $150,000 in 1961, it rose to $3,000,000 in 1971 and $5,000,000 in 1976. Baseball, too, has profited. When TV and radio rights are considered, nationwide and World Series rights grew from $3,250,000 in 1960 to $16,600,000 in 1970. In 1974 nationwide rights alone rose to $43,000,000; local rights for 1976 hovered around $35,000,000.[32]

How much money does television invest in sport coverage?

Table 12.2
Characteristics of Thirty-Two Standard Metropolitan
Statistical Areas (SMSAs)

Rank 1977 Census	SMSA Area	1977 Population	Rank ADI	Rank DMA	Rank Per Capita Wealth	% of U.S. TV Households
1	New York	18,358,800	1	1	1	8.84
2	Los Angeles	10,544,000	2	2	4	5.28
3	Chicago	8,318,600	3	3	13	3.84
4	Philadelphia	6,950,000	4	4	25	3.21
5	Boston	5,620,900	5	5	22	2.42
6	San Francisco/Oakland	4,871,100	6	6	5	2.41
7	Detroit	4,841,300	7	7	18	2.18
8	Washington	3,928,400	9	8	6	1.82
9	Cleveland	3,961,900	8	9	28	1.81
10	Pittsburgh	3,319,200	10	10	24	1.60
11	Dallas/Fort Worth	3,164,000	11	11	11	1.50
12	St. Louis	2,843,300	12	12	31	1.29
13	Houston	2,811,900	14	14	14	1.28
14	Miami	2,447,100	18	16	28	1.28
15	Minneapolis/St. Paul	2,832,400	13	13	12	1.27
16	Seattle	2,465,300	15	17	2	1.22
17	Atlanta	2,663,000	16	15	20	1.20
18	Tampa	2,146,300	20	18	30	1.17
19	Indianapolis	2,340,800	17	19	10	1.06
20	Baltimore	2,315,400	19	20	27	1.00
21	Portland	1,835,000	25	22	8	.90
22	Denver	1,879,100	28	28	7	.89
23	Cincinnati	1,929,800	23	24	21	.88
24	Milwaukee	1,913,400	26	23	19	.88
25	Kansas City	1,739,400	22	26	15	.84
26	Buffalo	1,813,600	24	25	26	.84
27	New Orleans	1,552,500	36	35	32	.69
28	Providence	1,749,000	29	29	23	.82
29	San Diego	1,655,900	34	32	9	.81
30	Phoenix	1,629,600	37	36	16	.74
31	Rochester	940,100	60	67	17	.44
32	Honolulu	891,200	81	80	3	.35

Source: *Spot Television Rates and Data*. Skokie, Ill.: Standard Rate and Data Service, April 15, 1973. DMA: Nielsen Station Index markings by households within Designated Market Areas, September 1975. Last column: U.S. Department of Commerce: County and City Data Book, 1972; A. C. Nielsen Company, 1978. Reprinted with permission.

Today the overall TV expenditures for sport is a staggering $500,000,000 and predicted to be close to $1 billion in 1980.[33] In an Olympic year one can conservatively add another $50-100 million. NBC bought the 1980 Moscow Olympics for $85 million.[34] Of utmost importance is the fact that 20 years ago these huge sums of monies were not available. According to Coakley, TV expenditures for sport are even higher than Michener's estimate:

> . . . during 1976 the three major television networks invested $315 million in sport coverage. ABC paid $50 million to professional baseball for television rights to many major-league games, $15 million to NCAA football, and $62 million for the winter and summer Olympic Games. NBC paid $42.8 million to professional baseball to televise the games ABC does not carry and $3.5 million to televise the Super Bowl. NBC and CBS share a $60 million package with the National Football League, and CBS has a $27 million 3-year contract with the National Basketball Association. The remainder of the $315 million is paid for events such as college bowl games, the Kentucky Derby, the Indianapolis 500, many golf tournaments, and tennis.[35]

In 1978, the total ticket for football, radio, and TV network rights for the professional and college ranks amounted to more than $200 million. This amount was nearly 2½ times as large as the rights of $82½ million for 1977. The 1978 radio-TV rights package broke down like this:

> *$193,700,000 from the television and radio networks for professional and college games. In 1977, this figure was $76,400,000.
> *$3,710,000 from local radio stations or rights holders for rights to NFL pre-season and regular-season games. In 1977, this figure was $3,645,000.
> *$676,000 in local TV rights to NFL pre-season games. In 1977, this figure was $653,000.
> *$2,063,352 for local radio and delayed TV rights to football of schools and colleges. In 1977, this amounted to $1,857,292.[36]

While broadcasters paid more, so, too, did the advertisers. The costs of thirty-second commercials for the Super Bowl and other games are found in Table 12.3.

SPORT COVERAGE IN THE PAST

The marriage of athletics to the electronic media, which appears to be so precariously successful today, was not without its crisis periods in bygone days.[37] The first year of serious commercial television was 1948. During this formative year, John Cameron Swayze, Howdy Doody, and Milton Berle were popular TV personalities. As equipment and technology were perfected, the dramatic impact of TV on sport began to be felt in the early 1950s. But several unanticipated consequences began to appear.

Football

Between 1949 and 1953 attendance at collegiate football games declined by nearly 3 million. Moreover, between 1966-73, ABC broadcast 87 football games nationally. In the latter years, each team was receiving $244,000 per appearance. The problem was that only the big football powers were the recipients of this windfall. In order to disperse this money, an agreement to restrict the

Table 12.3
Costs of Thirty-Second Commercials for Various
Sporting Events, 1977-78

NFL Games	Cost/1978	Cost/1977
Super Bowl	$185,000	$175,000
Regular Season Games	85,000	62,000
Preseason Games	42,500	

NCAA Games		
Rose Bowl	105,000	90,000
Orange Bowl	85,000	70,000
Cotton Bowl	70,000	
Sugar Bowl	50,000	50,000
Regular Season Telecasts	39,000	32,500
Fiesta Bowl	35,000	22,500
Gator Bowl	35,000	30,000
Hula Bowl	28,000	
Sun Bowl	24,000	
Peach Bowl	24,000	
Liberty Bowl	23,000	35,000
East-West Shrine	17,500	

Baseball		Cost/1977
World Series		75,000
All-Star Game		70,000
Monday Evening Game		26,000
Saturday Afternoon Game		15,000

Hockey		Cost/1977
Stanley Cup Playoff Game		12,500

Source: "Football Price Goes Right Out of the Stadium," *Broadcasting* (August 7, 1978), pp. 36, 38-41.

number of appearances by schools to three over a two-year period was instituted. In spite of this mandate, a frequency distribution of schools and appearances (1966-1975) was as follows: Notre Dame and Texas (21); Alabama, Southern California, and UCLA (19); Ohio State (17); Nebraska and Penn State (16); and following on their heels were Arkansas, Auburn, Louisiana State, Michigan, Michigan State, Oklahoma, and Tennessee.[38] The NCAA now has a TV committee and has instituted rules limiting the number of telecasts.

Between 1973 and 1975, ten football powers accounted for 59 percent (46 of 78 possible slots) of NCAA regular season telecasts. One anonymous Big Ten coach said: "We haven't been on TV even regionally for years . . . but some of the schools we recuit against, like Notre Dame, Nebraska, and Ohio State are on national TV twice or three times a year. National TV is where the good youngsters want to be . . . and they know our school isn't likely to get them there."[39] To counter this allegation, network spokesmen have retorted that about 50 of the NCAA's 140 major college teams (36%) receive some exposure on ABC TV each year. The spokesmen quickly add, too, that most conferences practice *revenue sharing*, that is, even if conference teams do not appear on TV, they usually share the TV-generated revenue.[40] What happens is that the rich get richer, and the poor poorer. At the close of the 1975 season, a contract between the NCAA and ABC was negotiated allowing the "biggies" to appear four times (not three) in two years and it was estimated that each team would receive in excess of $250,000 per TV appearance.

Boxing

Other sports, notably boxing, were not so fortunate. Between 1946 and 1964—the year when the last *Friday Night Fight of the Week* was telecast—there were hundreds of fights on television; in some areas nearly nightly boxing matches could be viewed. One consequence of this overexposure was a radical decline in club boxing; 250 of the 300 small fight clubs in the United States closed their doors between 1952 and 1959. The result was that there was no new talent—although old worn out boxers remained in abundance—to provide lifeblood to the sport. The return of boxing to TV has been slow, often by way of theatre TV.[41]

Baseball

Baseball presents another interesting case study. In 1939 minor league attendance exceeded that of the majors, 15 million for the former and about 9 million for the latter. A decade later the minor leagues saw 42 million people pass through the turnstiles. But by this time spectators could see their favorite big-time players on television for free. Minor league attendance figures plummeted to 13 million in 1959 and to 10 million in 1969. The number of minor league clubs declined from 488 in 1949 to 155 today.[42]

Initially, major league sport owners grabbed every opportunity to put their clubs on television. The results, in some cases, were nearly a fiasco. From a 1948 high of almost 21 million, attendance dropped to slightly less than 14½ million in 1953. One sobering example is the Cleveland Indians' attendance between 1948 and 1956. During that period, they won a World Series, an American League pennant, and had a string of fine players (Bob Feller, Bob Lemon, and Mike Garcia). The Indians televised many of their home games during that time and their attendance dropped a whopping 67 percent.[43]

The (then) Boston Braves also fell on hard times. In 1948, they won the National League pennant and drew nearly 1½ million fans, a season's attendance record. The management sold rights to televise all their 1949-50 home games and almost all home games for the 1951-52 seasons. Although finishing in the first division three of those four years, attendance dropped 81 percent—from 1,445,000 in 1948 to 281,278 in 1952. Lou Perini, owner of the Braves, moved to Milwaukee and refused to allow TV cameras at any of their games. Despite nearly one million paid attendance in

1964, Perini realized that the geographical location of Milwaukee—between Minneapolis and Chicago—was ill-suited and sold the franchise. The team made an exodus to "Dixie" and located in Atlanta, a virginal TV market.[44]

In 1969 major league baseball attendance reached an all-time high—27 million, although there were 24 rather than 20 clubs. The TV spectators watching the World Series averaged 23 million per game. Baseball attendance in 1976 set a record—31.3 million attendance. The 1977 season exceeded that at somewhere around 38 million and the 1978 attendance mark was nearly 41 million. The minor leagues were also having a banner year and nearly topped the 13 million regular season mark for the first time in 20 years. Total attendance at professional baseball games hovered around 51.3 million.[45] Many reasons have been advanced for baseball's comeback—the 1975 World Series between the Boston Red Sox and Cincinnati Reds, close pennant races, more home runs, a game not played against the clock like many sports, the changing social atmosphere after the upheavals of the late 1960s and early 1970s, promotional gimmicks, high salaries and last, but not least, television. Paul Weiss offered this comment:

> For a long time, TV didn't know how to show the game. They showed only the pitcher and batter. Now they show the whole field and have instant replays. These make a great difference in fan interest.[46]

The major television networks—ABC, NBC, and CBS—form the primary source of support and exposure for sport. A fourth network—the Hughes Sport Network, Inc.—is competing, albeit feebly, with the larger three. It would seem that the monies paid to sport franchises would be a harbinger of the networks' financial growth. Paradoxically, this does not appear to be the case. William Mac-Phail, CBS television sports director, has been quoted:

> Sports is a bad investment, generally speaking. The network needs it for prestige, for image, to satisfy the demands and desires of our affiliated stations. The rights have gotten so costly that we do sports as a public service rather than a profit-maker. We're doing great if we break even.[47]

Apparently, the TV networks are barricaded into a competitive situation over the right to televise sports. While the costs are becoming astronomical, none of the networks want to drop out for fear of losing prestige and advertising monies. It is interesting to speculate on what would happen if the networks refused or significantly reduced their coverage of sports. One sport sociologist said: "If television were ever to withdraw its financial support from sport, the existing structure of highly professionalized, commercialized sport could very easily crumble."[48] ABC's Roone Arledge echoes Nixon: "So many sports organizations have built their entire budgets around network TV . . . that if we ever withdrew the money, the whole structure would collapse."[49] The networks, however, would probably withdraw only if the ratings plummeted. Of course, that will happen only if Americans lose their taste and thirst for sports.

Since we have dwelled on the perceived negative consequences of TV on sports, let us balance the ledger by mentioning some qualifications and *positive* benefits. For one, the decision to play the first night (1975) World Series rather than during the day was made by baseball's management, not the TV networks. In fact, the TV networks were reluctant to do this since the World Series coincided with their new fall entertainment season. Commissioner of baseball Bowie Kuhn said:

"NBC did not want night-time television in the 1975 World Series. We did—because you may have a difference of 25 million people from afternoon to night. We're trying to promote baseball to the American public. How are we going to do that by playing these big games on a Wednesday afternoon?"[50] Baltimore Oriole's manager, Earl Weaver, remarked: "Not only does it provide big revenue . . .but it gives people all over the U.S. a chance to see all the great ball players."[51] Kowet concluded:

> TV created a new appetite for big-league sports, and the major leagues—to nearly everyone's satisfaction—were willing and able (in the jet age) to supply a new diet of big-league franchises. And besides contributing to the expansion of existing leagues, TV helped create entire leagues out of whole cloth (the AFL, the ABA, etc.). It raised pro football to a par in popularity with baseball. It introduced millions to tennis and golf (particularly women). It turned pro sports into a socially acceptable profession, and a desirable one.[52]

RECENT TV SPORT COVERAGE

Between 1971 and 1977, the number of sporting events telecast by TV networks increased by more than 60 percent (see Table 12.4). During this time span, tennis, basketball, and multi-sport spectacles witnessed the greatest increment in the number of telecasts. Although football's share of the telecasts has declined by 9 percent since 1971, the actual number of games telecast has increased by ten.[53]

A recent survey conducted by the Opinion Research Corporation provides some insights into Americans' attitudes toward television sports.[54] A random sample of more than 1000 adults across the United States—82 percent of whom were TV sport viewers—were phoned and asked a variety of questions. When queried as to what professional or college sports they watched during the past year, pro football and college football occupied the top spots. Sixty percent of those polled had viewed pro football and 55 percent had watched college football. The next most popular TV sports— baseball, college basketball, and pro basketball—were viewed by 49, 43, and 41 percent of the sample, respectively. After these sports, there was a sharp drop in the percentages that had viewed various sporting events. For example, pro tennis, hockey, boxing, golf, auto racing, soccer, bowling, college track and field, skiing, swimming, pro wrestling, and pro track and field all fell at 15 percent or below.

Are TV sports viewers participants or spectators? Almost 50 percent said they had attended a sporting event in the past year. Seventy-five percent indicated they had played organized sport at some time in their life, while 90 percent admitted to having participated in non-organized sport programs.

Do men or women watch more TV sports? Generally speaking, women view more television than men.[55] However, more men (90%) watch TV sports than women (76%).

Are there socioeconomic differences in TV sport viewing? TV sports viewing is correlated with educational level: the more the education, the more the sport viewing. Similarly, the survey found that 91 percent of men and women who earned $25,000 or more per year watched sports on TV the past twelve months.

Are there regional differences in TV sport preferences? Westerners and Southerners are the most avid pro football viewers. College football reaches its smallest viewing audiences in the East. Baseball viewing tends to be the reverse of that for football. The largest percentage of viewers is

Table 12.4
Network TV Sports Events: Distribution of Telecasts,
1971, 1974, 1977

Sports Event	1971		1974		1977		Rank Order, 1977
	n	%	n	%	n	%	
Football	99	28	113	23	109	19	2
Multi-Sports	58	17	112	23	118	21	1
Golf	44	13	57	12	73	13	3.5
Baseball	39	11	54	11	61	11	6
Tennis	7	2	51	10	47	8	7
Basketball	32	9	50	10	73	13	3.5
Bowling	27	8	15	3	19	3	8
Remainder	43	12	40	8	67	12	5
	349	100%	492	100%	567	100%	

Legend: n = number of telecasts
          % = share of total number of sports telecasts

Source: "Nielsen Television 78," A. C. Nielsen Company (Chicago, IL: Media Research Services Group, 1978). Used with permission.

found in the East and South; the smallest percentage in the West. The largest audiences for college basketball are found in the Midwest while the largest audiences for pro basketball are found in the West.

Do Americans prefer to see some sports more often and some less often than they presently do? Sixteen percent wished to see more baseball and 14 percent desired to view more pro football. On the other hand, 16 percent preferred to see less golf and 12 percent wished to see less pro wrestling. A. C. Nielsen's low 5.8 average rating for golf telecasts in 1977 suggests that there is probably an overexposure of this TV sport. Despite Americans' differential preference for certain sports, the survey data indicate that the majority of both men and women are generally satisfied with the current amount of TV sport coverage (although women wouldn't object to seeing less sport—both men and women's sporting events).

What do TV viewers like most about TV sport? The rank order of their *most liked* activities as evidenced by their desire for more of them include: officials wired for sound, instant replay, slow motion, cheerleader shots, coverage of on-field half-time activities at football games, split-screen action, shots of athletes on the sidelines, statistics projected on the screen, shots from the blimp, and crowd shots.

What do TV viewers like least about TV sport? Not surprisingly, viewers like least the commercial interruptions, particularly the sales pitches delivered in the guise of extra time outs.

Do the public prefer to watch sports in the comfort of their own home or do they prefer to attend events in person? When given this choice, most preferred their own home. However, the one exception was baseball. Another qualification is in order: younger viewers preferred attending sport events in person while females preferred TV viewing.

Finally, respondents were asked: "Of all the television sports announcers, which ones do you like the best?" Twenty percent said Howard Cosell, 13 percent said Frank Gifford, and 10 percent said Don Meredith. Other announcers—Joe Garagiola, Curt Gowdy, Jim McKay, Phyllis George' Chris Schenkel, Keith Jackson, Tony Kubek, Vin Scully, Tom Brookshier, Alex Karras, and Pat Summerall—garnered 6 percent or less of the vote. What sportcaster was liked the least? Nearly 40 percent said Howard Cosell! Three percent, 2, 2, and 1 percent said Gowdy, Garagiola, Meredith, and Schenkel, respectively.

SUMMARY

In this chapter we have examined the symbiotic relationship between the mass media and sport. The *mass media* are a by-product of industrial technology and refer to the transmission of a message to an audience that is geographically dispersed. The term is usually applied to the activities of broadcasting, telecasting, the press, and publicly screened films. The development of the mass media has been a basic determinant of *popular* or *mass culture*. Popular culture involves standardized material goods, art, life styles, ideas, tastes, fashions, and values.

Our review of the mass media began with the *press* (newspapers and magazines). Although isolated sport stories appeared in the press prior to the 1800s, it was not until the 1830s that two social conditions—urbanization and literacy—reached the point where the printed page could be financially solvent and socially appreciated. We then traced the emergence of the newspaper in general and the sport page in particular and the manner in which the sport section mirrored events in the larger society. From the first sport magazine—*The American Farmer* in 1819—to the popular *Sports Illustrated* in 1954, magazines devoted to sport began to grow and prosper.

Radio was pioneered in the 1920s with isolated broadcasts of sporting events sent over the "air" during this early period. Reports of the World Series, boxing matches, and college football games appeared during the early 1920s.

Television was introduced on a mass scale in the late 1940s and today dominates sport. Television has affected the economy, ownership and location of franchises, scheduling, staging, management, dynamics, and even the aesthetics of sporting events. Each of these areas was richly illustrated. Economically speaking, TV expenditures for sport hover around the billion dollar mark. Television's role in sport has been extravagently praised and unmercifully criticized. We discussed the pros and cons of TV's intrusion into sport by drawing upon popular and expert opinions.

IMPORTANT CONCEPTS DISCUSSED IN THIS CHAPTER

Popular (Mass) Culture

Mass Media (Mass Communication)

Sport Consumer:

  Indirect Sport Consumer

  Direct Sport Consumer

The Press (Magazines & Newspapers)

Broadcasting Media (Radio)

Television

Market Area

Area of Dominant Influence (ADI)

Designated Market Area (DMA)

ENDNOTES

[1] *Encyclopedia of Sociology* (Guilford, Conn.: Dushkin Publishing Group, 1974), p. 172.

[2] Paul Hoch, *Rip Off: The Big Game* (Garden City, NY: Anchor Books, 1972), p. 36.

[3] Barry D. McPherson, "Sport Consumption and the Economics of Consumerism," *Sport and Social Order*, ed. D. W. Ball and J. W. Loy (Reading, Mass.: Addison-Wesley, 1975), pp. 239-275.

[4] Ralph Nader and Peter Gruenstein, "Blessed Are the Fans, For They Shall Inherit $12 Bleacher Seats, Indigestible Hot Dogs, $2 Bottles of Beer and 100 Overpaid Superstars," *Playboy* (Spring, 1978), p. 98.

[5] John W. Loy, Barry D. McPherson, and Gerald S. Kenyon, *Sport and Social Systems: A Guide to the Analysis, Problems and Literature* (Reading, Mass.: Addison-Wesley, 1978), pp. 310-311.

[6] Nader and Gruenstein, "Blessed Are the Fans, For They Shall Inherit $12 Bleacher Seats, Indigestible Hot Dogs, $2 Bottles of Beer and 100 Overpaid Superstars."

[7] Loy, McPherson, and Kenyon, *Sport and Social Systems: A Guide to the Analysis, Problems and Literature,* p. 304.

[8] Frederick W. Cozens and Florence Scovil Stumpf, *Sports in American Life* (Chicago, Ill.: University of Chicago Press, 1953). The discussion on pages 263-264 is taken from this source.

[9] Ibid.

[10] Edwin Emery, *History of the American Newspaper Publishers Association* (Minneapolis, Minn.: University of Minnesota Press, 1950), p. 263.

[11] Several famous persons—Walter Cronkite, Ring Lardner, Grantland Rice, Red Smith, Ernest Hemingway, Bob Considine, James Reston, Paul Gallico, Shirley Povich, Damon Runyon, Heywood Broun, and John O'Hara—began their lustrous careers as sportswriters. See Michener, *Sports in America*, p. 315.

[12] Donald Brillhart, "The Sports Page and the Social Scene, 1929-1935" (Unpublished manuscript, University of California, Berkeley, 1951).

[13] Loy, McPherson, and Kenyon, *Sport and Social Systems: A Guide to the Analysis, Problems, and Literature,* p. 304.

[14] *Encyclopedia of Sociology*, p. 169.

[15] Loy, McPherson, and Kenyon, *Sport and Social Systems: A Guide to the Analysis, Problems, and Literature,* pp. 305, 307.

[16] Alfred M. Lee, *The Daily Newspaper in America* (New York: Macmillan, 1937). D. Stanley Eitzen and George H. Sage, *Sociology of American Sport* (Dubuque, Iowa: Wm. C. Brown, 1978), p. 36.

[17] *New York Times* (September 24, 1927), p. 14; Eitzen and Sage, *Sociology of American Sport*, p. 36.

[18] "Nielsen Television 78," A. C. Nielsen Company (Chicago, Ill.: Media Research Services Group, 1978).

[19] William Johnson, "TV Made It All a New Game," *Sports Illustrated* (December 29, 1969), p. 86.

[20] Joan M. Chandler, "TV and Sports," *Psychology Today* 10 (April 1977), pp. 64-76. Eldon E. Snyder and Elmer Spreitzer, *Social Aspects of Sport* (Englewood Cliffs, N.J.: Prentice-Hall, 1978).

[21] Jerry Kramer, *Instant Reply* (New York: World Publishing Co., 1968), p. 262.

[22] Don Kowet, "For Better or For Worse," *TV Guide* 26 (July 1, 1978), p. 2.

[23] James A. Michener, *Sports in America* (New York, Random House, 1976), p. 295. Michener (pp. 297-298) recalled a game played between the Philadelphia Eagles and New York Jets in Veterans Stadium that illustrates this travesty. With 3½ minutes to go, the Jets kicked a field goal, making the score 24-23 Eagles. Deep in their own territory, after the Jets kickoff following the field goal, the Eagles began running plays to "eat up the clock." The Jets had their hands tied as they had no time outs left. At this juncture the orange-vested TV man began frantically waving his hands—the sponsors had three more commercials to squeeze in. The referee called an arbitrary "network" time out to stop the clock. As any sport fan knows, this intervention could be enough—although the Eagles went on to win—to change the game's momentum and outcome.

[24] Johnson, "TV Made it All a New Game."

[25] Chandler, "TV and Sports"; Michener, *Sports in America*, p. 286.

[26] Chandler, "TV and Sports."

[27] Kowet, "For Better or For Worse."

[28] Chandler, "TV and Sports."

[29] Kowet, "For Better or For Worse," p. 3.

[30] Michener, *Sports in America*, pp. 305-309.

[31] Michener, *Sports in America*, p. 289.

[32] Ibid.

[33] Ibid.

[34] In 1960 CBS purchased TV rights for the Rome Olympics for $660,000. ABC paid $13½ million for telecast rights to the 1972 Olympic Games in Munich. ABC bought the rights to the 1976 summer games in Montreal for $25 million. See John T. Talamini and Charles H. Page, *Sport and Society: An Anthology* (Boston, MA: Little, Brown and Co., 1973).

[35] Jay J. Coakley, *Sport in Society: Issues and Controversies* (St. Louis, Mo.: C. V. Mosby Co., 1978), p. 192.

[36] "Football Price Goes Right Out of the Stadium," *Broadcasting* (August 7, 1978), p. 36.

[37] Johnson, "TV Made It All a New Game."

[38] Michener, *Sports in America*, p. 332.

[39] Kowet, "For Better or For Worse," p. 4.

[40] Ibid.

[41] Johnson, "TV Made It All a New Game."

[42] Ibid.

[43] Ibid.

[44] Ibid.

[45] "Behind Baseball's Comeback: It's An Island of Stability," *U.S. News and World Report* (September 19, 1977), pp. 56-57.

[46] Ibid., p. 57.

[47] Joseph Durso, *The All-American Dollar: The Big Business of Sports* (Boston, Mass.: Houghton Mifflin, 1971), p. 264.

[48] Howard L. Nixon, II, *Sport and Social Organization* (Indianapolis, Ind.: Bobbs-Merrill, 1976), pp. 61-62.

[49] Kowet, "For Better or For Worse," p. 6.

[50] Ibid., p. 3.

[51] Ibid., p. 6.

[52] Ibid.

[53] "Nielsen Television 78."

[54] Don Kowet, "TV Sports: America Speaks Out," *TV Guide* (August 19, 1978), p. 2.

[55] "Nielsen Television 78."

13

Sport, Collective Behavior, and Social Change

INTRODUCTION

Collective behavior is a concept encompassing a wide range of group phenomena, including crowds, riots, manias, panics, lynchings, stampedes, revivals, social and religious movements, revolutions, fads, fashions, crazes, public opinion, propaganda and rumor. Some forms of collective behavior are relatively spontaneous and of short duration (fads), while others are longer-lasting and require organization, planning, and coordination (social movements). All of these, however, are collective responses to and causes of socio-cultural change. The study of collective behavior is significant because it illuminates the dynamics—the *social processes*—of social and cultural change by which new norms, values, and traditions emerge. Figure 13.1 provides a model for understanding collective behavior. Notice that whereas much behavior is structured and governed by reasonably clear-cut social norms, such is not the case in incidents of riots, revivals, panics, and other kinds of crowd behaviors.

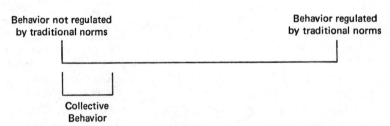

Figure 13.1
A Paradigm for Conceptualizing the Phenomenon of Collective Behavior
(From James W. Vander Zanden, *Sociology,* New York, Ronald Press, 1975, p. 253. Copyright, The Ronald Press, now a division of John Wiley & Sons, Inc., Reprinted by permission of John Wiley & Sons, Inc.)

Episodes of *collective behavior*—relatively spontaneous, unstructured, volatile, and transitory ways of thinking, feeling, and acting—abound in sport. Consider these:

On May 24, 1964, a soccer game between Peru and Argentina in Lima, Peru, resulted in the death of 293 persons. The brawl and genocide resulted from a disputed referee's call.[1]

In Glasgow, Scotland, June 2, 1971, 66 soccer fans were crushed to death after having left the stadium's exit only to return after their curiosity regarding a late score motivated them to do so.[2]

On June 4, 1974, the Cleveland Indians played the Texas Rangers on ($.10 a cup) "Beer Night" before a crowd of 25,134. While no deaths were reported, the Rangers' right field bull pen had to be closed down because Cleveland fans were bombarding the relief pitchers with fire crackers and beer cans. Streakers and other disruptive incidents necessitated irritating delays in the game. Fans climbed atop the Rangers' dugout threatening the players' lives and eventually Nestor Chylak (umpire), unable to control the melee, forfeited the game to Texas.[3]

Chris Chambliss sent the Yankees into the World Series with a ninth-inning home run against the Royals. Fans poured onto the field, knocked Chambliss down before he reached second base, mauled him at third base, and practically prevented him from scoring. Then they proceeded to tear up hundreds of feet of infield and outfield grass and the padding on the walls.[4]

The 1977 World Series ended in bedlam at Yankee Stadium when thousands of fans spilled onto the field after the final out, many to do damage despite their team's victory over the L.A. Dodgers, who themselves had taken the precaution of landing their team plane at a private field in an effort to avoid confrontation with the Yankee rooters. Before the stadium was cleared, there were almost 40 arrests and several dozen injuries.[5]

Recent Kentucky Derbys have seen horses and jockeys threatened by fans who throw paper cups and beer cans at them in the backstretch. In 1976 a smokebomb was thrown onto the track.[6]

After Mike Quarry beat the likeable Puerto Rican Pedro Soto in Felt Forum on December 9, 1974, in New York, Soto's boxing adherents ripped out seats, tore down ceiling panels, wrenched toilets from their moorings, and set fire to the room.[7]

On November 8, 1963, at Roosevelt Raceway in Long Island, NY, fans protesting a horse race smashed the tote board, set fire to a sulky on the home stretch, attacked a patrol judge inside his booth, destroyed concession stands, and overturned cars in the parking lot.[8]

On June 3, 1975, a game of box lacrosse between the Philadelphia Wings and Maryland Arrows was the equivalent of undeclared warfare. The state's attorney charged three players with having exacerbated the violence by attacking fans with their (potentially) lethal sticks.[9]

The U.S. Grand Prix at Watkins Glen, NY, has become so well known for its uncontained hell-raising at a mud-sopped area inside the track known as "The Bog" that the auto race featuring the world's greatest drivers has almost become secondary. In one such incident, a bus chartered by touring Brazilians was hijacked and taken to "The Bog" to be burned, with all the Brazilians' personal belongings still aboard.[10]

A 1975 NFL playoff game at Bloomington, MN, was interrupted when a Vikings' fan felled an official, with a whiskey bottle, knocking him unconscious. In another game, Viking fans got a taste of their own medicine when running back Chuck Foreman received an eye injury as the result of a snowball that hit him in Buffalo.[11]

During the third game of the 1973 baseball playoffs between the New York Mets and the Cincinnati Reds, fans at Shea Stadium, aroused by fisticuffs between Bud Harrelson and Pete Rose, showered the field with debris and caused an interruption in the game.[12]

At the University of Kansas in 1978, Jayhawk basketball fans pelted arch rival Kansas State University players with hot dogs. During the rematch KSU fans retaliated by deluging UK players with hundreds of ripe bananas, causing a 70-minute delay in the start of the game.[13]

The second game of a scheduled double-header between the Chicago White Sox and Detroit Tigers (July 12, 1979) had to be canceled when 7,000 rampaging fans took the field. The ensuing melee, apparently stimulated by a planned anti-disco demolition derby between games, found superfans toting anti-disco banners, igniting small fires and demolishing the batting cage. Comisky Park was in pandemonium. Thirty nine persons (many of whom the police believed to be intoxicated) were arrested for disorderly conduct although no serious injuries were reported.[14]

The entire spectrum of fandom is currently being extensively studied. Sport commissioners and observers of the sport scene seem to agree that a radical change has occurred in fans' behavior during the 1970s. The consensus seems to be that the "superfan" has emerged, an individual who wants to be a participant as well as a spectator. Arthur Fuss, assistant director of security for Major League Baseball, remarked recently, "Twenty years ago . . . professional sports were athlete-oriented. Now teams cater to the fan with jacket nights, bat days, beer nights and the like. Fans feel they can get closer."[15] Sociologist Irving Goldaber asserted: "Fans aren't just interested in winning games anymore . . . they have to vanquish the other team. When people come into the stands, they begin to feel the power to affect the outcome of the game. Now there is the feeling they can do something. America is a candidate for a new kind of violence—the fans' desire to achieve power vicariously."[16]

There is little doubt that both crowd and player *violence* in sport are increasing, and some would say at an alarming rate. Collective violence has marred soccer matches in England, Italy, Pakistan, Turkey, several Central and South American countries, and has accompanied a host of high school, collegiate, professional, and international sporting events in the United States, Canada, and elsewhere. The escalation of such episodes has prompted the formation of special commissions, at local, national and international levels, to investigate its roots and make policy decisions to mitigate such occurrences.

THEORIES OF CROWD BEHAVIOR

Sociologically, the study of *crowd behavior* has a fairly long and rich history. The roots and dynamics of crowd behavior have been explained in three different ways: (1) *contagion theory*, (2) *convergence theory*, and (3) *emergent norm theory*.[17] These different explanations are grounded on the manifestations of anonymity and de-individuation ("loss" of individual identity).

Contagion Theory

According to the *contagion theory's* originator, Gustave LeBon, a collective mind overpowers and submerges individuals in a crowd ("the law of mental unity of crowds"), through emotional contagion.[18] The consequence of individuals' submission to the crowd sufficiently alters their customary thoughts, feelings, and actions to produce a kind of "oneness." To contagion theorists, the crowd's influence on individuals is analogous to the spread of an infectious disease.

Three social psychological mechanisms are responsible for such action: (1) *suggestibility*— a psychological state which leaves individuals vulnerable and susceptible to the influence of others and acts as a catalyst to committing otherwise alien acts, (2) *imitation* and *contagion*—or the tendency to model one's own behavior after that of already-acting persons, and (3) *circular reaction,* or the social interaction process by which one's behavior is both a response and a stimulus to others' behavior.

For example, in 1972 the Ohio State and Minnesota basketball teams met in the latter's gym for the Big-Ten championship. Minnesota had been expected to win, and pregame activities—reminiscent of the Harlem Globetrotters' routine of dribbling, fast passing, and ball handling—were intended to hype up the players and 17,700 crowd. From the opening tip off to the final whistle, the game was fiercely contested. As the final period was drawing to a close, it became apparent that the home team would not be victorious, and angry fans hurled objects onto the court. Stimulated by these events, a Minnesota player committed a flagrant foul and a miniature riot took place on the court. The scuffle produced a contagion effect with both team members and partisan fans becoming involved in a melee.[19]

Convergence Theory

Whereas the contagion explanation highlights the temporary transformation of individuals' thoughts, feelings, and behaviors, *convergence theory* suspects that individuals' real selves, ordinarily covered up by a veneer of social propriety, are manifested under anonymous and de-individuated circumstances. In effect, convergence theories stress what might be termed the underlying asocial or antisocial proclivities of individuals whose behavior is ordinarily held in check by social norms. The convergence model underscores the *similar* predispositions people bring with them to social situations. For example, sport fans who turn out and eventually become uncontrollable generally "attack" the "foes"—visiting teams—rather than the home team (see the Cleveland Indians/Texas Rangers scenario, p. 283). The patients in a cancer ward provide a metaphor for comprehending the idea of convergence. They are not there because they have infected one another (as in the contagion approach) but because they share similar problems and have a common purpose.

Emergent Norm Theory

The *emergent norm* explanatory scheme challenges the underlying assumptions of the first two. Rather than an amorphous mass characterized by "unanimity," "uniformity," "oneness," and "similarity," this approach attempts to explain how the *illusion* of uniformity and unanimity develops since crowds contain motley types (core activists, cautious activists, passive supporters, opportunistic yielders, passersby, curiosity seekers, unsympathetics, dissenters). It stresses the initial *differences* in individual psychologies, motives, attitudes, behaviors, and predispositions that characterize crowd members. The emergent norm theory is aligned with the small group research of social psychologists Muzafer Sherif[20] and Solomon Asch[21] in which *norms*—behavioral expectancies— emerge to guide behavior in ambiguous contexts. Two kinds of social influence processes are at the heart of the emergent norm explanation. One is *normative social influence* and stems from the perception of the consequences of deviating from the majority's opinion and *informational social influence* in which people look to others for behavioral cues, particularly when they are not sure of their own interpretation of social situations or how to act. In the same vein, emergent norm theories maintain that "cultural scripts" (i.e., norms) emerge and channel behavior in these "new" social contexts.

In summary, while the three paradigms of crowd behavior—*contagion, convergence,* and *emergent norm*—differ, they are not mutually exclusive. Take crowd behavior at a sporting contest. Contagion, the reciprocal influence wrought by excitement among spectators, operates. Similarly, convergence is witnessed insofar as the stands are generally infested with partisan fans—some for the home team, others for the visiting team. Finally, a norm may emerge in the course of the contest which defines appropriate and inappropriate behavior and response to a particular event.

A THEORY OF COLLECTIVE BEHAVIOR

Neil Smelser's *value added* approach has attracted considerable interest among social scientists for its elegance in explaining collective behavior.[22] The notion of "value-added" is borrowed from economics and, in the present context, means that each collective behavior determinant "adds" its value to prior determinants and increasingly narrows and channels the subsequent collective acts.[23] According to the theory, there are six determinants of collective behavior and each of the six conditions is said to be "necessary," while all six are "sufficient" for collective patterns of behavior to emerge.[24] The six factors include: (1) *structural conduciveness,* (2) *structural strain,* (3) *growth of a generalized belief,* (4) *precipitating factors,* (5) *mobilization of participants for action,* and (6) *the operation of social control.* Smelser attempted to provide an answer to the question: "*Why* do collective behavior episodes occur *where* they do, *when* they do, and in the *ways* they do?"

Structural Conduciveness

Structural conduciveness refers to social conditions that are "ripe" for collective behavior to occur. Since sport stands are inhabited by partisan fans (see Vignette 13.1), the social basis for potential conflict exists. If, on the other hand, fans were a uniform and disinterested mass, the conditions for disruption would be minimal or even nonexistent. Structural conduciveness takes several forms:[25] (1) In sport, the presence of ethnic, racial, political, religious, social class, national, regional, and other cleavages provide the tinder for hostile outbursts. So-called "natural rivalries" can exploit existing antagonisms. In retrospect, it is not surprising that collective violence marred the September, 1947, soccer game between Hakoah, a Jewish Sports Club, and the Austrian Police Sports Club. The game, held in Vienna, was repeatedly punctuated by anti-Semitic slurs and spectators battled with each other until a riot police squad squelched the fracus. (2) Another form of structural conduciveness is the unavailability of alternate avenues of protest for grievances or the unavailability of targets to which blame can be displaced. Smelser hypothesized that underdeveloped countries generally are deficient in institutionalized channels for expressing disgruntlement, and this may be a partial explanation for the rampant sport riots in underindustrialized countries, for example, South and Central America and parts of Europe. (3) A third factor resides in the availability of objects to attack and upon which crowd hostility can be vented. If spectators can gain easy access to the playing surface, then, acts of violence may be more frequent when something "triggers" an episode of collective action. Managing the ecology of the field or stadium has increasingly been advocated as a counter-determinant to such outbreaks. (4) A final condition conducive to collective behavior is the existing communication channels. The mass media play a highly significant role in this process, particularly when disproportionate amounts of space and significance are alloted to sport events. Similarly, the congestion in sports stadia provides a stage for the rapid transmission of rumor and other unverified (or unverifiable) reports.

VIGNETTE 13.1
HOME TEAM AND VISITING TEAM FANS'
PERCEPTIONS OF A FOOTBALL GAME

Americans are sports fanatics and every year millions attend sporting events. It is of great social psychological importance that the game you see and the game they (i.e., rooters from the opposite side) see may be quite different. The present study involves the spectacle of collegiate football and is intended to convey the importance of individuals' personal characteristics— their needs, desires, motives, and particularly, group identification such as devotion to one's team.

A study conducted by Albert H. Hastorf and Hadley Cantril, "They Saw a Game: A Case Study," *Journal of Abnormal and Social Psychology* 49 (1954), pp. 129-134, had its setting in the final game of the season for two Ivy League collegiate football teams, Dartmouth and Princeton. Of significance, Princeton went into the finale undefeated and was led by a superstar quarterback named Dick Kazmaier who had received All-American honorifics. Shortly after the opening kickoff it became evident that the event was going to be a rough one. Kazmaier was taken off the field in the second quarter with a broken nose followed, in the third quarter, with the carrying off of a Dartmouth player with a broken leg. Tempers flared both during and after the game. Princeton won the fracus and had been penalized 25 yards during the game and Dartmouth 70 yards.

Accusations as to who started the "dirty" play emerged immediately following the game. Both campus and metropolitan news media added fuel to the already kindled fire. As one would probably surmise, Princeton accused Dartmouth for the less-than-desirable behavior and Dartmouth singled out Princeton for the same contemptible action. At this juncture Hastorf and Cantril intervened and collected data for subsequent analysis. First, they designed a questionnaire with the explicit purpose of determining how each side saw—perceived—the contest. Queries regarding how the game was played—"rough and clean," "rough and dirty," "clean and fair,"—who started the rough play, and the like, were asked of both Princeton (n=161) and Dartmouth (n=163) undergrads in introductory and intermediate psychology classes one week following the game. Second, at a later date undergraduates at both institutions were shown a film of the game and asked to take note and record the number of infractions and the nature of the rule breakage—"mild," "flagrant"—as well as who instigated the violations. At this point it should be mentioned that the researchers were not concerned with the accuracy (*veridicality*) of the perceptions; rather, they were focusing on the phenomenon of *social perception* itself.

Some of the empirical findings were these. Most importantly was the marked contrast in perceptions of what transpired that November 23, 1951 Saturday afternoon. Nearly all Princeton students described the game as "rough and dirty" and not a single student perceived it as clean and fair. Almost ninety percent of the Princeton undergrads wagered the Dartmouth team started the fracus in contrast to 53 percent (modal response) of Dartmouth students who deemed both teams were responsible. Interestingly, upon reviewing the game film Princeton students saw Dartmouth players violate the rules twice as often as their own team and furthermore, they saw the Dartmouth team make over twice as many infractions as did the Dartmouth students. When the severity of the infractions were judged, the ratio was about two "flagrant" to one "mild" on the Dartmouth team, and one "flagrant" to three "mild" on the Princeton team.

The Dartmouth students saw the game differently. While the plurality of answers fell in the "rough and dirty" category and over one-tenth thought the game "clean and fair," over one-third introduced a new category, "rough and fair" to describe the action. Although a third of the Dartmouth students felt their team had instigated the rough play, the majority thought both sides were to blame.

While additional specific findings could be reported, the discussion is sufficient to convey the flavor of the research report. Let us now offer some interpretative dimensions apropos social perception. It should be obvious that the game was perceived as a series of games by the bipartisan spectators. During an athletic event, a host of events are simultaneously happening (on and off the field) and a viewer catches only part of what is taking place. According to the authors, a happening only has significance when it reactivates something of significance in a person's assumptive form-world. That is, from the matrix of events occurring on the field only some will be experienced and usually those events "witnessed" will be affected by unique individuals' personal and social characteristics.

In summary, the empirical data suggest that it is dubious to conceptualize a football game as "something out there" that is objectively reacted to by the spectators. Rather, the content exists and is experienced only when the occurrences taking place have some kind of egoistic significance. Out of the web of events taking place, then, only those events imbued with personal significance will be abstracted and experienced. The next time you view or attend an athletic event it might be interesting to imagine what other spectators are actually "seeing."

Structural Strain

Structural strain refers to the experience of social malaise—frustration, deprivation, dissatisfaction, disgruntlement, conflict, tension, and ambiguity—by people. The 1969 "Soccer War" between Honduras and El Salvador demonstrates the ethnic, political, and economic foundations of collective violence. Prior to the three World Cup soccer games in June 1969, there was an illegal migration of an estimated 30,000 El Salvadoreans to Honduras. Although El Salvador was overpopulated, it was industrialized and rich whereas Honduras was a sparsely populated and economically underdeveloped, rural country. Such maneuvers deepened the resentments of Hondurans toward El Salvadoreans because of the latter's economic prosperity and domination of the Central American Common Market. These antagonisms were further kindled by border disputes between the two countries. Rumors of the decimation of El Salvadoreans in Honduras prompted the former country to mobilize troops and cross the border. Following the games and subsequent incidents, diplomatic and commercial ties between the two countries were severed.

The *hooliganism* of British soccer fans has been scrutinized under the heading of structural strain. Taylor has documented that this social phenomenon includes invasion of pitches by spectators, ransacking of soccer trains returning from games, throwing stones, beer cans and sundry objects at visiting team players, and invasions of the playing field by spectators to challenge the participants and the officials.[26] What is of social import is Taylor's provocative explanation for this collective activity. He wrote:

> The subculture of soccer in a working class community refers to the groups of working men bound together with a concern for the game in general (the soccer consciousness) and the local team in particular . . . . During the last quarter of the nineteenth century and throughout the Depression, the evidence is that players were very much subject to control by such local soccer sub-cultures; expected to receive advice, "tips," expected to conform to certain standards of behavior (as the sub-sultures' "public representatives"), and (in return) given a wage for so long as they fulfilled these expectations.[27]

What happened? This primary fan/player relationship was usurped. Bureaucratization (see pp. 41-42), professionalization, internationalization, and alterations in the control of the game alienated the working class fans. Taylor said:

> As structural changes in the game have threatened (the) central value (that the game is theirs) and have exposed it as an illusion, a reaction has occurred in the (working class) subculture, and in the process of reaction, other values have had to take a second place. In particular, where once the turf was sacred, now (working class fans are) prepared periodically to take up occupation of that turf in the assertion of other values.[28]

In short, Taylor interprets English hooliganism to be the result of working class fans' efforts to redress what they perceive as "injustices" and *reassert personal control* over the game. Rudé would call this series of events a "backward looking riot" in which disgruntled fans are attempting to restore a previous state of affairs.[29]

Growth of a Generalized Belief

A *generalized belief* provides people with an "answer" to their woes. It is two pronged in that it provides (1) a diagnosis of the forces and agents producing the strain, and (2) a response for coping with (easing or erasing) the strain. Frequently the generalized belief takes the form of an *ideology*—shared beliefs and definitions regarding the cause and/or the solution to the dilemma. The "Soccer War" provides a good illustration. Prior to and during the games the press reported charges of "mistreatment" of Honduran fans at the hands of El Salvadoreans, accusations of "brutality" directed at players on both teams, and stories of Honduran crowds taking El Salvadorean property and lives. These vague and sometimes conflicting reports, in an already strained atmosphere, provided volatile fuel for the development of hostile beliefs and presumably played a part in the crowd violence which marred the games.

Precipitating Factors

Collective behavior, as we've seen, does not occur in a vacuum. Something or someone must "trigger" or "touch off" the mass action. Smith's analysis of seventeen soccer riots found that many of the contests in which unruly crowd "misbehavior" occurred were particularly rough.[30] This was the case when Napoli met Rapid of Vienna in Brooklyn (NY) in June, 1959. During the contest tempers flared almost continuously. Interestingly, in many soccer riots the aggressive response of spectators seemed to have been precipitated by violent episodes: rough player interaction, spectator aggression (such as stone throwing between partisan fans in Dacca Stadium, Karachi in August, 1966), or police reaction to fan behavior (as when hoses were turned on the crowd after a call was disputed and prompted hurling "missiles" at the police). The most frequent events precipitating spectator hostility were disputed referees' calls—disallowing a goal, ejecting a player, an act of violence—in the last few minutes of a closely contested game. Fans' hostile reactions appeared to be attempts at redressing perceived injustices. Consider the following incident in pro football:

> With less than a minute remaining in a game between the Vikings and Cowboys in Bloomington, Minn., Dallas takes the lead on a disputed touchdown pass from Roger Staubach

to Drew Pearson, virtually assuring a Vikings' defeat, and disappointed fans to go bonkers. One end of the field becomes a rain of whiskey bottles, golf balls, beer cans, flasks; at the other, two police officers stop fights among drunks. A whiskey bottle, lofted from the stands, strikes referee Armen Terzian in the head, knocking him semiconscious and opening his forehead.[31]

Mobilization of Participants for Action

Once a precipitating event occurs the *mobilization of participants for action* begins to fester. Leadership, directed or diffuse, plays an important role at this juncture. To illustrate, consider the May 24, 1964, soccer game between Argentina and Peru in Lima's National Stadium.[32] The violence that ensued was "triggered off" by the referee's disallowance of a Peru goal (which would have tied the score with six minutes remaining). Following this decision, Matias Rojas, known as "Bomba" (The Bomb) for his previous attacks on officials, scaled a seven-foot high barbed-wire fence. Rojas was detained before confronting the referee but appeared to have provided a role model for several fans who followed suit. A second man over the fence was tripped by an officer, then struck with a truncheon, and appeared to divert the crowd's wrath to the police rather than to the referee. Others pushed and kicked rhythmically and tore large holes in the metal barricade and gained entrance to the playing field and began battling with the police. Others set fires in the stands. The result: three policemen dead and much property damage. Leaders like "Bomba" may incite the crowd; in other cases they may harangue the audience into action simply through derogatory chanting.

Operation of Social Control

Social control is a "counter-determinant" consisting of techniques to prevent, interrupt, deflect, or inhibit the accumulation of collective violence. Social control measures fall into two generic categories: (1) mechanisms aimed at preventing or minimizing the collective outburst, and (2) techniques that deter or repress an episode of collective behavior after it has begun. Once a collective episode is "in progress" quick and intelligent control on the part of authorities is necessary, albeit "tricky." Premature action has, on occasion, provided a catalyst to continued and escalated misbehavior. For example, there is some speculation that the use of tear gas in the Lima riot was, in hindsight, ill-advised. Even the display of physical force can be problematic; 500 policemen assigned to Glasgow's Ibrox Stadium for a Ranger-Celtic game on January 1, 1965, were not a sufficient "counter-determinant" as in excess of forty people were injured.[33]

Smelser proposed that in potential cases of collective violence, the ultimate determinant of the course of events is the behavior of those responsible for maintaining social control.[34] Given the desire for victory on the fans' part and the reality (in most sports) that one team must win and the other lose, fans' expectations for winning may be inflated by team officials, coaches, local announcers, and sportswriters who banter a team's unrealistic hope for "success." In short, expectations are not realized and magnified through "rising expectations." In an atmosphere pervaded by emphasis upon winning, it is not surprising that frustrations accumulate, perhaps to be vented when an event provides such an opportunity.

ADDITIONAL OBSERVATIONS ON AND REMEDIES FOR COLLECTIVE BEHAVIOR

Snyder and Spreitzer theorize that several conditions increase the likelihood of fans' disruptive behavior.[35] These include: (1) high and unrealistic expectations for the team's performance, (2) fans' strong attachment and identification with "their" team, (3) a closely contested event, (4) violent and hostile interactions between teams accompanied by the perception of a poorly regulated game, (5) lax, biased, and incompetent officiating. (6) law enforcement bodies appear reluctant, few in number, and ineffective, and (7) fans provided with role models for violent behavior. This interpretation of game violence attributes some of the problem to the *breakdown of social control* (or the perception of it) rather than an attempt to reassert personal control over the game.

Bryan and Horton studied fan violence and aggression in 79 university sporting events and offered the following hypotheses regarding the probability of collective violence occurring:[36]

1. Team sports are more likely to breed aggression and violence than are individual sports. Apparently, this is because it is easier to identify with teams than individual participants.
2. Football games are more prone to be marred by violence and aggression than basketball games. This grows out of the differential nature of the sports themselves.
3. Spectator violence is likely to be kindled by emotions of frustration and anger stemming from the losing team's loyal fans. The reason is that anger breeds anger.
4. Large schools tend to breed more aggression and violence than small schools. The researchers reason that there are more opportunities for student self-display at small schools and urban spectators seek more strongly individual identities in spectatorship.
5. Spectators appear to be stimulants to the display of team violence and aggression. This is consistent with the social psychological principle that the presence of others provides an added stimulant to activities in which participants are engaged.
6. Spectator violence and aggression are more likely to occur at the end of a sporting contest than at other times. The crowd needs to have experienced a common social event before their minds and activities become focused.
7. Spectator violence and aggression are more likely to emerge during Homecoming games than routine games. This apparently stems from the concerted effort to instill esprit de corps and solidarity among alumns and students.
8. Spectator violence and aggression are more likely to be manifest during traditional games with rivals. This is due to the same rationale as in point number seven.
9. The nature of collegiate violence and aggression is similar to that of the high schools. Education is apparently no deterrent to fan outbursts.
10. Spectator violence and aggression are more prone to occur when teams are from relatively close geographical distances than when widely separated. The researchers contend that in such circumstances nearness in space—propinquity—contributes to the rivalry.

Goldaber insists that concerted efforts at crowd control be made.[37] He suggests three remedial measures be taken: (1) consider alterations in the construction of sport facilities to make them less vulnerable to collective violence, (2) improve stadium management and law enforcement, and (3) study "sociological signals." "The problem is not the drunk after the tailgate party. The real problem is the mob. The officials, the scoreboard, the music and the cheerleaders have to develop ways to 'cheer down' the fans."

In the past years, deliberate attempts have been made to minimize or prevent destructive collective action. Because of what is known about the connection between on-the-field behavior and its off-the-field counterpart, codes to handle inflammatory behavior among players, coaches, and management have been established. At the high school level there is a guidebook entitled *Crowd Control for High School Athletics.*[38] There is also a proposal to ban a player for life if he assaults a referee in the Toronto and District Soccer League. Additionally, more player-official and player-fan-official fights have been dealt with in the courts (see account of box lacrosse game at beginning of chapter).

The ecology of the stadium has an effect on the nature of collective behavior. Sports that place fans and participants in close proximity—basketball—have had incidents in which fans have gone directly onto the playing surfaces. Other sports, (such as hockey) because of the boards and treacherous ice, have been bombarded with hurled air-borne objects. Hence, a second mode of minimizing such violence is to manage the physical environment of the playing area. Harrington advocated construction of tracks around soccer pitches to provide space between fans and players, especially near goal areas.[39] Other physical barriers include construction of steel barriers, bridged concrete ditches, and "unclimable" fences. Some soccer fields in foreign countries are surrounded by moats, iron palings, and barbed-wire fences. In the United States, on the other hand, while crowd control contingencies are employed, evidence suggests management is hesitant to do this for fear of angering and alienating paying customers.[40] Other forms of social control include the use of "mob squads," mounted constables, dogs, private and public police, state troopers, and soldiers, many carrying lethal weapons.

The solution to crowd behavior and collective violence is particularly problematic and paradoxical. Violence surrounds us, it is a pervasive theme in our culture, and, as H. Rap Brown said "violence is as American as cherry pie." Many sports are violent by their very nature (box lacrosse, hockey, boxing, football) and to this must be added fans' thirst for such hostility. Some sports are excessively violent and aggressive and such hostility may even be encouraged to promote gate receipts. Tutko and Bruns reported the following incident:

> In one of the NHL's most memorable battles, Terrible Teddy [Ted Lindsay, the former Detroit Red Wing great, who became their general manager in 1977] took on the fearsome Boston Hardrock, Wild Bill Ezinicki, who had never lost a fight. The fight was short and violent and both players were covered in blood when it ended. Most of it, though, belonged to Wild Bill. He needed 19 stitches to close the cuts on his face. Terrible Teddy needed one stitch on his eyebrow.[41]

Consider, too the case of Lynn Swann, acrobatic wide receiver of the Pittsburgh Steelers.

> The same body that could sprint and soar lay stretched out, motionless, on the grass of Oakland Coliseum. Swann had been poleaxed by safety [George] Atkinson, clubbed in the back of the head when the ball was thrown elsewhere. For one frightful minute, it looked as if Lynn Swann might never move again. And for months after the 1976 season ended, it seemed that he might decide never to play again in a game increasingly corrupted by illegal violence (*Sport*, January, 1978, p. 39).

High school games are not immune to collective violence, especially when it involves arch rivals. Hayes wrote:

> One consequence of the escalating player and crowd violence can be witnessed in crowd control measures in public schools. The Chicago Public League play-offs at the Ampitheater is but one illustration of control measures that have been instituted because of

violence in the past. Team spectators have separate bleachers, separate concession stands, and separate washroom facilities. The spectators enter and leave through different doors and the losing team's fans cannot leave until the winning teams's fans are gone . . . It is clear now that violence in sports is quickly becoming a major problem. Something must be done to alleviate it or sports will be in serious trouble. We cannot afford to let our sports degenerate into vicious spectacles and our sense of play deteriorate. As historians Hugh Davies Graham and Ted Robert Gurr state in *Violence in America*, "violent antagonisms expressed violently destroy peace and men and ultimately community."[42]

Many forms of entertainment are violence-laden—movies, children's cartoons, and news reports. Although professional opinion is divided, viewing/hearing violence may provide a stimulus to the same in an "audience." Goldstein and Arms studied fans attending two Army-Navy sporting events:[43] (1) football, and (2) gymnastics. Obviously, football is an aggressive sport while gymnastics is relatively nonaggressive. In comparing the pre- and post-game feelings of the fans, it was discovered that football spectators were more hostile, resentful, and irritable than gymnastics spectators. However, football fans' hostility level actually increased (by comparing their before and after game experiences), regardless of whether their team won or lost, while gymnastics fans showed no such escalation. One potentially confounding matter in their analysis was the self-selection factor, that is, hostile spectators may gravitate to aggressive games (like football) while non-hostile spectators may gravitate to nonaggressive games (like gymnastics). The bulk of research evidence suggests that sports do *not* produce a "catharsis effect"; instead, aggression tends to breed aggression.[44]

In any event, sports provide a medium conducive to the accumulation of conditions that provide the potential for collective uproar. To reduce the incidence of violence may necessitate a structural alteration in our society's values or the ways in which spectator sport is conducted and officiated.

SOCIAL MOVEMENTS IN SPORT

One of the most significant demonstrations of collective behavior that has relevance for sport is the notion of *social movement*. A "social movement" may be defined as a more or less persistent and orchestrated effort on the part of a relatively large number of people to either change a situation defined as undesirable or to prevent alteration in a situation deemed desirable. Social movements—collectivities acting with some continuity to promote or resist change in society—come in different sizes and forms. Among the most common types are migratory, expressive, utopian, reform, revolutionary, and resistance movements.[45] These social movements differ in their goals and objectives. For example, *revolutionary* movements advocate radical change in the existing social structure to the point of replacing the "old order" with a "new." *Reformist* movements, on the other hand, advocate changing the means to the given ends of the "old order." Let us consider the NCAA as a social movement.

The NCAA as a Social Movement [46]

The National Collegiate Athletic Association (NCAA) is the dominant organizational force in intercollegiate athletics today. Over 840 colleges and universities maintain some type of membership in the NCAA. This is almost double the corresponding membership two decades ago. All universities which operate "big-time" intercollegiate athletic programs are members of this *voluntary association.*

The financial status of the NCAA is very comfortable. The ABC television network paid the NCAA $36 million in 1975 and 1976 for the privilege of televising collegiate football games. This payment rose to $118 million in the years 1978 through 1981.[47] Hence, there is ample reason to examine the NCAA as a socioeconomic phenomenon.

The NCAA, originating as a reformist movement, has matured to the point where either the outright demise of the NCAA, or its substantial restructuring, can now be expected. The reform genre of social movements is characterized by an attempt to modify some component of society without radically transforming the entire social order. That part of society that the NCAA originally attempted to remedy was the unfashionable violence and other abuses that were occurring in intercollegiate athletics, football in particular, during the late nineteenth and early twentieth centuries. It is not unreasonable to suggest that the mayhem associated with intercollegiate football's "flying wedge" (an obsolete offensive formation in which blockers formed a wedge surrounding the ball carrier) was primarily responsible for the formation of the NCAA in 1906.

Social movements have a life cycle. It is seldom that two social movements have the same life history; however, there are sufficient common denominators among social movements to enable us to advance a typical *life cycle hypothesis.* Most "mature" social movements traverse through five stages: (1) *unrest,* (2) *excitement,* (3) *formalization,* (4) *institutionalization,* and (5) *dissolution.*[48] Movements, such as the NCAA, which pass through these formal stages become the *formal organizations* (see pp. 42, 295) which comprise the institutional fabric of society.

Unrest

The catalyst to most social movements is the perception that something is grievously wrong and must be rectified. *Social unrest* is often in the vanguard as a precipitating factor. In the early years of the twentieth century, intercollegiate athletics were disreputable and struggling. The rugged, violent nature of intercollegiate football, typified by mass formations and gang tackling, and desperately inadequate equipment, led to many injuries and deaths. In the 1905 season, 18 football players were killed on the gridiron. Unfortunately, colleges and universities were not organized in such a way that they could constructively change football's rules and regulations; therefore, many academic institutions reacted by eliminating football as a sponsored intercollegiate sport. It is accurate to state that the public at large was somewhat revolted at the violence which permeated intercollegiate football.

Midway through the 1905 football season, President Theodore Roosevelt became the catalyst for important changes in intercollegiate football. It is reported that after Roosevelt viewed a picture of a badly mauled football player, he threatened to abolish the game if remedial steps were not taken to modify the most objectionable aspects of the game.

Excitement

The transition from the unrest to the *excitement stage* is characterized by a clear identification of the problem needing attention. Whereas during the stage of unrest conditions are vague and ill-defined, during the stage of excitement, conditions are sufficiently identified so that specific action can be taken. To convert the unrest into action, a skillful and persuasive leader is needed—a Teddy

Roosevelt. Roosevelt's threat to discontinue intercollegiate football was taken seriously. As a result, an initial meeting of Ivy League schools to consider a course of action blossomed into a larger meeting attended by representatives of sixty two colleges and universities.

Formalization

On December 28, 1905, a committee of the sixty-two schools was appointed to seek merger with an already existing Football Rules Committee which had no real connection to academia. This resulted in the formation of the Intercollegiate Athletic Association, the forerunner of the NCAA. The *formalization stage* of the life cycle of a social movement is characterized by delegation and clarification of authority over business matters and rules, and a general statement of the organization's ideology. This is almost exactly what occurred during the formative years of the NCAA. One important product of this process was the approval of a dramatic innovation, the forward pass. Sanctioning of the forward pass clarified an otherwise murky situation in terms of football rules. More importantly, it opened up the game of intercollegiate football, and utlimately rendered obsolete the mass physical mayhem which had characterized the flying wedge. Finally, it also tremendously increased spectator appeal and hastened the development of big-time, commercialized intercollegiate football as we know it today.

Institutionalization

When a social movement such as the NCAA becomes a part of the established social order, it ceases to be a social movement in the traditional sense. Instead, it becomes a *formal organization* with characteristic bureaucratic structures (specific goals, highly specialized division of labor, a complex set of formal and informal rules and regulations, hierarchical authority, frequent impersonality, and visible concern for the perpetuation of its own existence).

The maturation of a social movement seems almost inevitably to result in a formalization of the movement's rules and traditions. Efficient bureaucrats replace agitators, and formal structure replaces informal customs. This stage of a social movement may last almost indefinitely; in the case of the NCAA, such activities commenced on the day of its founding, and have continued unabated to the present. A thick book of NCAA regulations prescribes a multitude of activities that have barely entered the minds of most fans, athletes and coaches. Further, the NCAA currently conducts thirty nine championship tournaments in eighteen sports.

The scope and complexity of intercollegiate athletics, as typified by athlete recruiting abuses, the multiplication of postseason games, and highly lucrative television revenues, have resulted in (some say for the better) a full-time NCAA professional staff which numbers among its members eleven full-time investigators of rules infractions, including at least five lawyers. The NCAA is frequently in the sports pages of daily newspapers because of its vitriolic conventions and its status as a litigant in a host of suits (see pp. 203, 296).

Dissolution

Some social movements never reach this stage; there is some evidence that the NCAA as we now know it may be developing intolerable internal fissures and stresses which will result in its *dissolution* as an organization. It is not outlandish to suggest that the NCAA may permute itself into a large number of sect-like bands, each doggedly pursuing parochial goals that have been found to be unrealistic for the entire NCAA "fraternity."

An athletic organization that attempted to write common rules for, and include under one roof, the Cincinnati Redlegs baseball team, and the Little League baseball teams of Cincinnati, Ohio, would undoubtedly have problems. This, however, is the situation in which the NCAA finds itself today. Its membership contains universities which operate athletic programs which are professional in everything except name, and also includes colleges which field club teams composed of amateurs in the traditional sense.

It is not clear that the NCAA can, despite its amoeba-like tendency to create new divisions, survive the tremendous heterogeneity of its membership. Very few such organizations[49] have ever succeeded in similar situations. Further, certain of the members of the NCAA are sufficiently well-heeled financially that they are able to delay and frustrate the NCAA with innumerable Lilliputian legal suits. The NCAA typically wins such legal battles in the end, but often only after the subject of controversy has become moot.

As early as 1910, the NCAA adopted the following formal objective: ". . . the regulation and supervision of college athletics throughout the United States in order that the athletic activities of the colleges and universities of the United States may be maintained on an ethical plane in keeping with the dignity and high purpose of education."[50] While it is tempting to argue that *goal displacement* has taken place, a more realistic scrutiny of the chronology of the NCAA must question whether this objective was ever realized at any time in any form.

The NCAA has evolved over time from a small, low pressure organization composed of members with similar interests. Such was the case prior to 1947. Today the NCAA is a large, unwieldy organization which seldom achieves consensus on any topic of substance. The "Golden Years" of the life cycle of the NCAA have probably passed. The future is likely to bring with it the demise of the NCAA as we now know it. In its place is likely to arise either a series of separate organizations with internally homogeneous memberships, or an NCAA which has decentralized nearly all important powers to its constituent divisions.[51] The key to this development will be, as in the past, the financial character of modern-day big-time intercollegiate athletics. The irony is that the very forces responsible for the growth of the NCAA—the commercialization, bureaucratization, and professionalization of collegiate sport—may be responsible for its disintegration.

CONTEMPORARY SOCIAL MOVEMENTS IN SPORT

Our case study of the NCAA as a social movement represented an historical example of the evolution of a social movement. Now let us turn to social movements that have evolved in recent years. Four such social movement in the realm of sport will be considered.[52] (1) *conventional labor activism,* (2) *egalitarian movement,* (3) *shamateur activism,* and (4) the *democratic movement.*

Conventional Labor Activism

This movement has been sparked by the monopolistic and capitalistic practices of professional sport owners (see Vignette 13.2) and the alleged economic exploitation of athletes contractually bound to them. In an article appropriately titled "The Owners are Destroying the Game," Wayne Embry, first black general manager (appointed by the Milwaukee Bucks, NBA) said:

VIGNETTE 13.2
FANS' PERCEPTIONS OF OWNERS

Despite the sharp attacks on professional sport owners some recent survey data suggest that not all fans are disgruntled by the modus operandi of owners. Most sport fans (56%) do not hold unfavorable impressions of sport owners; a little more than one-third (36%) did. On more specific issues 839 fans were asked (with the percentage in the various response categories indicated):

In your view, are sports owners:	Yes	No	Unsure
Basically honest business men?	62%	26%	12%
Dilettantes who just own teams for a hobby?	35	53	12
In sports for publicity and recognition?	50	41	9
Greedy?	52	38	10
Persons of civic responsibility?	41	45	14
Telling the truth when they say their teams lose money?	28	61	11
Taking unfair advantage of tax breaks?	55	21	24
Taking unfair advantage of athletes?	49	41	10

In the sports labor disputes of recent years, who do you think was generally at fault? The fans replied: owners (37%), players (24%), both equally (34%), and unsure (5%).

Do you believe that owners:	Yes	No	Unsure
Deserve the same tax breaks as anyone else?	76%	17%	7%
Should have to prove that they are not making little or no money before they are allowed to move their teams?	62	32	6
Deserve special antitrust laws, if that is what it takes for them to make a profit?	30	58	12

Source: Ray Kennedy and Nancy Williamson, "Money in Sports," *Sports Illustrated* 49 (July 31, 1978), p. 47.

Once this (basketball) provided a lot of fun, and a lot of good things came out of this game. But now it's a multi-million-dollar business. And some of the owners, out of ignorance, have taken basketball away from the players and the people who know the game . . . and those owners are destroying it.[53]

As we have seen (ch. 11), pro sports have historically operated under some form of a "reserve system" whereby athletes' movements and salaries were restricted by the team "signing" them. Several cases highlight the manner in which individuals have retaliated and attempted to redress these restricting conventions.

Former St. Louis Cardinal outfielder Curt Flood was traded in 1969 to the Philadelphia Phillies without having been consulted and without his consent. Such practices had been perfectly legitimate under pro baseball's "reserve clause." Flood fought the trade and took pro baseball to court arguing that such business transactions amounted to baseball players being relegated to slaves and chattel. He argued that such a move would necessitate abandoning his St. Louis business interests, uproot his family and, furthermore, was in violation of the federal antitrust laws since the trade obliged him to play for the team he had been traded to or quit baseball.

In a similar vein, Connie Hawkins' story as depicted by Wolf is testimony to the exploitation of college athletes.[54] As so often occurs in the recruitment of black stellar athletes, he was wined and dined by numerous college "cage" recruiters across the country. Despite his woefully inadequate "slum" educational background, Hawkins was not able to recall a single recruiter asking him about his academic background or career plans. His career ended shortly after it began when his name was (unfairly, according to Wolf) associated with the gambling scandal of the early 1960s. According to accounts, he was pressured by his former Iowa coaches to lie, in writing, absolving them from any guilt apropos recruitment irregularities and financial support. Many experts argue that such incidents are only the tip of the iceburg. Furthermore, it is not that pernicious personality types occupy positions of authority in sport, but rather that this phenomenon is *socially structured*. That is, such patterns of rule violations and exploitation of athletes may be understood in terms of the strains, tensions, and uncertainties associated with winning in big-game college programs.

Another illustration is the successful challenging of the "four year college rule" by Spencer Haywood. Haywood enrolled at the University of Detroit but subsequently quit school to sign an alleged million dollar contract with the Denver Rockets, then jumped to the Seattle Supersonics before moving to the New York Knicks. During this shuffle a rule—the *four-year college rule*—designed to protect the colleges intruded. It stated, in essence, that no athlete could sign a professional contract until his college class had graduated. In compliance with this rule, Haywood's contract with Seattle was voided. However, a judge struck the ruling down on the grounds that it restrained Haywood's right to earn a living.[55]

These cases are but a few highlighting the roots of *conventional labor activism* in sport. Moreover, professional players are increasingly turning to professional agents (see Vignette 6.1) to help them negotiate and secure an equitable contract.

Conventional labor activism can also be witnessed in such historically unprecedented occurrences as strikes (the football strike of 1974, the baseball strike of 1972, the umpire strike of 1978 and 1979, and the NASL 1979 strike), "holdouts," boycotts (particularly at the amateur, college and Olympic levels), and collective bargaining pursuits of pro athletes, and union-like player organizations. The labor movement in sport, like the labor activism counterpart in general, has been geared to produce more favorable salaries and fringe benefits (bonuses, retirement benefits), improve working conditions and enhance the job and financial security of athletes.

Egalitarian Movement

This social movement has been aimed at goals similar to those of the former one. It differs in that it focuses on improving the political, social, and economic status of *black* athletes. This practice has been precipitated by alleged racist practices (described in chapters 7 and 8) in amateur and professional sport.

Sport sociologist Harry Edwards has been a catalytic agent in this movement.[56] He organized the Olympic Project for Human Rights prior to the 1968 Mexico City Olympics. Although it failed to produce a black boycott of the Games, it has had a far-reaching effect on American athletics. His and other leaders' influence was seen in the wave of threatened and actual boycotts by black athletes in response to racist practices of academic institutions, coaches, athletic administrators, and others. "Rebellions" among black athletes declined from about 180 during the 1968-69 academic year, to less than 30 during the first half of the 1971-72 season, to practically none today.[57]

Edwards' attempt to enhance black pride and reject racist policies materialized in victory stand demonstrations of black athletes. For example, in the 1968 (Mexico City) Olympics Tommie Smith and John Carlos, after placing in the 200 meter sprint, raised their gloved hands and lowered their heads in giving the Black Power salute during the playing of the United States' national anthem. When asked why they had acted in this manner, they declared "to call attention to racial strife in America." Similarly, Wayne Collett and Vince Mattews, after running second and first in the 400 meter race in the 1972 (Munich) Olympics, stood casually, chatted, joked, and turned away from the American flag. When queried as to why they did this, they proclaimed "to personify whites' casual attitude toward blacks in the United States."

Finally, the egalitarian movement led to the ouster from Olympic competition of South Africa in 1968 and Rhodesia in 1972 because of their *apartheid* (the system of racial segregation practiced in South Africa) policies.

According to Edwards, the protagonists of the egalitarian movement are active or former college/professional black athletes who wish to bring about equal opportunity and rewards for blacks in sport. The movement is reformist in nature and aimed at restructuring sports' reward system for blacks.

Shamateur Activism

The term "shamateur" is a hybrid word derived from "sham" (meaning something which is not what it is purported to be) and "amateur" (a participant who plays for the love of the activity). The World Sports Federation (WSF), founded in 1972 by Suzy Chaffee and Jack Kelly, has advanced a platform for eliminating aristocratic exclusiveness, hypocrisy, and guilt experienced by "shamateur" athletes competing in the Olympics. For a thorough analysis of the political machinations of Olympic sport, see Lowe, Kanin, and Strenk.[58]

Olympic Sham

The foundation for the amateur movement can be grasped by comparing and contrasting Olympic symbolism and ideology with the historical realities of the Olympiads. The official Olympic symbol consists of five interlocking rings or circles representing sporting friendships among persons of different continents. The Olympic flag consists of the linked rings on a white background. Even the colors of the circles—blue, yellow, black, green, and red—are meaningful. At least one of these colors appears in the flag of every nation. The Olympic motto—"Citius, Altius, Fortius" means "faster, higher, stronger." The Olympic creed reads: "not to win but to take part, not to have conquered but to have fought well." All athletic participants take the Olympic oath in which they swear to respect and abide by the rules of good sportsmanship. Finally, the Olympic flame symbolizes continuity between the Ancient and Modern Games, for the torch is lit by the sun's rays in Olympia, Greece, and carried by relay runners to the host site.

These claimed ideals grip the heart and make the body shiver. "The problem is that so many vicious realities keep intruding into one's illusions about them." Additionally, it is difficult to escape the smell of jingoism incited by international sport. "Nationalistic gestures permeate just about every aspect of the games; flags, anthems, uniforms, and nation scores punctuate the action like a military exercise."[59]

Contrary to the Olympic ideals, international sporting activities may be subsumed under several overlapping categories: [60] (1) a political tool, (2) a mirror, barometer, or litmus reflecting domestic problems of a sociopolitical nature, (3) an outlet for national aggression, (4) propaganda and economic showcases, and (5) myopic nationalism.

Lyman reports the following goals of the *shamateur movement:*[61]

1. The individual athlete must have the right to determine the extent of training time required instead of the present sixty-day limit.
2. The National Olympic Committee and sports associations shall be responsible for arranging for athletes to be paid expense money, broken time payments and insurance coverage in connection with training and competition, whether these sources be private, governmental or commercial.
3. Athletes may receive scholarships and financial assistance while fulfilling educational requirements and may receive remuneration for actual employment in the athlete's sport, including positions as coaches.
4. Athletes may accept remuneration for television and other public appearances not involving actual competition in the athlete's sport. Remuneration for endorsements of commercial products connected with the athlete's sport may be accepted, but a share of such remuneration is subject to the rules of the International Federations and must be given to National Associations and other participating athletes.
5. National and International Federations and Olympic organizations shall be required to have competing or recently retired athletes as voting and fully participating members of such bodies.

For the most part, these stipulations appear to be reformist in character, simply making it easier for such athletes to reap rewards openly. Only the mandate that the athletes, not the customers, public, coaches, or mass media, be responsible for their practicing runs counter to the existing structure of sport. The condition that the Olympics be for the participants may, however, have broad "revolutionary" implications.

Democratic Movement

Jack Scott, an out-spoken critic of contemporary sport, has spearheaded this movement. [62] He explicitly criticizes the "winning at any cost" orientation and the dehumanization of athletes and athletic performances. It dovetails with what Edwards calls the "humanitarian counter-creed." The movement has been called "democratic" because of its tenets that sport and athletics be *of* the people (participants), *for* the pleasure of the people (participants), and run *by* the people (participants). It is "humanitarian" insofar as eliminating the theme of annihilating one's opponent and, instead, advocates genuine concern with the welfare of fellow competitors.

Scott denigrates the undesirable aspects of contemporary sport—excessive commercialism, authoritarianism, winning at any expense, drug-taking, recruiting violations, its elitist, spectator orientation, its overemphasis upon proving masculinity and denying females a role in sport, and the general conservative orientation, all of which the sport establishment appears to be bent upon preserving. Consequently, it is not difficult to see the fundamental fissures between sport as we know it today and the *democratic movement.*

Each of the four social movements—*conventional labor activism, egalitarian movement, shamateur activism,* and *democratic movement*—poses some threat, if successful, to the contemporary organization and character of American sport. The first two are reformist in nature since they call for alterations in the distribution of economic rewards. On the other hand, the success of the shamateur movement is likely to bring about the following changes:[63]

1. A liberalization of the amateur or Olympic eligibility criteria.
2. Expanded opportunities for participation by athletes of less privileged status.
3. Decreased hypocrisy and guilt about the acceptance of financial compensation.
4. Greater responsiveness by amateur officials to the needs of athletes whom they are supposed to serve.

There has been some success in the shamateur movement as witnessed by Olympic athletes being members of the U.S. Olympic Committee, the appointment of a former Olympic athlete to the vice-presidency of the U.S. Ski Association, and IOC President Lord Killanin's concession to regulate some of the inequalities in amateur sport.[64]

Scott's democratic movement is probably the most revolutionary of all since it calls for radical alterations in the contemporary structure of sport itself. It takes little imagination to see the profound alterations in sport as we know it today if his ideas were implemented. It is not likely, in the short run at least, that Scott's ideas will materialize since sport's dominant values—winning at any cost, commercialism, and competitiveness—are reinforced by the values in the larger society. Just the same, it is important to be cognizant of the sociocultural change these social movements may bring about in sport.

The Consumer Movement in Sports

F.A.N.S.

Consumer advocate Ralph Nader launched a campaign to defend the rights of sport fans in the summer of 1977. The new social movement is known as *F.A.N.S.*—the *F*ight to *A*dvance the *N*ation's *S*ports. To fully understand Nader's contention that the fans are being "ripped off" necessitates delving into the economics of sport. In this section, we will not do this (although it was fully discussed in chapter 11). Instead, we will consider some high points of the movement which Nader and others believe contribute to fan disgruntlement.

Fans are being exploited through the constant rise in ticket prices. For openers, the Washington Redskins charge up to $20 for a single game ticket; the New York Knicks charge $12.50. Until the 1976 season if you desired to purchase a season ticket to a Dallas Cowboys game you had to buy a $250 bond (to help pay stadium construction costs) in addition to the price of the ticket. The average costs of tickets for the 1977-78 season in football, basketball, baseball, and hockey were approximately $10, $7, $4, and $8, respectively.[65]

Fans are victimized as taxpayers, too. About 75 percent of all professional sports facilities are subsidized by the taxpayer. If these same taxpayers wish to attend a sport event, they must also purchase the tickets and pay to park in a lot they are helping to build.

In some sports, notably football, it is virtually impossible to secure tickets. The exhorbitant costs may be one reason. Take Robert F. Kennedy Memorial Stadium in Washington, D.C. Only one percent—500 seats—of R.F.K.'s 55,031 seats are sold to the public at large. In other words, 99 percent of the seats are sold to season ticket holders.

Prior to 1961 individual teams negotiated their own broadcast and telecast contracts with the media networks. This meant that in certain metropolitan areas several different games could be viewed on the same afternoon. In 1961, legislation authorized the leagues—not the individual teams—to negotiate for broadcast and telecast rights. The losers in this legislation were the fans (there were actually more hours of sport telecasting prior to 1961 than after) since there was less choice in games to watch and they paid more for them.

According to Nader and Gruenstein, the current state of affairs is the result of the "corporatizing" of sport, a subject we discussed at length in chapter 11.[66]

Nader and Gruenstein have advanced the following "bill of rights" for F.A.N.S.:[67]

F.A.N.S. proposes that fans have the right to:
1. Participate in the formation of the rules and procedures that govern the play and operation of professional and amateur sports competition.
2. Be informed about the operations and practices of professional and amateur sports.
3. Purchase reasonably priced tickets to sporting events and receive fair value for their money. Tickets to sporting events should be made available to the greatest number of fans and should not be reserved only for the wealthy and well-connected.
4. Ensure that food sold at those events is reasonably priced and well prepared.
5. Have their interest represented before Congress and other Governmental bodies.
6. Have their interests in the broadcasting of sports events effectively represented to the electronic media.
7. Have their interests in the resolution of labor, contractual and other disputes involving sports effectively expressed and represented. Additionally, fans have an interest in ensuring, to the maximum degree possible, the health and safety of athletes.
8. Have their interest in maintaining or establishing the integrity of a sport, team or event effectively expressed and represented.
9. Have knowledge of relevant information concerning sports enterprises that receive special public benefits in the form of low-cost leases of publicly owned facilities, tax benefits, and other subsidies and privileges. Those enterprises further have a special responsibility to serve the public interest.
10. Fans are also citizens, taxpayers and consumers and, as such, have an interest in seeing that the proper role of sports in America—as an enrichment of the quality of life—does not become exaggerated or distorted, and that those associated with sports do not receive special legal, tax or other privileges detrimental to the public interest.

There is some evidence from a recent survey by Yankelovich that Nader's efforts to rally fans to F.A.N.S. will be to little avail.[68] A nationwide poll of 839 self-described fans taken by the research firm was asked: "Would you be interested in joining a fans group formed by consumer advocates?" Eighty-five percent said, "no"; 14 percent said, "yes"; and 1 percent said, "unsure." The sample's responses may, in part, be due to the fact that they can express their dissatisfaction by staying home or tuning their televisions to another channel. But there is more to it than this:

It seems as though nothing can deter American sports fans from their preoccupation with professional sports or from their enthusiasm for it—not even expressed complaints about the commercialization that has occurred, the big salaries paid to the players, the motivations of the owners or the increase in unnecessary violence. . . . Instead, sport fans . . . state unequivocally that, compared to five years ago, they are enjoying professional sports even more now, are rooting harder than ever for their favorite teams, and are more enthusiastic about the star players than they were in the past.[69]

Using average attendance data as an indicator of enhanced enthusiasms, the *average* attendance statistics in at least two professional sports add substance to this quote. In the past five years (comparing 1972 and 1977 figures) baseball games' average attendance has increased from 16,203 to 19,991; NBA average attendance has increased from 9,259 to 11,198; NHL attendance has slightly dropped from 13,897 to 12,043 as did NFL figures, from 57,692 to 56,750. Another indicator of sport enthusiasm stems from average audience size (in millions of households tuned in) for these four team sports. Between 1972 and 1977 NFL averages increased from 16.2 to 19.5 million, baseball averages increased from 8.6 to 10.1 million, NBA average audience size declined slightly from 8.3 to 8.2 million, and NHL average audience size dropped from 6.4 to 0 (the latter figure was due to the league having no TV network contract that year).[70]

In comparing the Yankelovich, Skelly, and White, Inc. survey data with some of F.A.N.S.'s proposals, we note some discrepancies:[71]

1. Fans do not seem particularly interested in knowing the operations and practices of professional sport. Seventy-eight percent of those polled said no to the question: "Are you interested in knowing the details of contract negotiations and player salaries?"
2. Fans do not appear to be overly concerned about the present and future cost of tickets. Three items support this statement. (1) "Compared to other entertainment prices, do you think tickets to big-time sports events are too high, pretty reasonable or a bargain?" Fifty percent said "reasonable," 44 percent said "high," 3 percent said a "bargain." (2) "If prices for tickets to your favorite sports event increased by 10 percent, would you still go?" Seventy-six percent said "yes" and 24 percent said "no." (3) If prices increased by 25 percent, would you still go?" Fifty-six percent said "yes" and 44 percent said "no."
3. Fans don't seem to be overly dismayed by the cost of food served at sporting events. When asked, "Compared to prices at restaurants, theaters, and movies, do you think concession prices at sports events are too high, reasonable or a bargain?" Fifty-six percent said "high," 38 percent said "reasonable," and 1 percent said a "bargain."

In short, the public opinion survey indicates that while some fans may be disgruntled, they're more in a mood to revel than rebel. Compared to five years ago, the level of fan interest is up 24 percent, their fun in watching games is up 41 percent, their loyalty to their favorite teams is up 15 percent, and their enthusiasm for star players is up 10 percent. Peter Gruenstein, executive director of F.A.N.S. may be correct when he said: "We're in the Stone Age of consumerism in sports . . . . There's little recognition of fans as consumers and little understanding of the business of sports."[72] So long as contemporary sport fans endure the abuses of sport and accept the status quo, they will continue to provide some of the lifeblood for sport's current structure and functioning.

SUMMARY

This chapter has been devoted to a discussion of sport, collective behavior and social change. *Collective behavior* encompasses a wide range of group phenomena, including crowds, riots, mobs, revolutions, fads, fashions, and social movements. The study of collective behavior is significant because it illuminates the dynamics of *sociocultural change.*

We considered the increasing incidence of collective behavior in sport by relating some past and present vignettes. To understand this social phenomenon, we considered three explanations of crowd behavior: (1) *contagion theories* which maintain that a collective mind overpowers and submerges individuals in a crowd through emotional contagion; (2) *convergence theories* which argue that individuals' real selves are ordinarily covered up by a veneer of social propriety which unfolds under anonymous and de-individuated circumstances, and (3) *emergent norm theories* which suggest that norms or behavioral expectations emerge and guide behavior in certain crowd situations.

A theory of collective behavior—known as the *value added* approach—was considered for the light it sheds upon past and contemporary episodes of collective violence. According to this scheme, there are six determinants of collective behavior: (1) *structural conduciveness,* (2) *structural strain,* (3) *growth of a generalized belief,* (4) *precipitating factors,* (5) *mobilization of participants for action,* and (6) *operation of social control.* Each of these necessary conditions was amply illustrated from the sport literature.

Several *social movements* in sport—persistent and orchestrated efforts to change a situation defined as undesirable or maintain a situation deemed desirable—were considered. Among them were the NCAA as a social movement, *conventional labor activism, egalitarian movement, shamateur activism, democratic movement,* and the *consumer movement* (F.A.N.S.).

Finally, since fan behavior is generally considered more radical today than in yesteryear, speculations on its causes and remedies for its removal or minimization were addressed. In the end it appears that fans today are more in a mood to revel then rebel. So long as this attitude prevails, we will not anticipate radical alterations in the structure and functioning of contemporary sport.

IMPORTANT CONCEPTS DISCUSSED IN THIS CHAPTER

Collective Behavior

Theories of Crowd Behavior:

   Contagion Theory

   Convergence Theory

   Emergent Norm Theory

Normative Social Influence

Informational Social Influence

Value Added Theory of Collective Behavior

Structural Conduciveness

Structural Strain

Growth of a Generalized Belief

Precipitating Factors

Mobilization of Participants for Action

Operation of Social Control

Social Movement

NCAA

Conventional Labor Activism

Egalitarian Movement

Shamateur Activism

Democratic Movement

Consumer Movement (F.A.N.S.)

Hooliganism

Apartheid

ENDNOTES

[1] Michael D. Smith, "Hostile Outbursts in Sport," *Sport Sociology Bulletin* 2 (1973), pp. 6-10.

[2] Michael D. Smith, "Sport and Collective Violence," *Sport and Social Order*, D. W. Ball and J. W. Loy (Reading, Mass: Addison-Wesley, 1975), pp. 277-33.

[3] Ron Fimrite, "Take Me Out to the Brawl Game," *Sport Sociology*, A. Yiannakis et al. (Dubuque, Iowa: Kendall/Hunt, 1976), pp. 202-205.

[4] Eldon E. Snyder and Elmer Spreitzer, *Social Aspects of Sport* (Englewood Cliffs, NJ: Prentice-Hall, 1978), p. 134.

[5] Jim Benagh, "Rowdy Spectators—The 'Bad Apples' of Sports," *Family Weekly* (June 4, 1978), pp. 7-8.

[6] Ibid.

[7] James A. Michener, *Sports in America* (New York: Random House, 1976), p. 429.

[8] Ibid.

[9] Ibid., p. 430.

[10] Benagh, "Rowdy Spectators—The 'Bad Apples' of Sports," p. 7.

[11] Ibid.

[12] Ibid.

[13] Ibid.

[14] *The Daily Pantagraph*, Bloomington-Normal, Ill., 13 July, 1979, p. B1.

[15] Benagh, "Rowdy Spectators—The 'Bad Apples' of Sports," p. 8.

[16] Ibid., p. 7.

[17] James W. Vander Zanden, *Social Psychology* (New York: Random House, 1977), pp. 394-398.

[18] Gustave Le Bon, *The Crowd: A Study of the Popular Mind* (London, England: Ernest Benn, 1895).

[19] Michener, *Sports in America*, p. 428.

[20] M. Sherif, *The Psychology of Social Norms* (New York: Harper and Row, 1936).

[21] Solomon E. Asch, "Effects of Group Pressure Upon Modification and Distortion of Judgments," *Readings in Social Psychology*, E. Maccoby, T. Newcomb, and E. Hartley (New York: Holt, 1958), pp. 174-183.

[22] Neil J. Snelser, *Theory of Collective Behavior* (New York: Free Press, 1962).

[23] Smith, "Sport and Collective Violence." A substantial number of the illustrations that follow have been gleaned from this source, © 1978, Addism-Wesley. Reprinted with permission.

[24] A "necessary condition" is one that must be present if a certain effect is to be produced although it doesn't guarantee the effect. For example, it is necessary to be a female to become pregnant although not all females are or become pregnant. A "sufficient condition" is one that inevitably produces an effect in and of itself. For example, detaching a person's heart is sufficient to produce death although death can occur in other ways.

[25] Smith, "Hostile Outbursts in Sport"; Smith, "Sport and Collective Violence."

[26] Ian Taylor, " 'Football Mad': A Speculative Sociology of Football Hooliganism," *Sport: Readings from a Sociological Perspective*, Eric Dunning (Toronto, University of Toronto Press, 1972); Howard L. Nixon, II, *Sport and Social Organization* (Indianapolis, Ind.: Bobbs-Merrill, 1976).

[27] Ian Taylor, "Soccer Consciousness and Soccer Hooliganism," *Images of Deviance*, Stanley Cohen (Middlesex, England: Penguin, 1971), pp. 142-143.

[28] Ibid., p. 156.

[29] George Rudé, *The Crowd in History* (New York: Wiley, 1964).

[30] Smith, "Hostile Outbursts in Sport."

[31] Peter Greenberg, "Wild in the Stands," *New York Times* 9(10): 25-27, 62-64, Nov. 11, 1977.

[32] Smith, "Sport and Collective Violence."

[33] Ibid.

[34] Smelser, *Theory of Collective Behavior.*

[35] Snyder and Spreitzer, *Social Aspects of Sport*, p. 135.

[36] Clifford Bryan and Robert Horton, "Athletic Events and Spectacular Spectators: A Longitudinal Study of Aggression" (Paper presented at the American Educatonal Research Association, 1976).

[37] Benagh, "Rowdy Spectators: The 'Bad Apples' of Sports," p. 8.

[38] *Crowd Control for High School Athletics* (1970), cited in Smith, "Sport and Collective Violence."

[39] J. A. Harrington, *Soccer Hooliganism: A Preliminary Report to Mr. Denis Howell, Minister of Sport* (Bristol, John Wright and Sons, 1968).

[40] *New York Times*, October 14, 1973.

[41] Earl McRae, "The Aggressive Return of Terrible Teddy," *Sport* (MVP, Sports, Inc.), Decmeber, 1977, Vol. 65, No. 6, p. 86.

[42] Larry Hayes, unpublished manuscript, Illinois State University, Spring, 1978. Used with permission.

[43] Jeffrey Goldstein and Robert Arms, "Effects of Observing Athletic Contests on Hostility," *Sociometry* 34 (March, 1971), pp. 83-90.

[44] A. C. Fisher, *Psychology of Sport* (Palo Alto, Calif.: Mayfield Publishing Co., 1976).

[45] Herbert Blumer, "Collective Behavior," *New Outline of the Principles of Sociology*, A. Lee (New York: Barnes and Noble, 1951).

[46] Some of the following discussion has been taken from James V. Koch and Wilbert M. Leonard, II, "The NCAA: A Socioeconomic Analysis," *The American Journal of Economics and Sociology* 37 (July, 1978), pp. 225-239. Used with permission.

[47] Larry Van Dyne, "ABC Will Pay $118 Million to Televise College Football," *The Chronicle of Higher Education* (June 27, 1977), p. 6.

[48] Blumer, "Collective Behavior."

[49] Some have equated the operation of the NCAA to that of a *cartel*. A "cartel" is an agreement among firms in an industry—sport in the present—to regulate and monopolize transactions and entry barriers and usually consists of a relatively small number of members (although powerful) with similar interests, costs, and revenues. Both big-time collegiate and professional sport function in this manner. See James V. Koch, "A Troubled Cartel: The NCAA," *Law and Contemporary Problems* 38 (Winter-Spring, 1973), pp. 135-150.

[50] "Statement of Objectives," *NCAA* (1910).

[51] In January, 1978, the NCAA approved dividing its Division I football playing schools into two divisions: (1) I-A consisting of some 139 "elite" universities, and (2) I-AA consisting of 108 universities that do not have football programs but that do have basketball programs. Division II (195 schools) and Division III (233 schools) remained unchanged. The College Football Association, composed of the major conferences (with the exception of the Big-Ten and Pac-Eight—which became the Pac-Ten on July 1, 1978—and independents in the sport) was dissatisfied with the reorganization. The Association is trying again to create a "super division" of major football powers.

[52] Nixon, *Sport and Social Organization*, pp. 64-70. Some of the following discussion and examples are gleaned from this source. Used with permission. Jack Scott, *The Athletic Revolution* (see endnote 62).

[53] "The Owners are Destroying the Game," *Sport* (1977), p. 23.

[54] David Wolf, *Foul!* (New York: Holt, Rinehart, and Winston, 1972).

[55] Michener, *Sports in America*, p. 105.

[56] Harry Edwards, *Sociology of Sport* (Homewood, Ill.: Dorsey Press, 1973); Edwards, "The Black Athletic on the College Campus," *Sport and Society*, ed. J. Talamini and C. Page (Boston, Mass.: Little, Brown, 1973), pp. 202-219; Edwards, *The Revolt of the Black Athlete* (New York: Free Press, 1969).

[57] Edwards, *Sociology of Sport*, p. 151.

[58] Benjamin Lowe, David B. Kanin, and Andrew Strenk, *Sport and International Relations* (Champaign, Ill.: Stipes Publishing Co., 1978).

[59] Robert Kropke, "International Sports and the Social Sciences," *Sport in the Socio-cultural Process*, ed. Marie Hart (Dubuque, Iowa: Wm. C. Brown, Co., 1976), pp. 317-325; John McMurty, "A Case for Killing the Olympics," *Maclean's* (January, 1973), p. 34.

[60] Kropke, "International Sports and the Social Sciences."

[61] David H. Lyman, "The Future of the Olympics," *The Student Skier Three* (Holiday 8-9), 1972, p. 8.

[62] Jack Scott, *The Athletic Revolution* (New York: Free Press, 1971).

[63] Nixon, *Sport and Social Organization*, p. 69.

[64] Ibid.

[65] Ralph Nader and Peter Gruenstein, "Blessed Are the Fans, For They Shall Inherit $12 Bleacher Seats, Indigestible Hot Dogs, $2 Bottles of Beer and 100 Overpaid Superstars," *Playboy* (Spring, 1978), p. 98. Some of the following factual statements are gleaned from this source.

[66] Ibid.

[67] Ibid., p. 198.

[68] Ray Kennedy and Nancy Williamson, "Money in Sports," *Sports Illustrated* 49 (July 31, 1978), pp. 34-50.

[69] Ibid., p. 39.

[70] Kennedy and Williamson, "Money in Sports," p. 39.

[71] These comparisons combine the research outcomes of Kennedy and Williamson and the proposals of Nader and Gruenstein.

[72] Kennedy and Williamson, "Money in Sports," p. 41.

Index

transportation, 30-31
Tueart, Dennis, 241
Tumin, Melvin, 138
Tunis, John, 68
Tunney, Gene, 28, 265
Turowetz, A., 220
Tutko, Thomas, 68, 96-97, 102, 170, 292
TV Guide, 265
Tyus, Wyomia, 198

UCLA (University of California at Los Angeles), 55, 119
Uganda, 66
Umphlett, Wiley Lee, 48
umpires, 218
Unitas, Johnny, 77, 146
United States, 142
United States Olympic Committee (USOC), 41, 301
Updike, John, 5
urbanization, 15, 29, 32
USC (University of Southern California), 119
U.S.S.R., 66, 142-145

value added, 286
value orientations (American), 66, 103
value receptacle, sport as, 45
values, 45, 57, 65-73, 103
Vancouver Canucks, 236
Vander Velden, Lee, 95
Vander Zanden, James, 282
Van Lier, Norm, 133
Vare, Robert, 5
Veblen, Thorstein, 19
Veeck, Bill, 236
Veit, Hans, 215
Victorian Era, 141
Vilas, Guillermo, 243
violence, 284
Voight, David, 65
voluntary association, 294
Vorhies, Bob, 69

Wadkins, Lanny, 241
Waitz, Grete, 194
waivers, 244
Walcott, Jersey Joe, 51
Walker, Fleetwood, 158, 161
Walker, Weldy, 158, 161
Walters, Barbara, 269
Walton, Bill, 48, 123, 246
Waner, Paul, 140
Washington, University of, 202
Washington, Gene, 171
Watson, Tom, 51, 241
Weaver, Earl, 277
Webb, Harry, 55, 91, 94
Weber, Max, 9, 18

Webster, Marvin, 121
Weinberg, S. Kirson, 50, 220
Weismuller, Johnny, 28, 77, 264
Weiss, Paul, 19, 276
Wells, Warren, 133
Werblin, Sonny, 239
West, Jerry, 247
White, Rudy, 49
Whitworth, Kathy, 205
Widmeyer, W., 215
Wilkins, Lenny, 179
Williams, Cleveland, 133
Williams, Dick, 39
Williams, Jackie, 120
Williams, Robin, 66
Williams, Ted, 77
Williams College, 38
Williamson, Nancy, 49, 193, 227-228, 231, 233, 240-241, 251, 297
Wills, Helen, 28, 264
Wolf, David, 5, 118
Wolfgang, Marvin, 219
Women's Action Group (WAG), 190
women's movement, 190
Women's Professional Basketball League, 189
WomenSports, 189
Wooden, John, 68, 120, 123, 212
World Hockey Association (WHA), 33
World Series, 259
World Sports Federation (WSF), 299
Worthy, A., 172
Wright, Donald, 109, 140
Wright, John, 158
Wright, Orville, 31
Wright, Steve, 100
Wright, Wilbur, 31
Wrigley, Phil, 229
Wrigley Field, 32
Wyrick, Waneen, 195-196

Yale University, 25, 27-28, 30, 38
Yankee Stadium, 65, 237, 283
Yankelovich survey, 148, 302-303
Yarborough, Cale, 241
Yawkey, Tom, 229
Yee, Min, 109, 140
Yetman, Norman, 156-157, 165, 167-168, 171, 174-175, 178, 182-183, 216
YMCA, 33, 71
Young, Jimmy, 51
Youngman, Randy, 131, 133
YWCA, 71

Zeus, 189
Zuñi, 76
Zuppe, Bob, 102
Zurcher, Louis, 76

1920   Beginning of "Golden Age of Sports."

Radio station of the *Detroit News* broadcasted the World Series results on August 20.

First broadcast of a college football game from a station in Texas.

1921   KDKA Pittsburgh broadcast baseball games and fights.

National Football League (NFL) founded when eleven teams were granted charters.

Radio station broadcast the World Series results.

Judge Kenesaw Mountain Landis became pro baseball's first commissioner.

1922   Supreme Court decision in Federal Baseball Club of *Baltimore* vs. *National League* making baseball exempt from Sherman Antitrust Law of 1890.

1923   White House Conference on women's athletics.

1925   Gertrude Ederle became first female to swim the English Channel.

1928   Females permitted to participate in Olympic track and field events for the first time.

1929   Carnegie investigation of men's intercollegiate athletics.

1930   Rens (professional black) basketball team formed.

1932   Babe Didrikson "swept" Olympics.

1934   Men's collegiate basketball tournament, Madison Square Garden.

1935   Roller Derby invented.

First major league night baseball game, Pittsburgh vs. Cincinnati in Cincinnati.

1939   Little League started.

Heisman Trophy, after John Heisman, established.

First televised sporting event, a baseball game between Columbia and Princeton (announcer was Bill Stern).

First use of football helmets, All-Star Game.

1940   Olympics canceled (war).

Emergence of sport cartoons.

1944   Olympics canceled (war).

1945   The AP sports wires established for major league baseball.

1946   All-American Football Conference formed as a rival to the NFL.

Outland Trophy (for outstanding college lineman) established.

First time ever, all major league baseball games scheduled that day were played "under the lights."

Marion Motley became first black in the All-American Conference.

1947   Jackie Robinson, first (modern) black to play professional baseball.

First official motorcross race in Holland.

1948   First plastic flying disk—a frisbee—invented by Fred Morrison.

1949   Ladies Professional Golf Association (LPGA) formed.

National Basketball Association (NBA) formed.

1950   Three blacks broke the "color bar" in the National Basketball Association.

Congress created the United States Olympic Committee (USOC).

1951   College basketball scandal.

National Association for Intercollegiate Athletics (NAIA) founded.

1954   Debut of *Sports Illustrated*.

Fellowship of Christian Athletes (FCA) founded.